Agla + Pantarion + Gbcon + Carisin + Seraphim

Of Angels, Demons & Spirits

Daniel Harms is the author of *The Book of Oberon* (with Joseph H. Peterson and James R. Clark), *The Cthulhu Mythos Encyclopedia*, *The Necronomicon Files* (with John Wisdom Gonce III), and *The Long-Lost Friend: A 19th Century American Grimoire*. His articles have appeared in the *Journal for the Academic Study of Magic*, *The Journal of Scholarly Communication*, *Abraxas*, *Fortean Times*, *Paranoia*, and *The Unspeakable Oath*. His work has been translated into four languages. His blog, *Papers Falling from an Attic Window*, provides commentary on topics ranging from horror writer H. P. Lovecraft to the history of books of magic. He lives in upstate New York.

James R. Clark is a mathematician, artist, and philosopher living in Chicago. His illustrated work includes *The Book of Oberon*, *Arthurian Magic,* and the seventh edition of Israel Regardie's *Golden Dawn*.

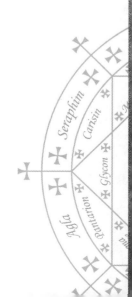

Of Angels, Demons & Spirits

A SOURCEBOOK OF BRITISH MAGIC

TRANSLATED & ANNOTATED FROM THE BODLEIAN LIBRARY'S 17TH CENTURY MANUSCRIPT

DANIEL HARMS · JAMES R. CLARK

LLEWELLYN PUBLICATIONS
Woodbury, Minnesota

FIRST EDITION
First Printing, 2019

Book design by Rebecca Zins
Cover design by Kevin R. Brown
Interior illustrations by James R. Clark

Llewellyn Publications is a registered trademark of Llewellyn Worldwide Ltd.

Note: The contents in this book are historical references used for teaching purposes, historical understanding, and reference only.

Library of Congress Cataloging-in-Publication Data
Names: Harms, Daniel, translator. | Clark, James R., illustrator.
Title: Of angels, demons, and spirits : a sourcebook of British magic /
    translated & annotated from the Bodleian Library's 17th century manuscript
    by Daniel Harms ; [illustrated by] James R. Clark.
Description: First edition. | Woodbury, Minnesota : Llewellyn Publications,
    2019. | "The [original] manuscript is chiefly in English, with about a
    quarter being Latin." | Includes bibliographical references and index.
Identifiers: LCCN 2018050632 | ISBN 9780738753683 (alk. paper)
Subjects: LCSH: Magic—England—History—17th century.
Classification: LCC BF1622.E55 O3 2019 | DDC 133.4/30942—dc23
LC record available at https://lccn.loc.gov/2018050632

Llewellyn Publications
A Division of Llewellyn Worldwide Ltd.
2143 Wooddale Drive
Woodbury, MN 55125-2989
www.llewellyn.com

Printed in the United States of America

TABLE OF
Contents

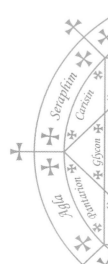

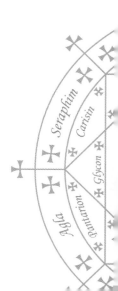

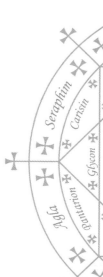

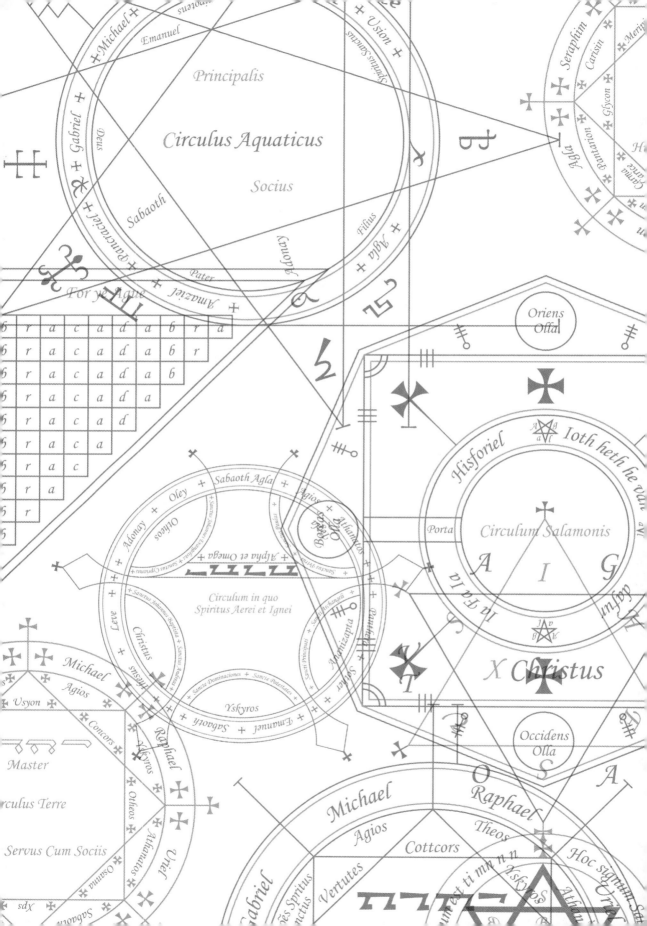

Introduction

The magician stands in the road as the snow falls on his hat and shoulders. A snowy winter in the countryside almost guarantees privacy, but if he leaves the road, his footprints will be visible on the ground. If a late-night traveler were to happen past, they might notice the tracks leading off the road, through the hedge, and toward the abandoned cottage in the hollow beyond. Would they speak to anyone in town? Would they care? Would he be shunned or prosecuted—or killed—if they found out?

He moves to the side, breaking off a small branch from the hedge. Balancing the basket on his other shoulder, he walks backward toward the gap in the hedge as he swishes the branch back and forth through the snow. Peering in the moonlight at his handiwork, he wonders whether he has made his trail more or less obvious. No time now; he can only hope that the falling snow does the work for him.

The cottage is dark and surrounded with snowdrifts. Its last tenants, as they hauled their few possessions to the city, spoke of unseen creatures laughing and invisible hands that pinched them under the covers. No one comes here now, save for the treasure hunters who showed up a few months ago and left town before dawn without speaking to anyone. At the bottom of the hill, a stream trickles quietly through ice. Something groans nearby—a tree branch?

Yet it seems safe. He was here last night, leaving a pail of water by the fireplace. After the sun rose, he found a curious film on the water's surface, which he collected with a silver spoon. It remains in a pewter vessel in one corner—so long as no one has disturbed it.

The house has but one room, cold and dark. The magician places a piece of charred linen into the cold fireplace, numb fingers fumbling in the dark with flint and steel until sparks turn to flame. A fragrant smell fills the room as the cherry sticks catch.

The man brushes off the table in the middle of the room before he covers it with a linen tablecloth, followed by three new knives with beautiful white hafts. From the basket he takes three loaves of the finest bread and a bottle of ale, brewed this morning, which he pours into wooden cups. The food and drink were so expensive that he skipped dinner in town. He reaches to break off a chunk of bread but then draws back his hand. Should he risk the anger of his guests?

An owl hoots as the man sits in a wobbling stool near the fireplace. Putting his back to the heat, he lifts up the saucer and anoints his eyes with the sticky substance it contains. His vision clouds and his eyes sting. He rubs, which makes it worse. After a few minutes, the prickling sensation stops and he settles onto the stool, drawing his cloak about him.

His head is drooping forward when the stool's leg shifts, startling him awake. He must not fall asleep—the three ladies of the fairies will be here soon, and he must be ready to greet the third so she will grant all his wishes. He hopes they will come. He hopes he will be awake when they do.

He hopes no one will see the tracks.

This scene might appear strange to us, but it is firmly based in views of the world that many of our ancestors held. The world was filled with nonhuman beings— good, evil, and indifferent—of great power and influence. Yet by virtue of the unique position of humanity in the cosmos, a person who was sufficiently pure, wise, and brave could convince or compel these beings to grant social standing, riches, or sex. To do this, a would-be magician required a book of magic, such as the one you hold now.

But what do we know about this book?

The Manuscript

Scholars are still discovering the surviving manuscripts on ritual magic held in libraries, archives, and private collections in North America, Europe, and in select institutions elsewhere. Modern literature for ritual magic practitioners often presents these as comprehensive treatises, along the lines of the *Key of Solomon*, the *Arbatel*, or *De Nigromantia*. Nonetheless, many of these manuscripts are less systematic compilations of material that practitioners assembled and edited from whatever manuscripts (or, later, printed works) they found accessible, interesting, or useful. Those familiar with the modern "Book of Shadows," or magical diary, will find its roots run deep.

In the collection of the Weston Library, part of the great Bodleian Library of Oxford, is one such manuscript, catalogued under the curious label "e Musaeo 173," usually shortened to e Mus. 173. It measures 8 x 6$\frac{1}{8}$ inches and is written on paper bound in vellum. The manuscript is chiefly in English, with about a quarter being Latin. The book is mainly written in secretary hand (a style of handwriting used for business purposes in the sixteenth and seventeenth centuries), with headings, holy names, and spirit names usually written in an italic hand. Both hands are consistent throughout, suggesting a single author. The ink is mostly black, with rubrics, or text in red ink, used to highlight particular words and passages. It may be that more such material was meant to be added later; some interesting blanks exist in the manuscript suggesting that the author intended to return to the passages with colored ink.

Where might this book have originated? As with so many other manuscripts of magic, it has no indication of authorship or ownership. The *Summary Catalogue* for the Bodleian manuscript collection informs us only that the work was copied in the early seventeenth century, and historian Frank Klaassen narrows these dates, based upon the secretary hand used within, to the first decade of that period. Some pages bear a watermark, a faint identifying mark, of a pot or vase with the initials "P. O." This would seem a promising lead, but the place and time of manufacturer are unknown, save that another sample of this watermark turns up in the papers of the Townshend family of Norfolk dating to 1575. Paper from such a batch could be used for decades, so this does little to narrow down the date.[1]

Who was the author? One of the love charms in the book bears the initials "A. B.," or possibly "J. A. B.," to signify the speaker. Given that most people in seventeenth century Britain lacked middle names, "A. B." is more likely—and since those are the first two letters of the alphabet, they may be generic holders for the magician to insert his name into the incantation when using it.

We do have two clues as to the manuscript's authorship, both on the same page. The first is the compiler's statement that a particular charm came from a Master Kymberleye, or Kimberly. The term "master" brings up a few possibilities. It could refer to a degree obtained at a university, but the name does not appear at an appropriate time in the (incomplete) alumni lists for Oxford or Cambridge. If it means a schoolmaster, our best candidate may be Jasper Kymberlye, who was

---

1   Foster, "Thomas Allen (1540–1632), Gloucester Hall, and the Survival of Catholicism in Post-Reformation Oxford," 110; Bodleian Library and Hunt, *A Summary Catalogue of Western Manuscripts in the Bodleian Library at Oxford*, 2, pt. 2:676–77; Klaassen, "Three Early Modern Magic Rituals to Spoil Witches," 4; Heawood, *Watermarks*, 143, plate 480.

appointed to that post at Asfordby, Leicestershire, on July 20, 1614. Of course, it could also refer to another person yet to be discovered.

The second clue is the appearance of one John Carpenter as a source for another charm on the same page. This is a common name, making its tracking difficult, but presumably, a place in which a Master Kymberleye and a John Carpenter lived at about the same time would be a possible candidate for the location in which the manuscript was written. Perhaps a specialist in local history or genealogy will be able to solve the mystery.

Thomas Barlow, who served as librarian for the Bodleian from 1652–60, received the manuscript in 1655, placing it in a cupboard in his study with other recent acquisitions on miscellaneous topics. Such works were labeled as being in the classification *in Musaeo*, Latin for "in the cupboard." When these books were taken out of the cupboard in 1728 for recataloguing, they were relabeled *e Musaeo*, or "out of the cupboard." Barlow claimed that the manuscript had come from the collection of Thomas Allen, who we shall meet shortly. Barlow arrived at Oxford as a servant in 1624, so his time and Allen's at the college did overlap, although it's unclear if they knew each other.

Yet the manuscript seems to have passed through another set of hands between Allen and the library. Allen was known for lending out books and not being fastidious about their return. Thus, even after he willed his remaining library to his friend Sir Kenelm Digby, who received them in 1632 and donated them to the Bodleian two years later, some works remained with others. A good number ended up in the collection of Sir Robert Bruce Cotton, later being donated to the British Library, while others are now part of collections as far-flung as Dublin's Trinity College, the University of Paris, and the Bibliothèque Nationale de France. It's possible e Mus. 173 may have been one of these misplaced works.[2]

When the book arrived at the Bodleian, it might not have arrived alone. In Thomas Barlow's notes, the work is listed alongside two other treatises of magic, since given the designations e Mus. 238 (also supposedly from Allen's collection) and 245. This might suggest that all three arrived simultaneously. There are no notes indicating whether these works were purchased or donated, although Barlow suggests they came from Joseph Godwin.[3]

2   Bodleian Library and Hunt, *A Summary Catalogue of Western Manuscripts in the Bodleian Library at Oxford*, 1:113; Watson, "Thomas Allen of Oxford and His Manuscripts."

3   Watson, "Thomas Allen of Oxford and His Manuscripts," 312. The work known as e Mus. 238 consists of two treatises on magic, one of which is a copy of *De Nigromantia*, with blank spaces for magical diagrams that were never filled in.

Godwin was a bookseller and publisher on Catte Street, on which the Bodleian's Weston Library stands today. We know relatively little about him, save that he was an active publisher from 1637 to his death in 1673. We know more about his son, Joseph, who apparently had matted hair, poor eyesight, and smallpox scars. Despite all this, a young woman living on the same street became infatuated with him, and when she could not have him, she poisoned herself with arsenic on October 12, 1655. When the elder Joseph died in 1673, this son, who had abandoned a fellowship at New College, took up the family business. A list of manuscripts acquired by the Bodleian from 1600 to 1695 includes five on magic, and four of these are from the elder Godwin, who donated no other works.[4]

Later scholars have recognized the value of e Mus. 173 in revealing the mindset and practices of the seventeenth century. The historian Keith Thomas's *Religion and the Decline of Magic*, a monumental work on early modern British mentality, refers to the manuscript repeatedly as a revealing source on magic of the time.[5] Frank Klaassen has used its contents to explore how cunning folk in the seventeenth century handled accusations of witchcraft.[6] Finally, the British folklorist Katherine Briggs has quoted from it repeatedly, beginning one enumeration of its contents as follows:

> One of the most interesting manuscripts which I have come across, from our point of view, is the early seventeenth-century treatise in the Bodleian, e Mus. 173. This has some general directions, but it is chiefly remarkable for the variety and scope of its recipes.[7]

Elsewhere, Briggs would say that the manuscript "contains in a small compass so great a variety of spells and treatises that it might be worth publication."[8] I hope that this work will fulfill her wish in some small way.

But what of the other potential owner of the book—Thomas Allen? What sort of man was he?

4   Plomer et al., *A Dictionary of the Printers and Booksellers Who Were at Work in England, Scotland and Ireland from 1668 to 1725*, 129; Wood, Clark, and Oxford Historical Society, *The Life and Times of Anthony Wood: Antiquary, of Oxford, 1632–1695, Described By Himself*, 199; Bodleian Library and Hunt, *A Summary Catalogue of Western Manuscripts in the Bodleian Library at Oxford*, 1:113–14, 120.

5   Thomas, *Religion and the Decline of Magic*, 220, 277, 649, 727.

6   Klaassen, "Three Early Modern Magic Rituals to Spoil Witches."

7   Briggs, "Some Seventeenth-Century Books of Magic," 456.

8   Briggs, *The Anatomy of Puck: An Examination of Fairy Beliefs among Shakespeare's Contemporaries and Successors*, 115.

The Life of Thomas Allen

EARLY LIFE

We know very little about the early years of Thomas Allen, astrologer, scholar, tutor, and reputed wizard. He was born in Staffordshire at Utoxeter or Bucknall on St. Thomas's Day, December 21, 1542, and was admitted to Oxford's Trinity College on June 4, 1561. The college had only been founded five years previously, through the generosity of Privy Council member Thomas Pope, and was intended for the sole purpose of educating future clergy. Allen was diligent in his studies, obtaining a BA on May 13, 1563, a fellowship in 1565, and a Master of Arts in 1567.[9]

Oxford had long been a stronghold of Catholic doctrine. During Elizabeth's reign, the government sought to bring the colleges into line with the Church of England. This was a slow process; in the 1560s no one insisted that all Oxford faculty conform to the church, perhaps for fear that too few would remain after the rest resigned. Nonetheless, the government overruled academic governance to appoint new heads of colleges who supported the queen's church. As Oxford changed, many Catholic sympathizers were expelled, convinced to leave, or chose to depart.[10]

Allen himself left in 1570, although his reasons remain unclear. It was customary—though not necessary—for a Trinity fellow to seek out a position in the clergy after six to eight years. Allen might have decided he no longer desired to serve in the new church. The atmosphere in Trinity was changing as well. By this time, the president of Trinity had been replaced—although with a stalwart of the school—and many of Allen's colleagues were departing. In 1570 three stone altars in Trinity's chapel previously used for Masses were destroyed. Further, the queen's commissioners and clergy threatened retribution against the college if it did not deface the plate used for Mass, thus causing it to lose any religious significance.[11]

No matter the reason, Allen left Trinity College and moved to Gloucester Hall, about a half mile away.[12] The hall was formerly part of Gloucester College, founded in 1283 by the Benedictine Order. It both fulfilled Benedictine edicts that a large number of its members be educated and allowed other worthy students to matriculate. The college was briefly assigned to the monastery of St. Peter's, Gloucester,

---

9   I have taken much of the information that follows from Foster, "Thomas Allen (1540–1632), Gloucester Hall, and the Survival of Catholicism in Post-Reformation Oxford." On Trinity, see Hopkins, *Trinity: 450 Years of an Oxford College Community*.

10   Williams, "Elizabethan Oxford: State, Church, and University."

11   Hopkins, *Trinity: 450 Years of an Oxford College Community*, 44–51.

12   Foster, "Thomas Allen, Gloucester Hall, and the Bodleian Library," 123.

thereby gaining its name.[13] After Henry VIII seized monastic property in 1536–41, the college closed, and the hall passed through various hands until becoming the property of St. John's College. It hosted few students, becoming "a quiet retreat to elderly men and women."[14] These included many recusants, such as Thomas Allen, who refused to conform to the new religious order.

Allen still possessed an important place at Oxford due to his mastery of mathematics. Knowledge of math beyond basic geometry was considered a luxury only to be pursued by those students who chose to do so. Allen became a private tutor for students across colleges and ideological lines, commanded packed houses for his lectures, and was labeled "the very soul and sun of all the mathematicians of his time."[15] Aubrey tells us that Allen was well-liked in Oxford, despite any misgivings about his faith. He was invited to the other houses for their gaudy days—feast days on which alumni gathered—on account of his wit and good humor. He had also mastered the customs and rules of the Oxford colleges, making him an individual to be consulted when questions on these arose.[16]

Allen also collected all sorts of manuscripts, most from far beyond Oxford. Half of the known surviving or described manuscripts from his collection deal with mathematics or science, while the others range over a wide variety of subjects, including magic. Works of incantations would not have been entirely out of place at a university of the period. It was unwise to make too public a show of one's conduct or to bring scandal upon the institution, but so long as a scholar kept an air of respectability about his inquiries, the university would usually tolerate it. Documents from the universities, including diaries, mock disputations, and manuscripts on a wide variety of occult topics, all show the universities of England to be places where astrological and magical studies were tolerated, if not encouraged.[17]

Although individual colleges owned their own collections, Oxford as a whole possessed no library since Duke Humfrey's library had been closed decades before. When Thomas Bodley sought to build a new library, the university appointed Allen to the committee assigned to the task. Allen was key in finding both funds and acquisitions for the library that would eventually become the Bodleian. He was

13   Salter, "Religious Houses: Gloucester College, Oxford."

14   Somerset and Salter, "The Colleges and Halls: Gloucester Hall and Worcester College, History," 299.

15   Feingold, "The Mathematical Sciences and New Philosophies"; Burton and Bathurst, *In viri doctissimi, clarissimi, optimi, Thomae Alleni, & philosophi & mathematici summi*; Wood, Bliss, and University of Oxford, *Athenae Oxonienses*, 1815, 2:542.

16   Aubrey and Clark, *"Brief Lives," Chiefly of Contemporaries, Set down by John Aubrey, between the Years 1669 & 1696*, 1:27.

17   Watson, "Thomas Allen of Oxford and His Manuscripts"; Feingold, "The Occult Tradition in the English Universities of the Renaissance: A Reassessment."

likely the one who cast the horoscope that established that the cornerstone of the library expansion, Arts End, be placed on July 19, 1610, at 10:30 AM. He contributed a small but significant collection of manuscripts to the library during his life, although the bulk of Allen's manuscripts would arrive at the Bodleian after his death. He was also a keen user; in 1613 the librarian claimed that Allen and his friend Brian Twyne were the only two who had consulted the Bodleian's manuscripts.[18]

Thomas Allen passed away on September 30, 1632. He was buried in Trinity Chapel with Church of England honors, although Hopkins proposes he converted formally to Catholicism upon his deathbed. Most of the money he left to poor family members in Uttoxeter, with nothing going to his fellow scholars or more wealthy relations. The amount he left to his longtime home of Gloucester Hall was half that he bestowed upon Trinity College, possibly due to a dispute with the new principal of the hall. Part of the gift to Trinity was spent on a portrait of Mr. Allen, which still hangs in the home of the college's president. As discussed before, the bulk of his books were routed to Sir Kenelm Digby.[19]

Allen might be much better known for his accomplishments had any works by him been published. Sadly, he only completed two manuscripts, commentaries on the second and third books of Ptolemy's *Tetrabiblios*, perhaps the most influential astrological tract of all time. The commentary on the second book survives in manuscript form, passing from William Lilly to Elias Ashmole, while the other has vanished. Further, no more than three letters of Allen's have survived. Thus, not only do many questions about his influence, knowledge, and accomplishments remain unanswered, but he has slipped into obscurity.[20]

GOOD AND FAMOUS FRIENDS

Readers might get the impression of Allen as a quiet, retiring man immersed in the academy, yet Allen had extensive contacts with many individuals both within and outside Oxford, including notable individuals such as the mathematician Thomas Harriot, the mystic Robert Fludd, and the author and courtier Sir Philip Sidney. Indeed, his ties extended to some of the most prominent people of the realm, as well as to some of the most famous wizards of any age.

18   Foster, "Thomas Allen (1540–1632)," 111–12; Foster, "Thomas Allen, Gloucester Hall, and the Bodleian Library," 126; Clapinson, *A Brief History of the Bodleian Library*, 5–8, 28.

19   Foster, "Thomas Allen (1540–1632)," 125–6; Hopkins, *Trinity: 450 Years of an Oxford College Community*, 54.

20   Ashmole 388, "Claudii Ptolomae, Pelusiensis de Astrorum Judiciis, aut ut vulgo vocant Quadripartitre Constructionis, liber secundus"; Feingold, *The Mathematicians' Apprenticeship: Science, Universities and Society in England, 1560–1640*, 155.

The first of these was Robert Dudley (1532?–1588), Earl[21] of Leicester and erst-while favorite of the queen. One of the most powerful men in the land, Dudley took on the role of university chancellor in 1564. The earl did much to reform the college, whether insisting on proper dress and high standards or leasing its land to his favorites. Most notably, he was one of the chief agents of asserting the church's control over the colleges. Despite the small number of Catholics at Oxford by 1581, the earl insisted in that year that all incoming students take the Oath of Supremacy to the Queen, and that any tutor suspected of Catholic sympathies would not be allowed to teach.[22]

One might expect the earl to have been Allen's nemesis, but nothing could be further from the truth. The magus John Dee had tutored Dudley in mathematics when the noble was a young man, and Dudley maintained a love of the subject that his rank never permitted him to indulge. He was also less strict about the beliefs of his personal associates, and Allen's convivial nature seems to have won Dudley over. Indeed, their relationship was so strong that Oxford historian Anthony à Wood later claimed that Allen was part of a small cabal that actually helped the earl run the college.[23]

As he sought to reform Oxford, the earl also desired to put bishops friendly to him into positions of power. It is said that the earl offered Allen a bishopric, which the scholar declined, either due to "the sweetness of a retired life," as Wood put it, or because his Roman Catholic sympathies outweighed the benefits of a church office. Nonetheless, the two men seem to have been close, as "no person was more familiar with" the earl than Allen—save if it were Dee himself.[24]

Did Allen have a relationship with Dee? Indeed, the magus was mentioned in Allen's funeral oration as singing the praises of his Oxford colleague's skills as a mathematician. We know very little of the interactions between the two men; I have found nothing in one man's writing that directly mentions the other. Still, they were certainly two individuals with friends and interests in common. In addi-tion, Dee was said to have given Allen a special lens that could project an inverted

21 To make this clear to non-British readers, an earl ranks below a duke or a marquess but above a baron. Given the lack of dukes and scarcity of marquesses for much of Elizabeth's reign, Allen was associated with some of the highest nobles in the realm.

22 Williams, "Elizabethan Oxford: State, Church, and University," 413–14, 423–31.

23 Wilson, *Sweet Robin: A Biography of Robert Dudley, Earl of Leicester 1533–1588*, 16; Williams, "Elizabethan Oxford: State, Church, and University," 424.

24 Wood, Bliss, and University of Oxford, *Athenae Oxonienses*, 1815, 2:542.

image of whatever was placed in front of it. Allen kept this glass until his death, leaving it to Thomas Aylesbury.[25]

On June 10, 1583, Oxford was graced with the presence of the Polish noble Albert Laski, Palatine of Sieradz. Four days of entertainments were provided for him, most notably a disputation between Doctor John Underhill and a fiery Neapolitan visitor, Giordano Bruno. During this time it was reported that Sir Philip Sidney introduced Laski to Allen. Laski was so impressed that he asked Allen to join him in his own country "to live there as he pleased, and accept of such honours and dignities which he could get for him."[26] Allen turned him down gracefully. On his way back to London, Laski stopped in Mortlake, where Sidney introduced him to Doctor John Dee, who later readily assented to Laski's offer of patronage in Poland. Would Laski have asked Dee if Allen had not refused? It seems likely; Dee had met Laski before Laski met Allen in Oxford, and Dee had conducted repeated attempts to contact the spirits for Laski.[27]

Allen might have been closer to Dee's scandalous partner and scryer, Edward Kelley. An anonymous young man who served as a secretary to Allen reported meeting the future magician and alchemist at Gloucester Hall. Wood could find no record for a Kelley present at that time, although he found some Talbots from Ireland. When Kelley first met Dee, he was using Talbot as an alias.[28] If Kelley was at Gloucester Hall, Kelley and Allen had an excellent opportunity to meet, though the evidence is questionable.

Later, Allen would become a favorite of Henry Percy, ninth Earl of Northumberland (1564–1632), popularly known as the "Wizard Earl." Northumberland was

---

25   Feingold, *The Mathematicians' Apprenticeship: Science, Universities and Society in England, 1560–1640*, 157; Bodleian Library, Madan, and Craster, *A Summary Catalogue of Western Manuscripts in the Bodleian Library at Oxford*, 2, pt. 1:646–47; Foster, "Thomas Allen (1540–1632)," 126.

   Allen also had several manuscripts in his library from Dee's collection. It is unclear whether most of these came directly to Allen from Dee or through intermediate sources. Bodleian Library, et al., *Digby Manuscripts*.

   It has been suggested that Thomas Allen was at one time a treasurer of the Company of Cathay, which bankrolled the expeditions of Sir Martin Frobisher, Dee's friend, in search of the Northwest Passage. It would appear that this Allen was actually a London leather merchant and member of the Skinner's Guild who was a major importer and exporter to Danzig in the late 1560s. Woolley, *The Queen's Conjurer: The Science and Magic of Dr. John Dee, Adviser to Queen Elizabeth I*, 128; Zins and Stevens, *England and the Baltic in the Elizabethan Era*, 101–2; Willan, *The Muscovy Merchants of 1555*, 75.

26   Wood, Bliss, and University of Oxford, *Athenae Oxonienses*, 1815, 2:542.

27   Wood and Gutch, *The History and Antiquities of the University of Oxford: In Two Books*, 215–18; McMullin, "Giordano Bruno at Oxford"; Woolley, *The Queen's Conjurer: The Science and Magic of Dr. John Dee, Adviser to Queen Elizabeth I*, 207; Parry, *The Arch-Conjuror of England: John Dee*, 162–70.

28   Wood, Bliss, and University of Oxford, *Athenae Oxonienses*, 1813, 1:639.

out of favor with the rulers of the time and even served sixteen years in the Tower of London due to his association with the Gunpowder Plot of 1605. One of the charges was that he had asked for a horoscope of James I to be drawn up, an activity considered treasonous, as it could reveal a monarch's date of death. Both at his estate at Syon and in the tower, Percy spent much of his time in contemplation of philosophical and scientific topics and consultation with the most brilliant men of his time. Although no one has suggested that his title "wizard" meant the earl was conjuring spirits, he did surround himself with men of learning and note, including Thomas Harriot and Sir Walter Raleigh.[29]

Even Queen Elizabeth once called upon Allen, or so Aubrey tells us. The occasion was the "new star that appeared in the Swan or Cassiopeia."[30] Today, a "new star" would be hardly worthy of note, but this one—the supernova that appeared in Cassiopeia in November of 1572—was a startling and frightening discovery. For centuries, academics had held to their Aristotelian view of the cosmos as predictable and unchanging above the lunar sphere. The supernova's appearance could be a sign that the views of the cosmos needed to be revised—or a portent from the Almighty, as was the Star of Bethlehem.[31]

Did the queen call upon Allen's expertise in the heavens? We have no evidence that she did, but the supernova did inspire interest at court. On December 11, 1572, the mathematician and astronomer Thomas Digges wrote William Cecil, Elizabeth's secretary of state, on his knowledge of the star.[32] The following year Digges published his treatise on the event, along with introducing another on the same topic by Dee, his good friend and mentor.[33] Given the interest in the event from both high levels of government and Allen's social circle, along with his ties to the Earl of Leicester, it is quite possible that Allen would have had the opportunity to discuss the supernova in a manner that would have reached the queen's ears.

At this time, knowledge of astronomy often overlapped with that in astrology, and Allen was no stranger to the practice. Two particular charts secured his fame. One, performed at the nativity of the future Earl of Kingston, Robert Pierrepont,

---

29 Batho, "The Library of the 'Wizard' Earl: Henry Percy, Ninth Earl of Northumberland (1564–1632)"; Nicholls, "The 'Wizard Earl' in Star Chamber: The Trial of the Earl of Northumberland, June 1606"; Batho, "The Wizard Earl of Northumberland: An Elizabethan Scholar-Nobleman."

30 Aubrey and Clark, *"Brief Lives,"* 1:28.

31 Baumgartner, "Starry Messengers: Supernovas, Comets, and Sunspots Heralded the Scientific Revolution."

32 Great Britain Public Record Office and Lemon, *Calendar of State Papers, Domestic Series, of the Reigns of Edward VI, Mary, Elizabeth 1547–1580, Preserved in the State Paper Department of Her Majesty's Public Record Office,* 454.

33 Digges, *Alae; seu, Scalae Mathematicae*; Dee and Digges, *Parallaticae Commentationis Praxeosq[ue] Nucleus Quidam.*

in 1584, was found to be accurate, based upon the family's own accounts, on everything from his treatment at court to his family. Allen drew up another horoscope for William Herbert, the third Earl of Pembroke, who had become chancellor of Oxford in 1626. According to Allen's chart, the earl would pass away at the age of fifty and one half. Pembroke died unexpectedly in 1630 a few days after his fiftieth birthday. Despite the gap in months, Allen received credit for his predictive talents.[34]

Was Allen a Magician?

Given the topic of e Mus. 173 and Allen's interest in astrology, we might very well ask if he was a practitioner of ritual magic. This places us into treacherous territory, but it deserves to be examined, especially in light of a large amount of anecdotal evidence that speaks of him as a magician. Some notable tales follow:

- John Power, likely a resident at Gloucester Hall, as was his younger brother Zachary, related a brief tale to the antiquarian John Aubrey. One of his servants had told Power that one of Allen's servants—possibly John Murtagh, to whom Allen referred in his will—used to proclaim to the gullible that he "should meet the spirits comeing up his staires like bees" from Allen's room.[35]

- The year 1584 saw the publication of a book seeking to libel the Earl of Leicester, Allen's first patron. The work, likely written by Charles Arundell, was entitled *The Copie of a Leter, Wryten by a Master of Arte of Cambridge* but became better known under its unofficial label of *Leicester's Commonwealth.* Among its accusations of all manner of crimes and foul deeds that the earl supposedly committed, the author criticized him for retaining "Dee and Allen (two atheists) for figuring and conjuring."[36] Elsewhere, the same book accuses the earl of employing magic to assault his foes and seduce women, although a Mother Davis or Davies was said to have cast a love spell against an unnamed woman—likely Her Majesty herself.[37]

- In the thirty-fourth year of Queen Elizabeth, a Thomas Fitzherbert made a series of accusations to the queen against William Bassett, the

34 Foster, "Thomas Allen (1540–1632)," 124; Aubrey and Clark, *"Brief Lives,"* 1:370–71.

35 Aubrey and Clark, *"Brief Lives,"* 1:27.

36 Peck, *Leicester's Commonwealth: The Copy of a Letter Written by a Master of Art of Cambridge (1584) and Related Documents,* 79.

37 Peck, *Leicester's Commonwealth,* 62, 125, 161–62.

sheriff of Derbyshire. One of these was that Bassett had consulted with Allen and a Mr. Davis regarding the fortunes of a sheriff in the event of a prince's death. Twelve or thirteen years before, Fitzherbert said, Bassett and Allen had tried to contact spirits as well. At the end of a year-long process, they dispatched one Richard Johnson to Langlay to obtain a hammer and anvil from a smith. When the sun shone at noon, they would strike the hammer against the anvil three times, and a spirit would manifest. Due to poor weather and the inability to determine the hour, the procedure was not completed—or so Fitzherbert ended his account.[38]

- Around 1600, according to Herefordshire folklore, the inhabitants of Bronsil Castle, Eastnor, were kept awake by repeated visits of a spirit at night. Gabriel Reede, the castle's owner, sought out Allen at Oxford to ask for a solution to the problem. Allen suggested to him that bringing in the bones of a former owner of the castle, Sir John Beauchamp, would silence the spirit. Reede did so, and the bones were still kept by the family at the end of the nineteenth century.[39]

- A document found in the manuscript collection of Elias Ashmole consists of a list of powers of an amulet supposedly owned by Allen and made under the power of Leo. Its capabilities include ease of childbirth, stopping the excessive flow of blood, protection from lightning, and putting demons to flight. It's unclear who wrote this passage or whether it attests to Allen's practice of magic or simply wishful thinking on the part of the scribe.[40]

Overall, most of the evidence for Allen as a magician falls into two categories: anecdotes, often related secondhand or further removed and told well after his death, and accusations by individuals who are attempting to embarrass others. We should not trust that they reveal anything definite about his interests. Allen did have magical manuscripts, but only a small fraction of the works traced back to his

---

38   Camm, *Forgotten Shrines: An Account of Some Old Catholic Halls and Families in England and of Relics and Memorials of the English Martyrs*, 387–88. I have not seen a spirit-summoning procedure that required striking an anvil three times after a year to summon one. The closest parallel I have seen is in the creation of the three cross knife in Pennsylvania German folklore, in which a knife must be made with nine strikes on the anvil, with a year between each three, during which time the devil appears to interfere with the process. Donmoyer, *Powwowing in Pennsylvania: Braucherei and the Ritual of Everyday Life*, 219–21.

39   Piper, "Bronsil Castle, Eastnor," 229–30.

40   Bodleian Ashmole MS 1441, 369r.

library deal with the topic, with much greater numbers dealing with mathematics, science, history, theology, the lives of the saints, medicine, and other topics. He seems to have been friendly with John Dee and possibly Kelley, but these gentlemen had other interests—optics, astrology, and mathematics, for starters—that they shared in common with Allen. Thus, we should approach any unsupported reports of magical practice from this period with some skepticism.[41]

Indeed, it was common for a man with scientific and scholarly interests to be associated with magic. An incident from one of Allen's trips to the Herefordshire home of his friend John Scudamore will illustrate this.

> ...he happened to leave his watch in the chamber window. (Watches were then rarities.) The maids came in to make the bed, and hearing a thing in a case cry, "Tick, tick, tick," presently concluded that it was his Devil, and took it by the string with the tongs, and threw it out of the window into the moat (to drown the Devil). It so happened that the string hung on a sprig of an elder that grew out of the moat, and this confirmed them that 'twas the Devil.[42]

What about our manuscript? Does it constitute proof? It is tempting to ascribe the work to Allen himself, but we have little evidence of this. I have also examined every known sample believed to be Thomas Allen's handwriting in order to identify similarities with the script in the manuscript. I am not an expert on handwriting differences, but I can say that there are substantial disparities between e Mus. 173 and the other documents. To be fair, the purported samples of Allen's handwriting also differ considerably from each other, as Michael Foster points out. Nonetheless, no evidence exists to suggest that Allen transcribed this manuscript.[43]

41 Foster, "Thomas Allen (1540–1632)," 109–10.

42 Aubrey and Clark, *"Brief Lives,"* 1:27–8. I have modernized Aubrey's text for ease of reading.

43 Foster, "Thomas Allen (1540–1632)," 111.

The Magic of the Manuscript

Described as a magical miscellany, e Mus. 173 is a collection of short magical operations, or portions thereof, intended to be a compendium from other works for study or practice. Past authors have often paid more attention to more systematic treatises, but the miscellanies suggest another approach to magic. Magicians might not work systematically with a single work, such as the *Key of Solomon* or *Lemegeton*, but instead take the names of spirits, conjurations, preparations, bindings, and licenses, with different variants, from various sources to assemble a ritual.

If anything, e Mus. 173 is more miscellaneous in content than others of the genre. The compiler has copied significant portions from other sources: talismans from Agrippa's *Three Books*, magic circles from *De Nigromancia*, a list of angels from the *Almadel* and another of planetary spirits from *Liber Juratus*. These fragments are not a sign of a disordered collector; the precise handwriting and carefully drawn illustrations argue otherwise. Instead, this is a collection intended to provide the user with a set of tools that could be used in spirit conjurations. Some of these might fill in gaps in the material elsewhere in the magician's collection. For instance, we have a license for the spirit Askariel, which would have been useful given multiple experiments for summoning the spirit without a dismissal.[44] Likewise, the sole choir of angels taken from the *Almadel* assists with conjurations, thus supplementing such operations. Some of the spirit circles relating to the elements might be used with conjurations to call up spirits connected with these forces, although the inclusion of the "Circle of the Horse" from *De Nigromantia* does seem to be missing a relevant operation from the same work. It might be that this work was intended to supplement another text or texts in possession of the author or was simply copied from another incomplete source.

Nonetheless, the text does include a number of fascinating rites in full, aimed at a wide variety of purposes. I have made some preliminary examinations of what the most common objectives for these rites might be. If we might venture some broad categories, it seems that the author was most concerned about calling up spirits to answer questions, usually of an unspecified nature (18 examples). Beyond this, the others include hunting for treasure (15), uncovering theft (12), healing (11, almost half of which are for stopping bleeding), combating witchcraft (10), and simply having spirits fulfill one's commands (9).[45] Such magical practices were largely the province of the cunning folk, so our scribe might have been such a

---

44   See later in this manuscript, as well as Harms, Clark, and Peterson, *The Book of Oberon*, 410–416.

45   The incantations in "The Chapters of All Offices of Spirits" are excluded from this listing but are included below on the list of spirits.

---

person, calling upon spirits in order to find thieves and riches, deal with the ills of his or her clients, and ward off hostile supernatural forces.[46]

Additionally, e Mus. 173 also includes different lists of spirits. First, we have a list of the four kings of the directions and their minions, as has previously appeared in *The Book of Oberon*, with a few noteworthy differences from that text. We also have two other lists of spirits and their seals. One of these is similar in format and content to others in Sloane MS 3853 and Chetham's Mun.A.4.98, although the one here has numerous differences in the spirits listed.[47]

The purposes of these spirits are much more variegated, and any categorization of their abilities can easily be debated. For instance, if a spirit transports the dead, should this be considered necromancy or transportation or some combination of the two? Should "answering questions" be subdivided into simple queries on one hand and those about the past or future on the other? Nonetheless, an attempt might give us some perspective.

Based upon my own categorization, it appears that the most common purpose for calling up these spirits is for the answering of the magician's questions (27 examples). Following this are the ability to influence people, whether favorably or unfavorably, toward the magician, and the teaching of various academic disciplines and types of natural magic (22 and 21, respectively).[48] The acquisition of treasure and money (18) follows these, and we have a wide gap before a profusion of other functions: the construction and manufacture of goods (9), erotic operations (9), making the magician invisible (8), and granting dignities and stations to the magician (9). Beyond these, we have other purposes that are only available in small numbers: granting wisdom, harming others, affecting the dead, consecrating items, and the like.

In some respects, such as the discovery of treasure and the seeking of information, this list supports the possibility of the compiler being a cunning person. What of the other interests—the obtaining of influence, the teaching of academic subjects, or invisibility? I believe these may be seen as a sign of broader curiosity from such a practitioner, involved very much in the life of his or her community but interested in the broader scope of magic and the power it promised.

---

46   Davies, *Popular Magic: Cunning Folk in English History*, 93–112.

47   Stam, "A Book Called the Dannel," 40–46.

48   If we include erotic operations among the latter, it would increase to 30.

Magic and Witchcraft in Seventeenth-Century England

THE LAW AND THE WITCH TRIALS

After Elizabeth's death in 1603, King James VI of Scotland acceded to the throne of England. James gained a reputation for being a man obsessed with witchcraft and magic. He himself had been the target of witch-raised storms and mists as he traveled to and from Denmark in 1589–90 to return to Britain with Queen Anne—at least, if the confessions of the North Berwick witches were to be believed. His book *Daemonologie* (1597), detailing the snares and wiles of demons and witches, became the only manual on witchcraft ever written by a monarch. Most notably, in 1604 Parliament passed a new act that portended dire calamities for anyone who would practice sorcery or witchcraft.[49]

This is not to say that the previous act, Elizabeth's of 1563, was not harsh in its penalties. Conjuration of evil spirits, causing death through magic, or aiding either of these two was punishable by death. Most other offenses, including magic for love, causing illness, destruction of property, or finding stolen property, would be punished with a year's imprisonment and four days in the pillory for a first offense, with either life imprisonment or execution for a second.

The Act of 1604 maintained most of the previous act, but it was intensified in most areas. Causing illness through magic was penalized with death instead of a year's imprisonment. The penalty for the second offenses for treasure hunting, solving theft, soliciting love, or the intent to cause injury or destruction of property was increased from life imprisonment to death. The act also prescribed death for two new offenses: dealing with a spirit outside of conjuration and stealing dead bodies or the parts thereof for use in magic.[50]

Nonetheless, the harsh penalties did not inspire most prosecutors and judges to greater fervor in seeking out wizards and magicians. As the century progressed, trials for magic and witchcraft waned in frequency overall, with some notable exceptions. King James himself seemed ambivalent about further prosecutions, sometimes encouraging them, sometimes investigating particular accusations and uncovering fraud. Nonetheless, belief in humans wielding supernatural powers was still prevalent, even at the highest levels of English government.[51]

Witchcraft was still very much a concern throughout the British Isles. People at all levels of society believed that individuals, usually female, possessed unnatural power that allowed them to destroy livestock, stop household production of beer or

---

49   Roberts and Normand, *Witchcraft in Early Modern Scotland*.

50   *Statutes of the Realm*, 5 Eliz. c. 16; Ibid., 1 Jac. I c. 12. For both acts and an analysis thereof, please see Newton and Bath, *Witchcraft and the Act of 1604*.

51   Roberts and Normand, *Witchcraft in Early Modern Scotland*, 106.

butter, and kill or injure people. The accused lived in the same areas as their victims, with multiple accusations following them over time. The Continental model of witchcraft, in which supposed groups of witches made covenants to serve Satan, met in sabbats, copulated with the devil, and embarked on sprees of destruction, only caught on in a limited fashion in England. By the time it was gaining widespread acceptance in popular belief, witchcraft charges were regarded with enough skepticism that the Continental model had no long-term effect on prosecution.[52]

Still, with such impressive legal remedies as given in the Act of 1604, one might have expected witchcraft suspicions to be dealt with through witch trials. Many court and jail records from the time did not survive, so our knowledge of these proceedings is limited. Still, records indicate that some regions, especially Essex and the Southwest, saw more witchcraft prosecution than others. Despite James's reputation as a witch hunter, his reign saw a decrease in prosecutions of witchcraft from the latter part of the Elizabethan period. It reached a new climax in 1647–9 with the East Anglian prosecutions of Matthew Hopkins, the "Witchfinder General," but this was the last British witch hunt.[53]

Still, English witch trials never became as endemic as they did in many parts of Europe. The reasons for this are myriad. Most charges originated in local disputes between neighbors, and the de-emphasis on the witches' conspiracy kept prosecutors from seeking the names of more witches from the accused. Popular belief held that a witch placed under the power of authorities could not do more harm, so this was to the afflicted's advantage. Nonetheless, many trials were held at the quarterly assizes (regional courts), presided over by judges from the capital who might be skeptical of local suspicions of witchcraft. The prosecuting individual was responsible for much of the cost of the trial, and conviction rates for all felonies were low. Thus, judicial remedies were often only sought as a last resort in the most dangerous cases.[54]

Thus, many who believed in witchcraft sought informal means to free themselves of enchantment. In the past, the Catholic Church proposed various remedies using holy words, objects, or rituals to counter misfortune.[55] The Church of England's position, calling for pastoral consultation or prayer, paled in comparison. At other times the afflicted would consult with local physicians or self-proclaimed experts in witchcraft. They might also resort to a variety of folk remedies, including scratching the suspected witch to draw blood, burning part of the person's

---

52 Sharpe, *Instruments of Darkness: Witchcraft in England 1550–1750*, 58–79.

53 Ibid., 105–47.

54 Ibid., 105–13.

55 British examples are lacking, but for similar examples on the continent, see De Waardt, "From Cunning Man to Natural Healer," 42–44.

thatch, or creating witch cakes or witch bottles to return the spell to the person. Sufferers might try several different methods, either consecutively or simultaneously.[56]

THE ROLE OF CUNNING FOLK

Another remedy was also available: consulting one of the cunning folk, or local magical practitioners, who had a thriving trade across England. Such individuals were usually members of the artisan and tradesmen classes, and the majority were male. Cunning folk offered a variety of services: healing, recovering stolen goods, treasure hunting, and unwitching. The latter might consist of providing charms against bewitchment, revealing the name or face of the witch, or performing rituals that would negate or reverse the witch's power. This did occasionally open up the cunning person to accusations of witchcraft, but evidence from cunning folk would often be presented in court—and accepted by the judge—as proof of witchcraft.[57]

We have little idea as to the activities of cunning folk outside the attention of judges and pamphleteers, but the London astrologer William Lilly (1602–1681) provides us with some insights into the magical market in his own city. When he was still a servant, his mistress died, and he found a pouch in her possessions with many different talismans within. Seeking to learn astrology, he turned to John Evans, who was known to call spirits using circles. Not only were stories about Dee and Simon Forman very much still the talk of London, but a large number of contemporary magicians—who created talismans for protection and healing, divined using the "mosaical rods," and crystal-gazed—still lived in the city. Lilly speaks of his own rituals, once hunting for treasure at Westminster, and at another time calling up the Queen of Fairies to the terror of a friend.[58]

The cunning folk were the chief practitioners of English magic in the seventeenth century, with the Renaissance magus epitomized in Dee vanishing entirely from the cultural landscape. Among the cunning folk was Simon Forman (1552–1611), who lived for some time in London. Forman was known at the time for his astrological medicine and his battles with the physicians of the era, vilified after his death through his peripheral involvement in a case of poisoning, and studied today due to his accounts of attending Shakespeare's plays and his well-documented sex life. One of his students, Richard Napier (1559–1634), went on to pursue a ministerial career at Great Linford, although he handed off his preaching duties in

---

56   Sharpe, *Instruments of Darkness: Witchcraft in England 1550–1750*, 155–62.

57   Davies, *Popular Magic*, 67–118; Ewen and Great Britain Courts of Assize and Nisi Prius, *Witch Hunting and Witch Trials: The Indictments for Witchcraft from the Records of 1373 Assizes Held for the Home Circuit A.D. 1559–1736*, 230, 363.

58   Lilly, *William Lilly's History of His Life and Times from the Year 1602 to 1681*.

favor of performing medicine, astrology, unwitching, and the creation of plane-tary talismans for all comers. His own magical experiments with ritual magic, including his calls to the angel Raphael, are less documented.[59]

Most cunning folk maintained good relations with their neighbors, but one infamous one did not: John Lambe of Tardebigge, Worcestershire, who was prose-cuted for witchcraft and spirit conjuration in 1607. He was charged again in 1608 for summoning a spirit known as Benias in a crystal placed upon his hat. Even imprisoned in Worcester Castle, he entertained guests by obtaining wine from a local tavern—without leaving his cell—and calling up spirits in the crystal. He was removed to London's King's Bench prison, from which he apparently gained his freedom and took up a lucrative practice in the city. In 1628, after being reprieved from a rape conviction, a mob beat him to death in the streets.[60]

WORKS ON MAGIC IN THE SEVENTEENTH CENTURY

Feeding the market for cunning magic was the florescence of publishing following the Civil War, which brought into print many books on magic in English for the first time. Notable among these were the translation by "J. F." of Agrippa's *De Occul-ta Philosophia* (1651), Giambattista della Porta's *Natural Magic* (1658), and the work of Robert Turner, who combined pseudo-Agrippa's *Fourth Book*, the *Magical Elements* or *Heptameron* attributed to Pietro d'Abano, and the book of mystical planetary magic titled *Arbatel*, into a compilation (1655, re-released in 1665). Such manuals soon became the stock-in-trade for many magicians of the period.[61]

To these publications we might add two works intended to discredit magicians. First, Reginald Scot's *Discoverie of Witchcraft*, originally published in 1584, appeared in new editions in 1651 and 1654. Scot's skeptical attitude toward witch-craft, more in vogue after the excesses of Matthew Hopkins, might have been the reason for these reprints. Such an explanation cannot account for the expanded edition of 1665, however, to which was added magical rituals and discussions of the nature of spirits. Second, Meric Casaubon's *A True & Faithful Relation of What Passed for Many Yeers Between Dr. John Dee...and Some Spirits* (1659) sought to discredit Dee and his spirit operations by portraying him as foolish. Instead, fasci-nated readers used it as a sourcebook, leading to the adoption of Dee's Enochian

---

59   Rowse, *Simon Forman: Sex and Society in Shakespeare's Age*; MacDonald, *Mystical Bedlam: Madness, Anxiety, and Healing in Seventeenth-Century England*.

60   *A Briefe Description of the Notorious Life of Iohn Lambe: Otherwise Called Doctor Lambe, Together with His Ignominious Death*.

61   Davies, *Popular Magic:*, 121–27.

procedures on a limited basis until his work gained greater recognition in the nineteenth century.[62]

Despite the apparent riches of printed occult books, their publication in Britain was confined to a mere two decades within the seventeenth century. No noteworthy book of English magic would appear for nearly a century and a half, and when Barrett published *The Magus* (1801), it was embarrassingly dependent upon the publications that came before. Thus manuscripts retained considerable importance. More manuscript works of British ritual magic survive from this period than from any century before, and many of these informed or borrowed from the print tradition, as well as oral magical traditions, to create a rich tapestry of operations for many different purposes. The most famous of these works, unpublished until the twentieth century, was the *Lemegeton*, which bundled two treatises on spirits with previous compilations such as the *Pauline Art*, the *Almadel*, and the *Ars Notoria*. For interested readers, a large number of other manuscripts, often more miscellaneous in focus, have been published more recently.[63]

Although many seventeenth-century scholars and clergy saw such manuscripts as blasphemous or worthless, we owe the survival of so many to antiquarian collectors of the time. Elias Ashmole (1617–1692) acquired the manuscripts of Simon Forman and William Lilly. He seems to have been inspired by them to craft astrological talismans for influence, curing diseases, and pest control, and he might have dabbled in fairy summoning as well.[64] Other prominent collectors who kept magical manuscripts in their libraries include the Cotton family, with Sir Thomas Cotton (1594–1662) providing Casaubon access to a work of Dee's spirit operations (now British Library Cotton Appendix MS. XLVI), which he published as his *True & Faithful Relation*. Most notable among these antiquarians was Sir Hans Sloane (1660–1753), whose collection of over two dozen magical manuscripts is now held in the British Library.[65]

---

62   Scot, *The Discovery of Witchcraft*; Asprem, *Arguing with Angels: Enochian Magic and Modern Occulture*, 29–42.

63   Klaassen, *The Transformations of Magic: Illicit Learned Magic in the Later Middle Ages and Renaissance*, 158–59; Peterson, *The Lesser Key of Solomon*; McLean, *A Treatise on Angel Magic*; Ashmole and Rankine, *The Book of Treasure Spirits*; Gauntlet and Rankine, *The Grimoire of Arthur Gauntlet*; Harms, Clark, and Peterson, *The Book of Oberon*; Skinner and Rankine, *The Keys to the Gateway of Magic*; Skinner and Rankine, *The Goetia of Dr. Rudd*; Skinner and Rankine, *A Cunning Man's Grimoire*; Young, *The Cambridge Book of Magic*.

64   Ashmole and Josten, *Elias Ashmole, 1617–1692: His Autobiographical and Historical Notes, His Correspondence, and Other Contemporary Sources Relating to His Life and Work*, 4:1523, 4:1629, 2:537. One of Ashmole's manuscripts includes two rites to summon fairies with the initials "E. A." inserted as the name of the summoner; see Ashmole MS. 1406, 16–24.

65   Dee, *A True & Faithful Relation of What Passed for Many Yeers Between Dr. John Dee…and Some Spirits*; Klaassen, *The Transformations of Magic*, 250.

In the latter decades of the seventeenth century, clerical and secular authorities turned their attention away from magic and witchcraft alike. The Church began to omit these offenses from the list of visitation articles sent to parishes, leading to fewer cases being pursued. Although the Act of 1604 remained on the books, it was largely ignored in practice. The focus for godly authors was no longer witches at the sabbat but materialism, as epitomized by Hobbes' *Leviathan*, and Deism, both of which they perceived as new fundamental threats to Christianity. Indeed, authors such as Joseph Glanvill, Richard Bovet, and even Reverend Robert Kirk collected and published reports of ghosts, witches, and other supernatural beings as proofs to shore up belief in God.[66]

Even in more skeptical times, belief in magic and witchcraft was still very much a part of the English mental landscape. Indeed, with the end of clergy, doctors, and judges dealing with purported witchcraft, the cunning men and women gained importance, with such situations being handled mostly outside the knowledge of the elites.

The Cosmology and Nature of Spirits in Early Modern Magic

Authors such as Greenfield and Kieckhefer have made great efforts to chart out the spiritual world of ritual magic texts and how they differed from conventional theology of their milieus. Both have said much that is worth seeking out, but I would like to touch upon some aspects of the present work and others, particularly *Oberon*, that have not been remarked upon before.

This book of magic, as many others of the sixteenth and seventeenth centuries, is part of a broader tradition of Christian theology and cosmology influenced by the Neoplatonists. Within Catholic theology the omnipotent God, composed of the Father, the Son, and the Holy Spirit, rules the universe. Beneath him are a number of celestial assistants, most notably the Virgin Mary, the angels, the saints, and the martyrs. All of these may manifest their power on earth, either through the words or actions of their human agents, including the pope, the clergy, and individuals who are particularly pious or beloved of God, such as widows or orphans, or through miraculous intervention. This intervention might be to protect God's chosen ones, to deliver a person from distress, or to overcome a demon possessing a person. This led to a profusion of spiritual practices, including blessings of people or crops, pilgrimages to holy sites, contact with relics, and myriad others that could

---

66 Davies, *Popular Magic*, 17–21; Sharpe, *Instruments of Darkness*, 244–52; Glanvil, *Saducismus Triumphatus*; Bovet, *Pandæmonium, or the Devil's Cloyster*; Kirk and Jamieson, *Secret Commonwealth*.

bring spiritual and material relief via the intercession of a lower member of the celestial court.

In a hierarchy below the celestial are the demons, former angels who fell from heaven, with their chief, known as Lucifer or Satan. These beings, although they seek to tempt humanity from salvation, are nonetheless obedient to and authorized by the will of God. This allows humans, empowered by the heavenly hierarchy, to obtain mastery over them. According to theologians, manifestations claiming to be fairies, or dead yet unsanctified individuals, should be considered infernal impostors or illusions. The existence of deceptive demons does raise serious questions about free will and the omnipotence of God that have never been resolved to a Christian audience's complete satisfaction.

Beyond orthodox theology, a popular tradition was also prevalent, making its way into the magical literature, that was different from orthodox theology in two major ways. First, not only could demons be driven off through exorcism, but similar techniques could be used to compel them to answer questions, reveal treasures, or perform other duties for the magician of which the church might not approve. Second, the world also included a wide variety of spirits neither angelic nor demonic: fairies, elementals, planetary spirits, or the unconsecrated dead. Not all magical practitioners held these views, of course, but they were prevalent enough to lead to a surreptitious ritual literature that circulated widely.

The rise of Protestantism brought with it a shift in the perceptions of the celestial hierarchy. Although the heavenly court remained intact after Protestantism, aside from most of the saints, the roles of many of its figures shifted. Most notably, the Virgin Mary, the angels, the remaining saints, and the holy dead of the Catholic Church were diminished in importance, as were its sacraments, shrines, relics, and other trappings. A personal relationship with God, without intermediaries such as churchmen or spiritual beings, came to the fore.

The compilation of e Mus. 173 and other manuscripts from this period occurred well after the Church of England had gained government-backed supremacy. Nonetheless, much of the language of their conjurations evokes elements of Catholic thought, such as the pope, the Blessed Virgin Mary, the saints, the angels, relics, and purgatory, which were either diminished in importance or discarded altogether in Protestant theology. Indeed, many of these incantations have strong parallels in orthodox Christian prayers, rituals, and exorcisms, and conjurors adapted standard prayers used by exorcists to their purposes—and the reverse was also true.[67]

Why would such Catholic elements be present in books of magic? We might consider three explanations. First, our scribes might have sympathies with the

---

67 Duffy, *The Stripping of the Altars: Traditional Religion in England, c.1400–c.1580*, 266–98; Young, *A History of Exorcism in Catholic Christianity*, 16–17, 73–77.

Catholic Church, as Thomas Allen himself did. Second, they might be aware that such material was outside church approval but found the efficacy of the rites more important than their orthodoxy. Such operations accomplished particular objectives that the corpus of the Church of England provided no corresponding tools to handle. Third, the rites could have been preserved simply out of curiosity, with no intent to use them. It is difficult to determine which one of these might have motivated our author, but given the large number of Catholic elements across magical manuscripts of the period, it is likely that all three of these might have been at play across the corpus.

These books of magic may refer to the beings summoned as "demons," "devils," "angels," and "fairies," but the most common term to appear is "spirits." This most likely reflects the attitudes that led to the Elizabethan and Jacobean witchcraft laws calling for the death of those who summoned "evil and wicked" spirits. We should be careful not to see the compilers of surreptitious works of magic as adhering strictly to the law, but given the heavy legal and cultural opprobrium against dealing with evil spirits, some effort to provide a neutral label to the members of these groups would not be surprising. Goodare has made a similar argument regarding testimonies of defendants at Scottish witch trials, as these often rely on labeling the encountered beings as "spirits." Even if this was the reason, the presence of "Sathan" and "Lucifer" in the present volume shows that not all scribes were fastidious about dissociating themselves from the demonic.[68]

Spirits of all sorts seem to have been composed of a different substance than the material bodies of humans. Still, in the folk tradition, a person was capable of interacting with them with properly consecrated tools and drawn diagrams. These beings had a broad base of knowledge, although explanations for such intellectual gifts varied: past or present proximity to the omnipotent God, their insubstantial nature allowing them to travel and view and hear secrets, or their great intellect and age. This knowledge often extended to hidden matters and thefts, as well as the past and the future.

Along with fulfilling requests for knowledge, some spirits might be able to perform other feats, such as teaching a set of knowledge, influencing others so as to obtain high stations or erotic desires, or the granting of riches—especially buried or sunken treasure. Europeans of the early modern era did not see buried treasure as material goods that could be unearthed simply with digging. Instead, spirits hid it, guarded it, brought it to the surface, pushed it deeper into the ground, or transformed its contents into worthless junk. When mysterious sights or sounds occurred at a location, many saw them as signs that spirits guarded treasure there

---

68   *Statutes of the Realm*, 5 Eliz. c. 16; Ibid., I Jac. I c. 12; Goodare, "Boundaries of the Fairy Realm in Scotland," 153.

and that the only way to free them would be to uncover these riches.[69] Thus, magicians offered their services to locate the treasure, command or drive off any spirits associated with it, and obtain the riches. In 1634 the astrologer William Lilly participated in a treasure expedition at Westminster Abbey, using hazel divining rods and dismissing the spirits when violent winds threatened to tear down the church. In 1680 Anne Kingsbury was brought before the mayor of Bridgwater, having been accused by Jane Crapp of performing treasure hunting in her house and attempting to speak with the spirit. Kingsbury confirmed that she owned dowsing rods for this; further, she claimed Lilly himself had taught her and that she had a royal commission to perform such a search, although she had left it at home in Taunton.[70]

When we arrive at the charges to the spirits to fulfill their purposes, the dynamic is quite different from the beliefs of either Catholicism or Protestantism. The spirit is commanded in no uncertain terms to appear immediately, in exactly the place the magician desires and in exactly the form commanded, to perform a service for him. One might see parallels here with Protestant beliefs in a perpetual spiritual war against the devil in which the faithful are victorious. Nonetheless, the more likely analogy is with folktales in which the devil pits himself against a particular person's ingenuity and comes up short. In one such tale, a man makes a deal with the devil for wealth for the next seven years. At the end of that time, he must show the devil a beast that the prince of hell has never seen before or his soul is forfeit. After seven years, the man's wife coats herself in feathers, gets on her hands and knees, and walks backward into the forest, frightening the devil and causing him to release the man from his bargain.[71]

Returning to these conjurations, the magician's ability to gain the upper hand in these contests is not through personal virtue and faith, as in Protestant theology, or cunning, as with the folktales. Instead, it comes through the purifications, ablutions, fasting, prayers, church-going, or other actions that the magician has undertaken before and during the ritual. Yet perhaps the magician has neglected one or more of these due to poorly copied operations, inability to find particular ingredients, or lapses in personal behavior. Thus the operations often build in multiple levels of purification, mysterious names, allusions to holy entities and events, and repetitions of all the above to ensure compliance. Many rites recognize this ambiguity, stating

---

69 Dillinger, *Magical Treasure Hunting in Europe and North America: A History*, 56–61.

70 Lilly, *William Lilly's History of His Life and Times from the Year 1602 to 1681*, 78–81; Trotman, "Seventeenth-Century Treasure-Seeking at Bridgwater."

71 W. N., *Merry Drollery, or A Collection of [Brace] Jovial Poems, Merry Songs, Witty Drolleries Intermix'd with Pleasant Catches. The First Part*, 7–11. We do have examples of grimoires from later periods elsewhere in Europe that seem to call for folkloric types of trickery (e.g., Faust, *Doctor Johannes Faust's Mightiest Sea-Spirit*, 56–7; Wentworth, *The Authentic Red Dragon*, 45).

that a conjuration will definitely cause the spirit to appear—but immediately thereafter providing another technique in case it does not. Modern magicians hypothesize that these lengthy rites might bring the magician into an altered state of consciousness where they would be more likely to perceive spirits—or what they might consider to be so.

Demons

If we must choose a category to which most of these "spirits" might be assigned, it most likely would be that of demons. Sometimes this connection is made explicit through an infernal name recognized in theology, such as Lucifer or Asmoday. At other times, it is by association with a spirit name mentioned in conjunction, or in command of, other demonic spirits. We might also include under this label a broad range of other "spirits" who are not placed in another category yet possess the same attributes as the demonic ones. Among these are some of the spirits to whom are dedicated discrete experiments, such as the operations for the spirits Birto and Askariel. Perhaps these categorizations will shift with more discoveries—although, based on what new discoveries have yielded so far, it is more likely that these will muddy the issues even further. The boundaries of this category are slippery, as are many aspects of these creatures.

The inclusion of explicitly demonic figures does not mean that the magicians were Satanists or operating outside a Christian framework. Nonetheless, popular Christian devotions that emphasize the demonic often slip into dualistic language and attitudes, and this does occur at times in ritual magic. We find operations in both magical manuals and trial accounts that are supposed to be accomplished by calling upon particular demons or stating that an action should be done "in the devil's name," ignoring or bypassing the divine hierarchy.[72] The scribe of Folger V.b.26 takes this one step further in two anti-theft operations, in which the paralyzed thief is called upon to leave in God's name, and if that does not work, to leave in the devil's name, implying limitations to the Almighty's power. No evidence exists that this is part of a coherent subversive theology, however.[73]

This did not make the demons irredeemably evil—at least, as they are presented in ritual magic texts. Orthodox theology did hold that such beings were evil and

---

72   e.g., Bever, *The Realities of Witchcraft and Popular Magic in Early Modern Europe: Culture, Cognition, and Everyday Life*, 31–32; Johnson, "Tidebast Och Vändelrot: Magical Representations in the Swedish Black Art Book Tradition," 273–75; Morton and Dähms, *The Trial of Tempel Anneke: Records of a Witchcraft Trial in Brunswick, Germany, 1663*, 86; Muyard, "Un Manuel de Sorcellerie en Basse Bretagne au XVIIIe Siècle," 293; Ohrvik, "'…For All Honest Christian and Science-Loving Readers': Religious Encounters in Early Modern Norwegian Black Books"; Wilby, *The Visions of Isobel Gowdie: Magic, Witchcraft and Dark Shamanism in Seventeenth-Century Scotland*, 39–40.

73   Harms, Clark, and Peterson, *The Book of Oberon*, 545, 549.

eternally damned. In 1398 the faculty of theology of the University of Paris declared beliefs in demons being good, or existing between salvation and damnation, to be in error. In the manuals of the magicians, however, some spirits are noted as being of a friendly or beneficent nature, and particular ones, such as Marchosias, Phoenix, and Focalor of the *Goetia*, hope to return to their heavenly thrones after some centuries. The texts of ritual magic give contradictory messages as to whether redemption of demons was possible. For example, *Oberon* notes that Satan "fell not of his own will" and thus resides in the air instead of hell. Nonetheless, a magician encountering him should refuse the spirit's request for prayer for his restoration to heaven, instead making a noncommittal and theologically correct statement that it could happen if it were God's will. Another spell in the same work, however, promises rebellious spirits that the magician will make just such an intercession if they prove obedient.[74]

Twentieth-century readers gained much of their understanding of these spirits from one particular set of manuscripts, edited by Samuel Liddell MacGregor Mathers and published by Aleister Crowley as the *Goetia*. That list presents seventy-two demons, each with its own name, a station or rank of nobility, a particular appearance, one or more areas of expertise or portfolios, a sigil, and the number of legions of spirits that it commands. This is only one of many spirit lists, including those from the *Pseudomonarchia daemonum* of Johann Weyer, the *Discoverie of Witchcraft* of Reginald Scot, the "List of Demons" from Munich MS. Clm 849, the "Livre des Esperitz" from Cambridge Trinity College MS. O.8.29, and the "De Officiis Spirituum" from Folger V.b.26.[75]

Examinations of such lists are valuable projects that have yielded useful insights into the spiritual beliefs of ritual magicians. Nonetheless, it should be noted that we also encounter information on demons elsewhere in these manuscripts. Sometimes we find lengthy lists, but others only provide short notes scattered through these manuscripts. We also have individual conjurations dedicated to particular demons, some of which include names not found elsewhere. All these sources should be examined when considering the nature and orders of spirits in these manuscripts.[76]

In many cases, spirits are assigned particular offices or titles; e Mus. 173 mentions Cantivalerion or Golgathell, the "emperor" of hell, and the four kings

---

74   Peterson, *The Lesser Key of Solomon*, 23, 24, 26; Boudet, "Les Condamnations de La Magie a Paris En 1398," 151; Harms, Clark, and Peterson, *The Book of Oberon*, 192, 101.

75   Weyer, *De praestigiis daemonum*, 913–31; Scot, *The Discouerie of Witchcraft*, 377–92; Kieckhefer, *Forbidden Rites: A Necromancer's Manual of the Fifteenth Century*, 291–93; Boudet, "Les Who's Who Démonologiques de la Renaissance et Leurs Ancêtres Médiévaux"; Harms, Clark, and Peterson, *The Book of Oberon*, 191–215.

76   For examples of analyses, see Stratton-Kent, *Pandemonium*; Boudet, *Les Catalogues de Démons Attribués à Salomon et à Saint Cyprien*.

attributed to the directions, a common element in many magical works dating back to the thirteenth century.[77] We also have procedures designated for the conjuration of particular stations of demons, including marquises, dukes, comites or counts, prelates, and knights. We certainly encounter such ranks in the *Goetia* and elsewhere, but they are strikingly absent in the lists in e Mus. 173, displaying that magicians did not consider these offices essential for working with spirits.

In popular tradition, demons could take on diverse forms, most strikingly those of animals or chimeras composed of different animal parts. In the popular *Faust Book*, translated into English by 1592, the infamous German magician encounters spirits who can take on the forms of "swine, harts, bears, wolves, apes, buffs, goats, antelopes, elephants, dragons, horses, asses, lions, cats, snakes, toads and all manner of ugly odious serpents and worms."[78] Such descriptions of demons as animals pre-date the English *Faust Book* by decades, but it does indicate that the appearance of demons as animals would not have been unknown to the reading and read-to British public.

Still, magical manuals do not give these descriptions for all spirits, especially in the longer operations, and these forms were inherently unstable. A spirit could take on a terrifying shape, sometimes accompanied by horrible sounds and smells, or pleasant forms, often those of a child or a monk. The key factor was the magician's power, gained by calling upon the heavenly realm, to compel the being into a pleasing appearance.

As with the *Goetia*, many of the spirit listings in books of magic note the purposes for which the particular spirit may be called. These may include teaching the magician a particular set of lore of nature or an academic topic, uncovering treasure, ensuring the favor of powerful people, granting erotic desires, constructing or destroying objects, or turning invisible. Multiple spirits may be able to perform the same function, and it is not uncommon for one spirit to provide multiple functions.

Not every spirit is provided with a purpose, however. One of our first conjurations in e Mus. 173, that dedicated to Mosacus, contains no indication of what this spirit could do in comparison with others. Indeed, many operations to summon specific spirits give only vague functions—such as answering questions or performing the magician's will—or none at all. This lack of information does not seem to have detracted from the popularity of these operations, as some were copied well into the nineteenth century.[79]

---

77   William of Auvergne, *Opera omnia*, 971; Agrippa von Nettesheim, *De Occulta Philosophia Libri Tres*, 471.

78   Jones, *The English Faust Book: A Critical Edition, Based on the Text of 1592*, 118.

79   Cf. Sibley, *The Clavis or Key to the Magic of Solomon*, 189–215.

Familiars—minor spirits who perform the magician's bidding—are mentioned on occasion in spirit lists, usually as being granted by particular demons as a benefit of conjuring them. References in Latin spirit lists to "familiares" granted by spirits date back at least to the fifteenth century. Seventeenth-century magicians would have had cause to be wary of such relationships; the King James Bible released in 1611 and some previous translations used the term "familiar" to refer to the spirits that served the witch of Endor in 1 Samuel 28. The word also referred to the belief of elites in early modern Britain that the devil, as part of a pact with a witch, would give him or her a servant. Such familiars could take the forms of animals or humans, and they suckled blood from the witch through a "witch's mark" on the body. No such characteristics appear in the descriptions of familiar spirits within the ritual magic texts examined, but it remains an open question how much of an overlap practitioners might have seen between the two types of spirits referred to by the same word.[80]

Within orthodox theology and popular tradition alike, relationships between humans and demons were considered pacts in which the human promised his or her soul in exchange for worldly goods or success. According to St. Thomas Aquinas, these could be divided into explicit pacts, in which the bond is known to the human, and implicit pacts, in which the magician unwittingly makes use of characters or signs with demonic elements. This element is missing from the texts we examine and indeed is absent from much of ritual magic. Instead, it is the demon who is often bound—to appear in a crystal, to be kept in a book, or to make itself available in another way whenever the magician desires—as a result of the conjurations noted above. The spirit must be compelled powerfully, lest it lie or lead the magician astray.[81]

ANGELS

Many manuscripts of medieval and early modern magic include operations for contacting angels. Such operations reflect long-standing official and popular beliefs regarding angels in Christian Europe that had a broad impact on the culture of the time, appearing in liturgy, art, and folklore. Angels were often subdivided into nine stations as proposed by Pseudo-Dionysius: seraphim, cherubim, thrones, dominions, virtues, powers, principalities, archangels, and angels. Among these were also named individuals, both the angels Michael, Gabriel, and Raphael, as named in the Bible, and others such as Uriel and Raguel, known better through popular or apocryphal tradition. People might plead with angels for intercession, especially the

---

80 Kieckhefer, *Forbidden Rites*, 292–3; Hutton, *The Witch*, 262–78; Sharpe, "The Witch's Familiar in Elizabethan England."

81 Aquinas, "Summa Theologiae," IIa, IIae, q. 96 a. 2 ad. 2.

guardian angel who was believed to protect each individual, although some clergy expressed concern about the orthodoxy of these angels.[82]

Magic could not ignore such powerful yet benevolent beings, and many magicians gave serious thought to consulting them. For example, Moses Long, in his manuscript "The Secret of Secrets" (1686), began with a discussion of the nature and powers of angels. He noted them as being stronger and more powerful than humans, possessing the ability to harm humans without being harmed, being invisible unless they choose otherwise, and moving as swiftly as wind or lightning. Certainly magicians would want these beings in their corner.[83]

Famous treatises such as the *Ars Notoria*, the *Almadel*, and the *Liber Iuratus*, as well as many individual operations, purported to give magicians great benefits from contacting and calling upon angels. Nonetheless, the context of such operations—in which they appear alongside and use similar language to demonic conjurations—opened them to censure and accusations that the spirits called were actually demons. Most notably, the faculty of the University of of Paris's 1398 propositions inveighed heavily against magic that involved angels.[84]

Angels appear in e Mus. 173 in lesser numbers than other spirits. This seems to reflect a reluctance for the magician to interfere with beings performing the will of God. The scribe of one spirit list promises to tell us about the summoning of angels, then quickly switches, proclaiming that he will only tell us of the spirits of the air. For the most part, references to angels appear among the numerous holy elements given in the conjurations, with the nine orders of angels and named individuals turning up frequently.

We do have two experiments explicitly directed at angels ("Experiment of the Three Good Angels") or a "spirit heavenly" ("To See a Spirit in a Crystal") in e Mus. 173. These are both scrying experiments in which an especially pure person, either a virgin boy or a pregnant woman, gazes into a crystal or beryl as the magician says a conjuration. These spirits might be called from all manner of realms, as one conjuration states the spirit might be in "heaven, or in hell, in earth, in air, in fire, in water, in stock, or in stone." Both operations include intended language to rule out the possibility of the angel lying to the operator, suggesting that sanctity did not necessarily lead to honesty.

We also have a ritual to create a wax image to bring back a thief, which involves various types of spiritual beings. The three that are chiefly invoked are Raguel,

---

82   Marshall, "The Guardian Angel in Protestant England."

83   Bodleian Rawlinson D.253, ii, published in Skinner and Rankine, *A Cunning Man's Grimoire*, 34.

84   Kieckhefer, "Angel Magic and the Cult of Angels in the Later Middle Ages;" Boudet, "Les Condamnations de la Magie a Paris en 1398."

Uriel, and Sabaoth. The latter is the Hebrew word for "hosts," while the other two are apocryphal members of the heavenly choir.

FAIRIES

What we know today as fairies in Britain were fed by three concepts originally separate in the medieval mind. First, elves, beings known since Anglo-Saxon times as bringers of misfortune, became the focus of a corpus of charms and rituals to ward off the dangers associated with them. Second, mysterious supernatural beings of uncertain origins who could help or hinder brave knights lent drama to the romances of chivalry that spread across northwest Europe in the twelfth to thirteenth centuries. Third, chroniclers reported stories of human-like beings who lived in their own realm but interacted occasionally with humans. By the fourteenth century, the idea of "fairies" had coalesced from these three. They might be found either in the household or far away in the wilderness. Their sizes varied considerably, most did not have wings, and their relationships with humans were fraught with ambiguity and peril.[85]

During the seventeenth century, the opinions of authorities were split on the nature of fairies or elves. Some, such as the anonymous author of the manuscript Bodleian Douce 116, asserted that they were angels who followed Lucifer but did not partake entirely in his rebellion, for which misdeed they were left on the earth. King James's *Daemonologie* portrayed them as demonic delusions and discouraged people from thinking of them too deeply. The most famous authority on them, the Reverend Robert Kirk, believed elves to be a separate species of beings like humans but of a spiritual nature closer to the angels. Finally, a minority believed them to be delusions of the common folk.[86]

No matter the uncertainty, many people did believe that some individuals could contact fairies—whatever they were—through magic. The astrologer William Lilly once summoned the Queen of Fairies in a wood near his house for a curious friend, who then begged him to send her away. In 1607 Susan Swapper (or Swaffer) and Anne Taylor of Rye, Sussex, set out to meet fairies that they hoped would bring them riches. The accused witch Isobel Gowdie spoke at her trial not only of deals with the devil, but also of visiting the King and Queen of Fairy, giving so many details that the scribe simply stopped recording them. Finally, the cunning woman Mary Parrish took Goodwin Wharton, a member of Parliament, on a wild series of treasure-hunting expeditions and other magical rituals among the "Lowlanders," or

---

85   Hutton, *The Witch*, 227–34; Hall, *Elves in Anglo-Saxon England*; Purkiss, *Troublesome Things*.

86   Bodleian Douce 116, 149–53; James I, *Daemonologie*, 76; Kirk and Jamieson, *Secret Commonwealth*; Hutton, *The Witch*, 239.

fairies, that led to him being declared their king, even though Mary made their excuses whenever he wished to speak with them.[87]

Operations of ritual magic to contact fairies turn up often in the manuscripts of ritual magic. Aside from the Douce manuscript listed above, most authors of these works pass over any speculations as to the origins of fairies, although their appearances along with various varieties of spirits indicate they are of a similar nature as demons. In two incantations in e Mus. 173, we see them in association with other spiritual beings—"spirits, devils, elves, or evils" that must vacate the guardianship of treasure.

Although some fairies remain anonymous, others have individual or collective names. Among them are the seven sisters of the "elphas," originally appearing as the names of fevers in a charm dating back to the eleventh century and here appropriated as the guardians of treasure. We also find a mention of the fairy queen Sibilia as a name to be written on the wax image against thieves mentioned above. The fairy king Oberion, famous for his appearance in *A Midsummer Night's Dream* under the name Oberon, may also be summoned through multiple procedures, some of which appear here and in *The Book of Oberon*.[88]

The rituals for fairies generally follow the outline of those for other spirits, but we also have two others that have a more folkloric quality. Both call for magicians to create or discover a mysterious substance that, when it is used to anoint the eyes, allows them to see spirits. Such a substance is first mentioned in the thirteenth-century work of Gervase of Tilbury, who tells of a woman who used such a substance in one eye and became able to view the invisible, to her eventual undoing. This tale has been adapted into many fairy stories, most notably the testimony of Joan Tyrrye at Taunton in 1555. While this ointment is usually taken surreptitiously from the fairies in folklore, we have detailed procedures and recipes given here for it—albeit none of which encourages one to put such matter into the eyes.[89]

In one of these ceremonies, once the magician obtains the ointment, he must set a table for the arrival of three spirits who will grant him his will. Rituals such as this, with a table being set for spirits to grant favor, have been practiced in Europe

87   Lilly, *William Lilly's History of His Life and Times*, 229–31; Gregory, *Rye Spirits*; Wilby, *The Visions of Isobel Gowdie*, 40; Clark, *Goodwin Wharton*; Timbers, *The Magical Adventures of Mary Parish*.

88   Wickersheimer, *Les manuscrits latins de médecine du haut Moyen Age dans les bibliothèques de France*, 32–33; Wallis, *Medieval Medicine: A Reader*, 69; Harms, Clark, and Peterson, *The Book of Oberon*, 21–24.

89   Gervase, *Otia Imperialia: Recreation for an Emperor*, 718–21; Holworthy, *Discoveries in the Diocesan Registry, Wells, Somerset*.

for a thousand years; in particular, one features prominently as the precipitating incident in the oldest known version of "Sleeping Beauty."[90]

The Dead, Ghosts, and Walking Bodies

The dead were not so far away from the British people of the seventeenth century. The mortality rate of the time was high, especially for children; during the early modern period, death would take a quarter of children before they reached ten years of age.[91] Churches were also the resting places of the local dead, so an encounter with the divine could also bring reminders of one's own mortality.

The dead were very much part of the spiritual landscape. One passage from the Thirty-Nine Articles, finalized in 1571 and setting forth the doctrines of the Church of England, is particularly enlightening to the orthodox belief of the time:

> The Romish doctrine concerning purgatory, pardons, worshipping and adoration, as well of images as of reliques, and also invocation of the saints, is a fond thing vainly invented, and grounded upon no warranty of Scripture, but rather repugnant to the word of God.[92]

This passage effectively separates the departed into two categories: the apostles, saints, and martyrs, for which a level of veneration had been offered in the past, and the spiritual remnants of ordinary people.

Early Christianity placed a heavy emphasis on the apostles and followers of Jesus who died for the faith. These became enshrined among the cult of the saints, the numbers of which burgeoned as missionaries encountered tribulation in new lands, and far-flung Christians incorporated local mythological figures into the new faith or combined them with local proselytizers. These deceased individuals could hear prayers, and their special position allowed them to intercede with the Holy Trinity. Further, the body parts and personal possessions of these individuals could become relics, which were believed to have special powers of their own to consecrate or heal. Stories about saints, most famously those told in Jacobus da Voragine's *Legenda Aurea*, or *Golden Legend*, became incredibly popular.

By the sixteenth century, western Europe was filled with relics, shrines, pilgrimages, prayers, and other places, practices, and objects of devotion, much of which were only peripheral or unmentioned in Scripture. The Church of England and other reformers who wished to re-emphasize God and the Bible saw this popular

---

90   Harms, "Spirits at the Table: Faerie Queens in the Grimoires"; Bryant, *Perceforest: The Prehistory of King Arthur's Britain*, 387–88, 409. For more information on fairies in ritual magic, see Harms, "Hell and Fairy."

91   Pollock, "Little Commonwealths I: The Household and Family Relationship," 61.

92   Bicknell, *A Theological Introduction to the Thirty-Nine Articles of the Church of England*, 276.

devotion as problematic, and they did what they could to stamp out the cult of the saints, with varying levels of success.

The holy dead and their relics rarely appear in conjurations, save collectively as one of the litany of holy elements called upon to compel the spirit to appear. Most instances of individual saints do not dive deeply into the church's catalogue; few incantations cite any figures beyond the apostles, St. Michael, and the women from the lineage of Jesus. We do have one unusual operation in Folger V.b.26, in which St. George, one of the few Catholic saints to be recognized in England after the Reformation, is conjured into a thumbnail so a boy may see him and ask him questions.[93]

The ordinary dead were also very much part of the spiritual landscape of the seventeenth century, despite the best effort of the reformers. According to Catholic doctrine, before most Christians could go to heaven, they spent time in purgatory, where they would suffer for their sins before becoming pure enough to enter heaven and the divine presence. While in purgatory, spirits could leave to visit the living for brief times as part of carrying out this process of repentance. Purgatory was not a desirable place for a dead person to remain, so the church authorized practices to shorten a person's stay, including the saying of Masses and the sale of indulgences, church documents that mitigated or removed penalties for sin.

One of the main impetuses for the Reformation was the abuse of indulgences. A key argument against indulgences was the denial of purgatory's existence, and with it the ability of the dead to return to our world. If one of the deceased appeared, it was either the work of the divine to warn humanity or that of the devil to mislead them—and the devil was a much more likely candidate. King James recognized another reason why a dead person might appear to the living: a demon could inhabit the body of a dead person from which the soul had fled and impersonate the individual, passing on false advice and comfort.[94]

These cautions from the intellectual elite seem to have had little effect on popular beliefs about ghosts and spirits of the dead. Well after the Reformation, people still held that ghosts could appear to the living, usually due to unfinished business from their lives: warning or advising those dear to them, revealing the murderers responsible for their deaths, or signaling the location of buried treasure.[95]

With regard to magic, most Bible readers would have been aware of the warnings against dealing with the dead (Deuteronomy 18:11). On the other hand, they might also refer to the narrative of the witch of Endor's summoning of Samuel on

---

93 Harms, Clark, and Peterson, *The Book of Oberon*, 432–34.

94 Roberts and Normand, *Witchcraft in Early Modern Scotland*, 403–8.

95 Oldridge, *The Supernatural in Tudor and Stuart England*, 108–17.

behalf of King Saul (1 Samuel 28). Although theologians had reinterpreted the tale in terms of a demonic delusion, the overt language of the passage describes a woman calling up the spirit of a dead prophet with magic. Nonetheless, the heavy opprobrium with which religious authorities treated the witch of Endor's story made summoning the dead less popular than the invocation of demons.

Still, necromancy was indeed practiced. The *Fourth Book* attributed to Agrippa promised that such a summoning was possible in churchyards, execution sites, battlefields, or the presence of unburied corpses, with blood and bones being used as incense. Reginald Scot's *Discovery of Witchcraft* began its rite to call the queen of the fairies with the conjuration of a dead man, and its expanded 1665 edition included instructions for necromantic circles and an operation to summon the ghost of a hanged man. A well-known story relates how Edward Kelley, the scryer for John Dee, called up a dead man in a Lancashire churchyard. The explorers Humphrey Gilbert and John Davis may have participated in their own summoning of dead magicians, including King Solomon.[96]

One case of a supposed necromantic summoning was conducted near Stamford, Lincolnshire, according to a pamphlet published in 1679. A man split up his inheritance among his two sons, and the elder conspired to murder the younger to gain the rest. A terrible apparition was seen in this area, making horrible noises and taking on the forms of a bear, a lion, and the murdered man bearing terrible wounds. The brother called upon a man who "pretended to Astrology," and presumably to magic, to put down the ghost. The would-be conjuror did so and was so terrified when the spirit appeared that he attempted to run away. The ghost called him back and told him the identities of his killer, and the magician brought this information to a magistrate. The murderer was brought in and made a full confession.[97]

The accuracy of such an account is open to question, but the story itself is important. A magician calls up the ghost of a murdered man, learns the truth, and reports it to the authorities. The response is not a denunciation of the spirit as a demon or an arrest of the magician for the practice of black arts, but instead bringing in the suspect. The author of this text knew that readers would accept this story as plausible, even though it varied widely from orthodox doctrine. This attests to the long-standing and powerful belief in the spirits of the dead and the ability of magicians to approach them.

---

96   Agrippa von Nettesheim, Turner, and Petrus, *Henry Cornelius Agrippa, His Fourth Book of Occult Philosophy*, 69–71; Scot, *The Discouerie of Witchcraft*, 401–8; Scot, *The Discovery of Witchcraft*, 215–18; Weever, *Antient Funeral Monuments*, lxv–lxvi; Klaassen, *The Transformations of Magic*, 167–70.

97   *Strange and Wonderful News from Lincolnshire*.

When we encounter the dead in the grimoires, however, it is difficult to consider them apart from demons. This is not to say that their status is confused, as it rarely is. Rather, demons and the dead are often related to each other, usually with the departed under the mastery of the infernal, but sometimes simply appearing within a similar context. In *Oberon*, for example, we do have one rite of a tablet to summon a dead man, but it also notes an herb that can be used to constrain both demons and the dead, as well as providing a word from the Semeforas that Adam used to do the same.[98]

Two entities on the spirit lists in e Mus. 173 are capable of bringing spirits out of purgatory, the realm in Catholic theology where souls made penance for their sins. Notably, the same spirits appear on the lists in *Oberon* and perform similar functions without mentioning purgatory. Henry VIII prohibited the use of the term in prayers in 1536, and many books of hours have the term "purgatory" excised from them. This suggests that the list in *Oberon* may have undergone revision due to Protestant sensibilities, and that its continued usage in e Mus. 173, which appeared decades after *Oberon*, may indicate Catholic sympathies on the part of its scribe.[99]

Bodleian e Mus. 173 provides two different versions of a rite to contact a spirit of the dead in order to reveal thieves. The magician should go to the tomb and call the name of the dead person three times. With his head next to the tomb, the magician then calls upon Sezel, who is said to be "God." Other versions of the operation elsewhere name the spirit in question "Azazel Asiel" or "Azafell," giving the rite a more demonic cast.[100] In the manuscript at hand, Sezel governs bones, and he is asked to come forth and bring the information desired. That night, the magician must sleep with the head upon grave dirt tied up in a cloth in order to meet the spirit through dream incubation. The theology behind this is not spelled out, but it would appear the magician is appealing initially to a particular spirit of the dead to contact Sezel.

Yet was there resurrection of the body as well? One list of spirits includes Nereus, who can be conjured to bring the dead to life for forty-four days when the magician anoints a body in its tomb with oil. This could be an actual spell intended for resurrection, but within the beliefs of the time, it is more likely that it was intended to either bring back the spirit of the dead person or to infuse a demon into a body.

---

98 The Semeforas is a treatise, likely dating to the thirteenth century, detailing the seven names of power God gave to Adam. *Oberon*, 318, 158, and 163, respectively.

99 Duffy, *Marking the Hours*, 158; *Oberon*, 213, 214. As a caution, another section of *Oberon* includes a mention of popes, which many Protestants would have excised as well; Ibid., 58.

100 Newberry Vault Case 5017, 12r; Bodleian Ballard 66, 35–9.

At the same time, we also have one spirit list entry that seems to endorse the orthodox theological view that the conjured dead were actually demons in disguise. This is the spirit Busyn, who is able "to make one of his subjects to enter into the dead bodies and carry it about, and to speak and go where you will, and do all things as the body did living, except eating." The last piece is comparable to one of the earliest aspects of the zombie myth: that a resuscitated dead person must not be fed salt, lest they recall their former life and take revenge on the magician who changed them. In both cases, the boundaries between the living and the dead, already strained by the concept of a mobile corpse, snap back when the dead body tries to eat like a living creature.[101]

PLANETARY AND STELLAR SPIRITS

Spirits connected with celestial bodies, whether planets or stars, also appear within these texts. The learned recognized the influence of the planets on the macrocosm and microcosm through the science of astrology. Signs in the heavens, most notably the star of Bethlehem, foretold future events, and the movement of the stars and planets had their influences upon humanity. A person's body was itself subject to various stellar influences that a doctor should take into account when treating illness, although these factors could not overrule free will, thus maintaining personal choice as the key element of salvation. The same heavenly forces, according to the theologically marginal doctrines of natural magic, had influence on animals, plants, stones, and metals, and the wise could use these virtues to bring about change in the world.

Nonetheless, viewing these celestial bodies as sentient beings was less frequent or acceptable. Certainly people of the time were familiar with the personified planets and the symbols of the zodiac from antiquity through literature and art, but there is little sign that these were considered a true picture of the skies. Medieval people believed that an angel or intelligence was responsible for the movement of each planet, although the mechanism by which this was accomplished was open to debate. Works such as the *Picatrix* and Agrippa's *Three Books* presented names and processes relating to the angels and intelligences of the planets, but these were not considered orthodox theological works.[102]

Bodleian e Mus. 173 possesses a list of spirits taken from the *Arbatel*, a treatise on magic that first appeared in Basel in 1575.[103] As presented in the *Arbatel*, the

---

101 Lauro, *The Transatlantic Zombie*, 45.

102 Godwin, *The Pagan Dream of the Renaissance*; Grant, *Planets, Stars, and Orbs*, 524–45; Pingree, *Picatrix: The Latin Version of the Ghiyat al-Hakim*, 112–37, 140–45; Agrippa von Nettesheim, *De Occulta Philosophia Libri Tres*, 310–18, 389–93.

103 Gilly, "The First Book of White Magic in Germany."

seven "Olympic" spirits are each associated with a particular planet, seal, and set of powers quite similar to the ones discussed for the spirit lists above, including teaching various areas of knowledge, healing, treasure finding, honours, and wisdom. What sets the presentation in e Mus. 173 apart is that each spirit is a bearer of medicine against a set of ailments particular to the qualities of that planet. The origin of this interesting fusion is unknown.

The seven stars of the Pleiades seem to be invoked in one brief operation to empower a wax image to be enchanted to attract a person for the purposes of love or theft. Based upon this rite, each of them apparently possessed a name, a seal, and governance over a particular part of the body. This is reminiscent of their role as seven spirits commanded by Solomon in *The Testament of Solomon*, although no known connection exists between these two documents.[104]

WITCHES

Ritual magic texts say little about the methods of witches and witchcraft, but they do engage with a larger cultural picture of witches that appeared in early modern England. Witch accusations often followed a particular set of characteristics and circumstances. Suspected witches came from a variety of genders, ages, and social classes, yet the most likely people to be accused were women, usually advanced in years, whose ties to the local community had been strained due to poverty or widowhood. Their power was conveyed through social ties—often with words during or after an argument, but in other cases through a gift from the victim, the creation of an image of the victim, a visit from the witch in spectral form or a familiar, or even a simple gaze. Through these means, a witch could cause sickness among livestock, delay the fermenting of beer or the churning of butter, or cause the wasting illness or death of people.[105]

Within this milieu, the power that the witch possessed had two other aspects. First, it created a tie between the witch and the victim. Second, it existed in tension with other powers that could reveal, avert, end, or reverse its effects. The copyists of ritual magic texts were aware of these principles, setting forth a number of operations for use in cases of witchcraft.

Undoubtedly, the best way to handle witchcraft was to ensure that it bypassed its intended victim, often through an object with protective virtue. Bodleian e Mus. 173 provides a written talisman for this purpose, and *Oberon* provides a formula in which the names of three archangels are written on laurel leaves. Given the many

---

104 Duling, "Testament of Solomon," 969–70.

105 Sharpe, *Instruments of Darkness*, 60–65, 152–55.

challenges of daily life, such talismans were often multipurpose objects, providing protection against enemies, natural disasters, illness, or childbirth as well.

Discovering bewitchment and the identity of a witch was a popular part of cunning practice and was often key to ending the curse. Bodleian e Mus. 173 provides a brief example of staring into the person's eyes to see if they reflect the viewer, showing that the person is not bewitched. Another ritual, attributed to the likely fictitious William Bacon, requires the creation of an image with the appearance of the suspected witch. When this is pricked with pins, the person's reflection will appear in a pool of water, where he or she will confess. This ritual is part of a broader corpus of rites involving images known today as "voodoo dolls," which actually have been a staple of European magical practice for millennia.[106]

As might be expected, the most frequent usage of anti-witchcraft magic was for its reversal. Ritual magic works provide us with a wide variety of techniques that might be used. One of the simplest is the "three biters" charm, which appears twice in e Mus. 173, along with another charm that requires that salt be placed on the affected person or liquid. In another ritual, the magician cuts a wand from a tree at sunrise and beats a carpet with it, symbolically striking the witch. If the person finds a "witch knot," or tangle in the hair of an animal, the magician may burn it with an incantation—a small-scale enactment of a folk belief that sometimes led to the burning of an entire animal alive to ward off harm. Another involves the creation of two images on lamb parchment that are pricked with a dagger to torment the witches. *Oberon* and other texts provide us with another set of procedures in which the victim's urine is heated and used either to cook a pigeon heart filled with pins or to create a cake that will return the harmful magic to the witch.[107]

Even the spirit lists in e Mus. 173 include entities who have special offices relating to witches. On one hand, the spirit Barbays or Barbais works to undo witchcraft. On the other hand, we have Mistolas, who teaches the magician how to engage in witchcraft. One should be cautious about deriving an overarching theory from one example, but Mistolas suggests that most magicians considered their operations as separate from those carried out by witches, although the spirits they called upon might themselves be connected with witchcraft.

---

106 Faraone, "Binding and Burying the Forces of Evil"; Armitage, "European and African Figural Ritual Magic"; Harms, *Wax Images, "Voodoo Dolls," Figurines, Manikins, and Poppets in Magic*.

107 British Library Additional MS. 36674, 145r.

Editor's Principles and Notes

One great barrier to the understanding of the history of Western magic has been the lack of reliable and commonly available texts. Much of our notions of a "proper" grimoire, for instance, are heavily influenced by the publications of Samuel Liddel MacGregor Mathers, Aleister Crowley, and Arthur Edward Waite, which has led to problems of interpretation. For example, most readers have come to see a book of magic as a unitary creation, as is the case with the volumes these individuals edited, and not the miscellanies that are an important part of the corpus. Even today, as more editors publish the works they uncover, the tendency is often to consider each book in isolation, which sometimes leads to errors in interpretation even among the most knowledgeable. (I am certain that I have committed some of my own.)

The best remedy to this is to make the corpus of magic as widely available as possible. Here we run into an ongoing problem: the lack of scholarly publishers willing to issue such works in translation or at all. Even as the history of magic has gained more respect among scholars, the number of such works released by scholarly presses is small, and even smaller if we consider those released only in Latin. Once we arrive at those from post-medieval times, the number is almost nonexistent.[108] The gap has been filled with a rising number of texts published by non-academic authors, mostly by small presses.

The purpose of this book, as well as *The Book of Oberon* and *The Long-Lost Friend*, is to try to create an edition for the lay reader that nonetheless has enough critical apparatus to be useful to scholars. With this in mind, the text has had its spelling modernized and both capitalization and punctuation added or amended to make it more accessible to modern readers. Nonetheless, the wording of the English text remains faithful to the original. I have translated the Latin passages into English to the best of my ability.

ABBREVIATIONS: Expanded whenever possible. This is particularly the case for abbreviations for the names of the Christian Trinity, which are often abbreviated in various forms.

---

108 For scholarly publications of magical manuals in general, see Betz, *The Greek Magical Papyri in Translation*; Meyer and Smith, *Ancient Christian Magic*; Lidaka, "The Book of Angels, Rings, Characters and Images of the Planets: Attributed to Osbert Bokenham"; Weill-Parot and Véronèse, "Antonio Da Montolmo's De Occultis et Manifestis or Liber Intelligentiarum"; Braekman, *Magische Experimenten en Toverpraktijen uit een Middelnederlands Handschrift*; and Kieckhefer, *Forbidden Rites*. The post-medieval examples I have been able to find include Spamer and Nickel, *Romanusbüchlein*; Brown and Hohman, "The Long Hidden Friend"; and Ebermann, "Le Médecin des Pauvres."

ET: The Latin "and" has been left in some lists of voces magicae for consistency.

FIAT: Latin "let it be done." Usually appearing in groups of three.

LATIN: The original spelling in these passages has been maintained, even when it is idiosyncratic or even possibly inaccurate. For example, it is typical for the classical "ae" to be transformed into "e," and for "c" and "t" to be used interchangeably. Abbreviations have been expanded whenever possible. A few words turn up often enough to be left untranslated; these are included on this list.

MARGINALIA: Placed in footnotes, where applicable.

N.: An abbreviation where the name of a spirit or client should be inserted into an incantation.

OBERON: *The Book of Oberon*, Harms, Clark, and Peterson (Llewellyn, 2015). This information comes from Folger Shakespeare Library V.b.26, but the published edition is referred to for ease of reference. (This is an exception to the "published versions of manuscripts" guideline below.)

PAGE NUMBERS, ORIGINAL: Placed in brackets. The abbreviations [r] for "recto" (front of the page) and [v] for "verso" (rear of the page) are used frequently.

PSALMS: Given the frequent usage of Latin Psalms, numbering and texts are assigned according to the Vulgate. It should be noted that this differs from the Masoretic order of common usage in Protestant bibles.

PUBLISHED VERSIONS OF MANUSCRIPTS: When available to the editor, manuscripts have been cited instead of published editions. Given the large numbers of cited manuscripts, however, this was not always possible. Here are some common works:

Bayerische Staatsbibliothek Clm 849: Kieckhefer, Richard. *Forbidden Rites: A Necromancer's Manual of the Fifteenth Century*. University Park, PA: Pennsylvania State University Press, 1998.

British Library Sloane 3824: Ashmole, Elias, and David Rankine. *The Book of Treasure Spirits: A 17th Century Grimoire of Magical Conjurations to Increase Wealth and Catch Thieves through the Invocation of Spirits, Fallen Angels, Demons, and Fairies*. London: Avalonia, 2009.

British Library Sloane 3851: Gauntlet, Arthur, and David Rankine. *The Grimoire of Arthur Gauntlet: A 17th Century London Cunning-Man's Book of Charms, Conjurations and Prayers*. London: Avalonia, 2011.

Cambridge University Library, Additional 3544: Foreman, Paul. *The Cambridge Book of Magic: A Tudor Necromancer's Handbook*. Edited by Francis Young. Cambridge: Francis Young, 2015.

RED INK: The usage of red ink is common for chapter headings, numerals, crosses in the text, and the name Tetragrammaton. It can hardly be said to be used consistently throughout—and occasionally it is unclear what color the copyist intended to make a word or character—so the best effort has been made to use colors consistent with the manuscript.

SPELLING IN ILLUSTRATIONS: Efforts have been made to correct the spelling in these, save in cases in which inserting the proper letters—e.g., an omitted "m" in "Tetragrammaton"—would lead to a serious distortion of the image. Please see the notes on individual diagrams for more information.

THEE/THOU/YOU: "You" is sometimes used in the modern sense and sometimes as a plural form of "thou" or in contexts in which it could be singular or plural.

VOCES MAGICAE: Given the unclear nature of some of the writing, including clear misspellings, an effort has been made to ensure the best possible rendering, although this might not always be accurate. If a phrase is plain in the Latin, it is translated, but some others are garbled and have been left in their original form. "Tetragrammaton" has been corrected from "Tetragramaton," the form in which it appears in most instances.

Acknowledgments

Thanks to Al Cummins, Bobby Derie, Eric Purdue, Richard Powell, Clayton Townsend, Daniel Clark, the Interlibrary Loan department at SUNY Cortland, and the staff at the New York Public Library, the British Library, the Wellcome Institute, University College Dublin, and most importantly, the Bodleian Library at Oxford.

Special thanks to Joseph Peterson for his timely and extremely helpful comments. Also thanks to James Clark, who has endured discussions over practically every stroke of the art in this manuscript.

Disclaimer

The contents in this book are historical references used for teaching purposes only.

All herbal formulas are given for historical understanding and reference. Please consult a standard reference source or an expert herbalist to learn more about the possible effects of certain herbs used within spells and charms.

Llewellyn Worldwide does not suggest, support, or condone the animal mistreatment or sacrifices detailed in this book. These practices should be viewed as a historical curiosity that has no place in our modern world; the reader may revivify these practices with symbolic substitutions rather than harming live animals.

Burning any substance should be conducted in a well-ventilated area with appropriate precautions against fire having been made.

The author and publisher make no claims that the spirits Zorobaym or Benias are present in this book, nor that the spirits Satrapis, Beluginis, and Baramptis will return it to you if you lose it.

Works Cited

MANUSCRIPTS

Bodleian Library, Oxford. Ashmole 388, 1406, 1441; Ballard 66; Douce 116; e Mus. 173, 238; Rawlinson D.253.

British Library, London. Additional 36674.

Newberry Library, Chicago. Vault Case 5017.

PRINTED WORKS

Agrippa von Nettesheim, Heinrich Cornelius. *De Occulta Philosophia Libri Tres*. Edited by V. Perrone Compagni. Leiden/New York: E. J. Brill, 1992.

Agrippa von Nettesheim, Heinrich Cornelius, Robert Turner, and Petrus. *Henry Cornelius Agrippa, His Fourth Book of Occult Philosophy of Geomancy, Magical Elements of Peter de Abano, Astronomical Geomancy, the Nature of Spirits, Arbatel of Magick*. London: Printed by J. C. for John Harrison..., 1655.

Aquinas, Thomas. "Summa Theologiae," 2011. http://www.corpusthomisticum.org/sth3092.html.

Armitage, Natalie. "European and African Figural Ritual Magic: The Beginnings of the Voodoo Doll Myth." In *The Materiality of Magic: An Artifactual Investigation into Ritual Practices and Popular Beliefs*, edited by Ceri Houlbrook and Natalie Armitage, 85–101. Oxford: Oxbow Books, 2015.

Ashmole, Elias, and Conrad Hermann Josten. *Elias Ashmole, 1617–1692: His Autobiographical and Historical Notes, His Correspondence, and Other Contemporary Sources Relating to His Life and Work*. 5 vols. Oxford: Clarendon Press, 1966.

Ashmole, Elias, and David Rankine. *The Book of Treasure Spirits: A 17th Century Grimoire of Magical Conjurations to Increase Wealth and Catch Thieves through the Invocation of Spirits, Fallen Angels, Demons, and Fairies*. London: Avalonia, 2009.

Asprem, Egil. *Arguing with Angels: Enochian Magic and Modern Occulture*. Albany: State University of New York Press, 2012.

Aubrey, John, and Andrew Clark. *"Brief Lives," Chiefly of Contemporaries, Set down by John Aubrey, between the Years 1669 & 1696*. Oxford: At the Clarendon Press, 1898.

Batho, G. R. "The Library of the 'Wizard' Earl: Henry Percy, Ninth Earl of Northumberland (1564–1632)." *Library* Series 5, XV, no. 4 (1960): 246–61.

Batho, Gordon. "The Wizard Earl of Northumberland: An Elizabethan Scholar-Nobleman." *Historian* 75 (2002): 19–23.

Baumgartner, Frederic J. "Starry Messengers: Supernovas, Comets, and Sunspots Heralded the Scientific Revolution." *The Sciences* 32, no. 1 (1992): 38–43.

Betz, Hans Dieter. *The Greek Magical Papyri in Translation, Including the Demotic Spells*. Chicago: University of Chicago Press, 1986.

Bever, Edward Watts Morton. *The Realities of Witchcraft and Popular Magic in Early Modern Europe: Culture, Cognition, and Everyday Life*. New York: Palgrave Macmillan, 2008.

Bicknell, Edward John. *A Theological Introduction to the Thirty-Nine Articles of the Church of England*. New York: Longmans, Green and Co., 1955.

Bodleian Library and R. W. Hunt. *A Summary Catalogue of Western Manuscripts in the Bodleian Library at Oxford*. Vol. 1. 7 vols. Oxford: Clarendon Press, 1953.

Bodleian Library, Richard William Hunt, Andrew G. Watson, and William Dunn Macray. *Digby Manuscripts: 1. A Reproduction of the 1883 Catalogue by W. D. Macray; 2. Notes on Macray's Description of the Manuscripts by R. W. Hunt & A. G. Wilson; Appendix: An Edition of Thomas Allen's Catalogue of His Manuscripts by A. G. Watson*. Oxford: Bodleian Library, 1999.

Bodleian Library, Florence Madan, and H. H. E. Craster. *A Summary Catalogue of Western Manuscripts in the Bodleian Library at Oxford*. Vol. 2, pt. 1. 7 vols. Oxford: Clarendon Press, 1922.

Bodleian Library, Florence Madan, H. H. E. Craster, and N. Denholm-Young. *A Summary Catalogue of Western Manuscripts in the Bodleian Library at Oxford*. Vol. 2, pt. 2. 7 vols. Oxford: Clarendon Press, 1937.

Boudet, Jean-Patrice. *Les Catalogues de Démons Attribués à Salomon et à Saint Cyprien*. Florence: SISMEL edizioni del Galluzzo, forthcoming.

———. "Les Condamnations de la Magie a Paris en 1398." *Revue Mabillon* n. s. 12 (2001), 121–57.

———. "Les Who's Who Démonologiques de La Renaissance et Leurs Ancêtres Médiévaux." *Médiévales* 44 (2003). http://medievales.revues.org/1019.

Bovet, R. *Pandæmonium, or the Devil's Cloyster. Being a Further Blow to Modern Sadduceism, Proving the Existence of Witches and Spirits, Etc.* London: For J. Walthoe, 1684.

Braekman, Willy Louis. *Magische Experimenten en Toverpraktijen uit een Middelnederlands Handschrift: With an English Summary*. Gent: Seminarie voor Volkskunde, 1966.

A Briefe Description of the Notorious Life of Iohn Lambe: Otherwise Called Doctor Lambe, Together with His Ignominious Death. Printed in Amsterdam [i.e., London]: [G. Miller?], 1628.

Briggs, Katharine Mary. *The Anatomy of Puck: An Examination of Fairy Beliefs among Shakespeare's Contemporaries and Successors.* London: Routledge & Paul, 1959.

———. "Some Seventeenth-Century Books of Magic." *Folklore* 64, no. 4 (1953): 445–62.

Brown, Carleton F., and Johann Georg Hohman. "The Long Hidden Friend." *The Journal of American Folklore* 17, no. 65 (1904): 89–152.

Bryant, Nigel. *Perceforest: The Prehistory of King Arthur's Britain.* Cambridge, UK/Rochester, NY: D. S. Brewer, 2011.

Burton, William, and George. Bathurst. *In viri doctissimi, clarissimi, optimi, Thomae Alleni, & philosophi & mathematici summi, ultimo Septembris MDCXXXII Oxonijs demortui, exequiarum Iustis ab alma academia postridiè solutis, orationes binæ: Prior habita est in Aula Glocestrensi, unde pompâ Academicâ est elatus. Posterior, cum, ad Tumulum, in Collegium S. Trinitatis receptus est. ...* Londini: Excudebat G. Stanesbeius, 1632.

Camm, Bede. *Forgotten Shrines: An Account of Some Old Catholic Halls and Families in England and of Relics and Memorials of the English Martyrs.* London: MacDonald & Evans, 1910.

Clapinson, Mary. *A Brief History of the Bodleian Library.* Oxford: Bodleian Library, 2015.

Clark, J. Kent. *Goodwin Wharton.* Oxford: Oxford University Press, 1984.

Davies, Owen. *Popular Magic: Cunning Folk in English History.* London: Hambledon Continuum, 2007.

De Waardt, Hans. "From Cunning Man to Natural Healer." In *New Perspectives on Witchcraft, Magic, and Demonology 5: Witchcraft, Healing, and Popular Diseases,* edited by Brian P. Levack, 39–47. New York [u.a.: Routledge, 2001].

Dee, John, *A True & Faithful Relation of What Passed for Many Yeers Between Dr. John Dee...and Some Spirits: Tending (Had It Succeeded) to a General Alteration of Most States and Kingdomes in the World: His Private Conferences with Rodolphe Emperor of Germany, Stephen K. of Poland, and Divers Other Princes about It: The Particulars of His Cause, as It Was Agitated in the Emperors Court, by the Pope's Intervention: His Banishment and Restoration in Part: As Also the Letters of Sundry Great Men and Princes (Some Whereof Were Present at Some of These Conferences and Apparitions of Spirits) to the Said D. Dee: Out of the Original Copy, Written with Dr. Dees*

Own Hand, Kept in the Library of Sir Tho. Cotton...: With a Preface Confirming the Reality (as to the Point of Spirits) of This Relation, and Shewing the Several Good Uses That a Sober Christian May Make of All. London: Printed by D. Maxwell for T. Garthwait, 1659.

Dee, John, and Thomas Digges. *Parallaticae Commentationis Praxeosq[ue] Nucleus Quidam. Authore Ioanne Dee, Londinensi.* London: Apud Iohannem Dayum typographum, 1573.

Digges, Thomas. *Alæ; seu, Scalæ Mathematicæ, Quibus Visibilium Remotissima Cælorum Theatra Conscendi, & Planetarum Omnium Itinera Nouis & Inauditis Methodis Explorari: Tùm Huius Portentosi Syderis in Mundi Boreali Plaga Insolito Fulgore Coruscantis. Distantia, & Magnitudo Immensa, Situsq: Protinùs Tremedus Indagari, Deiá; Stupendum Ostentum, Terricolis Expositum Cognosci Liquidissimè Prossit.* London: Apud Thomas Marsh, 1573.

Dillinger, Johannes. *Magical Treasure Hunting in Europe and North America: A History.* Houndmills, New York/Basingstoke, Hampshire: Palgrave Macmillan, 2012.

Donmoyer, Patrick. *Powwowing in Pennsylvania: Braucherei and the Ritual of Everyday Life.* Kutztown, PA: Pennsylvania German Cultural Heritage Center, 2018.

Duffy, Eamon. *Marking the Hours: English People and Their Prayers, 1240–1570.* New Haven: Yale University Press, 2011.

———. *The Stripping of the Altars: Traditional Religion in England, c.1400–c.1580.* New Haven; London: Yale University Press, 2005.

Duling, Dennis C., trans. "Testament of Solomon (First to Third Century A.D.): A New Translation and Introduction." In *The Old Testament Pseudepigrapha*, 935–87. Garden City, NY: Doubleday, 1983.

Ebermann, Oskar. "Le Médecin des Pauvres." *Zeitschrift des Vereins für Volkskunde* 24 (1914): 134–62.

Ewen, C. L'Estrange, and Great Britain Courts of Assize and Nisi Prius. *Witch Hunting and Witch Trials: The Indictments for Witchcraft from the Records of 1373 Assizes Held for the Home Circuit A.D. 1559–1736.* New York: Barnes & Noble, 1971.

Faraone, Christopher A. "Binding and Burying the Forces of Evil: The Defensive Use of 'Voodoo Dolls' in Ancient Greece." *Classical Antiquity* 10, no. 2 (October 1, 1991): 165–220. https://doi.org/10.2307/25010949.

Faust, Johannes. *Doctor Johannes Faust's Mightiest Sea-Spirit*, edited and translated by Nicolás Álvarez Ortiz. n. p.: Enodia, 2018.

Feingold, Mordechai. "The Mathematical Sciences and New Philosophies." In *The History of the University of Oxford*, edited by Nicholas Tyacke, 4:359–448. Oxford: Clarendon Press, 1997.

———. *The Mathematicians' Apprenticeship: Science, Universities and Society in England, 1560–1640*. Cambridge: Cambridge University Press, 1984.

———. "The Occult Tradition in the English Universities of the Renaissance: A Reassessment." In *Occult and Scientific Mentalities in the Renaissance*, edited by Brian Vickers, 73–94. Cambridge: Cambridge University Press, 1984.

Foster, Michael. "Thomas Allen (1540–1632), Gloucester Hall, and the Survival of Catholicism in Post-Reformation Oxford." *Oxoniensia* 46 (1981): 99–128.

———. "Thomas Allen, Gloucester Hall, and the Bodleian Library." *Downside Review* 100, no. 339 (1982): 116–37.

Gauntlet, Arthur, and David Rankine. *The Grimoire of Arthur Gauntlet: A 17th Century London Cunning-Man's Book of Charms, Conjurations and Prayers: Includes Material from the Heptameron, the Arbatel, the Discoverie of Witchcraft; and the Writings of Cornelius Agrippa and William Bacon*. London: Avalonia, 2011.

Gervase of Tilbury. *Otia Imperialia: Recreation for an Emperor*. Edited by S. E. Banks and J. W. Binns. Oxford: Clarendon Press, 2002.

Gilly, Carlos. "The First Book of White Magic in Germany." In *Magia, Alchimia, Scienza Dal '400 al '700: L'influsso di Ermete Trismegisto = Magic, Alchemy and Science 15th–18th Centuries: The Influence of Hermes Trismegistus /Ca Cura Di*, edited by Carlos Gilly, Cis van Heertum, 1:209–16. Firenze: Centro Di, 2002.

Glanvil, Joseph. *Saducismus Triumphatus: Or, Full and Plain Evidence Concerning Witches and Apparitions*. London: Printed for J. Collins at his shop under the Temple Church, 1681.

Godwin, Joscelyn. *The Pagan Dream of the Renaissance*. Boston, MA: Weiser Books, 2005.

Goodare, Julian. "Boundaries of the Fairy Realm in Scotland." In *Airy Nothings: Imagining the Otherworld of Faerie from the Middle Ages to the Age of Reason: Essays in Honour of Alasdair A. MacDonald*, edited by K. E. Olsen, Jan R. Veenstra, and A. A. MacDonald, 139–69. Brill's Studies in Intellectual History 222. Leiden: Brill, 2014.

Grant, Edward. *Planets, Stars, and Orbs: The Medieval Cosmos, 1200–1687*. Cambridge, UK: Cambridge University Press, 2009.

Great Britain Public Record Office, and Robert Lemon. *Calendar of State Papers, Domestic Series, of the Reigns of Edward VI, Mary, Elizabeth 1547–1580, Preserved in the State Paper Department of Her Majesty's Public Record Office*. London: Longman, Brown, Green, Longmans & Roberts, 1856.

Great Britain. *Statutes of the Realm*. London: Dawsons, 1963.

Gregory, Annabel. *Rye Spirits: Faith, Faction, and Fairies in a Seventeenth Century English Town*. London: Hedge, 2013.

Heawood, Edward. *Watermarks: Mainly of the 17th and 18th Centuries*. Monumenta Chartae Papyraceae Historiam Illustrantia 1. Hilversum: The Paper Publications Society, 1969.

Hall, Alaric. *Elves in Anglo-Saxon England: Matters of Belief, Health, Gender, and Identity*. Woodbridge, Suffolk, UK; Rochester, NY: Boydell Press, 2007.

Harms, Dan. "Hell and Fairy: The Differentiation of Fairies and Demons within British Ritual Magic of the Early Modern Period." In *Knowing Demons, Knowing Spirits in the Early Modern Period*, edited by Michelle D. Brock, Richard Raiswell, and David R. Winter. Palgrave Historical Studies in Witchcraft and Magic. Houndmills: Palgrave Macmillan, 2018.

———. "Spirits at the Table: Faerie Queens in the Grimoires." In *The Faerie Queens: In Magic, Myth and Legend*, edited by Sorita D'Este, 41–58. London: Avalonia, 2013.

———. *Wax Images, "Voodoo Dolls," Figurines, Manikins, and Poppets in Magic*. Burbage: Caduceus Books, forthcoming.

Harms, Daniel, James R. Clark, and Joseph H. Peterson. *The Book of Oberon: A Sourcebook of Elizabethan Magic*. Woodbury, MN: Llewellyn, 2015.

Holworthy, Richard. *Discoveries in the Diocesan Registry, Wells, Somerset: A Paper Read before the Society of Genealogists, 10th March, 1926*. Wells, Somerset: Diocesan Registry, 1926.

Hopkins, Clare. *Trinity: 450 Years of an Oxford College Community*. Oxford: Oxford University Press, 2005.

Hutton, Ronald. *The Witch: A History of Fear from Ancient Times to the Present*. New Haven: Yale University Press, 2017.

James I. *Daemonologie: In Forme of a Dialogue: Diuided into Three Bookes*, edited by Robert Waldegrave. Edinburgh: Printed by Robert Walde-graue, Printer to the Kings Majestie, 1597.

Johnson, Thomas K. "Tidebast Och Vändelrot: Magical Representations in the Swedish Black Art Book Tradition." PhD diss., University of Washington, 2010.

Jones, John Henry. *The English Faust Book: A Critical Edition, Based on the Text of 1592*. Cambridge: Cambridge University Press, 1994.

Kieckhefer, Richard. "Angel Magic and the Cult of Angels in the Later Middle Ages" in *Contesting Orthodoxy in Medieval and Early Modern Europe: Heresy, Magic, and Witchcraft*, edited by Louise Nyholm Kallestrup and Raisa Maria Toivo, 71–110. Palgrave Historical Studies in Witchcraft and Magic. Cham, Switzerland: Palgrave Macmillan, 2017.

———. *Forbidden Rites: A Necromancer's Manual of the Fifteenth Century*. University Park, PA: Pennsylvania State University Press, 1998.

Kirk, Robert, and Robert Jamieson. *An Essay of the Nature and Actions of the Subterranean (and for the Most Part,) Invisible People, Heretofoir Going under the Name of Elves, Faunes, and Fairies, or the Lyke, among the Low-Country Scots, as They Are Described by Those Who Have the Second Sight; and Now, to Occasion Further Inquiry, Collected and Compared, by a Circumspect Inquirer Residing among the Scottish-Irish in Scotland; with an Appendix, Consisting of Extracts from A Treatise on Second Sight, by Theophilus Insulanus*. [Second Title: Secret Commonwealth.] Edinburgh: J. Ballantyne, 1815.

Klaassen, Frank F. "Three Early Modern Magic Rituals to Spoil Witches." *Opuscula* 1, no. 1 (2011), 1–10.

———. *The Transformations of Magic: Illicit Learned Magic in the Later Middle Ages and Renaissance*. Magic in History. University Park, PA: The Pennsylvania State University Press, 2012.

Lauro, Sarah Juliet. *The Transatlantic Zombie: Slavery, Rebellion, and Living Death*. American Literatures Initiative. New Brunswick, NJ: Rutgers University Press, 2015.

Lidaka, Juris G. "The Book of Angels, Rings, Characters and Images of the Planets: Attributed to Osbert Bokenham" in *Conjuring Spirits: Texts and Traditions of Medieval Ritual Magic*, 32–75. University Park, PA: The Pennsylvania State University Press, 1998.

Lilly, W. *William Lilly's History of His Life and Times from the Year 1602 to 1681*. Reprinted for C. Baldwin, 1715.

MacDonald, Michael. *Mystical Bedlam: Madness, Anxiety, and Healing in Seventeenth-Century England*. Cambridge: Cambridge University Press, 1981.

Marshall, Peter. "The Guardian Angel in Protestant England." In *Conversations with Angels: Essays towards a History of Spiritual Communication, 1100–*

1700, edited by Joad Raymond, 295–316. Houndmills, Basingstoke, Hampshire, UK/New York: Palgrave Macmillan, 2011.

McLean, Adam. *A Treatise on Angel Magic*. San Francisco, CA: Weiser Books, 2006.

McMullin, Ernan. "Giordano Bruno at Oxford." *Isis* 77, no. 1 (1986): 85–94.

Meyer, Marvin W., and Richard Smith. *Ancient Christian Magic: Coptic Texts of Ritual Power*. HarperSanFrancisco, 1994.

Morton, Peter Alan, and Barbara Dähms. *The Trial of Tempel Anneke: Records of a Witchcraft Trial in Brunswick, Germany, 1663*. Peterborough, Ont.: Broadview Press, 2006.

Muyard, F. "Un Manuel de Sorcellerie en Basse Bretagne au XVIIIe Siècle." *Annales de Bretagne et des Pays de l'Ouest* 99, no. 3 (1992): 291–97.

Newton, John, and Jo Bath, eds. *Witchcraft and the Act of 1604*. Studies in Medieval and Reformation Traditions 131. Leiden; Boston: Brill, 2008.

Nicholls, Mark. "The 'Wizard Earl' in Star Chamber: The Trial of the Earl of Northumberland, June 1606." *The Historical Journal* 30, no. 1 (1987): 173–89.

Ohrvik, Ane. "'...For All Honest Christian and Science-Loving Readers': Religious Encounters in Early Modern Norwegian Black Books." *ARV: Nordic Yearbook of Folklore* 68 (2012): 7–25.

Oldridge, Darren. *The Supernatural in Tudor and Stuart England*. London: Routledge, 2016.

Parry, G. J. R. *The Arch-Conjuror of England: John Dee*. New Haven: Yale University Press, 2011.

Peck, D. C. *Leicester's Commonwealth: The Copy of a Letter Written by a Master of Art of Cambridge (1584) and Related Documents*. Athens: Ohio University Press, 1985.

Peterson, Joseph H. *The Lesser Key of Solomon: Lemegeton Clavicula Salomonis: Detailing the Ceremonial Art of Commanding Spirits Both Good and Evil*. York Beach, ME: Weiser Books, 2001.

Pingree, David Edwin. *Picatrix: The Latin Version of the Ghiyat al-Hakim*. London: Warburg Institute, 1986.

Piper, G. H. "Bronsil Castle, Eastnor." *Transactions of the Woolhope Naturalists' Field Club*, 1880, 228–31.

Plomer, Henry Robert, Harry Gidney Aldis, E. R. McC. Dix, G. J. Gray, and R. B. McKerrow. *A Dictionary of the Printers and Booksellers Who Were at*

Work in England, Scotland and Ireland from 1668 to 1725. London: Printed for the Bibliographical Society at the Oxford University Press, 1922.

Pollock, Linda. "Little Commonwealths I: The Household and Family Relationship" in *A Social History of England, 1500–1750*, edited by Keith Wrightson, 60–83. Cambridge: Cambridge University Press, 2017.

Purkiss, Diane. *Troublesome Things: A History of Fairies and Fairy Stories*. London/New York: Allen Lane, 2000.

Roberts, Gareth, and Lawrence Normand. *Witchcraft in Early Modern Scotland: James VI's Demonology and the North Berwick Witches*. Exeter: University of Exeter Press, 2000.

Rowse, A. L. *Simon Forman: Sex and Society in Shakespeare's Age*. London: Weidenfeld & Nicolson, 1974.

Salter, H. E. "Religious Houses: Gloucester College, Oxford" in *The Victoria History of the County of Oxford*, edited by William Page, 2:70–71. London: Archiband Constable & Co. Ltd., 1907.

Scot, Reginald. *The Discouerie of Witchcraft: Wherein the Lewde Dealing of Witches and Witchmongers Is Notablie Detected, the Knauerie of Coniurors, the Impietie of Inchantors, the Follie of Soothsaiers, the Impudent Falshood of Cousenors, the Infidelitie of Atheists, the Pestilent Practices of Pythonists, the Curiositie of Figure Casters, the Vanitie of Dreamers, the Beggerlie Art of Alcumystrie, the Abhomination of Idolatrie, the Horrible Art of Poisoning, the Vertue and Power of Naturall Magike, and All the Conueiances of Legierdemaine and Iuggling Are Deciphered: And Many Other Things Opened, Which Have Long Lien Hidden, Howbeit Verie Necessarie to Be Knowne: Heerevnto Is Added a Treatise Vpon the Nature and Substance of Spirits and Diuels, & c.* Imprinted at London: By William Brome, 1584.

———. *The Discovery of Witchcraft Proving That the Compacts and Contracts of Witches with Devils and All Infernal Spirits or Familiars Are but Erroneous Novelties and Imaginary Conceptions: Also Discovering, How Far Their Power Extendeth in Killing, Tormenting, Consuming, or Curing the Bodies of Men, Women, Children, or Animals by Charms, Philtres, Periapts, Pentacles, Curses, and Conjurations: Wherein Likewise the Unchristian Practices and Inhumane Dealings of Searchers and Witch-Tryers upon Aged, Melancholly, and Superstitious People, in Extorting Confessions by Terrors and Tortures, and in Devising False Marks and Symptoms, Are Notably Detected...: In Sixteen Books*. London: Printed for Andrew Clark..., 1665.

Sharpe, James. "The Witch's Familiar in Elizabethan England" in *Authority and Consent in Tudor England: Essays Presented to C. S. L. Davies*, edited by

George William Bernard, Clifford Stephen Lloyd. Davies, and Steven J. Gunn, 219–32. Aldershot: Ashgate, 2002.

Sharpe, James A. *Instruments of Darkness: Witchcraft in England 1550–1750*. London/New York: Penguin, 1997.

Sibley, Ebenezer, Frederick Hockley, and Joseph H. Peterson. *The Clavis or Key to the Magic of Solomon*. Lake Worth, FL/Newburyport, MA: Ibis Press; distributed by Red Wheel/Weiser, 2009.

Skinner, Stephen, and David Rankine. *A Cunning Man's Grimoire: The Secret of Secrets, A Sixteenth Century English Grimoire*. Singapore: Golden Hoard Press, 2018.

———. *The Goetia of Dr. Rudd: Angels and Demons of Liber Malorum Spirituum Seu Goetia Lemegeton Clavicula Salomonis*. London: Golden Hoard Press, 2010.

———. *The Keys to the Gateway of Magic: Summoning the Solomonic Archangels & Demon Princes Being a Transcription of Janua Magica Reserata, Dr Rudd's Nine Hierarchies of Angels & Nine Celestial Keys, The Demon Princes: In MSS Sloane 3825 and Harley 6482 with Other Pertinent Discourses from Sloane 3821, Sloane 3824, Sloane 3628, and Rawlinson D. 1363*. London: Golden Hoard Press, 2005.

Somerset, H. V. F., and H. E. Salter. "The Colleges and Halls: Gloucester Hall and Worcester College, History" in *The Victoria History of the County of Oxford*, edited by H. E. Salter and Mary D. Lobel, 3:298–301. London: Dawsons of Pall Mall, 1965.

Spamer, Adolf, and Johanna Nickel. *Romanusbüchlein: Historisch-Philologischer Kommentar Zu Einem Deutschen Zauberbuch*. Berlin: Akademie-Verlag, 1958.

Stam, Janneke. "A Book Called the Dannel: An Edition and Study of Sixteenth Century Necromancy." MA Thesis, Radboud Universiteit, 2016.

Strange and Wonderful News from Linconshire, Or, A Dreadful Account of a Most Inhumane and Bloody Murther Committed upon the Body of One Mr. Carter, by the Contrivance of His Elder Brother, Who Had Soon After Found Out, by the Appearance of a Most Dreadful and Terrible Ghost, Sent by Almighty Providence for the Discovery: As Also, the Manner of Its Appearance in Several Shapes and Forms, with Fresh Bleeding Wounds, Still Pursuing the Murtherer from Place to Place, with the Relation How He Endeavoured to Conjure It Down, and of Its Appearance and Declaration of the Murtherers, and of the Confession of the Murderer When Apprehended, with Many Other Remarkable Circumstances. London, 1679.

Stratton-Kent, Jake. *Pandemonium: A Discordant Concordance of Diverse Spirit Catalogues*. West Yorkshire: Hadean Press, 2016.

Thomas, Keith. *Religion and the Decline of Magic*. Harmondsworth, Middlesex: Penguin, 1971.

Timbers, Frances. *The Magical Adventures of Mary Parish: The Occult World of Seventeenth-Century London*. Kirksville, MO: Truman State University Press, 2016.

Trotman, E. E. "Seventeenth-Century Treasure-Seeking at Bridgwater." *Notes and Queries for Somerset and Dorset* 27 (1961): 220–21.

W. N. *Merry Drollery, or A Collection of [Brace] Jovial Poems, Merry Songs, Witty Drolleries Intermix'd with Pleasant Catches. The First Part*. London: Printed by J. W. for P. H. and are to be sold at the New Exchange..., 1661.

Wallis, Faith. *Medieval Medicine: A Reader*. Toronto: University of Toronto Press, 2010.

Watson, Andrew G. "Thomas Allen of Oxford and His Manuscripts" in *Medieval Scribes, Manuscripts & Libraries: Essays Presented to N. R. Ker*, edited by Malcolm Beckwith Parkes and Andrew G. Watson, 279–313.

Wentworth, Joshua A., trans. *The Authentic Red Dragon (Le Veritable Dragon Rouge), or the Art of Commanding the Celestial, Aerial, Terrestrial, and Infernal Spirits, with the Secret of Making the Dead Speak; of Winning Every Time One Plays the Lottery; of Discovering Hidden Treasures, etc., Followed by The Black Hen (La Poule Noire), Cabbala Unknown until Now, Translated from the French Edition of 1521*. York Beach, ME: Teitan Press, 2011.

Weever, John. *Antient Funeral Monuments of Great-Britain, Ireland, and the Islands Adjacent, with the Dissolved Monasteries Therein Contained; Their Founders, and What Eminent Persons Have Been Therein Interred; As Also, the Death and Burial of Certain of the Blood-Royal, Nobility, and Gentry of These Kingdoms, Entombed in Foreign Nations; Intermixed and Illustrated with Variety of Historical Observations, Annotations, and Brief Notes; Extracted out of Approved Authors, Infallible Records, Leidger Books, Charters, Rolls, Old Manuscripts, and the Collections of Judicious Antiquaries; Whereunto Is Prefixed, A Discourse on Funeral Monuments, Containing an Account of the Foundation and Fall of Religious Houses—Of Religious Orders—Of the Ecclesiastical State of England—And of Other Occurrences Touched upon throughout the Work*. London: W. Tooke, 1767.

Weill-Parot, Nicolas, and Julien Véronèse. "Antonio Da Montolmo's De Occultis et Manifestis or Liber Intelligentiarum: An Annotated Critical Edition with English Translation and Introduction" in *Invoking Angels:*

Theurgic Ideas and Practices, Thirteenth to Sixteenth Centuries, edited by Claire Fanger, 341–66. Magic in History. University Park, PA: Pennsylvania State University Press, 2012.

Weyer, Johann. *Ioannis Wieri De praestigiis daemonum, & incantationibus ac ueneficiis libri sex, postrema editione quinta aucti & recogniti. Accessit Liber apologeticus, et Pseudomonarchia daemonum …* Basileae: Ex Officina Oporiniana [per Balthasarum Han, Hieronymum Gemusaeum & Polycarpi fratris haeredes], 1577.

Wickersheimer, Ernest. *Les manuscrits latins de médecine du haut Moyen Age dans les bibliothèques de France.* Paris: Centre National de la Recherche Scientifique, 1966.

Wilby, Emma. *The Visions of Isobel Gowdie: Magic, Witchcraft and Dark Shamanism in Seventeenth-Century Scotland.* Brighton/Portland, OR: Sussex Academic Press, 2010.

Willan, Thomas Stuart. *The Muscovy Merchants of 1555.* Clifton, NJ: A. M. Kelley, 1973.

William of Auvergne. *Guilielmi Alverni episcopi Parisiensis, mathematici perfectissimi, eximii philosophi, ac theologi præstantissimi, Opera omnia: quæ hactenus reperiri potuerunt, reconditissimam rerum humanarum, ac divinarum doctrinam abundè complectentia, ac proinde bonarum artium ac scientiarum studiosis, maximè verò theologis, ac divini verbi concionatoribus apprimè necessaria: nunc demùm in hac novissima editione ab innumeris errorum chiliadibus expurgata, instaurata, elucidata, atque sermonibus & variis tractatibus aucta ex m.ss. codd. ut et præfationibus ad lectorem apertius intelligetur: quorum catalogum proxima post præfationes pagina indicabit cum indicibus locupletissimis rerum notabilium.* Aureliæ; Londini: ex typographia F. Hotot; apud Robertum Scott, bibliopolam, 1674.

Williams, Penry. "Elizabethan Oxford: State, Church, and University" in *The History of the University of Oxford*, edited by James McConica and T. H. Aston, 3:397–440. Oxford: Clarendon Press, 1986.

Wilson, Derek. *Sweet Robin: A Biography of Robert Dudley, Earl of Leicester 1533–1588.* London: Allison & Busby, 1997.

Wood, Anthony à, Philip Bliss, and University of Oxford. *Athenae Oxonienses: An Exact History of All the Writers and Bishops Who Have Had Their Education in the University of Oxford. To Which Are Added the Fasti, or Annals of the Said University.* Vol. 1. 4 vols. London: Rivington, 1813.

———. *Athenae Oxonienses. An Exact History of All the Writers and Bishops Who Have Had Their Education in the University of Oxford. To Which Are*

Added the Fasti, or Annals of the Said University. Vol. 2. 4 vols. London: Rivington, 1815.

Wood, Anthony à, Andrew Clark, and Oxford Historical Society. *The Life and Times of Anthony Wood: Antiquary, of Oxford, 1632–1695, Described by Himself*. Oxford Historical Society 40. Oxford: Printed for the Oxford Historical Society, at the Clarendon Press, 1900.

Wood, Anthony à, and John Gutch. *The History and Antiquities of the University of Oxford: In Two Books*. Oxford: [publisher not identified], 1796.

Woolley, Benjamin. *The Queen's Conjurer: The Science and Magic of Dr. John Dee, Adviser to Queen Elizabeth I*. London: HarperCollins, 2002.

Young, Francis. *The Cambridge Book of Magic: A Tudor Necromancer's Handbook*. Cambridge: Francis Young, 2015.

———. *A History of Exorcism in Catholic Christianity*. Palgrave Historical Studies in Witchcraft and Magic. Cambridge: Palgrave Macmillan, 2016.

Zins, Henryk Stanislaw, and Henry Charles Stevens. *England and the Baltic in the Elizabethan Era*. Totowa: Rowman [and] Littlefield, 1972.

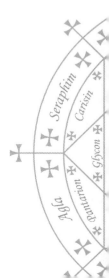

Of Angels, Demons & Spirits

E MUS. 173

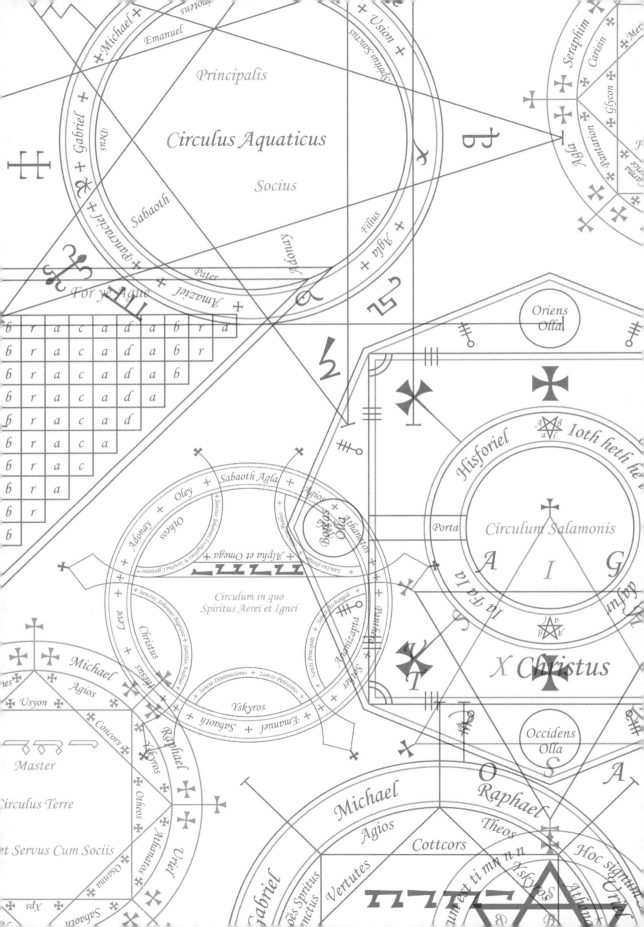

---:◆:---

Consecratio Libris [Consecration of the Book]

"O most amiable God, O God incomparable, O God incomprehensible, O most meek and merciful God, O most excellent and glorious God, O omnipotent and insearchable God, and God of all mercy, I, N., although unworthy and full of all iniquity, deceit, and malice, meekly do come unto thy mercy, desiring and praying thee most humbly that thou wilt not behold my great and innumerable number of my sins, but, according to thy great mercy, vouchsafe to hear the prayers of me, N., thy unworthy servant, and grant that, with thy most holy names in signs and writings hallowed, that that [sic] this book may receive such virtue and strength, that the fierce potentates and princes and all spirits, by this prayer of consecration, and by this holy book, may be constrained and compelled, whether they will or not, to obey my will and commandments, and whosoever I shall take upon me or any other with this book to exorcise withal, that all spirits thereby may be reclaimed unto our wills and minds, and by the virtue of these holy names of God, written with four letters: Ioth + Theos[109] + Ozam + Agla + Deus + Eloy +, therewith they heard and returned back, and gave way in sunder, the air was fixed and set, the earth trembled, the fire was quenched, and all powers both celestial and terrestrial doth quake and are troubled, and by these holy names of God On + Alpha + et Ω + Eloy + Eloim + Sother + Emanuel + Sabaoth + Adonay + Egge + Yaya + Yeye + that this book may be consecrated, and all experiments and characters written therein. Grant this, O Lord + which are worthy all honours and praises, world without end. Amen."

The Consecration for the Stone

"O thou creature of God, thou crystal stone, I conjure thee and command thee that you be blessed, and by that authority given unto me by the holy church, so bless I thee and adjure thee to be blessed through Jesus + Christ + the son of the living God, that you mayst have power and virtue for the purpose that thou art ordained for. I do charge thee and command thee to receive such virtue, that by the power of

---

109 *Theos*: Greek for "God." When spelled in the Greek alphabet, this is four letters long.

---

these names of God, thou mayst have virtue to give a true sight unto any spirit that shall be called into thee to appear, that by the holiness and virtue, he or they may give true answers of all things that shall be demanded, of him or them, and I, N., by all

[1v]

the names of all the orders of angels, and by all the movings of the seven planets and sphere, and by the high and most worthy name of God + Tetragrammaton +, that you do receive such virtue and influence of grace of Jesus + Christ + that what spirit or spirits soever shall be called into thee, he or they may be brought into such fear and favour unto the bearer through these blessed names of God, and this con-secration, that he or they through fear may obey all the precepts and will of thy faithful servant of God N., and soever he or they continue except N. license thee or you to depart, and that thou shalt have no power to lie, nor tell any fables, nor work no guile nor falsehood when thou art called into this stone, through the grace of God, which worketh in thee, a blessed and consecrated stone, to subdue and make obedient all spirits, that shall be called into thee, through the most blessed Son of God, who liveth and reigneth with God the Father and the Holy Ghost, world with-out end. Amen."

Then say, "*Deus, deus meus.* [God, my God.]"[110] *Finis.*

110 Psalm 21 in the Vulgate numbering (which will be used for all subsequent psalm references).

Planetary Hours

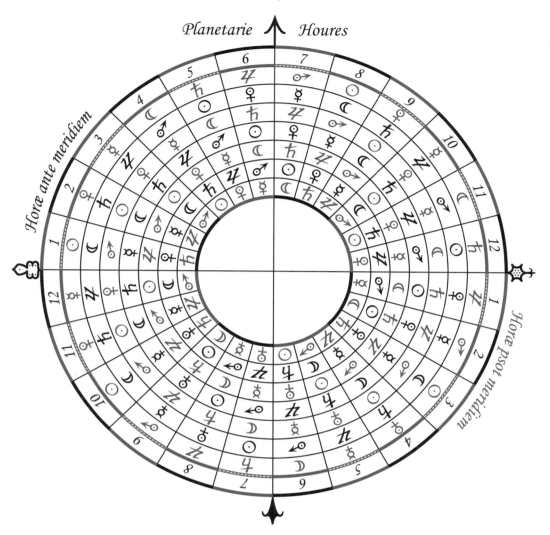

[How to Use the Incantation Above][111]

When you find a + in any place, you must say, "*In nomine patris, et filii et spiritus sancti.* [In the name of the Father, and the Son, and the Holy Ghost.]" And the stone must not be touched with any man's bare hand again before the spirit be called into it, etc.

[A Call to a Spirit]

"In the name of our Lord Jesus Christ, the Father, the Son, and the Holy Ghost, Holy Trinity and Inseparable Unity, have mercy upon us. **Amen.**"

And then say, "*Deus, deus meus, respice in me*" et "*Miserere mei, domine,*" et etc. ["God, my God, look back upon me" and "Have mercy on me, Lord," and so forth.][112]

For the Wind and the Earth

"I conjure thee, wind and earth, by Jesus Christ, which hath made thee so thick by his virtue and blessing and walking upon the sea which he gave to Peter, commanding him to come to him, and by the virtue of Jesus Christ, that thou cease and wax all clear, that I may hear and see the spirits appearing in this stone to shew unto me all things lawfully, by the blessing of God almighty. The virtue and power of the Father, the Son, and the Holy Ghost come down upon me and remain over me, the servant of God. The praise of our Lord, the health of our Lord, the wounds of our Lord, the virtue and kindness of our Lord, the body and blood of our Lord Jesus Christ be my health and help to subdue to me a spirit in this stone to answer and to shew to me the truth in every matter that I shall ask or enquire of him, *per virtutem dei qui venturus est iudicare vivos et mortuos et seculum per ignem* [by the virtue of God who shall come to judge the living and the death, and the world by fire]. Amen.

"I conjure thee, light, by the virtue of the Father, the Son, and the Holy Ghost, and by that which God made only by his word, saying, 'Let light be made,' and light was

---

111 Headings in brackets are conjectural titles for those sections, which were not titled in the original.

112 Psalms 21 and 30.

---

made, and by all the virtues of our Lord Jesus Christ, and by the power of God, and by all the might of God, and by all things that God hath power of in heaven, in earth, in the sea, and in hell, that you cease and wax clear to the sight of me, so that I be not troubled by the light, but that I may see the spirit appearing in this stone with these mine eyes, and all things that thou spirit appearing would do, say, or shew unto me. Also I conjure the light by these names of God + On + Tasion + Sepeton + and by the virtue of all the holy names of God, and by his power and his passion, and by his holy mother St. Mary our lady, and by all her virtue, and by all the apostles, patriarchs, and prophets, and by all the power of the names of the holy angels and archangels of God and by the baptism of Christ, and by his fasting and Christendom, and by and by all things that God hath power upon, that you have no power on me, nor to draw thyself from us. Otherwise thou shalt do, and that you help us and be assistant unto us, that the spirit appearing may shew unto us, by signs, writings, or speeches, the truth of all such things as we shall ask of him, by the virtue and power of Almighty God, whom we ought to praise evermore. Amen."

[2v]

Then look into the air and call the spirit, saying, "O thou spirit N. with thy fellows, know you that Christ conquereth and Christ reigneth and commandeth in the air." Then say three times, "O thou spirit N. with thy fellows, come and enter into this glass or crystal visibly to the sight of our corporeal eyes, in a fair form of a man or an angel. O thou spirit N., I conjure thee by the living God and by the true God, the which is the first and the last, and I call thee by the virtue of our Lord Jesus Christ, the which descended from heaven for the health of mankind, born of St. Mary the virgin. And I adjure thee, N., by the three persons in Trinity, and I constrain thee by the virtue and power of these three persons, and I call and adjure thee by the Holy Ghost proceeding from the Father and the Son, and did light upon Christ in the flood of Jordan, and did fill the apostles which spake to the praise of God in diverse languages and but with one tongue. Also I constrain thee by the lamb sitting on the throne of God, and by the seven sacraments, and I conjure thee by angels, archangels, thrones, and dominations, principates, and potestates,[113] and by all the virtues of them, I call and constrain thee by the company of them that are before God continually singing, '*Sanctus, sanctus, sanctus* [holy, holy, holy]' with continual voice. And I conjure thee by the 24 seigneurs kneeling before God, and I conjure thee by the seven gold candlesticks that stand shining before God with their lights. I conjure thee by the golden censer, and I command thee by all

---

113 A reference to the ninefold celestial hierarchy of Pseudo-Dionysius. The list given here omits cherubim, seraphim, and virtues.

patriarchs, prophets, and by all holy saints of God, and by the four evangelists, and I require thee and conjure thee by the company of all the holy martyrs and servants of God which suffered for the love of God. I conjure thee by all masses that ever was said or sung through all the world, and by the nine learned priests and by the nine children christened and by the nine answers of God. I conjure and require thee by the incarnation, nativity, baptism, fasting, and transfiguration of Christ, and I command thee by the passion of Christ, and by the crown of thorn which the Jews put upon his head and by the reed which they put in his right hand and kneeled down before him and mocked him, saying, 'Hail, king of the Jews,' and by the strokes that the Jews gave him, and by the cross that our Lord was hanged on, and by the cry of the Son of God to his father, saying, 'Eloy, Eloy, Lama Zabathanie,' that is to say, 'My God, my God, why hast thou forsaken me?' and by the death of Christ, and by the spear which pierced his side, and by the nails that he was nailed with, and by the wounds of Christ and by the bread that he took and broke and gave to his disciples, saying, 'Take, eat, this is my body,' and by his precious blood that he gave to his disciples, saying, 'Take and drink, for this is the drink of my blood of the new testament, which is shed for you and for many for the remission of sins,' and by the sheets that our Lord was lapped[114] in, and by the grave that his body was buried in, and by his descension into hell, and by his resurrection and ascension, that, wheresoever you be, that you come without any tarrying, and that you enter and appear visibly unto my sight in this crystal stone or glass in a fair form or shape of a man or angel, and give unto me a true answer of all such things as I shall ask of thee, and that you do not trouble me neither in my senses, body, or soul, but that you come gently and quietly and speak meekly unto me or give me in writing all such things that I shall demand of thee under the pain of everlasting damnation, fiat. O ye spirit N., I charge and command thee to come at this call at the time appointed, without hurting or harming of me or any other creature of God under the pain of eternal damnation. *Fiat* [let it be done], *fiat, fiat*. Amen."

Finis.

[3r]

In nomine domini Jesus Christus, [In the name of Lord Jesus Christ], amen.

---

114 *Lapped*: Wrapped or folded.

In all these days of the moon, all experiments may be proved, and in no other days: As in the 2nd, 4th, 6th, 8th, 10th, 12th, and 14th.

[An Experiment of Mosacus][115]

First make a circle for the spirit to appear in, in some secret place from people, and let the circle be two foot broad, and write therein the name of the spirit, and then command him to appear in the likeness of a child of three years of age with a red head, and when he cometh, he will hover from the ground a shaftment[116] as still as a stone, but look not too much on him, I warn thee, for it is not wholesome, and you mayst have two fellows with thee in the circle, and you mayst call what spirit thou wilt for what faculties thou desirest, and what thing soever thou wilt have done, write it in a piece of new vellum, and cast it out of thy circle to the spirit when he doth appear, and bid him fulfill thine intent and purpose as it is there written, and anon it shall be done, for he will go forth and do more in one hour than thou canst go or do in seven years, and he will tell thee all things that thou wilt ask of him, or else he will tell thee who may fulfill thine intent and purpose.

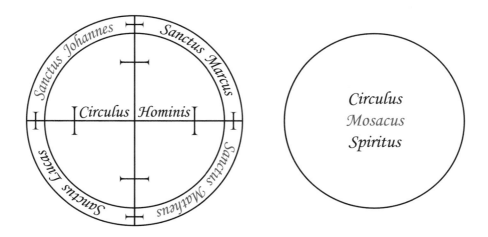

---

115 *Mosacus*: For other operations, see *Oberon*, 446–53, and Cambridge Additional 3544, 10–22.

116 *Shaftment*: The distance from the end of an extended thumb to the opposite edge of the hand.

Make a circle on the ground for thee[117] and thy fellows to be in, and make it seven foot from the spirit's circle, and make it seven foot of breadth from the midst to the sides with a palm tree that was hallowed on Palm Sunday, saying these words following: "+ *In nomine patris paracliti + et filii + et spiritus sancti, amen* [+ In the name of the Father the defender + and of the Son + and of the Holy Ghost, amen]," and then strew ashes of the same palm in the circle, saying the aforesaid words. Then make a + with the same ashes on thy forehead, saying even the aforesaid words.[118]

Then cast holy water in the circle, saying these words:

"Aspargis [Aspergo] te aqua benedicta in circulo isto, et loco isto, in nomine dei patris omnipotentis, qui aquam fecit, benedixit, et consecravit et dedit potestatem famulis suis sacerdotibus, et precipue diebus dominicis in ecclesia sua, illum benedictum consecrare, in nomine

[3v]

suo benedictione et consecratione qui est pater et fillius et spiritus sanctus. Ego te, aqua benedicta, invoco et exorzizo te in nomine et virtute dei et sancte marie matris sue, nec non in nomine et virtute omni sanctorum et sanctarum eius cum comfortia omni celestium, ut tu, aqua benedicta, hoc circulum consecres per illum deum qui te fecit, et consecrari iussit, ut eras michi defentio et protectio ab omnibus diaboli temtationibus, infestationibus, insidiis, et fraudibus. Presentia, sancti spiritus, nobis misericordium tuum posteritibus ubique. Adesse dignatur, per dominum nostrum Jesum Christum, filium tuum, qui vivit et regnat deus, per omnia secula seculorum. Amen."

["I sprinkle you, holy water, in this circle, in this place, in the name of God the omnipotent father, who made, blessed, and consecrated water, and gave power to the priests his servants, and taught them, on Sundays in his church, to consecrate that blessed substance with blessing and consecration in his name, who is Father and Son and Holy Ghost. I invoke thee, holy water, and I exorcise thee in the name and virtue of God and the holy Mary his mother, and also in the name and the virtue of all his male and female saints with the corroboration of all the heavens, so that thou, holy water, mayst consecrate this circle by that God that made thee, and

---

117 Text in the first circle: *Sanctus Marcus, Sanctus Matheus, Saunctus Lucas, Sanctus Johannes.*
    Center: *Circulus hominis* [circle of the man].
    Second circle: *Circulus / Mosacus / Spiritus* [Circle / Mosacus / Spirit].

118 From this point, the operation diverges sharply from that in *Oberon*.

---

he orders you to be consecrated so that thou wert defense and protection to me from all temptations of the devil, troubles, enemies, and deceits. Deliver, Holy Ghost, thy mercy to the children everywhere. It is deemed worthy to be present, by our Lord Jesus Christ, thy son, who lives and reigns God, forever and ever. Amen."][119]

"Coniuro te, circulum, et locum istum, per illud verum deum qui ista terram creavit. Sanctifico + et consecro te circulum, et locum istum, per ipsum creatorem qui totum mundum de nichilo fecit, et per ista eius nomina sanctissima + Theos + Otheos + Yskyros + Athanatos + Agla + Ia + Ym + Deus + Oley + Beoth + Otheo + Sabaoth + Fanaboth + Hell + Habyell + Anathay + Matiell + Amaziell + Gudumell + Agios + Thekymas + Thelias + Ymas + Ely + Messias + Eloy + Elyon + Agan + Ya + Ya + Ye + Ye + Yoat + Yamell + Van + Than + Hele + Hubbe + Thu + Valburi + Tablens + Sem + Hallata + Coynothomen + Sabalay + Trotiamos + Orepym + Haglata + Uytell + Ytell + Abna + Amya + Hoye + Noys + Yahena + Yara + et omnia nomina dei sacratissima, in nota et ignota, sit locus iste et circulus iste, ex dono omnipotentis, benedictus et consecratus, et sancta maria, matrem domini nostri Jesum Christi, plena gratia, consecratus, sanctificatus, et custoditus, et a societate omni sanctorum et sanctarum dei, omnium angelorum, archangelorum, thronorum, et dominationum, principatum et potestatum, et virtutem quoque cherubyn et seraphyn, prophetarum, appostolorum, evangelistarum, martyrum, patriarcharum, confessorum, atque virginum, potenter consecratus, confirmatus, et recensiliatus (reconciliatus) circulus iste, et locus iste, quatenus tantem virtutem, potestatem, sanitatem capiat et obtineat, a signo dei vivi et veri, et a sancta Christi cruce + qui nullus spiritus malignus aliquam potestatem terminum istum ingredi, nec contagiones valeat inferre, nec aliquo modo michi movendi, ipso adiuvante et discendente [defendente] cui celestia, terrestria, et infernalia semper obedient. Amen."

["I conjure thee, circle, and this place, by that true God who made this earth. I purify + and I consecrate thee, circle, and this place, by the same creator who made all the universe out of nothing, and by these his most holy names + Theos + Otheos + Yskyros + Athanatos + Agla + Ia + Ym + Deus + Oley + Beoth + Otheo + Sabaoth + Fanaboth + Hell + Habyell + Anathay + Matiell + Amaziell + Gudumell + Agios + Thekymas + Thelias + Ymas + Ely + Messias + Eloy + Elyon + Agan + Ya + Ya + Ye + Ye + Yoat + Yamell + Van + Than + Hele + Hubbe + Thu + Valburi + Tablens + Sem + Hallata + Coynothomen + Sabalay + Trotiamos + Orepym + Haglata + Uytell + Ytell + Abna + Amya + Hoye + Noys + Yahena + Yara + and by all most

---

119 Compare to Sloane 3853, 67r–v.

holy names of God, known and unknown, this place and this circle may be blessed and consecrated, by the gift of the Omnipotent, and holy Mary, mother of our Lord Jesus Christ, full of grace, may be consecrated, purified, and guarded, and from out of the fellowship of all male and female saints of God, of all angels, archangels, thrones, and dominions, principalities and powers, and virtues, also of cherubim and seraphim, prophets, apostles, evangelists, martyrs, patriarchs, confessors, and virgins, may this circle and this place be powerfully consecrated, fortified, and restored, so that it may capture and maintain such virtue, power, and health, by the sign of the living and true God, and by the holy cross of Christ + that no evil spirit mayst have any power to penetrate this limit, and not have power to bring in contagions, nor raising discord for me in any manner, with his help and protection, whom celestial, earthly, and infernal things always obey. Amen."][120]

Then go thou into the circle with thy right foot before, and standing or kneeling therein, say as followeth:

"*Benedicat nos/me + imperialis maiestas protegat nos/me + regalis divinitas custodiat nos/me + sempiterna deitas foveat nos/me + gloriosa unitas defendat nos/me + imensa trinitas dirigat nos/me + inestimabilis bonitas regat nos/me potentia + patris vivificat nos/me + sapientia filii, illuminat nos/me.*

[4r]

+ *virtus spiritus sancti, Alpha et Ω, deus et homo, sis nobis/michi tuis/tuo famulo/famulis salus et protectio. Amen.* [May thou bless us/me + may the imperial majesty protect us/me + may the royal divinity guard us/me + may the everlasting deity support us/me + may the glorious unity defend us/me + may the immeasurable Trinity guide us/me + may the inestimable benevolence rule us/me + the power of the Father revives us/me + the wisdom of the Son illuminates us/me + the virtue of the Holy Ghost, Alpha and Ω, God and man, may be to us/me your servant/servants health and protection. Amen."][121]

Then kneel down upon thy knees saying thy Pater Noster and Ave Maria and a Creed, Confiteor, et Misereatur.[122]

---

120 Compare to *Oberon,* 241–2, and Sloane 3853, 68r–v.

121 See *Oberon,* 247–8, 447.

122 *Confiteor, misereatur:* Prayers said as part of confession. These prayers were omitted in many Protestant liturgies.

"Iudica me deus," cum "gloria patri," et "Deus in nomine tuo," cum gloria patri, "Deus misereatur" cum gloria patri. [And say "Judge me, God"[123] with a Gloria Patri,[124] and a "God in thy name"[125] with a Gloria Patri, and "God may pity"[126] with a Gloria Patri.]

This done, thou art safe and thou needest not to be afraid, for there may come no wicked spirit within thy circle, but I warn thee, come not out of thy circle till thou hast avoided[127] the spirit as thou shalt know hereafter, for if you do, he will devour thee, therefore take heed.

Ista oratio e[s]t dicenda ante invocationem cuiusque spiritus. Ad inveniendum psalmi supra dicitur, sed "Iudica me, Deus" cum gloria patri, "Deus, in nomine tuo," cum gloria patri, "Deus misereatur," cum gloria patri, in quo loco stant in psalterio. Quere et invenies. [This prayer is said before the invocation of whatever spirit. When coming to the psalms spoken above, but "Judge me, God" with a Gloria Patri, "God, in thy name" with a Gloria Patri, "God may pity" with a Gloria Patri, in what place they are in the psalter. Seek and ye shall find.][128]

Feria tertia, feria quarta, feria quarta [Tuesday, Wednesday, Wednesday] 58 70 83[129]

"Omnipotens sempiterne deus, qui in principio cuncta ex nihilo creasti, cui obedient omnes creature tue, cui omnes genuflectitur celestium, terrestrium, et infernorum, quem timent angeli, archangeli, dominationi, trones, potestates adorant, tremunt, qui manu claudis omnia, et Adam et Evam similitudinem tuam fecisti, et angelos tuos incredulos propter eorum superbiam in profundum inferni, eiecisti. Te rogo, te peto clementissime, pater omnipotentis, et obsecro per Jesus Christum dominum nostrum, filium tuum, in cuius potentia sunt omnia, qui sedet ad dexteram patris omnipotentis. Inde venturus est iudicare vivos et mortuos. Tu, qui es Alpha et Ω, principium et finis,

---

123 Psalm 42.

124 *Gloria Patri*: "*Gloria patri, et filio, et spiritui sancto. Sicut erat in principio, et nunc, et semper, et in saecula saeculorum. Amen.* [Glory to the Father, and to the Son, and to the Holy Ghost. As it was in the beginning, and is now, and always, and will be forever. Amen.]"

125 Psalm 53.

126 Psalm 66.

127 *Avoided*: Banished.

128 Matthew 7:7.

129 *Numbers of unknown significance.* Given that they are similarly spaced apart as the numbers of the psalms above, I speculate that they are page numbers in a psalter, although none of the English Latin psalters I have examined fit the numbers in question.

---

primus et novissimus, rex regum et dominis dominantium, Ioth, Agla, Nabnothell, Abnell, Enathi, Anatell, Maziell, Zodomell, Ayos, Colimas, Elias, Iskyros, Athanatos, Ymas, Ely, Messias, et per ista nomina sanctissima tua, et per omnia tua nomina alia, te invoco, obsecro, per nativitatem domini nostri Jesu Christi, et per sapientium tuam, per passionem tuam, per resurrectionem tuam, per assentionem tuam, per sanctum paraclitum tuum, per amaritudinem passionis tue, et per quicunque vulnera tuam, per mortem et sanguinem et aquam qui exierunt de corpore tuo, et per manum omnipotentiam tuum, et per ineffabilem virtutem tuam, per sacramentum quod dissipulis tuis, propriis membris, tradidisti, per sanctam et individuam trinitatem, et per beatam virginem mariam, matrem tuam, per angelos [et] archangelos, per patriarcas, et per omnes sanctos et sanctas tuas, et per omnia sacramentum [sacramenta] et misteria que sunt in honore tuo ministrata, et per omnia sanctissima nomina tua, cognita [et] incognita. Adoro et rogo te, ut acceptabiles habeas omnes coniurationes et verba ea, cum quibus uti potero, et dies [des] michi virtutem et

[4v]

potestatem super omnes angelos tuos qui de celo eiecti sunt ad dissipiandum humanum genus, et loquelam eorum attrahendum ad constringendum, et ad solvendum ad ligandum eos coram nobis/meus, et ad precipiendum eos omnia que sunt eis possibilia tacere, et ut nullo modo vocem meam contemptuant, sed in dictis meis semper obedient, et nos/me timent per humilitatem tuam et gratiam tuam. Deprecor et peto te, Athanathon, Anay, Anthon, Arathon, Negedo, Iay, Ray El, Usion, Bo, Ra, Nix, et per omnia alia tua sancta nomina, et per sanctes sanctas tuas, et per angelos, archangelos, potestates, dominationes, et virtutes, et per illa nomina per que Salamon constringebat diabolum, et conclusit illum, et [per] Agla, Yoth, Othae, Nabnothe, et per omnia nomina sancta tua, et per omnia tua que scripta sunt in toto mundo, et per virtutem eorum, ut concedere digneris nobis/michi hanc potestatem, ut constringere possim et nobis/ michi respondere de omnibus que queram, sine letione corporis et anime mee, et alicuius rei, et sine fallatione et mendatione, per domine noster Jesus Christus, filium tuum, qui tecum vivit et regnat deus, per omnia secula seculorum. Amen."

["Almighty everlasting God, who in the beginning created all out of nothing, whom all thy creations obey, to whom all beings of the heavens, the earths, or the hellish realms genuflect, whom the angels, archangels, dominions, thrones, and powers fear, entreat, and tremble before, that, with thy hand, thou encompasseth all things, and thou made Adam and Eve in thy likeness, and thou didst eject thy disobedient angels, on account of their pride, into the depths of hell. I ask thee, I beg thee most gently, Father of omnipotence, and I beseech by Jesus Christ our Lord, thy son, in whose power are all things, who sits to the right of the Omnipotent Father. From there he will come to judge the living and the dead. Thou, who art Alpha and Ω, the beginning and the end, the first and the last, king of kings and lord of lords, Ioth, Agla, Nabnothell, Abnell, Enathi, Anatell, Maziell, Zodomell, Ayos, Colimas, Elias, Iskyros, Athanatos, Ymas, Ely, Messias, and by these thy most holy names, and by all thy other names, I invoke thee and I beseech thee by the nativity of our lord Jesus Christ, and by thy wisdom, by thy passion, by thy resurrection, by thy ascension, by thy holy defender, by the bitterness of thy passion, and by thy five wounds, by thy death and the blood and the water that escaped from thy body, and by thy omnipotent hand, and by thy ineffable virtue, by the sacrament that thou didst hand over to thy disciples, the members of thy own church, by the holy and individual trinity, and by the Blessed Virgin Mary, thy mother, by the angels and archangels, by the patriarchs, and by all thy male and female saints, and by all sacraments and mysteries that were dispensed in thy honor, and by all thy most holy names, known and unknown. I implore and ask thee that thou mayst consider acceptable all conjurations and these words, which will be able to be used, and thou mayst give me virtue and power over all thy angels who were ejected from heaven for the scattered human race, and the word of these for bringing, constraining, loosing, and binding of these to us/me face to face, and for commanding all of these possible to be silent in them, and so that in no way they may be contemptuous of my voice, but they will always obey at my words, and they fear us/me by thy humility and your grace. I entreat and ask for you, Athanathon, Anay, Anthon, Arathon, Negedo, Iay, Ray El, Usion, Bo, Ra, Nix, and by all your other holy names, and by the angels, archangels, powers, dominions, and virtues, and by those names by which Solomon was constraining the devil, and he confined him, and by Agla, Yoth, Othae, Nabnothe, and by all thy holy names and by all thy names that were written in all the world, and by the virtues of these, so that thou mayst deem worthy to grant to us/me this power, so that I may be able to bind them and they may respond to us/me of all things that I will ask, without hurt of my body and soul, and of any thing, and without deceit or falsehood, by our Lord Jesus Christ, thy son, who lives and reigns with thee, God, forever and ever. Amen."]

Alia oratio ante invocationem spiritus. "*In nomine domini nostri Jesu Christi, et totius trinitatis, patris, et filii, et spiritus sancti, amen. Sancta trinitas et insepera[bi]lis bonitas, et invoco te obsecro ut sis michi salus et defentio et protectio anime mee, nunc et in perpetuum, per virtutem sancte crucis + et passionis tue. Te depreco, domine Jesu Christus, fili dei vivi, per merita et intercessiones beatissime maria virginis et matris tuo, atque omnium sanctorum tuarum, ut michi concedas gratiam tuam atque potestatem tuam super istum spirituum N., ut quandocumque eum in veritate et virtute nominorum tuorum invocavero. Statim michi conveniat Nichell michi ledens neque timorem inferens, sed in omnibus obediens, et mandata mea implens, per te, Jesu Christe, salvator mundi, qui vivis et regnas cum deo patre et sancto spiritu deus, per omnia secula seculorum. Amen."*

[Another prayer before the invocation of the spirit. "In the name of our Lord Jesus Christ and of all the Trinity, of the Father, and of the Son, and of the Holy Ghost, amen. Holy Trinity and inseparable goodness. I invoke thee and implore that thou mayst have for me health and defense and protection of my soul, now and in perpetuity, by the virtue of the holy cross + and of thy passion. I beg thee, Jesus Christ, son of the living God, by the merits and intercessions of the most blessed Mary, virgin and thy mother, and of all thy saints, that thou mayst grant to me thy grace and thy power over that spirit N., that whenever I will invoke thee in truth and in the virtue of thy names, immediately Nichell may come to me,[130] neither hurting me nor introducing fear, but obeying and satisfying my commands in all matters, by thee, Jesus Christ, savior of the world, that thou livest and reignest with God the Father and the Holy Spirit, God, forever and ever. Amen."]

Nota: Here begins the invocation of the spirit and the secretness of Salamon.

Nomina spiritum veneris [names of the spirits of Venus], Rignell, Sathan, Astarth.[131]

Say this 3 times:

"*In nomine patris paracliti et filii et spiritus sancti* [in the name of the Father the defender, and the Son, and the Holy Spirit], amen."

"*Mosacus spiritus veni festinanter. Coniuro te, spiritum nomine Mosacus, per deum patrem omnipotentem, per deum vivum, per deum verum, per deum sanctum, per deum qui te de paradisi gaudio eiecit, et per hec sancta nomina dei vivi + Messias + Sother + Emanuell + Sabaoth + Adonay + Otheos + Athanatos + Ely + Panthon + Craton + Ysus + Kyrus + Alpha et Ω + Jesus Christus nazarenus, et coniuro te, Mosacus spiritus, per hec sancta nomina dei principa-*

[5r]

---

130 *Immediately, Nichell...me*: In Clm 849 and Sloane 3826, a similar passage reads "you will immediately come to me to do my will."
131 *Astarth*: Possibly a variant of Astaroth.

---

lia + Tetragrammaton + Onale + Domandelabo + Gramaton + Omoyson + Alconale + Sparon + Agla + Hely + Lamazabatony + Egon + Regon + Bo + Ra + Nix + et per omnia alia nomina dei, et per sanctum Mariam, matrem domini nostri Jesu Christi, et per omnes ordines angelorum et per omnes virgines, et per quinque vulnera dei, et per virginitatem beate Iohannis Evangeliste ac Baptiste, et per hec nomina dei, Mageth Maothe, per que Salomon te constringebat, ut ubicunque fueris, statim monstres te michi in circulo tuo in pulcra forma humana, cum rubro colore vel albo, in similtudinem pueri trium annorum, habens rub[r]um caput. Mosacus spiritus, iubeo te per fidem quam debes. Demo, in eterno private gaudio, et per virtutem dei vivi et vero purissimi, et per illos angelos, archangelos, tronos, dominationes, principates, potestates, cherubin, et ceraphin, et per omnes alios angelos, et omnes reliquas sanctorum et sanctarum qui continentur in universo mundo, et sicut hoc est verum, quod Maria fiat virgo in partu, et post partum virgo premansit, et sicut hoc est verum quod hostia de pane virtetur in corpus domini nostri Jesu Christi, et per ista nomina que sunt maxime nigromantia artis, viz., Belsac, Sari, Sarie, Superbelffat, Pamulon in potestate Aye Dessebe, nominates, aque resistunt, et elementa concominantur ista nomina. Iubeo et coniuro te, per charitatem dei, et per oculos eius, et per omnia membra eius, et per divinitatem eius, et per bonum et malum qui quatuor elementa sustinent, ut cuicunque fueris, statim in ictu oculi, aperies et monstres te michi in circulo tuo in pulcra forma humana, et imple omne desideriunt [desiderium] meum, nullo modo animam meam nec corpus meum nec membris meis, nec alicui creature, neque alicui animali domini, nec ecclesie sue campanili, quovismodo necare seu agravare presumas, et michi demonstras ac respondeas veraciter, et in sophisticaliter, nec figmentaliter, nec respotionibus sophistalibus, sed sicut fuerit in facto de preteritis, de presentibus, et futuris, et omnia que ab eis interogabuntur. Sic fiat, per ipsum domini imperium est honor, vertus, pax, eternitas, et bonitas, per infinita seculorum secula. Amen."

["Spirit Mosacus, come quickly. I conjure thee, spirit with the name Mosacus, by God the omnipotent Father, by the living God, by the true God, by the holy God, by God who ejected thee from paradise with delight, and by those holy names of the living God + Messias + Sother + Emanuell + Sabaoth + Adonay + Otheos + Athanatos + Ely + Panthon + Craton + Ysus + Kyrus + Alpha and Ω + Jesus Christ of Nazareth, and I conjure thee, spirit Mosacus, by these chief holy names of God + Tetragrammaton + Onale + Domandelabo + Gramaton + Omoyson + Alconale + Sparon + Agla + Hely + Lamazabatony + Egon + Regon + Bo + Ra + Nix + and by all other names of God, and by the holy Mary, mother of our Lord Jesus Christ, and by all orders of angels and by all virgins, and by the five wounds of God, and by the virginity of the blessed John the Evangelist and the Baptist, and by these names of

God, Mageth Maothe, by which Solomon bound thee, so that wherever thou wilt be, thou shouldst appear to me immediately in thy circle in a beautiful human form, with a red or white color, in the likeness of a boy of three years with red hair. Spirit Mosacus, I order thee by the faith that thou hast. I remove thee, stripped of eternal joy, and through the virtue of the living and truly most pure God, and by those angels, archangels, thrones, dominions, principalities, powers, cherubim, and seraphim, and by all other angels, and all relics of male and female saints that are contained in the whole world, and just as this is true, that Mary may have been made a virgin in birth, and after birth remained a virgin, and just as this is true that the Host of the bread is transformed into the body of our Lord Jesus Christ, and by these names that are greatest in the art of nigromancy,[132] that is, Belsac, Sari, Sarie, Superbelffat, Pamulon, in the power Aye, Dessebe, which, having been named, the waters still, and the elements attend those names. I order and conjure thee, by the charity of God, and by his eyes, and by all his limbs, and by his divinity, and by the good and evil that the four elements support, so that, whatever thou mayst be, thou mayst appear immediately in a blink of the eyes, and show thyself to me in thy circle in beautiful human form, and satisfy all my desire, in no way mayst thou dare as far as to kill or to oppress my soul nor my body nor my limbs, neither any creature nor any animal of God, nor his church with belltowers, and thou showest to me and respond truly and with answers neither specious, nor fictitious, nor sophistic, but just as thou shouldst be in deed regarding the past, present, and future, and all that out of these will be answered. Thus let it be done. By the great dominion of the Lord is honor, virtue, peace, eternity, and goodness, forever and ever. Amen."][133]

"*Coniuro te, Mosacus spiritus, per iudicem [iudicium] vivorum et mortuorum, factorem mundi, et creationem celi et terre, et eum qui te de celo eiecit, et per crucem + passionis sue, ut au-*

[5v]

dias vocem meam, et veni, et cum omni potentia mea, coniuro te, spiritus nomine Mosacus. Adiuro te, et per hec omnia nomina sanctissima et sacratissima et potentissima dei vivi. Exorzizo te et constringo te, ut sito, velociter et festinanter venias et demonstres te michi in pulcra forma humana cum omni pietate, et per hec nomina omnipotentis dei, viventis in secula seculorum. Veni, veni, + Agla + Tetragrammaton + Alpha et Ω + Agios + Otheos + Yskyros + Athanatos + Panton + Craton + et Ysus

---

132 *Nigromancy*: Magic, with the term suggesting practices of which the author approved. Klaassen, *The Transformations of Magic*, 10–11.

133 Compare to *Oberon*, 448.

+ Salvator + Beena + Ylaye + Say + et Helamo + Mahate + Hehahub + Azepa + Hyheha + Aracya + Hahanat + Agla + Tetragrammaton + Alpha + et Ω + Agyos + Otheos + Yskyros + Athanatos + Panton + Craton + et Ysus + Messias + Sother + Emanuell + Sabaoth + Adonay + Unigenitus + Via + Vita + Manus + Omo + Usion + El + Elya + Hely + Heloy + Lamazabathony + Tetragrammaton + Adonay + Adonay + On + Cados + Accinemos + Elaaymo + Saday + Aglata + Ya + Yot + Yeell + Annova + Yava + Anabona + per virtutem istorum nominum productorum, veni, tu spiritus *Mosacus* nomine, ubicunque es, et per ista nomina dei omnipotentis, et per omnia nomina eius qui omnis lingua confiteatur. Ego te constringo, te adiuro, te invoco, + Vagon + Iregon + Gramaton + Tetragrammaton + Tegeton + Pantheon + Maldall + Amandall + Agla + Basion + Urion + Barion + Baron + Bucton + Zelen + et per vertutem istorum nominum, et per virginitatem istorum nominum. Veni, veni, et in nomine omnium nominum que dixi et nominavi, et in nomine omnium nominum que dicam, tibi dico, spiritus, veni, et iterum veni in nomine + Anepheneton + Egylla + Abmago + Erith + Ebrutone + Talsea + Semeth + Agla + Iesus + Christus + Tetragrammaton + et per omnia altissimi dei vivi, effabilia et ineffabilia, tu, spiritus *Mosacus*, veni, et monstra te michi in circulo tuo, sine letione corporis mei et anime mee et sensus mei et visus mei, et per ista ineffabilia nomina dei patris, et filii, et spiritus sancti. Tu spiritus nomina (nomine) *Mosacus*, festinanter et mihi visibiliter veni, et imple omne desiderium meum, + Oristeon + Uzirion + Egirion + Onella + Eriona + Usyor + Nutonys + Barasym + Nohym + Ioseph + et exorzizo, te spiritus *Mosacus* per septem nomina dei Roell + Yoth + Ynos + Mabnos + Vesprolyo + Nouthy + Christus + et coniuro te, spiritus *Mosacus*, per omnia sancta et sacratissima nomina dei, et in virtute nominum ordinum angelorum, seraphin, cherubin, tronum, dominationum, potestatum, principatum, archangelorum, Raphael, Caphaell, Dardyell, Harataphell, Anaell, Paavtyell, Anabiell, Innael, Carmelyon, Storax,[134] Inquiell, Salgiell, Gabryell, Michaell, Myhell, Faraphyell,

[6r]

Samyell, Yssytres, Atythaell, Uryell, Rasell, Boell, Caszepell, Mekuton, Hocraell, Satquiell, Ubnell, Ragnell, Lancyell, Robyell, Pantetaron, Baracheell, Lucyell, et in virtutem omnium appostolorum, Petri et Pauli et aliorum. Et coniuro te, spiritus *Mosacus*, ut sito venias et monstres te mihi visibiliter, per omnia que prodixi, et per virtutem omnium patriarcharum, et virtute omnium martyrum Christi, et in virtute omnium confessorum, et in virtute septem lampadarum que sunt ante tronum dei, et in virtute septem sacramentorum ecclesie, et in virtute septem ordinum sacrorum, et in virtute

---

134 *Carmelyon, Storax*: Spirits or angels said to be one of the counselers of Oberion; *Oberon*, 455.

passionis et martirii domini nostri Jesu Christi, qui est filius dei vivi sempiterni, et in virtute animalium plena oculis ante et retro, et per meum proprium angelum, et per celum et terram, mare, et omnia que in eis sunt, et omnes missas et elemosinas quas fiebant in ecclesia dei, et per septem planetas celi, per solem et ☉ Sycoracem angelum eius vel Storax, per saturnum ♄ et Malathym angelus eius, per Iovem ♃ et Phytone-um angelum eius, per martem ♂ et Cornigerum angelum eius, per mercurium ☿ et Iperon angelum eius, per veneram ♀ et Albanyxa vel Albanixta angelum eius, per luna ☽ et Cormelyon[135] angelum eius. Et coniuro te, spiritus Mosacus, per tremedum iudi-cium altissimi dei, et adiuro te, spiritus, per ista nomina sancta quibus omnis crea-tura timet, que sunt hec, Anexniton + Ioazac + Patir + Semeforas + Alleluya + Alpha + Beth + Symell + 4 Gymell + Deleth + He + Van + Say + Heth + Thethe + Iothe + Caph + Lameth + Mein + Min + Minii + Miin + Min + Sameth + Aymse + Zade + Coph + Caaph + Regsim + Ihan + Maledicto tibi, spiritui, per hec nomina, et per omnia nomina que nomina in ante, in lacum ignis et sulphuris, ut permaneas in infernum usque in diem iudicii. Ideo veni, veni, veni, ubicunque es, veni, per secretis-sima secretorum, et veni per secretissima nomina dei. Et coniuro te per omnia sanctis-sima nomina dei et per omnia nomina eius que scripta sunt toto mundo, ut cito mihi venias. O tu spiritus, audi que dixi et que dicam tibi, et veni monstrans te mihi in circulo tuo in pulcra forma humana, et quicquid a te petam statim voluntatem meam et subicias et obedias dictis meis, et sine mora imple sub pena perpetua dampnationis et maledictionis dei patris omnipotentis desiderium meum, et veni per secretissima secretorum."

["I conjure thee, spirit Mosacus, by the judgment of the living and the dead, maker of the world, and the creation of heaven and earth, and he who cast thee out of heaven, and by the cross + of his passion, so that thou mayst hear my voice and come, and with all my power, I conjure thee, spirit named Mosacus. I adjure thee, and by all these most holy and sacred and powerful names of the living God. I exorcize thee and bind thee, so that soon speedily and hastily thou mayst come and show thyself to me in a beautiful human shape with all dutifulness, and by these names of omnipotent God, living forever and ever. Come, come, + Agla + Tetra-grammaton + Alpha et Ω + Agios + Otheos + Yskyros + Athanatos + Panton + Craton + and Ysus + Salvator + Beena + Ylaye + Say + and Helamo + Mahate + Hehahub + Azepa + Hyheha + Aracya + Hahanat + Agla + Tetragrammaton + Alpha + and Ω + Agyos + Otheos + Yskyros + Athanatos + Panton + Craton + and Ysus + Messias + Sother + Emanuell + Sabaoth + Adonay + Unigenitus + Via + Vita + Manus + Omo + Usion + El + Elya + Hely + Heloy + Lamazabathony +

---

135 *Storax and Carmelyon*: As above. It is notable that they are connected with the sun and moon here, as *Oberon* lists Oberion as being "under the government of the Sun and Moon" (207).

Tetragrammaton + Adonay + Adonay + On + Cados + Accinemos + Elaaymo + Saday + Aglata + Ya + Yot + Yeell + Annova + Yava + Anabona + by the virtue of those names disclosed, come, thou spirit named Mosacus, wherever thou art, and by those names of God omnipotent, and by all these names that the tongue may confess. I bind thee, I adjure thee, I invoke thee, + Vagon + Iregon + Gramaton + Tetragrammaton + Tegeton + Pantheon + Maldall + Amandall[136] + Agla + Basion + Urion + Barion + Baron + Bucton + Zelen + and by the virtue of those names, and by the purity of those names. Come, come, and in the name of all names that I said and named, and in the name of all names that I will say, to thee I say, spirit, come, and again come in the name + Anepheneton + Egylla + Abmago + Erith + Ebrutone + Talsea + Semeth + Agla + Iesus + Christus + Tetragrammaton + and by all names of the living most high God, effable and ineffable, thou, spirit Mosacus, come, and show thyself to me in thy circle, without harm of my body or my soul or my reason or my vision, and by these ineffable names of God the Father, and of the Son, and of the Holy Ghost. Thou, spirit named Mosacus, come quickly and visibly to me, and satisfy all my longings, + Oristeon + Uzirion + Egirion + Onella + Erio-na + Usyor + Nutonys + Barasym + Nohym + Ioseph + and I exorcise thee, spirit Mosacus, by the seven names of God Roell + Yoth + Ynos + Mabnos + Vesprolyo + Nouthy + Christus + and I conjure thee, spirit Mosacus, by all holy and most con-secrated names of God, and in the virtue of the names of the orders of the angels, seraphim, cherubim, thrones, dominions, powers, principalities, archangels, Raphael, Caphaell, Dardyell, Harataphell, Anaell, Paavtyell, Anabiell, Innael, Carmelyon, Storax, Inquiell, Salgiell, Gabryell, Michaell, Myhell, Faraphyell, Samy-ell, Yssytres, Atythaell, Uryell, Rasell, Boell, Caszepell, Mekuton, Hocraell, Satqui-ell, Ubnell, Ragnell, Lancyell, Robyell, Pantetaron, Baracheell, Lucyell, and in the virtue of all apostles, of Peter and Paul and the others. And I conjure thee, spirit Mosacus, so that soon thou mayst come and thou mayst show thyself to me visibly by all that I said, and by the virtue of all patriarchs, and by the virtue of all martyrs of Christ, and in the virtue of all confessors, and in the virtue of the seven lamps that are before the throne of God, and in the virtue of the seven sacraments of the church, and in the virtue of the seven sacred orders, and in the virtue of the passion and of the martyrs of our Lord Jesus Christ, who is the son of the living eternal God, and in the virtue of the living creatures full of eyes before and behind,[137] and by my own angel, and by heaven and earth, the sea, and all things that are in them, and by all masses and alms that were made in the Church of God, and by the seven planets of heaven, by the sun ☉ and its angel, Sycoracem or Storax, by Saturn ♄

---

136 *Amandall*: Perhaps a reference to the magical work "Almadel" or "Almandal." See Véronèse, *L'Almandal et l'Almadel latins au Moyen Âge*.

137 Revelation 4:6–8.

and its angel Malathym, by Jupiter ♃ and its angel Phytoneum,[138] by Mars ♂ and its angel Cornigerum, by Mercury ☿ and its angel Iperon, by Venus ♀ and Albanyxa or Albanixta its angel, by the moon ☽ and its angel Cormelyon. And I conjure thee, spirit Mosacus, by the great judgment of the most high God, and I adjure thee, spirit, by these holy names by which every creature fears, that are here: Anexniton + Ioazac + Patir + Semeforas + Alleluya + Alpha + Beth + Symell + 4[139] Gymell + Deleth + He + Van + Say + Heth + Thethe + Iothe + Caph + Lameth + Mein + Min + Minii + Miin + Min + Sameth + Aymse + Zade + Coph + Caaph + Regsim + Ihan + I curse thee, spirit, by these names, and by all names that have been named before, into the lake of fire and sulfur, so that thou shalt continue in hell until the day of judgment. Thus, come, come, come, wherever thou art, come, by the most secret of secrets, and come by the most secret names of God. And I conjure thee by all the most holy names of God, and by all his names that are written in all the world, so that soon thou mayst come to me. O thou spirit, hear what I said, and that I will say to thee, and come showing thyself to me in your circle in a beautiful human form, and whatever I shall ask my will from thee, immediately thou shouldst both submit and obey my words, and satisfy my desire without delay, under perpetual pain of damnation and curses of God the omnipotent Father, and come by the most secret of secrets."]

[6v]

"Deus angelorum, deus archangelorum, deus prophetarum, deus martirum, deus appostolorum, deus patriarcharum, deus confessorum, deus virginum, deus pater, domini nostri Jesu Christi. Invoco nomen tuum sanctum in hac per clara maiestati et tuam potentiam. Supplex exposto ut mihi auxilium prestare digneris adversus istum spiritum N., ut ubicunque latet, ad auditum meum festinanter accedat. Ipse imperat tibi, diabolo, de supernis celorum sedibus teque ad inferiorem precipit. Audi, argo spiritus N., inimicus fidei generis humani, mortis temptator, a iusticia declinator, radix malorum, fomes vitiorum, seductor hominum, socius demonum, illum graviter metue, qui in Isaac immaculatus est, in Iosephe mundatus est, in agro occisus est, in homine crucifixus est, deinde surrexit trumphator. Audi, ergo, spiritus, et time iudicium dei, nam est mihi benigne, paratus in omnibus negotiis meis perficiendis. Amen."

138 *Phytoneum:* Could also be "Phytoneun."

139 4: A character of unknown import, not present in a similar list of voces magicae, also based on Hebrew letters later in this manuscript. It might be an attempt to stylize an additional cross accidentally inserted in the manuscript.

["God of angels, God of archangels, God of prophets, God of martyrs, God of apostles, God of patriarchs, God of confessors, God of virgins, God the Father, our Lord Jesus Christ. I invoke thy holy name in this matter by the brilliant majesty and thy power. Kneeling, I implore that thou mayst deem worthy to furnish me help, setting against that spirit N., so that wherever he lurks, he may quickly approach to my hearing. The same orders thee, devil, from the lofty seat of the heavens, and he casts thee down to hell. Hear, slothful spirit N., enemy of the faith of the human race, tempter of death, rejector from justice, root of evils, kindling of crimes, seducer of men, friend of demons, fear that one greatly who is immaculate in Isaac, and is cleansed in Joseph, in the field he is slain, in man he is crucified, then the triumpher rises. Hear therefore, spirit, and fear the judgment of God, for he is kindly to me, ready in all my completed affairs. Amen."]

"Coniuro te, serpens antiquus, per iudicem vivorum et mortuorum, et per deum qui habet potestatem mittere te in gehennem, ut sito perficias quicquid te precipiam, eo iubente qui sedet in summis. Amen."

["I conjure thee, old serpent, by the judgment of the living and of the dead, and by the God who holds power to send thee into Gehenna, so that soon thou mayst complete whatsoever I command thee, commanding by him who sits in the highest. Amen."]

"Quicunque vult," et cet. ["Whosoever wishes,"[140] and so forth.]

NOTA

Say this conjuration nine times. If the spirit be rebellious and will come not erst[141] and then this psalm "Quicunque vult,"[142] and before you hast done, he will in his circle, and he will ask thee what thou wilt have. Then by and by speak to him and dread not saying these words heareafter written:

Coniuratio super spiritum [conjuration over the spirit]

NOTA

"Coniuro te, spiritum, qui coram me est, per patrem, et filium, et spiritum sanctum, et per ista nomina dei, Saday + Tetragrammaton + Adonay + Algamay + Bo + Ra + Nix

---

140 The Athanasian Creed.

141 *Erst*: First.

142 As above; often used in place of a psalm.

+ et per omnia nomina sancta dei, et per omnia opera eius, in celo et in terra, et per virginitatem beate Maria virginis et nostris domini nostri Iesu Christi, et per virtutem celi et terre, et per veram christianitatem, et per virtutem horum verborum, quibus astrictus es huc venire, ut non habeas aliquam potestatem mihi/nobis, nocendi in corde, corpore, et anima, nec a visu meo recedere, donec fueris a me licentiatus, ac coniuro te ut daris mihi verum responsum ad omnia que interrogabo, sine mendationem, dissimiliatione, fallatia, fraude, vel terrore, et ut permaneas in pulcra forma queri, ac perficias veraciter et velociter quicquid tibi precipiam sub pena perpetua dampnationis ac maledictionis dei patris omnipotentis."

["I conjure thee, spirit, who is face to face with me, by the Father, and by the Son, and by the Holy Ghost, and by these names of God, Saday + Tetragrammaton + Adonay + Algamay + Bo + Ra + Nix +, and by all holy names of God, and by all his works, in heaven and on earth, and by the virginity of the Blessed Virgin Mary, and by ours, our Lord Jesus Christ, and by the virtue of heaven and earth, and by the true Christianity, and by the virtue of these words, by which thou wert constrained to come here, so that thou mayst not have any power injuring me/us in mind, body, or soul, and not to fall back from my vision, while thou shalt be licensed by me, and I conjure thee so that a true answer to all that I will ask is given to me, without falsehood, dissembling, trick, fraud, or terror, and so that thou mayst continue to be questioned in a beautiful form, and that thou mayst finish truly and quickly whatever I will command thee, under the perpetual pain of damnation and curse of God the omnipotent Father."]

Then cast thy mind in writing out of thy circle to the spirit,

[7r]

and bid him fulfill thine intent, and anon he will do it, and he will give thee an answer thereof, and when he hath done thine intent and bidding, say thus to the spirit as followeth hereafter:

LICENTIA [LICENSE]
"Coniuro, spiritus, ad requiem. Mosacue spiritus, vade ad locum predestinatum, ubi deus noster te ordinavit, quousque alias te invocavero et cum alias te invocavero. Presto sub mihi. Et pax sit inter me et te, in nomine patris paracliti et filii et spiritus sancti. Facio hoc signum + thau."

["I conjure thee, spirit, to rest. Spirit Mosacus, go to thy predestined place, where our God has ordered thee, until that time I will invoke thee elsewhere, and at another time I invoke thee. I discharge thee beneath me. And let there be peace between me and thee, in the name of the Father the defender, and the Son, and the Holy Ghost. I make this sign + Tau."]

Then say, "Quicunque vult," etc. And as he came, so he will go, and if he be rebellious and will not away, say this following:

"*O maligne spiritus, principus totius nequitis, recede, Effimaliom, qui demones tibi precipiunt.* [O wicked spirit, prince of all wantonness, withdraw, Effimaliom, who demons command thee.]"

And then anon he will be out of thy sight, for he may not abide.

Then go, whether thou wilt break thy circle or thou go for sight of the people, saying, "*In nomine patris paracliti, et filii, et spiritus sancto, facio hoc signum thau* [in the name of the Father defender, and of the Son, and of the Holy Spirit, I make this sign Tau] + my Lord God, be my governor now and evermore. Amen."

Licentia Salomonis [The License of Solomon]

"By all things which I have said and conjured, and by all things that I have done under the power of our Lord Jesus Christ, the which is three and one in deity of majesty, I do bind thee or you altogether and all your bodies, from the crown of your heads unto the soles of your feet, and no members of you forsaken, but that you be obedient to me in all things and in all other times, and be seen to me whensoever and wheresoever, and so often as I am in the place that I am, within house, or without house, and shall call thee or you altogether, or one, or two or more, and without any impediment, so long as I will, ye do fulfill my desire, without lie or sorrow, without strife or fraud, without fear, or any other falsehood, and without hurt of me, or any other creature of God, as well of body as of soul, and that thou or you do serve no man of the form of mankind, when that I have any thing to do with you, but come alone, except you do receive license of me or the worker being licensed of me, and always to my working of these books, or any other invocation, without respect of any party wheresoever ye shall become. Likewise ye shall be ready to my presence and also you yourselves, your fellows or friends prepared. Ye do give to these holy names, you constraining in all hours of the day or night, whether they be, or spiritual named of me, that is to say + Adonay + Sabaoth + Adonay + Cados + Adonay + Amora + Sother + Emanuell + Tetragrammaton + Jesus + in all hours of the day and night, so long as ye may be under the condition of this present license, so often as I shall call you and others, always you be obedient to me, other ways not."

Then you shall make the sign of the holy + upon thee, saying, "*In nomine patris, et filii, et spiritus sancti. Amen.* [In the name of the Father and the Son and the Holy Ghost, Amen.]" If they be horrible, say St. John's Gospel unto the end.[143] "*In principio erat verbum.* [In the beginning was the word.]" Then say, "Christ doth overcome, Christ doth right, Christ his servants doth defend from all evils. *In nomine patris, et filii, et spiritus sancti. Amen.*"

Licentia Generalis [General License]

"I conjure thee or you, spirits N. I charge thee or you, spirits N., by the Father and the Son and the Holy Ghost, and by the four names of God + Tetragrammaton + Saday + Aquamay + Tetragrammaton + and by all the names of God by the which I have bound thee or constrained thee or you spirits N., that thou or you go from me gently and peaceably and quietly and quickly without blame, and without hurt or harm of any soul or body, and that quick and ready thou or you be to me, and to my calling or naming, whensoever and so often as I shall call thee or you wheresoever ye shall be, come, that you come to me wheresoever I shall be, under the pain of the great sentence of God, and other ways I do curse thee or you, spirits N."

Licentia Salomonis [The License of Solomon]

"I conjure you, gentle spirits, by that same judicial temple of Solomon, the which he hath repaired[144] unto the high God, and by all the elements, and by that same high name set and graved in my scepter above, so that for this time, ye do go peaceably and quickly without tempest of lightning or rain or thunder or cold or other tempest, as well of you as of other your fellows, so that I may the sooner call you again to me without hurt, and so coming to me, not troubling me nor vexing me. Fare ye

---

143 *To the end*: Likely meaning only to the end of the first chapter.
144 *Repaired*: Delivered or restored.

well, by the virtue of our Lord Jesu Christ, the son of the living God, the which doth live in this world and in the world to come. Amen."

Then say *Pater Noster, et Ave Maria, et Credo in deum patrem.*[145]

[8r]

[A Call to Zorobaym, the Spirit in This Book, and Iuramiter][146]

Hi sunt qui dant gradias donis et magistris, si velis invenire favorez et granz de eo, itu in domum eius, dic ut sequitur: [These are those that give favors with gifts and with teachers.[147] If you may wish to come upon favors and grants[148] from him, with going into his home, say as follows:]

"*Zorobaym, Zorobaym,*[149] *adiuro vos*[150] *per ipsum qui vos inclusit in hoc libro, et per ista nomina, Bicomon, Moonon, et Zenen, Amon, Thodo, Cenryos,*[151] *Seyros, Ymaser, ut vos detis domino meo N. cor et mentem, ut ita me vel alios quem vel quos voluero diligat, et omnia que voluero faciat per velle meo, et veniatis in ea forma vel specie in qua a me vel ab aliis vobis precipietur, et hoc sine querella faciatus, et statem et perfectem spiritum, eius in amore mei accendatus, utrum vir vel mulier ~ ut me diligat cum praecipio vobis ipsis vel ipsum in meo amore secundum voluntatem meam accendatus per istas karacteres.*"

["Zorobaym, Zorobaym, I adjure you all by the same one that imprisoned you in this book, and by these names, Bicomon, Moonon, and Zenen, Amon, Thodo, Cenryos, Seyros, Ymaser, that you may give heart and mind to my lord N., so that them or those I will wish may love me or others, and all that I wish may be done by my will, and you may come in this form or appearance in which you will be commanded by me or by others, and this without making a complaint, both stable and

---

145 An Our Father, and a Hail Mary, and an "I believe in God the Father" (Nicene Creed).

146 See Sloane MS 3853, 222r.

147 *Teachers*: Other readings might include "commanders" or "advisers."

148 *Grants*: Conjectural.

149 *Zorobaym*: Sloane MS 3853 has "Sorobayhym."

150 *Vos*: A plural pronoun, suggesting multiple spirits are being called.

151 *Moonon…Cenryos*: The manuscript sometimes truncates m's and n's using the same character. Due to this, these words of power could also be read as "Bicomom, Moonom, Zenem, Amom, Thodo, Cemryos." I feel the "n" is more likely.

perfect spirit, any man or woman kindled of me in love to me, so that he or she may love me when I command to you these ones or this one, kindled in love of me, following my will, by these characters."]

4 p e ℬ ℬ ⊚ ⊚ Ⰷ ⅛ Ⅽ Ⅽⅇ xt neon ⊚

Hic sunt qui faciunt mulieres ardere in amore tuo, cum velis habere aliqua mulierez te amare, i tu ad lectum tuum et dic ~ ~ ~ [These are the ones that make women to burn in your love. When you may wish to have any woman to love you, go to your bed and say:]

"Coniuro te vel vos, Iuramiter, cum xxii sociis tuis, per Neonem principem vestrum, et per deum meum, si per ista nomina, Gratius, Leges, Odor, Carus, Christi, Leger et Inger, Tobus, ut faciatis talem N. vel talis exardere in amore meo vel amore illorum de quibus ego voluero, et veniatis in ea forma vel specie in qua a me vel ab aliis vobis precipietur et statim et incontinenti et sine aliqua molestia vel querella, mihi obedias et in quacunque die vel nocte, vobis per septum fuerit veniatis et voluntatem meam vel aliorum de quibus voluero, adimpleatis, per istas caracteres."

["I conjure thee or you all, Iuramiter, with twenty-two of your associates, by Neonem your prince, and by my God, if[152] by these names Gratius, Leges, Odor, Carus Christi, Leger and Inger,[153] Tobus, so that you all may make such a one N. or such ones to burn in love of me or love of others of whom I will desire, and you may come in this form or appearance which has been ordered to you by me or by others, and immediately and incontinently, and without any trouble or complaint, you may obey me and in whatsoever day or night it may be ordered to you, you may come and may complete my will or that of others of whom I wish, by these characters."]

e p Ⅽ l ⌧m e p⸰ Ⅶ o e p ⅌ ⅌ Ⱬ neon 2

---

152 *If:* "And" is a more likely conjunction here.
153 *Gratius...Inger:* Roughly "More thankfully, laws, incense, beloved of Christ, I may be appointed and inspire!"

These Be the Characters of Asazell or Aszazell and Naris
And this is the seal of the same.

The License of Askariell[154] to Depart

"Ite ad locum predestinatum. Pax sit inter nos et vos, in nomine patris, et filii, et spiritus sancti, amen. ⊗ *Signum solis.* ["Go to your appointed place. Let there be peace between us and you, in the name of the Father, and of the Son, and the Holy Ghost, amen. The sign of the sun."] *Finis.*

[8v]

For a Spirit that Walketh[155]

"I conjure thee, you spirit N., wheresoever that you be, in the air, in the earth, in the water, or in the fire, east, west, south, or north, wheresoever thou art, be thou to me obedient in all things which I shall demand of thee or require of thee. I conjure thee, spirit N., by the judgment of them that live and die, and by their judge also, and by the maker of the world, and by the creator of heaven and earth, and by him that did passion thee and made thee, and by his passion and pain, that thou hear my voice, and whatsoever that I do ask of thee, by and by incline thyself unto my

---

154 *Askariell*: See *Oberon*, 410–6. That version lacks a license. For other spells to call this spirit, see Sloane 3849; 3851, 93b; 3853, 142r, and below. It is also likely the spirit "Scariot" called into a crystal by William Wycherle, who was put on trial in 1549. Foxe, Cranmer, and Nichols, *Narratives of the Days of the Reformation*, 333.

155 Sightings of a spirit in a location were often taken as a sign that it protected treasure.

---

petition, and submit thyself to be quick in coming, and also quiet, gentle, and meek. By the virtue of the incarnation of Jesus Christ I command thee; the Holy Lamb Immaculate doth command thee; let angels and archangels reprove thee; let the elect of God reprove thee, and leave thee desolate as the Ayriltis and Crassitus[156] of the Moabites, and cease that soon without any tarrying, that you come to me and obey me and my words and my will that you dost truly fulfill in all things and be obedient unto me. Amen.

"O Lord, I desire thee by thy bitter pain and passion, thou Son of the living God. Give power and grace unto me by thy divine power, that this spirit, named of me N., wheresoever that he lieth, thy name heard, may come forth and do my will, according to my will and desire, by the virtue and in the virtue of our Lord Jesus Christ, which is Alpha + et Ω +, the first and the last, the beginning and ending. I conjure thee, you spirit N., by him that said, and all things were done, made, and created, and by him to whom the highest of angels be obedient, celestial, terrestrial, and infernal, and by the virtue of him that is omnipotent, and by the fearful day of judgment of God, and by all his holy names, as hereafter followeth + On + El + Ely + Eloy + Messias + Sother + Emanuel + Sabaoth + Tetragrammaton + Via + Vita + Manus + Homo + Usyon + Principium + Primogenitus + Sapientia + Virtus + Alpha + Caput + et Finis + Vocitatur + et est oo[157] + Fons + Origo + Boni + Paraclitus + ac Mediator + Agnus + Ovis + Vitulus + Serpens + Aries + Leo + Vermis + Flos + Mons + Os + Virbum + Splendor + Soll + Gloria + Lux + et Imago + Panis + Flos + Vitis + Mons + Ianua + Petra + Lapisque + Angelus + et Sponsus + Pastorque + Propheta + Sacerdos + Athanatos + Kyros + Theon + Panton +

[9r]

---

156 *Ayriltis and Crassitus*: Unknown. The latter is perhaps a reference to King Eglon, referred to in Judges 3:17 as "crassus," or fat.

157 oo: Possibly an infinity symbol, but most likely meant to signify omega.

et Ysus + Agyos + Otheos + Agyos + Yskyros + Agyos + Athanatos + Eleyson + Ymas[158] + that thou come readily, without any tarrying, visibly and in a fair form of a man, not hurting me, nor fearing me, nor harming me nor any creature that ever God made or ordained, quick or dead, and that you obey me and my precepts, by the virtue of God and his holy secret names, the which I have rehearsed and shall rehearse, and by the virtue of all that is beforesaid, I constrain thee to come and do my will by Him that shall judge thee. I adjure thee by his names whom in form of bread you fear, to whom the virtues of your heavens, the power and dominations of the throne of cherubim and seraphim be subject and do fear and honor, and with their incessant voice doth laud and exclamant,[159] 'Holy, holy, holy, Lord God of Sabaoth, the heavens and the earth be full of thy glory, Hosanna in his high places.' Jesus of Nazareth, the King of the Jews, commandeth thee that you obey me, and whatsoever I ask of thee, thou do it diligently in all things, by the power of him that sitteth in the highest place and looketh down to hell, to whom be laud, power, honour, and grace, and accion,[160] glory, and victory, which livest and reignest, and doth imperate[161] in the Trinity perfect the glorious God throughout, world without end. Amen.

"The God of Abraham, the God of Isaac, the God of Jacob, the God of patriarchs, the God of prophets, the God of martyrs, the God of confessors, the God of virgins, the God and father of our Lord Jesus Christ, I do invocate thy holy name and peculiar majesty, that if this spirit have hid treasure which lieth unoccupied, under the earth or above the earth in any place, that thou, Lord, wilt grant me the disposition thereof to obtain it to the use of us living creatures, and that none of all the devils, spirits, elves, or evils which keepeth this treasure do not prevail against me, nor none of my company."

---

158 *Via…Ymas*: "Way + Life + Hand + Man + Essence + Beginning + Firstborn + Wisdom + Strength + Alpha + Head + and End + He is named + and he is Ω + Source + Beginning + Of the good + Advocate + and Mediator + Lamb + Sheep +, Bull-calf + Serpent + Ram + Lion + Worm + Flower + Mountain + Mouth (or Face) + Word + Brilliance + Sun + Glory + Light + and Likeness + Bread + Flower + Grapevine + Mountain + Gate + Rock + and Stone + Angel + and Bridegroom + and Shepherd + Prophet + Priest + Undying +Opportune Moment + God + Everywhere + and Jesus + Saint + God + Saint + Mighty + Saint + Undying + Have Mercy + Upon Me." This prayer of the names of Jesus is present in many English books of hours, and variants of it turn up repeatedly in this manuscript. See Duffy, *The Stripping of the Altars*, 274– 75. The last part ("Agyos + Otheos…") is the Trisagion, which appears in the Byzantine, Coptic, and other rites.

159 *Exclamant*: Latin, "they cry out."

160 *Accion*: Action.

161 *Imperate*: Command.

Of Asazell and Naris

"Thou great lord, Asazell or Aszazell and Naris, I bind thee and you by the head of your prince and by the characters that thou or you ought to obey, *et per nomen* [and by the name] Abgramaton + that thou givest leave to this spirit to depart, and send him to me with his character by night, without hurt or harm of my body or soul, or any other creature, by the virtue of all that is spoken or said, or shall be spoken of men. I conjure you, spirits, devils, elves, or evils which are associate with him in torment, that you avoid[162] from him till such time as I have obtained my will by the mercy of God, and if you do rebel against me, I do conjure thee or you by the virtue and power of Almighty God, that thou or you do descend into hell, and that heaven and earth do excommunicate thee or you, and all the creatures that are contained into them do excommunicate thee and you, and the twenty-four senators doth excommunicate thee or you and cast thee or you into hell, into the deepest pit of hellfire, there to be burned with wildfire and brimstone, and the seven names of God, which shall not be named, doth excommunicate thee and you and do cast thee and you down into the fire of hell by the most mighty names of God, most of power, most excellent, most strong, which can accord to no man, but only to God. See that you know and except[163] and fear this hour, that you so mayst be thrown down with hunger, hatred, and dolour into a place of darkness, where there is no order, but sempiternal[164] fearfulness doth inhabit. *Fiat, fiat, fiat.* Amen.

"I N., the son of N., I bind thee by one God, by the true God, and by the holy God, and by him that said and all things were done, and by him that over all angels do triumph, and archangels, hosts, and all things celestial, terrestrial, and infernal, and by all that I have spoken or may cogitate, and by all things that God hath done to the laud and glory of his holy name, and by the ineffable names of Christ Jesus + Messias + Sother + Emanuell + Sabaoth + Adonay + Alpha et Ω + Yskyros + Kyros + Otheos + Tetragrammaton + Anepheneton + Mephenaye + Satyll + And by the bond of Solomon the sapient, with the which Solomon bound spirits into a vessel of glass, and by the most corroborant[165] messenger of God, and by the name of God + Ell + and by a charge admirable, I conjure thee and bind thee, thou spirit that hid

162 *Avoid:* Depart.
163 *Except:* Take objection to.
164 *Sempiternal:* eternal.
165 *Corroborant:* invigorating.

this treasure and you spirits and devils that keepeth it, by all the secret names of God which would not be named with an unclean mouth, and by the name Ya + Ya + and in the name Ya + Ya + which Adam heard, and by the name Yfas + and in the name Yfas + which Noy[166] heard and was delivered from the deluge with his octavy[167] family, and by the name Yott + and in the name Yott + triplex, which Abraham

[10r]

heard and did know God omnipotent, and in the name Array Farray + which Moses heard in the hill of God, and spake with God, and in the name Elyon + that Elias did name that it should not rain on the earth, and it did not rain for the space of three years and six months, and by the name Smagogyon + and in the name Sniagagion + that Elias did name, and the elements did rain and the earth gave her fruits, and by the name Gekyon + and in the name Gekyon + which Mary did hear and she was delivered,[168] and by the name Pandacraton + and in the name Pandacraton + and by the name Adonay + and by the name Emanuell + and by the name Alpha + et Ω + and by the holy name of God Semopheras + and by all the holy names of God, and by this name Arsetyce + and by this name Ya + Ya + and by this name Isance + and by this holy name Agla + and by this holy name Adonay + and by all the great, mighty, and holy names of God, and by the virtue of all that I have said and shall say, I conjure thee and constrain thee, I bind thee and charge thee, that you fulfill my will in that way and manner that I would have thee to do, and I will pray to God for thee thy creator and mine, for to have mercy upon thee, thou spirit N. or creature, by the baptism of Christ, I require thee, by the which sacrament you hast received or ought to have received, and by the manhood of Christ, I conjure thee that you come, and by the manhood of Christ, which was dead and rose again, I conjure thee, you spirits N., *per verbum caro factum est* (by the word that was made flesh). I conjure thee by the pain and passion of our Lord Jesus Christ, and by the blood and water that ran out of his blessed side, and by all the wounds of Christ, and by the lungs and liver of that Lord that died for us upon a cross. Also I conjure thee by that only sacrifice that he offered up for us to his heavenly Father to pacify his wrath and to take the cross upon him. I conjure thee by the great agony that he had hanging on the cross when he said, 'Heloy, heloy, lamazabathanye,' I conjure thee by his death and burying, and by his resurrection,

---

166 *Noy*: Noah.

167 *Octavy*: Unknown, but most likely referring to Noah's eight-person family.

168 *By the name Ya…delivered*: For similar passages, see Additional MS. 36674, 7v; Gal, Boudet, and Moulinier-Brogi, *Vedrai Mirabilia*, 357, 380–1; *Oberon*, 98.

and by his glorious ascension, and by the coming of the Holy Ghost, and by the dreadful day of judgment when he shall come to judge both thee and me, and as you thinkest to be saved at the last day, I charge thee to obey me, and I charge thee by the obedience that you owest to the almighty God in Trinity, and by the great name of God, *deus deorum* [God of gods], that made all heavens

[10v]

with all wise and glorious diginities, worthiness, and worships and sufferages, and by all his glorious dignities that be in heaven, and by all princes under heaven, and by all signs, characters, and stars of the firmament of heaven of our Lord, and by the four elements, and by all that groweth upon the earth, and by all waters, seas, woods, lands, stones, and all other things, and by all serpents and things that creepeth upon the earth, and by all the birds of heaven and fowls flying, and by all beasts upon the earth. I conjure thee by the tops of hills and mountains, and by all wells and deepness in the earth, and by all the graciousness of God from your first creation, that the cause of thy walking may be known and rehearsed. I conjure thee by thy own creation, and by thy life and death[169] that thou never rest day nor night in the air, nor in the fire, nor in the earth, nor in the water, nor in the wind, nor in no other place that ever God ordained or created, till that you shew me the truth, where and in what place thy treasure is hid, that I may obtain that without hurt of my body or of my soul, or if any thing be out of right cause, and unrightfully occupied, that it may be amended. I conjure thee and you devils, spirits, and elves associate with this spirit, that I call that you avoid and not to hinder me in no point of my purpose. I adjure you by the living God that you come not nigh, you spirit that I call, till I have obtained my will and my purpose, by the virtue of God and all the holy company of heaven. Amen.

"I do excommunicate and curse all the devils, spirits, and elves which do rebel and will not obey. The great curse that God gave unto Sathan and Lucifer light upon you spirits, devils, or elves that hinder and let my purpose. The pain of the same curse that God gave to Lucifer and unto all his wicked angels light upon you devils, spirits, or evils that rebel against me. The great curse that God gave and cursed the earth light upon thee, thou spirit that hid this treasure, if you do rebel against me and not consent to me.

---

169 *Thy life and death*: This might imply that at least some of the spirits addressed here were once human.

"I conjure you all, spirits, devils, elves, and evils, from the place where the treasure lieth, and command you by all the secret names of God as you trust and would be saved at the dreadful day of judgment, by Christ's most precious blood, that you by your craft do not change it nor alter it nor draw it away, or delude me or us by any of your falsecrafts, even

[11r]

as you would have mercy and grace of the eternal God, but that you benignly and gently obey to your creator, for he sayeth by his promise, I shall constrain you as thus: 'They shall cast out devils in my name, and speak with new tongues,[170] and say to mountains, 'Plant thyself, and cast thyself into the sea, and it shall be done.'[171] In the name of Jesus of Nazareth, I claim the victory of your wicked creatures, by whose promise I trust to obtain my desire, by the mercy of the Father, the Son and the Holy Ghost, three persons and one god in substance, living and reigning for ever and ever, to whom be all laud, praise, honour, and glory, without beginning and without ending. Amen.

"O you rebelling spirits, why do you rebel? All the curses of all things cursed light upon you. And so, you being cast down into hell among the devils, where there is no joy but eternal torments, dolour, and gnashing of teeth, the curse that God gave unto Cain may throw you down into a fire of brimstone, and all the torments that ever were ordained by God may torment you forever in everlasting fire and may consume thee or you. O you wicked spirits, I curse you by that power of the great sentence of God. I curse you by all God's holiness. I curse you by all angels and archangels. I curse you by all the prophets and patriarchs. I curse you by all the apostles and disciples of God, and by all holy things. I curse you by heaven and earth, and by the sea and land, by nights and days and by the lightnings, by heat and cold, by ice and snow, and by all that groweth upon the earth. Be you accursed, you rebelling spirits. Void you into everlasting torments, you malignant spirits, prepared for the devil and his angels, world without end. Amen." +

170 Mark 16:17
171 Mark 11:23; Matthew 21:21.

The Circle of Defense for the Master and His Fellows to Stand In, Either in Field or Town, and This Is the True Working of This Science.[172]

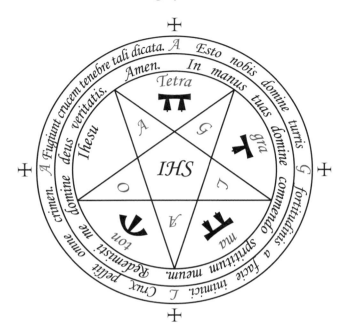

[11v]

When thou makest thy circle, first say this orison into the east, kneeling: *"Derige, domine deus meus, vias meas et actos meos in beneplacito tuo, et viam iniquitatis amove a me, et delege tua miserere mei.* [Steer me, Lord my God, in my ways, and my actions in thy good pleasure, and remove the way of iniquity from me, and elect to give thy mercy to me.]" This devoutly said, then make the first circle and say, *"In nomine dei patris omnipotentis, qui, solo verbo, cuncta creavit ex nihilo.* [In the name of God the omnipotent Father, who, by one word, created all things out of nothing.]" Then make the second circle within the first circle and say, *"In nomine filii*

---

172 Text in circle, outer ring: *A. Esto nobis domine turris. G. fortitudinis a facie inimici.* [You shall
be a tower of strength, Lord, in the face of the enemy (derivative of Psalm 60:4).] *L. Crux pellit
omne crimen. A. Fugiunt crucem tenebre; tali dicata* signo, mens fluctuare nescit. [The cross expels
every sin. The darknesses flee the cross; with such a consecrated sign, *the mind does not know
to doubt* (from Prudentius's *Hymn ante Somnum*, with the missing words filled in and set in
roman).]

　　Inner circle: *In manus tuas domine commendo spiritum meum. Redimisti me, domine, deus
veritatis.* [Into thy hands, Lord, I commend my spirit. Redeem me, Lord, God of truth (Psalm
30:6, Luke 23:46).] Amen.

　　Around pentagram: *Tetra gra ma ton.* Jesus. In rays of star: *O AGLA.* In center: *IHS.* Jesus.

unigeniti, qui humanum genus precioso sanguine redemisti vel redemit. [In the name of the only begotten Son, who redeemed or redeems the race of humans with his precious blood.]" Then make the third circle within the middlemost, and let each circle be a foot from other, and say this orison following, *"Hoc est circulo sancto in nomine dei paracliti, qui corda appostolorum et prophetarum transivit potentia.* [This is the holy circle in the name of God the Guardian, who surpasses the souls of the apostles and prophets in power.]" Then write the character and names that long to thy oration. After that, perfume it with incense and balsam, and then set up thy circle, which is made of parchment, and say

The blessing of the circle

"I do bless this + circle and this place by Jesus the true God which hath made this earth. I do sanctify + thee and hallow + the circle and this place by him our creator, the which hath created the world of naught, and by these most holy names + Theos + Otheos + Yskyros + Athanatos + Ioth +Tetheos + Aglaytha + Indeus + Eloy + Beoth + Hebanth + Tethe + Othee + Sabaoth + Panabaoth + Halhalyell + Anathy + Ionatyell + Amazyell + Gudoniell + Agyos + Thekymas + Thelyas + Ymas + Ely + Messias + Onelos + Eloe + Elyon + Agge + Ya + Ya + Ye + Ye + Yoat + Yemaell + Van + Than + He + He + Hubbethu + Vabbar + Tolleus + Som + Haglata + Thay + No + Thomon + Sadalay + Trohamos + Zepim + Haglata + Bythel + Ytel + Abra + Amya + Haye + Nooe + Yahena + Yara + and by all the most holiest names of God to me known and not known, this circle and this place, let it be of the gift of the grace of the omnipotent and most high God blessed + hallowed + sanctified and kept of the holy company of the saints of God and of the angels, archangels, thrones, and of dominations, principates, potestates, and of the virtues, of cherubim and seraphim, of patriarchs and prophets, apostles and evangelists, martyrs, virgins, and of widows, and of all the elect and chosen of God confirmed and hallowed + and granting this circle and this place, that it may obtain and receive such virtue, power, and holiness, with the sign of the living God, true and everlasting God, and of the holy Cross + of Christ, and likewise that it may be filled full of all grace of the Cross + through the intercession of the most holy and blessed mother of our Lord Jesus Christ, that no evil spirit have any power at any time, nor any manner of ways to enter into this circle, neither to overcome it any manner of way, nor to bring at any time temptation in this circle or place, or fewes[173] or fantasies, God being our helper and defender, to whom heavenly things, earthly things, and infernal things be in subjection, to whom be praise throughout the

---

173 *Fewes*: Traces, usually of an animal.

---

world of worlds. Amen."

This ought to be said nine times, when your new circle shall be made. Further-more, let it be sprinkled with holy water, saying, *"Aspergo te, aqua benedicta,"* ut *supra in experimento Mosacus spiritus.* ["'I sprinkle thee, holy water,' as above in the experiment of Mosacus the spirit…], et cetera."

This orison following doth stir up one's mind to God:

"O Agyos, summe, O Adonay, conditor universe carnis, et creatoris, O Hely, universe maiestatis, ne derelinquas me miserum in tempore necessitatis me[o], magna rex orbis universe, deus Abraham, deus Ysaac, deus Iacob, ad iuvandum me festina, Eleyson + Primogenitus + Principium + et Finis + Vita + et Veritas + Sapientia + Virtus + Para-clitus + Ego Sum Qui Sum + Qui Est Mediator + Agnus + Ovis + Serpens + Aries + Leo + Vermis + Os + Verbum + Splendor + Soll + Gloria + Lux + et Ymago + Panis + Vitis + Mons + Ianua + Petra + Lapisque + Rex, Christ, Pater, Filius, Homo, Spiritus, Omnipotens, salvum me fac modo in hac hora et in isto opere, et in omni tempore. Amen.

["O Agyos, the greatest, O Adonay, founder of the universe of flesh, and creator, O Hely, of the universe of majesty, mayst thou not abandon wretched me in my time of need, great king of the orb of the universe, God of Abraham, God of Isaac, God of Jacob, make haste for the purpose of helping me, Eleyson + Primogenitus + Principium + et Finis + Vita + et Veritas + Sapientia + Virtus + Paraclitus + I am that I am + Who Is the Mediator + Agnus + Ovis + Serpens + Aries + Leo + Vermis + Os + Verbum + Splendor + Soll + Gloria + Lux + Et Ymago + Panis + Vitis + Mons + Ianua + Petra + Lapisque + King, Christ, Father, Son, Man, Spirit, Omnip-otent, make me safe presently in this hour and in that work, and in all time. Amen."]

When you hast said this orison, stand or sitting whether thou wilt, and hold thy sword in thy hand and call on this wise. This is the privy key of nigromancy, and say as followeth hereafter:

"Gyel, Gyal, Esay, Velyon, Trwdrie, Ruchen, Arvyr, Rowdeys, Suriflyen, Zacos, Zalas, Erathon, Alays, Ysyne, Kyas, Kuthan, Appatay, Tropayca, Yka, Ykar, Rufalas, Bruschan, Ducales, Grynaca, Orgeas, Calkfulgra, Aquos, you devils before named, ye the which have power to wrath[174] by night everywhere round about, by the east part;

"And you, Burcham and Sathan, Chule, Gorgorydas, Astole, Moson, Slaugnes, the which do walk betwixt the night and the day by the parts of this sign, which is called Cancer,[175] by the which sign ye have power to make storms and rain, clouds, and thunder;

"And you devils, Misinall, Orcormislas, Pistraye, Elyas, Orecha, Ybles, Oresos, Chanturo, Eusule, the which ye do walk in the hour of noon[176] by the plain ground, until the earth be corrupted of your humours;

"And you Yska, Panchasy, Melse, Chadonas, Appellonii, Tubull, Crissia, they which do walk by the septentrionalem[177] plague, that is the plague of midnight, in the last hour of the day;

"And you devils Athasan, Achios, Yssery, Ranas, Arnace, Saymbrie, the which do walk at the third hour of the day;

"And you devils, Atyes, Ysraradus, Relfem, Relsez, the which do walk early in the morning;

"And I conjure thee, Sathan, the which both morning and evening thou dost lead all other spirits and by all the parts of the world.

"I do conjure you that you do satisfy me, and that you do come and give answer to my request and petition. O thou Valgus or Malchus, the which dost keep the infernal gates, I do

[12v]

174 *Wrath*: Rage, annoy, or harm.
175 This section includes spirits associated with both certain times of the day and certain constellations. How these two conditions are to work together is not stated.
176 *Noon*: Folklore holds that such ailments as sunstroke, which may afflict the careless in the middle of the day, were the work of midday demons. Worrell, "The Demon of Noonday and Some Related Ideas"; Blum and Blum, *The Dangerous Hour: The Lore of Crisis and Mystery in Rural Greece*.
177 *Septentrionalem*: Northern, or having to do with the constellation Ursa Major. This might also be a reference to a biblical plague of locusts (Joel 2:20).

conjure thee that you dost not keep nor hold them against my words, but without let so quickly open thou them to the voice of my prayers. O thou king Yfera or Ysera, O thou king Galfane, and you prince Lucifer, arise from your chairs, and you quickly, in what manner you may, come ye with them and give ye forth of the gates infernal quickly together. O thou prince Lucifer with all the whole company gathered together, and all thy infernal fellows accompanied and spirits aforenamed, and all keepers of spirits, thou dost make to come from thence without let, and without respite, for I do conjure you and all you by equal law."

When the master hath said this conjuration, let him turn into the septentrionalem part, where the sun is hidden, and hold up his sword in his hand and say as followeth:

"O thou Prince Lucifer, and all thy whole heaps[178] gathered together, and all thy fellows, you and also you altogether, I do conjure you by God's body in form of bread and wine, by the water and air, by the Father, and the Son, and the Holy Ghost, and by all the which God hath created and made, and by him that hath and made you. I do conjure you by heaven, and by the sun and moon, and by the stars, and by all heavenly things, so that without let from thence ye do satisfy truly to my petition, and that you do come to my calling, O thou Prince Lucifer, with all other devils aforenamed. I do conjure you by all the goodness of the earth, and by all that is thereon, and by all things that be present, that be past, and that be to come. O thou Prince Lucifer and all other devils aforenamed, I do conjure you by the same nature, the which god hath formed Adam and Eve, of the which all we be formed, that ye do make perfect my will and petition. O you princes and infernal devils, both great and small, and you altogether, I do conjure you by all holy saints, and all holy gramaticals,[179] dieleticals,[180] astrologicals,[181] magicals,[182] matematicals,[183] visible and invisible and intelligible, that you do arise sweetly, and that you do make perfect my will, and that you do fulfill my petition and that soon, and by all the virtues and powers which ye have, or may have, you I do conjure. Send ye one, and come you without let and fear and trembling quickly, one of your devil's messengers whom ye may, which may have power in fulfilling my desire, and all things which I shall or will ask of him, in the fairest shape of a man. Come you, come you,

---

178 *Heaps*: Hosts, multitudes. The word's usage in this sense may postdate those in the *Oxford English Dictionary*.

179 *Gramaticals*: Likely grammars, or experts in grammar. Not in *Oxford English Dictionary*.

180 *Dielecticals*: Reasonings.

181 *Astrologicals*: Likely astrological matters or astrologers. Not in OED.

182 *Magicals*: Likely magics or magicians. Not in OED.

183 *Matematicals*: Mathematicians.

come you soon, come you and that you dost obey to me and I to thee, and that you dost form, and I will do for thee. Come thou, come thou, come you quickly to me, come thou."

Finis.

[13r]

A Citation of What Spirit Thou Wilt

N. Note that the master, three days before his works, he ought to acite[184] spirits viz. in the rising of the sun and at noon, and at the sun setting, the which done they shall appear wheresoever the master be, upon the pain of the great sentence.

"O thou or you spirit Vazago,[185] or you spirits or kings, mighty princes and wise, they or you I do conjure N., and I do command thee or you by the virtue of the names of the almighty God + Iesu + Ioth + Iene + Roell + Agla + Thau + Yana + Ya + He + Va + Ve + Yoon + Adonay + Cados + Anora + Dedragramay + Saday + Ynos + Mabnos + Vesperlio + Nonthy + Anaitheon + Stimulamaton + Elze + Phares + Tetragrammaton + Metheorton + Trissono + Gay + Lotheoron + Alpha + et Ω + Aligeperul + Oryon + Cachefurto + Synon + Yskyros + Dodrast + Stelco + Ditro + Girast + Messias + Sother + Emanuell + Onandoct + Orio + Lather + Tericon + Tonon + Fercon + Stillico + Sureban + Achinodabyr + Aliglassateron + Aliglator + of thrones, dominations, principates, potestates, virtues, cherubim, and seraphim, of angels and archangels, Michaell, Gabriell, Capiell, Sabquiell, Samaell, Kaphaell, Anaell, Uryell, Michaell, Myhell, Sarypyell, Abla, Rex, Sabaoth + Emanuell + Pantiferon + Tobyell + so thou spirit or you spirits, in the virtue and by the virtue of all these names before said, and by the virtue of this holy book, be ye cited and most sweetly that you come and be the most readiest in this hour without all hurt of my body and of my soul, coming in my help, and that you dost fulfill my will in all things, for because you art said to be meek and gentle, and to be in presence I desire, and I will thy power to be raised up for heavenly virtues.

---

184 *Acite*: Summon. "Ascite" elsewhere in this work.

185 *Vazago*: Also Vassago or Vasago, one of the seventy-two spirits of the *Goetia*, who appears in other contexts as well up until the nineteenth century. See *Oberon*, 205; Sloane 3824, 110r–111v; Peterson, *The Lesser Key of Solomon: Lemegeton Clavicula Salomonis: Detailing the Ceremonial Art of Commanding Spirits Both Good and Evil*, 8; Sibley, Hockley, and Peterson, *The Clavis or Key to the Magic of Solomon*, 370–72, 414–17; Hockley, Hamill, and Gilbert, *The Rosicrucian Seer: Magical Writings of Frederick Hockley*, 81–8.

Be ye cited in this hour that you dost come hither, and dost absolve of duty all my petitions and questions, and you shall make answer to me of all unknown things, and shall satisfy me fully of them without craft. O thou spirit or you spirits N., be thou or you ready now to come to me, and make thee or you ready to come from thence hither to make perfect my will. I do call thee N., I constrain thee, and I conjure thee N. by the virtue of the holy + Cross, and by the virtue of the incarnation of Jesus Christ, and by the passion, resurrection, and ascension of our Lord Jesus Christ, and by the fearful day of judgment, by the Father, the Son, and the

[13v]

Holy Ghost, and by these ineffable names of God, Oristeon + Uzirion + Egirion + Onella + Eviona + Usioz + Nutonis + Barasim + Nohim + Ioseph + and by many names of him Sother + Messias + Emanuell + Sabaoth + Adonay + and by the seven names of god Roell + Yoth + Ynos + Mabnos + Vesperlio + Nonthy + Christum + of whose virtue all truth is kept, I do exorcise you by the virtue of these names of God, and by the virtue of all the conjurations before said, and by the virtue of this book, so that most sweetly you do appear in this hour, and that you dost come before me without any hurt of my body or of my soul to help me, and that you dost fulfill my will in all things. And I myself being whole and sound together and joyful, so you dost forsake me, and leave me in that state, and that I may prosper in my work which I have now in hand, and you to fulfill my will perfectly, and that you hast no power of hurting me, deceiving me, nor tempting me, neither in the day nor night, by all my life, nor any other Christian creature that you do hurt, nor any thing in the world that you dost destroy, but whensoever I shall call thee, then peaceably, quietly, and quickly thou do come unto me. In a fair shape of mankind you dost appear, both to obey me and make steadfast my will, and I do swear thee by heaven and earth and by all things which be therein, and by the virtue of this holy book and by the virtue of our Lord Jesus Christ, you which shall come to judge the quick and the dead and the world by fire. Amen."

And the master shall say this conjuration that hereafter followeth:

"And in the virtue of the nine orders of angels, cherubim, and seraphim, of thrones, dominations, principates, potestates, and virtues, of archangels, or angels, Raphaell, Caphaell, Dardyell, Harataphell, Anaell, Paantyell, Anabyell, Lunaell, Carmelyon, Storax, Inquiell, Salgyell, Gabryell, Michaell, Myhell, Saraphyell, Samyell, Yssykes, Atythaell, Uryell, Rasell, Boell, Caszepell, Mettuton, Hocraell, Satquiell, Ubnell, Raguell, Lancyell, Robyell, Pantetaron, Baracheell, Luciell, and in the virtue of all the apostles, Peter and Paul and others, and in the virtue of all the patriarchs, and in the virtue of all the martyrs of Christ, and in the virtue of all confessors, and in the virtue of the seven lamps being before the throne of God, the which be the seven spirits of God, the spirit of counsel, the spirit of strength, the spirit of wisdom and understanding, the spirit of science and peace, the spirit of the fear of God, and in the virtue of the seven sacraments, baptism, confession, confirmation, the sacrament of the altar orders,[186] matrimony, and extreme unction, and by the virtue of the seven cardinal virtues, faith, hope, charity, justice, temperance, strength, and prudence, and in the virtue of the seven orders, the which be conjuror, a door keeper, acolyte, a reader, subdeacon, deacon, and priesthood, and in the passion and

[14r]

martyrdom of our Lord Jesus Christ the true living son of God, everlasting and unmeasurable, and in the virtue of the two seats, of the four elders sitting above the seats, and in the virtue of the four beasts full of eyes before and behind going round about, and in the virtue of all heavenly spirits, so that ye be cited, and that thou or you do forsake all your places and come meekly in a fair form, and honestly, without any manner of hurt of my body or of my soul, both now and hereafter for evermore, and also without hope or asking of any reward, or any manner of offering or sacrifice of me, or any other, and that you be obedient to all my precepts, and by and by without any let or tarrying, as I said before, you or ye do fulfill my desire, forsaking and leaving meekly all pride and illusions, and make appearance as well within the circle as without, if it may be possibly done, so be it. Amen.

"And if thou or you do resist to this, I do constrain and blaspheme thee or you, and likewise I do exorcise and conjure thee or you, N., that here, without tarrying and without any transgression, that you dost come and fulfill my will by the bonds of Solomon, and by the rings of Solomon, Antytacuy, Antygehyly, Antynhobetye, Antynadenarii, and by the sign of him, and by the clear conjurations of him, and and [sic] by the crown of thorns, the which Christ for me and for the nature of all mankind upon his precious head he vouchsafed meekly to bear, and by the spear the which he was stricken with, and by the three nails the which hath pierced him, both hands and feet, for the love of all mankind, and by the Five Books of Moses, and by the wisdom of Solomon, and by the whips that Christ was scourged withal, and by the thirty pence of silver for the which he was sold, and by the Host of Christ, and by the word that was made flesh, by Christ, by the precepts of

---

186 *Sacrament of the altar orders*: Most likely the Eucharist and holy orders.

---

decalogy,[187] and by the twelve articles of the Christian faith, and by the four evangelists, and by the tree of life, being in the midst of paradise, and by your prince Belzabub, and by the seats of Belchye, and by Mathye, and Appologye, and by the seats of Samaym here consecrate and holy angels keeping the same, and by my proper angel, and by heaven and earth, the sea, and all that is therein, and by all the masses and almsdeeds,[188] the which at any time were done in the militant Church of God, and by the seven planets of heaven, by Sol ☉ and Sycoracem or Storax his angel, and by Saturn ♄ and Malathym his angel, and by Iovis ♃ and Philoneum his angel, and by Mars ♂ and Cornegerum[189] his angel, and by Mercury ☿ and Iparon his angel, and by Venus ♀ and Albanixa or Albnixta his angel, and by Luna ☽

[14v]

and Carmelyon his angel, and by the fearful judgment of the high God, and by the fire devouring all fires, and to this I do conjure thee or you spirits N., and by all the fearful and marvelous names of God, the which ye have heard, that all heavenly things, earthly, and infernal things do fear, tremble, and be subdued, and made meek, so that thou or you spirits N. do fulfill as is before spoken, the which precepts is to thee or you spirits N. So be it. Amen."

For to Excommunicate Spirits that Will Not Appear in Their Invocation

"O thou or you spirits N., which lawfully of me have been cited and have been called to appear here in this crystal stone, or in this glass, or in this circle appointed for thee before me, the master of this art, and my fellows, and as yet you wouldst not come, nor appear, in the great contempt of our Lord Jesus Christ and yours, which hath created us and you. And for this cause, I, by the authority of our Lord Jesu Christ, in the part to me given or committed, I do unto it, that the law shall extend to, either in writings, or in scriptures, so that thou or you be excommunicated, and accursed, execrate, and deprived, from all your places, your offices, and your degrees, and cast into the extreme infernal pains of fire and brimstone, there to dwell, suffer, and to burn, until such time as you be obedient unto my precepts, at all times and hours, to fulfill all my desire. And I now by God's divine license,

---

187 *Decalogy*: The Ten Commandments.

188 *Almsdeeds*: Acts of giving alms.

189 *Cornegerum*: Could also be "Cornegerun."

and by all same authority of our Lord Jesus Christ, to all the aforesaid things concerning your pains, I do ratify, prove, and confirm so that you never have rest nor hope of forgiveness, in the day of judgment, nor unto the day of judgment, but that your pains shall grow and multiply upon you from day to day, from hour to hour, from time to time, from month to month, from evil unto worse, and in the same evermore to continue, and from the face of God forevermore to be excommunicate until such time as you be obedient unto my desires and owes, and to fulfill perfectly all the same. *Fiat, fiat, fiat.* Amen.

"And yet I do ascite you spirits N. preemptorily, that you do appear before me or us, in the next invocation, in this crystal stone, glass, or in this circle appointed for you, of me your master, and that visibly in a fair form of mankind, and quickly, under the pains of damnation and the foresaid condition, whensoever it shall please me to call you or any of you, by the virtue of our Lord Jesus Christ, Jesus of Nazareth, our king and yours, and king of the Jews, and by his holy mother St. Mary, and by all the holy and elect of God, and by the virtue of the Holy Ghost, and by the precious blood of our saviour Jesus Christ, the which he shed in his blessed bitter passion, who liveth and reigneth now and ever, world without end. Amen."

[15r]

[The Nature of Cantivalerion]

The emperor of all spirits, **Cantivalerion** or **Galgathell**.

[The Nature of Alyzaire and His Princes]

The 12 and the east altitude[190] is called **Alyzaire**,[191] and the prince **Alyzaire** hath power thereof to compel spirits to serve the commandments of God, and to defend men from them, and freely they teach all men the fables of spirits, and they holden Lucifer bound until the day of doom and judgment, and all damned spirits and wicked men, they shall bind freely, and pain, and these be of the order of dominations, the names of the princes thereof be these that follow: **Falneyl, Alymos, Allybyn, Lubyras, Ana, Anay, Andromalchinwce**.[192]

---

190 *East altitude*: What follows derives from a section of the magical manual Almadel. The Almadel includes twelve altitudes of angels that may be contacted. See Véronèse, *L'Almandal et l'Almadel latins au Moyen Âge*, 161–62.

191 *Alyzaire*: Véronèse has "Elyzan."

192 *Falneyl...Andromalchinwce*: Véronèse has "Salnet, Alymos, Alybyn, Lubras, Anas, Anay."

[The Seventh Science of Sciences, or How to Treat with Spirits]

The seventh science of sciences is to learn after these things. Let the conjurer shew forth his pentacle, and let him ask of him or them the beginning and ending of all things that thou wilt, and he, by and by, will grant it to thee. If it be one spirit alone, or two that was called, which thing thou knowing, the master shall say to every one of them, "Do ye return every one of you to his own place, and the peace of God, be betwixt us and you." After that say the Gospel of Saint John the Evangelist, "*In principio erat verbum* [in the beginning was the word],"[193] and "*Credo in deum patrem*. [I believe in God the Father],"[194] and let them go out of the circle, one after another, and wash their faces, one after another, with holy water, as it is spoken before of water and hyssop,[195] and let them go or return another way that they know to be sure.

And mark that this conjuration be at the least wise heard, and if the spirits be bound with chains of iron or fire, no spirit dare to abide, and if they be in any part conjured or constrained, thou shalt say in the conjuration "that his messengers he shall send, having power to fulfill my will and commandments in all things," saying what they shall do, and if they rebel before the conjurer and will not come, then let him write their names in a place prepared of clay and dust, and let him kindle a new fire, and let him put in the fire, brimstone, and of other horrible things, as asafoetida, or assacasinus,[196] the dung of a horse, or other filthy kind of dung, and say over the fire this conjuration following, holding their names aloft over the fire:

"I conjure thee, fire, by him that hath made all the world to fear, tremble, and quake, so that these spirits may be made pale, and that thou wouldst make hot and burn these spirits whose names and characters that I have put or cast into thee, so that in his or their persons they do feel it everlastingly. *Fiat, fiat, fiat*. Amen."

---

193 John, Chapter 1.

194 The Apostle's Creed.

195 This passage indicates that it was taken from a longer work.

196 *Assacasinus*: Not found in any contemporary source that I have located. Removing the "assa" prefix, possibly derived from the Persian "asa," or "mastic," leaves us with "casinus." I would like to suggest that this might refer to *Cassia fistula*, or the golden rain tree. Its medieval name, "cassia," is superficially similar to as a remedy in medieval times, and burning a sample showed it to have a strong effect on the sinuses. An Italian book of magic includes two operations that involve fumigating with cassia for love, and another guideline which states it should be burned with sulfur, pitch, and ink to fumigate images for hate. Gal, Boudet, and Moulinier-Brogi, *Vedrai Mirabilia*, 249, 333, and 227, respectively. Nonetheless, a period source confirming or disproving the identity of this particular word would be most welcome.

Then cast their names into the fire and say, "Do ye not know that ye be accursed and blasphemed perpetually, and in pains eternally, and ye shall have no rest neither in the day nor in the night, nor in no hour, if by and by ye do not ap-

[15v]

pear visibly into my sight in the fair form of a man, that you be obedient to the words that be spoken and to me, of these things by Him the which hath made the world to tremble, and by His name and in the name of all these names to whom all creatures do fear, and in them thunder and lightning be created, by the which you and your subjects shall be destroyed, the which names be here following: Anerniton + Ioazac + Pater + Semeforas + Alleluya + Aleph + Beth + Symell + Gymell + Deleth + He + Vau + Say + Heth + Thethe + Iothe + Caph + Lameth + Mim + Nin + Miriis + Miiu + Min + Sameth + Aymse + Zade + Coph + Coaph + Regsim + Thau +[197] and by these names we do curse you, and from your office and from your dignity we do deprive you, and by the virtue of them, be thou or you cast into the lake of fire and brimstone, and into the bottom of the nethermost pit, we do bind you again. *Fiat, fiat, fiat.* Amen."

Then without any let, they shall roam everywhere about you, saying, "Master or lord, command thou what thou wilt, and loose us from the pains of this conjuring." Then in the same hour, write the names of them and make to them a fragrant odor with frankincense, mastic, and other sweet things, and shew to them the pentacle, and ask what you will and thou shalt have it done, and answer to them and say thus:

"By the great sentence of relection,[198] and by the virtue of pentacles, will you be obedient to this pentacle and to the words of our creator. The peace of God be betwixt you and us, and be ye adored with frankincense of most sweetest odor. Go you in peace with the blessing of him that doth give to you to know such things, and be ye ready always to come when ye be called of me, without solemnity to be kept of any man. Amen, amen, amen. *Fiat, fiat, fiat.* Amen."

197 *Aleph...Thau*: A list inspired by the names of the letters of the Hebrew alphabet.
198 *Relection*: Reading again, or a treatise.

Experimentum de Elphas quod Est Verum
[Experiment of Elves That Is True]

In primus magister assignatus erit ad locum vel homines, dicens. "In nomine patris et filium et spiritus sancti." ["In the beginning, the master shall be appointed to the place or people, saying, 'In the name of the Father, and the Son, and the Holy Spirit.'"] Amen.

T I conjure you, elphas,[199] which be seven sisters and have these names: Lilia, Restilia, Foca, Folla, Affrica, Iulia, Veinilla.[200] I conjure you and charge you by the power and virtue of the Father, and the Son, and the Holy Ghost, and by holy Mary, the mother of our Lord Jesus Christ, and by the annunciation of the blessed Virgin Mary, and by the virtue of the nativity of our Lord Jesus Christ, and by his circumcision, and by his baptism, and his holy fasting, and by his passion, death, and resurrection, and by the ascension of our Lord Jesus Christ, and by the coming of the Holy Ghost our comforter, and by the twelve apostles, and martyrs, and confessors, and also virgins, and all the elect of god, and of our Lord Jesus Christ, that from henceforth neither you nor none other, for thou have any rule nor power of this ground, neither within nor without, nor upon this servant of God N., neither by day nor night, but the Holy Trinity. Let it be always upon him. Amen. Sator, Arepo, Tenet, Opera,

[16r]

Ratas,[201] Kyrie Eleyson, Christe Eleyson, Kyry Eleyson,[202] Adonay cui pater, cui filius, cum spiritus sancti [to whom the Father, to whom the Son, with the Holy Spirit] affa affa affa.[203] Also I conjure you always, sisters of elphas, and all your subjects by these holy names of our Lord Jesus Christ, Messyas, Sother, Emanuell, Sabaoth, Adonay, Unigenitus, Via, Vita, Manus, Homo, Usyon, Primogenitus, Sapientia, Virtus, Alpha, Caput, Finis et Ω, Fons et Orygo, Boni Paraclitus ac Mediator, Agnus, Avis, Vitulus, Serpens, Aries, Leo, Virmis, Os, Virbum, Splendor, Sol, Gloria, Lux et Imago Patris, Flos, Vitis, Mons, Ianua, Petra Lapisque, Angelus et Sponsus, Pastor, Propheta, Sacerdos, Athanatos, Kyros, Panton, Craton, et Jesus. That

---

199 *Elphas*: Elves.

200 *Seven sisters…*: See *Oberon*, 24, 179.

201 *Sator…Ratas*: A derivation of the famous Sator square, used in many different contexts.

202 *Kyrie Eleison*: The beginning lines from an important prayer in Christian liturgy.

203 *Affa*: Abbreviation for alleluia.

same God which is signified by these holy names, let him save this earth, or this man N., to whom be praise above and by all joys. Amen.

"By these holy names of God I conjure thee, and I do swear thee and you, and I do charge thee and you sisters of elphas, and all you subjects, that from henceforth you have no power upon this earth, nor upon this servant of God N., by day nor by night, nor that you do carry away this treasure that is hidden in this earth, nor diminish that, nor alter it into any other kind, but that you do suffer it to remain freely and holy, and that ye go from it gently. In the name of the Father, and of the Son, and of the Holy Ghost. *Fiat, fiat, fiat.* Amen."

Let the master say this conjuration openly into the east, and then the elements shall not discomfort him.

"O you elements four, the fire, the air, the water, and the earth, I exorcise you by these four names of God, by the virtue of whom you do bear rule, Didragramay, Saday, Ya, Yoth, and by the six names, with the virtue of the which heaven and hell with the six days is Dodrast, Gymell, Ditro, Alpha, Congor, Coren, and by the five fires burning before the sight of God, of whose virtue the stars do receive light, Nogdor, Romathy, Dinider, Grudorio, Piri, and by the seven angels singing before the throne of God new songs by whom all the world is saved, Uriel, Afoirco, Salvator, Ronos, Perth, Pariel, Entro, and by the six beasts walking before God, having eyes before and behind, by whose virtue eyes do receive light, the generations do continue, the seas and the earth doth move, Parcoth, Ustiron, Nossor, Surth, Detriel, Ardo, and first by the coming of God, and by Smargeos, by whose power Adam was made and did speak, and by whose virtue hath bound Adam and Eve with the devil's bond and hath brought forth sorrow, and by the incarnation of God, and by the baptism that which he hath received in the flood of Jordan, in saying and giving example

[16v]

to all Christians, and by his circumcision, and by his fasting, and by his passion and his cross + in the which he hath received death for the health of all mankind, and by his glorious resurrection and by these holy names, Dripo, Fulon, Norey, Rymeloth, and by his vervelous[204] ascension, and by the throne where doth sit Aymaeleon, and by him the which hath made his angels spirits and his ministers flaming fire,

---

204 *Vervelous*: Unknown, possibly a variant of marvelous.

the which doth take virtue of the light of Nosgov, Irculo, the which shall come to judge the quick and the dead, in the virtue of Tebtevy, Milmel, and by these names of God, Regge, Misol, Duspersa, Palusper, Novoth, Tetragrammaton, Vilco, Nicros, Lillo, of whose power the universal church is contained, and by all things which shall be of you in the virtue of Noscor, Regge, Pllo, Seriatell, and by the virginity of God which we know in the virtue of Stelco, and by his power, and by his excellency and majesty and dignity, the which we know to be kept in the virtue of Poliol, Didragramay, Ditro, Northi, Paldo, Pal, Loqui, and by the holy cherubim and seraphim whom we know to reign with nine names of orders of angels, Serph, Velto, Putrost, Vertes, Velgo, Verteri, Nogell, Antro, Insaul, and by the virginity of blessed Mary, of whose chastity is in Northa and Ditroel, Noudoel, Nemper, in the virtue of whom God was born of the virgin, and by Gulprul, in the virtue of whom God hath made all things of naught. *Fiat, fiat, fiat.* Amen."

[A *Call to the* Four Kings]

Note that the master, three days ere he begin his work, he must abstain his body from women and from all other inconveniences, and put out clean vestures, for by this invocation, conjuration, and orations, that master may call whom he will to this work, that is to say these four kings, **Oriens, Egyn, Paymon, and Mayemon,** *quatuor reges planetarum* [four kings of the planets],[205] and others whom the which doth know [blank]. Say this prayer once with a good mind as hereafter followeth.

"O God, which hast assigned thy holy cross and hast lightened the darkness of this world, grant it to me, thy unworthy servant, that all my working begun in thee, and it so begun in thee, may be continued and ended in thee, almighty and everlasting God, which hast infinite power, and most noblest virtue and most worthy empeere,[206] and the most marvelous names in all the world. I beseech thee by the virtue of thy holy virginity and thy holy death, that no wicked spirit may withstand

---

205 *Oriens…*: Kings of the four directions, not planets. These four, bearing different names in different contexts, are attested in magical traditions back to the early thirteenth century. For examples, see William of Auvergne, *Guilielmi Alverni Opera Omnia*, vol. I, 1030; Rosen and Thorndike, *The Sphere of Sacrobosco and Its Commentators*, 404; Boudet, "Les Condamnations de La Magie a Paris En 1398," 146, 151; Gal, Boudet, and Moulinier-Brogi, *Vedrai Mirabilia: Un Libro di Magia del Quattrocento*, 291; Agrippa von Nettesheim, *De Occulta Philosophia Libri Tres*, 268, 471; *Oberon*, 170, 208–13, 285–6, 297–301; Sloane 3853, 258r; McLean, *The Magical Calendar: A Synthesis of Magical Symbolism from the Seventeenth-Century Renaissance of Medieval Occultism*, 35; ben Simeon et al., *The Book of Abramelin: A New Translation*, 148, 171; Skinner and Rankine, *The Veritable Key of Solomon*, 312; Delatte, *Un Office byzantin d'exorcisme*, 89–92; Peterson, *The Lesser Key of Solomon*, 40.

206 *Empeere*: Possibly empery, the position of emperor.

---

the commandments, the which I command them in thy name, and in the name of all thy holy saints, through our Lord Jesus Christ, the same that liveth and reigneth with God the Father, forever and ever. Amen."

Furthermore, say this prayer following, devoutly beseeching God of this grace, that ye may have power to constrain and conjure all spirits meekly, saying this prayer: "In the name of the Father, and of the Son, and of the Holy Ghost. Amen.

[17r]

"O God of Abraham, God of Isaac, God of Jacob, God which madest Adam of the earth like to thy image, O God which madest Eve of the rib of Adam, O God which hast suffered Cain to slay his brother Abel, O God which camest from the bosom of the Father for the redemption of the world, O God which wouldst be born of a virgin, our lady being a maiden, O God which didst suffer thyself to be taken of thy enemies the Jews, grant to me thy unworthy servant well to do, and well to speed, without hurt of my body or of my soul, and grant that all the spirits of the air or of the earth which I shall call to this work to me, may be obedient to me, and serve me, and not to do or say anything against me, but that I may have a pure sight to see in this glass or crystal or circle, these four kings, that is to say, Oriens, Egyn, Paymon, and Mayemon. O Lord Jesus Christ, you are the health, saviour, and the redeemer of this world. I beseech thee that I may be worthy to see thy holy angels in this glass or in this stone or in this circle. O Lord, I pray thee and humbly beseech thee with all my whole mind, that thou wouldst vouchsafe to give me license to see these spirits N. N., without any hurt of my body or of my soul or of my wits, and that they may serve me, and be obedient unto me, through the power of thy holy name Tetragrammaton. Amen.

"O almighty and everlasting God, which is the way, the truth, and the life, which vouchsafest to be brought of the Jews before Pilate, and to be accused of false witnesses, and in the great hall of King Caeser to be condemned to death, and to be led unto the Mount of Calvary, and in that place to be done on the cross and crucified. So everlasting Father, I desire thee, which art three in person and one in substance, that by the same manner all the spirits of the air by thy holy power and virtue, and by the virtue of thy holy names they may be taken and brought unto me, and that these spirits which I shall call may fly no way from me. O Lord Jesus Christ, king of glory, which vouchsafest of the wicked Jews to be nailed on the cross, grant that on the same manner these four kings, Oriens, Egyn, Paymon, and Mayemon, may be as surely bound of me thy unworthy servant, by the virtue of thy holy names, and also to me be obedient, patient, and serviceable, until I have my will perfectly fulfilled, and that they rebel no more against me, than thou didst, O Lord, against thy enemies the Jews. O Lord Jesus Christ, which suffered Longinus the blind knight[207] to thrust his spear into thy blessed side, I humbly beseech thee, O Lord Jesus Christ, to vouchsafe to send thy license to me, through the power of thy holy name to speak to those spirits, and to thrust through their sides, like as thy side was pierced through

[17v]

with the spear of Longinus the blind knight. O king of kings and lord of lords, which hast suffered blood and water to come out of thy blessed side, to fulfill the holy prophecy of thy holy prophets. O merciful Jesus, I beseech thee and pray thee that thou wilt grant to me dominion and power to name thy holy names, and to fulfill my desire as you hast fulfilled the holy prophecy through thy grace. Amen.

"O Lord which art the way, the life, and the true virtue and health, which hast suffered thyself to be crucified between two thieves, and also to drink aysell[208] and gall, grant, everlasting God, I beseech thee, that these four spirits N. N., through thy holy names spoken of me, thy unworthy servant, may be crucified and also drink most by their aysell and gall, except they fulfill and bring to pass my desire in all things. O my Lord, the son of God, over whose head it was written in Hebrew, Greek, and Latin, 'Jesus of Nazareth, King of the Jews,' grant me well to do and well to speed, without hurt or damnation, either of body or soul. Lord Jesus Christ, full of infinite virtue, which in dying hast restored everlasting life, and also was two days in the grave, and on the third day, rose again from death, grant to me, I beseech thee, thy wretched servant, that spirits may arise from all seats and places in this long and wide world, and come to me in fair forms of fair men, at my first, second, or within the third call, visibly to my sight, without letting of any thing, but coming to me, and these that I shall call to this work through the virtue of these thy principal names + Agla + Tetragrammaton + Alpha + et Ω + Agyos + Otheos + Yskyros + Athanatos + Panton + Craton + et Ysus + Salvator + Beena + Ylaye + Say et Helamo + Matiate + Haehahub + Azepa + Hyheha + Aracya + Hahanat + O omnipotent and everlasting God, which didst cast out seven devils forth of the body of Mary Magdalene, O omnipotent and everlasting God, which wouldst that

---

207 *Longinus the blind knight*: The centurion who stabbed Christ in the side with his sword. According to legend, this event cured his blindness. De Voragine, *The Golden Legend: Readings on the Saints*, 184.

208 *Aysell*: Vinegar.

Saint Thomas the Apostle, not believing that you wast risen again, should feel thy wounds. O Lord Jesus Christ crucified, which did ascend from Galilee to heaven, by his own power and sitteth in heaven on the right hand of God the Father, and shall come to judge the quick and the dead, grant to me that I may see in this glass or stone of crystal or beryl, these spirits N. N., visibly in the forms or likenesses of fair men, without any hurt of my body or of my soul, through the virtue of thy holy name, which is blessed, world without end. Amen."

This done on this manner, thou shall call them one after another until you have them all **four** in the stone or in the glass, this blessing begun on thyself.

"In the name of the Father and of the Son, and of the Holy Ghost. Amen.

[18r]

"O you king N., which hast power on all the spirits of the air which be under thy regality, I warn thee, and constrain thee, I command thee, and now I call on thee and conjure thee by these holy names of God the Father, almighty king of kings and lord of lords + Agla + Tetragrammaton + Alpha + et Ω + Agyos + Otheos + Yskyros + Athanatos + Panton + Craton + et Ysus + Messyas + Sother + Emanuell + Sabaoth + Adonay + that you appear before me that I may see thee in this glass, stone, or crystal, or beryl. And I command thee, I conjure thee, I bind thee, and I constrain thee. I adjure thee with all my might, and I command thee to obey me and fulfill my mind by all the holy names of God, and by thine own power, which you hast above all the spirits of the air being under thy regality and power, that I may have my will faithfully fulfilled in all things, according to my desire. And to these things I command thee and adjure thee, by the high names of Jesus Christ, El + Elya + Hely + Heloy + Lamasabathany + Tetragrammaton + Altonay + Adonay + On + Cados + Accinomos + Elaaymon + Saday + Aglata + Ya + Yot + Yeel + Annora + Yana + Anabona + and by these two names Ioth + Naboth + I command thee, I adjure thee, and I constrain thee that, wheresoever you be, that you come to me, by the nine names of angels, that is to say, Michaell, Raphaell, Gabriell, Daniell, Tobyell, Uryell, Barachyell, cherubim, and seraphim, and by our blessed lady, the holy mother of Jesus Christ, and by her five principal joys, which she had of her son our redeemer, that by and by without any tarrying, thou enter into this stone of crystal or beryl or glass, and faithfully fulfill my will in all things. In the name of the Father, and of the Son, and of the Holy Ghost. Amen."

And this conjuration must be said three times, and he will come, or ever the third time be said, and when you hast them all together on this manner, thou shalt salute them, saying:

"Welcome you God's sons,[209] that thus appear in this glass or stone, for to shew and tell me the truth of all things, by the leave of God." And then thou shalt say to them thus:

"Ego vos coniuro qui apparietis hic, in isto vaso vitreo vel christallo, per patrem, et filium, et spiritum sanctum, et per illum deum qui precioso sanguine nos redemitt, et per omnes virtutes, et potestates illius, et per omnia nomina dei omnipotentis, et per ista nomina dei Ungon + Iregon + Gramaton + Tetragrammaton + Tegeton + Pantheon + Maldall + Amandall + Agla + Basyon + Uryon + Baryon + Taron + Budon + Zelen + et per virtutem istorum nominum, et per virginitatem dei, et per vitam eius, et per omnia nomina eius, et per omnia mirabilia eius, et per omnia miracula eius, et per istam potestatem quam deus habet super omnes malignos

[18v]

spiritus, et per honorem quem debetis creatore vestro, et per Iohannem Baptistam, et per caput eius, et per decolationem eius, et per eius virginitatem eius [sic], et per sanctum Iohanem Evangelistam, et virginitatem eius, et per omnes virgines, et per mundicium virginum, et per tremendum diem iudicii, et per de quibus deus habet vel habetit [habebit] potestatem in eternum, quod vos, N .N., qui apparietis hic coram me in isto vaso vitreo vel christallo a visu meo, ne recedatis propter ullam invocationem vobis factam, nisi per me fueritis licentiati, nec aliquam potestatem habeatis mentiendi, nec fallendi, nec mihi aliquam fatiendi fallatiam, sed quod verum est, sine terrore et chachinis ostendendi, et respondendi per eum qui venturus est iudicare vivos et mortuos et seculum per ignem. Amen."

["I conjure you who may appear here in this glass vessel or crystal, by the Father, and the Son, and the Holy Spirit, and by that God who redeemed us with [his] precious blood, and by all virtues, and the powers of those, and by all these names of God omnipotent, and by these names of God, Ungon + Iregon + Gramaton + Tetragrammaton + Tegeton + Pantheon + Maldall + Amandall + Agla + Basyon + Uryon + Baryon + Taron + Budon + Zelen +, and by the virtue of these names, and by the virginity of God, and by his life, and by all his names, and by all his won-

---

209 *God's sons*: An unusual statement, based upon conventional theology that only one Son of God exists.

ders, and by all his miracles, and by that power that God holds over all malignant spirits, and by the honor that you owe to your creator, and by John the Baptist, and by his head, and by his decapitation, and by his his [sic] virginity, and by the holy John the Evangelist, and by his virginity, and by all virgins, and by the cleanness of virgins, and by the great day of judgment, and by the power in eternity of these things which God holds or will hold, that you, N .N. , who should appear here, face to face, in this glass vessel or crystal to my sight, that you not withdraw on account any incantation made to you, unless you should be licensed by me, and that you may not hold any power of lying, nor of cheating, nor of making any deceit to me, but that which is true, without fear or displaying laughter, and responding by him who will come to judge the living and the dead, and the world by fire. Amen."]

Then ask what thou wilt with this conjuration:

"I charge you and command you, and also I warn you, N. N., by all that I have said before and rehearsed, and by all things, that any spirit may be constrained, commanded, and compelled by that ye say and shew me the truth in this matter."

And if the spirits be rebelling and will not come for the first call, then thou shalt call them on this wise, one after another as before:

"O thou king N., I command thee, and I conjure thee by the living God, and by thee alone God, which is Alpha et Ω, and I call upon thee by the virtue of our Lord Jesus Christ, which, for the health of mankind, came down from heaven, born of the Virgin Mary. I conjure thee, N., by the Holy Ghost our comforter, which preceded from the Father and the Son, and rested upon Christ in the likeness of a dove, in the water of Jordan, and fulfilled the apostles, which spake in diverse tongues the great mysteries of God. I conjure thee, by the three persons in trinity, and I constrain thee by the virtues and powers of these three persons. I call upon thee, and adjure thee, by the Father, and the Son, and the Holy Ghost, and I constrain thee by the virtue of one undivided Trinity, and by the lamb sitting on the throne of God, and by the seven horns the which God hath ordained to be the seven gifts of the Holy Ghost. I conjure thee by angels and archangels, by thrones and dominations, by principates and potestates, and by all virtues I call on thee, and by all the ceremonies of them. And I conjure thee by the virtue of them that do cry and never rest before our Lord Jesus Christ, 'Sanctus, sanctus, sanctus, dominus deus Sabaoth. [Holy, holy, holy, lord God Sabaoth.]' I conjure thee by the twenty-four elders bearing their wings in their hands and coming forth after God, and by their white crowns and seats.

"I conjure thee by the twenty-four martyrs, and I conjure thee by the thunders of god, lightnings, and lettings,[210] and I conjure thee by the seven candlesticks of gold that standeth before God always burning. I call upon thee, and I conjure thee by the golden censer, and I call upon thee and command thee by all patriarchs and prophets, and I constrain thee by all the holy apostles, and by the four evangelists, and I require thee and conjure thee by all the holy martyrs, which have suffered for the love of God, and I conjure thee by all the masses which have been sung and said at any time in all the world, and by the nine well-learned priests, and by the nine children newly christened, and by the nine altars of God. I constrain thee by the shewing of Christ and require thee by the birth of Christ, and I conjure thee by the baptism of Christ, and I adjure thee by the fast of Christ, and I call upon thee by the transfiguration of Christ, and I command thee by the Passion of Christ, and I bind thee by the crown of thorn, the which the Jews put upon the head of Jesus Christ, and by the rod, the which the Jews put in his right hand and did kneel down before him, mocking him and saying, 'Hail King of the Jews,' and by the buffets, the which the Jews gave him looking on him, and by the cross, the which our Lord was done on, and by the cry of our Lord Jesus Christ, saying to his father, 'O God, my god, why hast thou forsaken me?' and by the death of Christ, and by the spear with the which the side of Christ was opened, and by the whips of Christ, and by the nails with the which the body of Christ was nailed, and by the wounds of Christ, and by the bread which Christ took and blessed it, and brake it, and gave it to his disciples, saying, 'Take, eat, this is my body,' and by the blood of Christ, which he gave to them, saying, 'Take and drink you all of this, this is the cup of my blood of the New Testament which is shed for you and for many in remission of their sins,' and by the sheet the which the body of Christ was lapped in, and by the sepulcher in the which the body of Christ was buried in, and by the going down of Christ into hell, and by his resurrection on the true day, and by all the great deeds and wonders of God, that wheresoever that thou be, thou do appear in all haste and enter into this crystal stone, glass, or beryl, visibly unto my sight in the likeness of a fair man, having a red or white colour, of a fair king crowned with a golden crown, and give me a true answer, as far as you hast knowledge, of any thing that I shall ask of thee, speaking to me without any impediment of my wits, and without any deceit, and without any hurt of my body or of my soul, or any creature under the high power of the majesty of God. Amen. *Fiat, fiat, fiat.* [Let it be done, let it be done, let it be done.] Amen." *Finis.*

---

210 *Lettings*: Obstacles, or allowing matters to occur.

An Experiment of Askaryell[211]

When thou shalt work this experiment, you must take a clean crystal stone without cracks, filth, or holes, and you must have a thong of a hart's skin to lap or wind the stone in, so that the stone may be in the midst of the binding, and ever when you wrappest the thong about the stone, say thus:

"*In nomine sancte trinitatis, patris veritatis, hanc gemmam respicio. In nomine sancte deitatis, et trinitatis, patris veritatis, hanc gemmam respicio.*" ["In the name of the holy Trinity, of the true Father, I reflect upon this gem. In the name of the holy divinity, and of the Trinity, of the true Father, I reflect upon this gem."]

And then hold the stone that is so dight[212] in thy right hand against the sun, when the sun is in the south and at the highest and hottest, and thou shalt see what thou wilt in all countries, and shalt see both thy friends and foes, what they do, and what they say, and of them that be dead as well as of them that be alive. And for treasure that is hid in any place you mayst see it, and for theft he will shew thee the thief and the place that he entered in at, and he will bring to thee the thief, and with his finger he will shew to thee the stolen goods, and the spirit will tell thee all that thou wilt ask of him, and thou shalt command him that he bring his fellows with him, and that he bear the sign of the cross on his head, and he will bring one Mathepart with him, and another will come with him in another clothing, and this is true, for we have proved it and found it true.

"*Centony, Messitone, Messiton, Myssyron, qui habitatis in bosto. Ego coniuro vos, sitis perati ad omnia mea precepta obediendo mihi. Coniuro te, Askariell, Abybo, Theal, Beabo, per patrem, et fillium, et spiritum sanctum, qui est Alpha et Ω, et per tremendum diem iudicii, et per vertutem dei vivi, et per omnia nomina dei ineffabilia, quatenus tu in ista gemma christeline sine mora sertissim venias, in persona tua propria et sertum in capite tuo. Demonstres te mihi, et omnibus circumstantibus, et si hoc non feceris, ego condemnabo te, Askaryell, in infernum, in ignem eternum, in virtute et per virtutem dei vivi.*"

211 See *Oberon*, 534–8, Sloane 3846, 34r. Neither of the rituals in question mentions Askariel, but they do have striking similarities.

212 *Dight*: Properly.

["Centony, Messitone, Messiton, Myssyron, you that inhabit woods. I conjure you, that you may be ready to all my commands, obeying me. I conjure you, Askariell, Abybo, Theal, Beabo, by the Father, and the Son, and the Holy Ghost, that is Alpha and Ω, and by the great day of judgment, and by the virtue of the living God, and by the all unutterable names of God, till you may come into that crystalline gem without delay most certainly, in your own person and a wreath on your head. You may show yourself to me, and in all circumstances, and if you will not do this, I condemn you, Askaryell, into hell, into eternal fire, in the virtue and by the virtue of the living God."]

And except he come at the third call, condemn him, saying thus:

"Ego condemno te, Askaryell, in ignem eternum, et per virtutem dei vivi, et per virtutem omnium nominum eius, et per potestatem quam deus henc super te, ut sis in penam eternam, in ignem eternam ibi permanes, donec appeares mihi et tu tum voluntatem meam adimpleas."

["I condemn thee, Askaryell, into eternal fire, and by the virtue of the living God, and by the virtue of all these names, and by the power that God possesses over thee, so that thou mayst be in eternal punishment, and thou remainest there in eternal fire, until thou mayst appear to me and thou then may satisfy my will."]

And if he come not the first day, call him the second day, and if he come not the second day, call him the third day, and then he shall come and then say again as followeth:

"I conjure thee, Askariell, Abybo, Arboab, Sentony, Messitone, Messiton, Messyron, *qui habitatis in bosto* [who reside in the woods], I conjure thee *per patrem, et filium, et spiritum sanctum, qui est Alpha et Ω* [by the Father, and Son, and the Holy Spirit, who is Alpha and Ω], and by the dreadful day of doom of God, and by the virtue of God's life and by the strength of God, and by all the holy truth of God, and by all the holy names of God, that you come in thy proper person, truly and

[20r]

in form of man personally, with a certain sign of thy head of the cross + into this stone of crystal or beryl, in this hour anon without any tarrying, and bring thy fellows with thee, and visibly shew thee and them to me, and to all that stand about me, and soon appear, that I may openly send them, by my precepts and conjurations, and truly to answer to my questions and be obedient to all my commandments." And then say again:

"I conjure thee, Askariel, by all these holy names of God almighty + Erysell + Deus + Ieta + Apres + Eloy + Vita + Gloriosus + Voniys + Bonis + On + Unigenitus + Via + Manus + Homo + Usyon + Principium + Primogenitus + Principatus + Sapientia + Vertus + Alpha + et Ω + Caput + et Finis + Orygo + Paraclytus + Mediator + Agnus + Ovis + Vulpes + Aries + Lux + et Ymago + Panis + Flos + Vitis + Mons + Ianua + Petra + Lapisque + Pastor + Propheta + Sacerdos + Athanatos + Kyros + Theos + Otheos + Panton + Craton + et Ysus + Anepheneton + Egylla + Abmago + Erith + Ebrutone + Talsea + Semeth + Agla + Jesus + Christus + Tetragrammaton + Adonay + Sabaoth + Sother + Emanuell + and by all these names of God, and all other holy names of almighty God both effable and ineffable, I conjure thee, Askariell, that you hide nothing from me, nor nothing withhold, but truly answer to my commandments and demands, and I charge thee and constrain thee, Askaryell, by the virtue of all that I have said before and rehearsed, and in pain of eternal damnation, until the day of doom, that you shew thyself to me and to my sight, and to them that be with me, that I and they may see thee even now in the fair form of a man."

And then say again as here followeth, with these words:

"I conjure thee, Askaryell, by the virtue of all the holy sacraments, of all holy church, and by the virtue of the holy sacrament of Christ's body in form of bread, and by the virtue of his prudence, and by the virtue by the which God hanged heaven above, and the earth beneath, and by the virtue which God had in mind, ere that the world was made, and by the virtue of the throne, which is the separating of the elements that he drowned the world, of his mercy, and by the sea and all that is therein, and by the deep, and by the deepness, and by the wisdom and virtue by the which God ordained both day and night, and by all angels and archangels, thrones and dominations, principates and potestates, virtues, cherubim, and seraphim, and by him who passeth over heaven and hell, and by him that is wondrous mighty, and by these that God made and formed, to the laud, praise, and honour of the majesty of his name. And by the firmament of heaven, and by all the virtues of it, and by the virtue of all the saints in heaven, and by all things that are in heaven,

[20v]

and by the virtue of all the relics of all the saints in heaven, and by the virtue of all that ever God made, thought, or wrought, that you in this crystal, stone, or glass shew thyself to me, by and by, without any tarrying, and certainly and truly come and enter in in the proper person truly and the form of a man personally and certainly unhid, and visibly shew thyself to me and to all that stand about me, and soon appear and bring thy fellows with thee, that I may openly send thee and them, by my precepts and conjurations, and that truly you answer to my commandments. And if thou dost not this, then I, in the virtue, and by the virtue and power of God and of all his holy holiness and this conjuration, I condemn thee, Askaryell, into hell into everlasting pain, in fire burning until the day of doom. *Fiat, fiat, fiat.* Amen. But if thou sooner come to my presence, and truly give me answer of all things which I shall demand of thee."

These characters will assign[213] any spirit, without a child.[214]

Finis.

Pro Furto [For Theft][215]

Write all the names that you hast in suspicion, each name by itself as they be most commonly called, and take as many balls of clay as you hast written names, and put each name into a several[216] ball of clay, and let the clay be tough as it cometh out of the earth, then put the balls into a vessel of holy water, and say this psalm three

---

213 *Assign*: Direct.

214 It was a common practice over the years for a virgin child to serve as a scryer in spirit operations. Given the likely reluctance of most parents to hand over their children to engage in spirit-summoning ritual magic, rites that did not require them would have had a particular appeal.

215 For longer rituals using this process, see Sloane MS 3846, 43r–v, 71v; Sloane 3851, 55r–v; Cambridge Additional 3544, 46–7; Kittredge, *Witchcraft in Old and New England*, 192–93. Such practices were condemned at the Synod of Exeter in 1287. Wilkins, *Concilia Magnae Britanniae et Hiberniae*, vol. 2, 162.

216 *Several*: Separate.

times kneeling: "*Si vere uticque* [if in very deed...]"[217] and his that is guilty, the ball shall cleave, and the name shall hover above the water.

Ite pro Furto [Again for Theft]

Scribe in pergameno virgine, die marcurii, figuras sequentes, et pone sub capite tuo. Eum is dormitum, et videbis eius furtum. [Write on virgin parchment, in the day of Mercury, the following figures, and put them under thy head. Go to sleep, and thou wilt see the stolen thing of this one.]

Ad Cognoscendum Societas
[A Partnership for the Purpose of Knowing]

Si velis cognoscere secretas hominis vel mulieris, accipe herbam quam vocatur selon-dyne, et pone sub aurem dexteram, et quodcumque velis cognoscere revelabitur tibi in sompno tuo.

["If thou wishest to know the secrets of a man or of a woman, get the herb that is called celandine[218] and put it under thy right ear, and whatsoever thou wishest to know will be revealed to thee in thy sleep."][219]

Ad Amorem [For Love]

Scribe signum, sequis, et mirabile videbis, qui si canem tetegeris, sequatur te. Scribatur in carta pergameni, et quacunque muliere nuda carna tetegeris, dileget te. Fyet in die ♀. ["Write the sign, thou attendest, and thou wilt see a marvelous thing, that if thou mayst touch a dog, it may follow thee. It should be drawn in parchment paper, and thou mayst touch the nude flesh of whatever woman, she will love thee. Let it be done in the day of Venus."]

217 Psalm 57.
218 *Celandine*: Probably greater celandine (*Cheildonium majus*).
219 Prolonged contact of celandine with skin could result in staining or irritation.

Sigillum Solis [Sigil of the Sun], Sigillum Lune [Sigil of the Moon]

[21r]

Circulus Terre [Circle of Earth][220]

220 Bacon's *Nigromantia* includes a similar circle for the earth. Additional MS. 36674, 158r. Bacon and Macdonald, *De Nigromancia: Sloane Ms. 3885 & Additional Ms. 36674*, 55. A more exact match is below at 59r.

Text in outer circle: + Michael + + Raphael + + Uriel + + Pancraciel + + Usyon + + Agla + + Seraphim + + Gabriel +.

Middle circle: + Agios + + Yskyros + + Athanatos + + Sabaoth + + Amaliezyn + + Pantarion + + Carisin + + Dominaciones +.

Inner circle: + Usyon + + Concors + + Otheos + + Osanna + + Xps (Christus] + + Carmacarice + + Glycon + + Meripin +.

In the center: Yod-He-Vau-He / Master / *Circulus Terre* (Circle of the Earth) / *hic sedet servus cum sociis* (here sits the servant with his associates).

Hec Sunt Nomina Spiritum Narrandi
[These Are the Spirit Names Which Are to Be Called]

Yay, Abay, Milony, Semar, Alkadeus, Walkadeus, Askadeus, Floran, Hermely, Daragybya, archbishop, with a cross + in his hand, and doth give a true answer to the master.

Mychaell, Myhell, Sarapiell, Abba, Askariell, Bybon, and Beal, Askades, Beray, Walkades, Balbo and Bosto, Oberyon, and Blyth. S. and Beall, Eaioy, Hermely, Doragybyn, Samanus, and for theft, Tyltryon, Botheron, Spirgon, Macryon, the emperor of all spirits, Cantivalerion *vel* [or] Golgathell, Terre, Andromalcus, Ennoy.

[21v]

Here Followeth the Names of the
Seven Kings of the Seven Planets[221]

♄ Maymon, king of Saturn; ♃ Formone *vel* (or) Formyone,[222] king of Jupiter; ♂ Iammax, king of Mars; ☉ Barthan, king of the sun; ♀ Farabores *vel* [or] Tres,[223] king of Venus; ☿ Abba,[224] king of Mercury; ☽ Harthan, king of the moon.

Ut Scias de Thesauro Obscondito
[So That You May Know of Hidden Treasure][225]

Scribe in carta aliqua ista carecteria sequentia, die saturni et hora luna, et pone chartam illam in terra ubi credas thesaurum esse obsconditum, et si aliquid thesauri ibi existit, charta conbuvit, aliter non, et hec sunt charecteria sequentia.

[Write on some paper these characters following, in the day of Saturn and the hour of the moon, and put this paper into the earth where thou mayst believe there to be

---

221 These come from the *Liber Juratus, or The Sworn Book of Honorius*. See Honorius and Hedegård, *Liber Iuratus Honorii: A Critical Edition of the Latin Version of the Sworn Book of Honorius*, 117–19; Peterson, "Liber Juratus Honorii, or The Sworne Booke of Honorius," 200–205.

222 *Formone vel [or] Formyone*: Honorius has "Formione."

223 *Farabores vel [or] Tres*: Honorius has "Sarabocres."

224 *Abba*: Honorius has "Habaa."

225 See Scot, *The Discouerie of Witchcraft*, 408, for a version in English of the same ritual.

hidden treasure, and if any treasure be there, the paper burns up, otherwise not, and these are the characters following:]

Finis huius operis. [The end of this operation.]

[Letters and Characters of the Planets]226

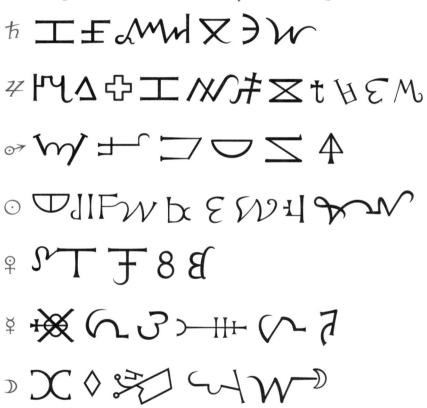

226 Agrippa von Nettesheim, *De Occulta Philosophia Libri Tres.*, (i.33), pp. 148–9. The text: *Litterae seu Caracteres Saturni* [The Letters or Characters of Saturn], *Litterae seu Caracteres Iovis* [The Letters or Characters of Jove (Jupiter)], *Litterae seu Caracteres Martis* [The Letters or Characters of Mars], *Litterae seu Caracteres Solis* [The Letters or Characters of the Sun], *Litterae seu Caracteres Veneris* [The Letters or Characters of Venus], *Litterae seu Caracteres Mercurii* [The Letters or Characters of Mercury], *Litterae seu Caracteres Luna* [The Letters or Characters of the Moon].

Hec sunt littera sive caracteres quae septum planetas pertinent, quas hic depictum vides. [These are the letters or characters that belong to the seven planets, that here thou seest depicted.]

[22r]

An Experiment of Saymay, for Treasure in the Seas to Be Brought Up. Most Certainly Proved.

The master must rise in the morning, being Thursday before the sun arise, in the sign of Gemini, and apparel himself in clean clothes, then take into his hand a vial glass full of fair water and cover it with a fair linen cloth, and set the glass upon a marble stone, saying this conjuration:

"I conjure you, spirits Samay, Saymay, Caymay, Zaphey, Pestron, Caronem et Priamon, by the Father, the Son, and the Holy Ghost. I conjure you by the righteousness of God, which brought forth water out of a stone, and by the things that be above the heavens and under the earth, and by all things which be upon the seas, in the seas, and under the seas, and by all the infernal powers, and by all things that are in hell, and by the goodness by the which God made man to his own similitude and likeness, and by the righteousness by the which he condemned him, and by all the holy martyrs, patriarchs, and prophets, and by their faith and merits, and by the twenty-four seigneurs and elders, which are before the seat of God, and by their crowns and treasures, and by the golden vial, and by the seven planets, and by the holy seat of God, and by the 144 thousand innocents which do sing before God a new song.

"I conjure you, Saymay, Samay, Caymay, Zaphey, Pestron, Caronem, and Priamon, that immediately you do come from your places, wheresoever you be, and that you appear unto me visibly in this water in a fair human shape and similitude, and you to be favourable unto me, not fearing me nor doing any hurt, damage, or detriment to me, nor any other creature in the world, and that with all expedition, you do enter into this vial of water, and that you do fulfill all my commandments, with the clearness of the said water, and that to my sight, your bodies may seem fair and well to behold."

Then say this prayer:

"O Lord Jesus Christ, which hast given to thine apostles virtue to heal all diseases, to raise the dead, to cleanse the lepers, and to cast out devils, grant unto me thy grace, that by thy mighty power and by the virtue of the holy name, I may bind these spirits which I have now called, and that they may do all things, what-

[22v]

soever I shall command thee to do, in all things that are made by thee. And you, Lord, hast said to thine apostles and disciples, 'Ask and you shall have, seek and you shall find, knock and it shall be opened unto you.'[227] Therefore, O Lord, I ask, I seek, I knock, I desire, and I beseech thee, by the goodness and merits of thy holy mother and Virgin Mary, and of all thy holy saints in heaven, that as thou hast promised to give all things to them that ask in thy name, grant that immediately before me, the spirits before named may come and appear without delay, and that I may bind them that they may obey me and my commandments, whatsoever I shall command them to do through thy merits. O blessed Jesu, who liveth and reigneth with the Father and the Holy Ghost, one god, world without end. Amen."

Tunc dic: [Then say]:

"I conjure you spirits, Saymay, Samay, Caymay, Zaphey, Pestron, Caronem et Priamon, by the Father, the Son, and the Holy Ghost. I conjure you by the righteousness of God, and by the Blessed Virgin Mary, and by the conception of our Lord Jesus Christ, and by his nativity, and circumcision, by his baptism and fasting, and by his holy and blessed passion, and by his power, by the which he raised up the dead and healed the sick, and by his supper which he did eat with his disciples, and by his humility, by the which he did wash his disciples' feet, and by the spear with the which his body was pierced, and by the gall which he tasted upon the cross, and by the blood and water which he shed out of his most precious side, body, and heart, and by his invocation which he made upon the cross, and by the darkening of the sun and moon, and by the virtue by the which the earth did tremble, by the sweat that was upon his head, and by the virtue by the which he spoiled hell and brought forth his elect, by his glorious resurrection, and by his ascension into the heavens, and by the coming of the Holy Ghost. I conjure you spirits, by all the holy names of God, and by that unspeakable name of God which no man ought to

227 Matthew 7:7

name, that you do come incontinently and immediately and truly your own selves, and appear visibly unto me in this water, and that you do whatsoever I shall command you, and that you answer me truly without falsehood or deceit, to all my questions and demands, by the virtue of all the holy names aforesaid.

"I conjure you, Caron and Priamon, by the unspeakable name of God + Tetragrammaton + and by the precious bloodshedding of our Lord Jesus Christ, which he shed upon the altar of the cross, and by the fearful day of judgment, in the which you

[23r]

trust to be saved or damned, that you be obedient unto me and appear visibly to me, in this vial, and in this water, without any fear or hurt doing unto me or any other creature in the world. And that you, Caron and Priamon, do not depart out of my sight, out of this water, until I shall give you license, by him which shall come to judge both the quick and the dead and the world by fire. *Fiat.* Amen."

And when he is appeared, then say:

"I conjure you, Caron and Priamon, with all your subjects, by the Father, the Son, and the Holy Ghost, by the Holy Trinity and unspeakable unity, and by these holy names of God + Tetragrammaton + Sabaoth + Adonay + Algramay + Jesus + On +, by all the aforesaid names and by the precious bloodshedding of Jesus Christ, that you, Priamon, do bring unto me the value of 5000£ in gold and silver, without any tarrying and want, and without any fraud, hurt, or dissimulation, whersoever that be in the seas or out of the seas, and that you bring it, or cause the same to be brought by one of thy subjects unto me, and so lay it and leave it in such a place N. quietly, without any hurt or disturbance of any creature, or other things in the world, and then presently and quietly to depart, by the virtue of him that holdeth in his hand the scepter of glory, which liveth and reigneth God, world without end. Amen."

Repeat this conjuration aforesaid seven times from the beginning to the end and the spirit shall appear, and when he hath fulfilled all thine intent and purpose, then license him to depart, *ut patet aliis experimentis* [thus he may be subject to other experiments]. *Finis.*

Take a thin plate of virgin wax, and make it four square. Draw a picture of a woman thereon, and write in the fore part of the head with a needle this word: Ascariell,[228] and in the breast the woman's name, and, at the nether end of the picture, the man's name, and on the right side of the picture make this character ⌐_⌐ , and on the left side this character ♀, then bury this plate in a crossway where two ways meet, half a foot in the ground on the day of ♀ after sun setting, where you shall let it remain three days and three nights, and go round about the place, saying:

"I conjure and adjure thee, thou spirit Ascariel, which hast power over the love of women, by God the Father, the Son, and the Holy Ghost, and by the Blessed Virgin Mary, and by the love that she bare to her child Jesus, and by the merits, passion, death, and resurrection of the same Jesus, and by these holy, fearful, and terrible names of God, Agla, On, Tetragrammaton, *Ego sum qui sum* [I am that I am], Alpha et Omega, and by all the other holy names of God, and by all the holy company of heaven, that you constrain and cause this woman N. to burn in love with this man N. N., so that she never take rest, sleeping, waking, eating, drinking, laying, nor walking, until she have willingly consented to love me,[229] the said N. N., in the name of the Father, the Son, and the Holy Ghost. Amen."

This being said, round about the place three nights together after sunset. Next, after the change of the moon, make this character every time upon the ground ⌐ЦГ⌐ with your forefinger and depart, and she will either come or send for the party before the three days' end. *Probatum est.* [It is proven.]

Finis.

[23v]

---

228 *Ascariell*: Note that the Sibilia wax image experiment below also places a name on the head. This indicates that the use of "Sibilia" may be a reference to a spirit, and not just a coincidental *vox magica*.

229 *She never take…me*: Adjurations that a target of love magic may not eat, drink, sleep, or engage in other actions are common in magical literature, back to the magical papyri of the first century. Martinez, "Narrating Power: The Theory and Practice of the Magical Historiola in Ritual Spells"; Toporkov, "Miracles and Impossibilities in Magic Folk Poetry."

Aliud Experimentum Verissimum pro Furto
[Another Most True Experiment for Theft][230]

This is the way to make a thief come again and bring the thing which he hath stolen with him at the will and pleasure of the Master of the work, and it is the experiment of the philosopher Phrayes, translated out of Hebrew into Latin.

There be four kings of the air, which have power to hurt and annoy the earth and the sea, under which four kings there be four spirits having power to rule and bring again a thief with the things stolen.

The first legion obeyeth the south king, the second is under the west king, the third is under the north king, and the fourth is under the east king, whose names with their signs appear in the circle following, and note that whatsoever thou wilt work, take heed you be in clean life of thy sins towards God. Go to the church and leave service,[231] this done upon the Monday before the sun arise.[232] After that go home[233] secretly, and take a quantity of new wax,[234] of the finest and cleanest, as big as the palm of thy hand, and make a laminam quadratum[235] thereof, and write the names of the spirits as appeareth in the figure following. Then in the midst of thy lamina, make a round circle, and in the midst thereof, write this name, Sathan,[236] unto whom these four spirits obey. Then write the name or names of the things stolen, then the name or surname of him that hath lost the goods and was owner of those things. This done, then say this conjuration hereafter following[237] the same day four times, first with your face towards the south, second towards the west, third towards the north, and the fourth towards the east.

---

230 For similar experiments, see *Oberon*, 179–83; Sloane 1727, 50r–51r; Sloane 3824, 16r–20r; Sloane 3853, 73v–74v; Bodleian Rawlinson D.252, 103r–107r; Cambridge Additional 3544, 41–4; Wellcome 110, 99v; Dawson, *History of Skipton*, 392–3.

231 *Go…service*: *Oberon* and Cambridge Additional 3544 state a Mass of the Holy Ghost must be attended, with 3544 specifying that it occurs in the home. Sloane 3824 stipulates repeated trips to the church to pray at the altar.

232 *Monday…arise*: *Oberon* and Sloane 3824 state this must occur on Monday or Wednesday during the waxing of the moon. Sloane 3824 adds that the air must be "serene & Still." Cambridge Additional 3544 calls for the rite to begin before Monday or Wednesday before sunrise.

233 *Home*: Both *Oberon* and Sloane 3824 place the experiment in a wood.

234 *Wax*: Both *Oberon* and Sloane 3824 make multiple tablets out of lead, while Cambridge Additional 3544 stipulates silk.

235 *Laminam quadratum*: A square lamina.

236 *Sathan*: Sloane 3824 has "Sheho."

237 *Conjuration hereafter following*: Sloane 3824 has a longer set of conjurations before directly addressing the four spirits. The conjurations from three sources are different in many respects.

"O you, spirits Teltron, Spirion, Boytheon, and Maveryon,[238] whose names be here written, I conjure you and exorcise you by the living God, by the true God, by the holy God, by the Father, the Son, and the Holy Ghost, by the high and invisible Trinity, by the principal name of God, Alpha + et Ω + and by the name of our Lord Jesus Christ, by the which names patriarchs and prophets did invocate him, and he did help them, by the high and most mighty name of the Lord + Tetragrammaton + by the precious death and passion of our Lord Jesus Christ, that wheresoever you be in the earth, in the sea, in the fire, in the air, or in the water, that you may come together into one place, in which the thief or thieves be, that have stolen N. or taken it away from N. into any other place, and you, him, her, or them, within such a time (here name the time) to return and restore it into the same place, from whence it was taken (such a day and the hour). Otherways I will condemn you, and do condemn you, by the resurrection of our Lord Jesus Christ and his blessed mother, and Saint John Baptist, that you be bound in chains of fire, and to be tormented with most hard punishment, except you shall bring again him, her, or them, with such a thing N. stolen from N. or K. I conjure you by the most Blessed Virgin Mary, mother of God, and by all the evangelists, and by the twelve apostles, and by all the martyrs, confessors, and virgins, and by your king, that in what place soever you be, in water, earth,

[24r]

fire, or air, you come together in that place where or in which the thief or thieves be, which have stolen and carried away the foresaid things N. from such a place N., and that you cause them to return and bring again the same things into such a place N. from whence it was taken, such a day N. and the day of the month, within such an hour."

Say this conjuration aforesaid at morning, noon, and night, towards the four parts of the world, and after bury the plate of wax in the ground the same day, and the thief or thieves shall come at the time appointed with the things stolen.

Sequitur figura lamine, qui factura est in cera virginea.

---

238 *Teltron…Maveryon*: Sloane 3824 has "Theltrion, Sperion, Mayerion, and Boytheon"; *Oberon* has "Theltrion, Speryon, Boytheon, et Mayeryon"; Additional 3544 has "Theltrion, Spyrion, Boytheon, Maheryon."

[The figure with the lamen follows, which is going to be made in virgin wax.][239]

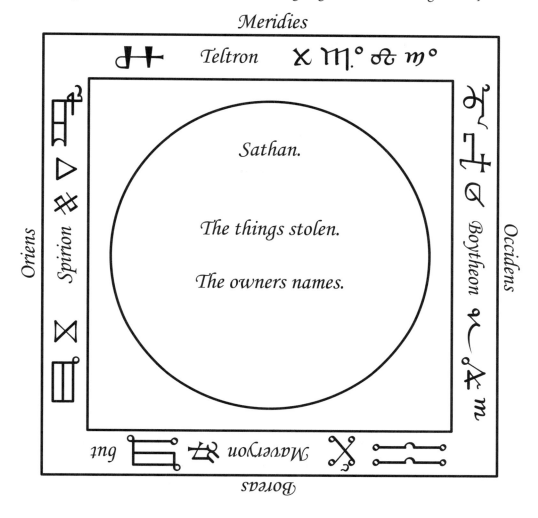

This must always be done, the ☽ crescent.

Note: when the wind is in the south or west, you shall not work.

Finis huius operis. [The end of this operation.]

[24v]

239 Magic square text, outer edge: *Meridies / Occidens / Boreas / Oriens* [South / West / North / East].
      Inside square: Teltron / Boytheon / Maveryon but/ Spirion.
      Inside circle: Sathan / The things stolen. / The owners [sic] names.

Experimentum ad Includendum Spiritum Bilgal in Christallo [Experiment for the Purpose of Enclosing the Spirit Bilgal[240] in a Crystal]

"Exorsi[s]o te, spiritum Bilgall, per deum patrem qui mundum creavit, per deum filium qui mundum suo preciose sanguine redemit, et per spiritum sanctum qui mundum illuminavit, per deum vivum, per deum verum, et per deum sanctum, et per deum qui te de paradiso gaudio eiecit, per beatam mariam virginem et matrem dei, et per omnes sanctos, appostoles, martires, confessores, et virgines, per celum et terram, et per omnia que in eis sunt, per quatuor elementa, et per ineffabilem potestatem dei. Coniuro et exorziso te, spiritum Bilgal, per omnia ista nomina sancta dei + Messyas + Sother + Cinanuell + Sabaoth + Adonay + Theos + Athanatos + Eloy + Panton + Craton + Ysus + Alpha + et Ω + Christus + Jesus + Nazarenus + On + et El + et per hec sancta nomina, exorziso te, Bilgal, per nomen principalem dei + Tetragrammaton + Hanabaco + Mandell + Aho + Gramaton + Atanell + et per vulnera preciosa Jesu Christi, et per hec nomina Nioth + Neoth + per que Salamonem te in vasa vitrio constringebat, quatenus ubicunque fueris, nunc statim mihi vel isto N. in isto christallo te ipsum monstres, in pulcra forma et decora humana, habentem colorem rubeum vel album, sine aliquo dampno, timore, tremore, et detrimento corporis, et anyme mee vel istius vel istorum, hic in societate mea existeum, et sine molestia et fallacia tu ipse in isto christallo mox hic veneras et appareas visibiliter, per dominum nostrum Jesum Christum, qui venturus est iudicare vivos et mortuos et seculum per ignem. Amen. Fiat, fiat, fiat. Amen."

["I exorcise thee, spirit Bilgall, by God the Father who created the world, by God the Son who redeemed the world with his precious blood, and by the Holy Spirit who illuminated the world, by the living God, by the true God, and by the holy God, and by the God who cast thee out of joyous paradise, by the Blessed Virgin Mary, and the mother of God, and by all saints, apostles, martyrs, confessors, and virgins, by heaven and earth, and by all that are in them, by the four elements, and by the unutterable power of God. I conjure and exorcise thee, spirit Bilgal, by all those holy names of God + Messyas + Sother + Cinanuell + Sabaoth + Adonay + Theos + Athanatos + Eloy + Panton + Craton + Ysus + Alpha + and Ω + Christus + Jesus + Nazarenus + On + and El + and by these holy names, I exorcise thee, Bilgal, by the principal name of God, + Tetragrammaton + Hanabaco + Mandell + Aho + Gramaton + Atanell + and by the precious wounds of Jesus Christ, and by these names Nioth + Neoth + by which Solomon was binding thee in a glass vessel, as wherever thou mayst be, now show thyself immediately to me or to this one N. in this crystal,

---

240 *Bilgal*: For operations for the same spirit, see *Oberon*, 401–3; Sloane 3846, 109r–110r.

---

in a beautiful form and human beauty, having a red or white color, without any injury, fear, trembling, or harm of the body, or my or this one's or these one's soul (or souls), remaining here in my society, I may (you mayst) appear, and without trouble or deceit thou thyself may come and appear here visibly in this crystal soon, by our Lord Jesus Christ, who will come to judge the living and the dead, and the world by fire. Amen. Let it be done, let it be done, let it be done. Amen."]

Et cum apparet tibi vel socio tuo, ligatis eum sic: [And when he may appear to thee or thy companion, thou mayst bind him thus:]

"*Coniuro te, spiritum Bilgal, coarto, constringo, ligo, et impero te, corpus et sanguinem domini nostri Jesu Christi, per oculos eius, et per omnia membra eius, et per vulnera eius qui in are crucis sustinunt, per mundi redemptione [redemptionem], per potestatem divinam domini nostri Jesu Christi, et per hec sancta nomina et gloriosa per que deus creavit celum et terram, et omnia que in eis sunt, Legethomonon, Legelegna, Ledeforon, Arbelgenerocon, Lederogaon, Ledepoton, Ledefeleson, et per illum casum per quem cadebas a throno celi, et per illa nomina per quem maledictus es, Perynnoy Monton, quatenus in isto christallo firmiter permantas, et ab illo non recedas, donec te licentiavero nec dum omne velle meum veraciter adimplevisti, secundum potestatem tuam, et nobis quod querimus manifeste et sine fallacia, mendatione, vel ambiguitate ostendas et facias, et sine timore aut detrimento mei corporis, vel alicuius in societate mea existentium. Sta, sta, sta, Bilgal, in nomina Saphar et Saphiron, Jesus, Tetragrammaton, fiat, fiat, fiat. Amen.*"

["I conjure thee, spirit Bilgal, I constrain, I hinder, I bind, and I rule thee by the body and blood of our Lord Jesus Christ through his eyes, and by his eyes, and by all his limbs, and by his wounds that were sustained in the altar of the cross, by the redemption of the world, by the divine power of our Lord Jesus Christ, and by these holy and glorious names by which God created the heaven and the earth, and all things that are in them, Legethomonon, Legelegna, Ledeforon, Arbelgenerocon, Lederogaon, Ledepoton, Ledefeleson, and by that misfortune by which thou wert falling out of the throne of heaven, by those names by which thou wert cursed, Perynnoy Monton, in order that thou shouldst remain in this crystal steadfastly, and thou mayst not withdraw out of this until I will license thee, and not until thou hast completed all my will, according to thy power, and that thou shouldst show to us and do what we seek clearly and without deceit, lying, or ambiguity, and without fear or harm of my body, or of anyone appearing in my fellowship. Stand, stand, stand, Bilgal, in the names Saphar and Saphiron, Jesus, Tetragrammaton. Let it be done, let it be done, let it be done. Amen."]

Sed si noluerit aperire, tunc dic: [But if he will not appear, then say:]

"Maledictio dei patris omnipotentis + et filii + et spiritus

[25r]

sancti + defendat super te, et a dignitatibus tuis omnibus dedeprivat, et in stagnum ignis terribilis et sulphuris te projiciat, nisi cito sine mora veneris, et voluntatem meam perfeceris et perimpleas. Fiat, fiat, fiat. Amen."

["The curse of God the omnipotent Father + and of the Son + and of the Holy Ghost + may repel thee, and deprive thee[241] from all thy diginities, and into the lake of terrible fire and sulfur he may throw thee, unless thou mayst come soon without delay, and thou mayst complete and satisfy my will. Let it be done, let it be done, let it be done. Amen."]

And when he hath fulfilled thine intent, then give him leave to depart *sic* [thus]:

"Coniuro te, Bilgal, per illam virtutem et potestatem per quam dominus ligavit te, et super sua sancta nomina, ego precipio tibi, Bilgal, quod cum recedas ab isto loco sine nostro tedio, timore, aut nocumento alicuius creature dei, et paratus sis iterum venire quandocunque te iterum habere voluero, et istud sit verum per nomen domini nostri Jesu christi. Vade in locum tibi a deo predestiantum. In nomine patris, recede, Bilgal, in pace. In nomine filii + recede, Bilgal, in pace. In nomine spiritus sancti + recede, Bilgal, in pace, et pax domini nostri Iesu Christi sit inter me et te. Fiat, fiat, fiat. Amen."

["I conjure thou, Bilgal, by that virtue and power through which the Lord bound thee, and his holy names above, I command thee, Bilgal, that when thou mayst depart from this place without our weariness, fear, or injury of any creature of God, and thou mayst be ready to come again whenever I will want to have thee again, and this may be true by the name of our Lord Jesus Christ. Go into the place predestined to thee by God. In the name of the Father, leave, Bilgal, in peace. In the name of the Son +, leave, Bilgal, in peace. In the name of the Holy Ghost +, leave, Bilgal, in peace, and let there be the peace of our Lord Jesus Christ between me and thee. Let it be done, let it be done, let it be done. Amen."]

Si non vult recedere, dic: [If he does not wish to retire, say:]

---

241 *Deprive thee*: Latin *dedeprivat* is unknown, and the first syllable might have been accidentally repeated.

"Maledictio dei patris omnipotentis + et filii + et spiritus sancti + defendat super te, et tecum maneat, nisi discedas et desedas in pace ad locum tibi predestinatum et per Jesum Christi ordinatum, sine aliquo terrore et dampno corporis et anime mee, et cum alias te invocavero, cum omni festinatione in isto christallo apparias, ubicunque te invocavero, in domo vel extra vel in campo, et omnia precepta adimpleas. Fiat, fiat, fiat. Amen. Pax christi sit mecum et socie, et vade in pace, in nomine patris, et filii, et spiritus sancti. Amen. In nomine Iesu, hoc signum facio."

["The curse of God the omnipotent Father + and of the Son + and of the Holy Ghost + may repel thee, and let it remain with thee, unless thou mayst disperse and depart in peace to the place predestined and decreed for thee by Jesus Christ, without any fear or harm of my body or soul, and another time when I will invoke thee, thou mayst appear in that crystal with all haste, whenever I will invoke thee, in the house or without or in the field, and thou mayst carry out all my commands. Let it be done, let it be done, let it be done. Amen. May the peace of Christ be with me and my companions, and go in peace, in the name of the Father, and of the Son, and of the Holy Ghost. Amen. In the name of Jesus, I make this sign."] **T**

Finis huius experimentum. [The end of this experiment.]

Experimentum de Forma Spatulae
[Experiment of the Form of the Spatula][242]

TBy this experiment is constrained man, woman, or beast, of what condition soever it be, so that their names be written in manner as it is shewed in the figure of the spatula following. When you wouldst do this thing, choose which of them you likest best to do. And if you wouldst constrain any spirit, write his name between L and A., and if you wouldst any woman should love thee, write her name between A and V. and write the colour of him or her. For the love of man or woman is had in the same hour in the which it is done and fulfilled, and the deed done in the spatula as it behoveth thee. First you must get the wood of white thorn, *vel per aqua* [or through water], the which doth grow in the water. Thou shalt dry the same and make thereof coals of fire, and gather them together, and put them in a new earthen pot, and hold the spatula over the pot that it may be a little warm, and say to the spirits this conjuration following:

242 For similar operations, see Bayerische Staatsbibliothek Clm 849, 32r–33r; Sloane 3850, 28r–v. This is not to be confused with another group of spatula rituals, usually intended to summon the spirit Vassago.

"Coniuro vos, spiritus Asiell, Casiell, Lamfriell, Iamfriell, Palam, Herlam, Olam, Bolam, per deum vivum, per deum verum, et per deum sanctum, tres personas, unum verum deum, qui cuncta creavit ex nihillo, verbo suo, per eum qui vos fecit, et Adam et Evam cre-

[25v]

avit et totum genus humanum, et per eum qui celum, terram, et mare creavit, et omnia que in eis sunt, et qui sigillavit mare in alto nomina suo, et terminum sibi possuit quem preterire non possit, et ardam in medie eius stabilavit, et per eum qui fecit angelos suos spiritus, et ministros suos ignem ardentum, qui preterita, presencia, et futura cognoscit, et per eum qui habet claves inferni et mortis, per eum qui est Alpha + et Ω + principium et finis, qui vivit et regnat, vinxit et gubernat, qui mortuus fuit et tercio die resurrexit, et qui vocatus est + Tetragrammaton +

["I conjure you, spirit Asiell, Casiell, Lamfriell, Iamfriell, Palam, Herlam, Olam, Bolam,[243] by the living God, by the true God, and by the holy God, three persons, one true God, who created all out of nothing, by his word, by him who made you, and created Adam and Eve and all the race of humans, and by him who made heaven, earth, and sea, and all things that are in them, and that he sealed up in the sea in his high name, and he was able to set a limit for himself that he may not be able to disregard, and he made firm the dry land in the middle of these, and by him who made the angels his spirits, and a burning fire his ministers, who knows past, present, and future, and by him who holds the keys of hell and of death, by him who is Alpha + and Ω + first and last, who lives and reigns, conquers and governs, who was dead and resurrected on the third day, and who was called + Tetragrammaton +]

"Coniuro vos, spiritus, per spiritum sanctum, paracletum, et per illud nomen gloriousum et ineffabilem, cuius virtutem nullus cognovit nisi illae solus, qui est verbum dei, et per hec sancta nomina dei, Messyas + Sother + Emanuell + Sabaoth + Adonay + Agla + On + Tetragrammaton + El + Ely + Eloy + Elyon + Sadday + Algramay + Dedragamay + Ioth + Yara + Pahena + Alleya + Forsythan + Fortiston + Almaron + et per omnia alia nomina dei et per eorum virtutes.

["I conjure you, spirit, by the Holy Ghost, defender, and by that glorious and unutterable name, the virtue of which none knew unless these alone, that is the word of

---

243 *Asiell...Bolam*: "Asyel, Castiel, Lamisniel, Rabam, Erlain, [et] Belam" in Clm 849.

God, and by these holy names of God, Messyas + Sother + Emanuell + Sabaoth +
Adonay + Agla + On + Tetragrammaton + El + Ely + Eloy + Elyon + Sadday +
Algramay + Dedragamay + Ioth + Yara + Pahena + Alleya + Forsythan + Fortiston
+ Almaron +, and by all other names of God and by their virtues.]

*"Coniuro vos, spiritus Asyell, Casyel, Lamfriel, Iamfriell, Palam, Herlam, Olam, et
Bolam, per patrem, et filium, et spiritum sanctum, per sanctam trinitatem et unitatem,
et per corpus et sanguinem domini nostri Jesu Christi, per omnia membra eius sancta,
et per omnia vulnera eius que per redemptione mundi in ara crucis sustinnat, per coronam spiniam quam dominus noster Jesus Christus in capito sed portavit, et per lac
beate Marie, virginis, et per omnia sancta dei nomina predicta, et per omnes eorum
virtutes, et per virtutem et potestatem domini nostri Jesu Christi, et per hanc coniurationem vobis precipio.*

["I conjure you, spirit Asyell, Casyel, Lamfriel, Iamfriell, Palam, Herlam, Olam, and
Bolam, by the Father, and the Son, and the Holy Ghost, by the Holy Trinity and
Unity, and by the body and blood of our Lord Jesus Christ, by all his holy limbs,
and by all his wounds that he sustained on the altar of the cross for the redemption
of the world, by the crown of thorn that our Lord Jesus Christ nonetheless carried
on his head, and by the milk of the Blessed Mary, virgin, and by all aforementioned
holy names of God, and by all virtues of these, and by the virtue and power of our
Lord Jesus Christ, and by this conjuration I command you.]

*"Quatenus cito et sine dilacione, constringatis cor et animam illius hominis vel mulieris
N. quod sicut haec spatula calefacta est ab hoc igne, ita illum hominem vel mulierem N.
accendatis, et calefaciatis amorem in meum, ita quod requiescere non possit, in
dormiendo vel vigilando, edendo vel bibendo, stando vel sedendo, equitando vel eundo,
per fervorem amoris mei, donec ad me veniat, et omne velle meum et voluntatem meam
proficerit, et preimplevit cum effectu. Fiat, fiat, fiat. Amen."*

["In order that soon and without delay, you may restrain the heart and soul of that
man or woman N., that this spatula was heated out of this fire, thus you may
approach that man or woman N. and you may excite love into mine, that thus he or
she may not be to rest, in sleeping or waking, eating or drinking, standing or sitting, riding or walking, by the boiling heat of love of me, until he or she may come
to me, and she may place in command all my will and my volition, and it is fulfilled
with effect."]

Say this conjuration three times in the hour of Venus, if it be for a man or woman that you wouldst have kindled in thy love or in the work of Venus.

And if you wouldst constrain any spirit, write his name as is aforesaid, and say the former conjuration three times, "*Coniuro vos, spiritus* [I conjure you, spirit]" *et cet*, and at the end of the conjuration, say as followeth:

"*Quatenus illum spiritum N., quem quero, qui potestatem habet super illum quem quero, faciatis venire ad me in pulchra forma humana, et mihi fideliter obedire et respondere, et omnia que desiderabo perfecte et veraciter praeimplere.*"

["In order that spirit N. that I seek, who holds power over that one that I seek, you may make to come to me in a beautiful human form, and faithfully obey and respond to me, and all that I will desire perfectly and truly to be fulfilled."]

And if you desirest any beast, say the former conjuration, "*Coniuro vos, spiritus* [I conjure you, spirit]" *et cet*, and at the end of the conjuration, say as followeth:

[26r]

"*Quatenus constringatis et ligatis illam bestiam N., quod non exire possit a loco in qui iam est, vel stat, nec removere aliquo modo, donec omne velle meum et desiderium super ipsam praefeci et praeimplevi. Coniuro vos per Christum, qui venturus est iudicare vivos et mortuos, et secula per ignem. Amen.*"

["In order that you may restrain and bind that beast N., that it may not be able to depart out of the place in which it is now, or stands, and not to remove in another way, until I set and fulfill all my will and desire over this one. I conjure you by Christ, who will come to judge the living and the dead and the world by fire. Amen."]

This you may do upon deer, hare, coney, pigeon, capon, rook, hen, or what you will.

When the Master will do these things, it is to be noted that he must be in such a place where he may be found, for except he may find thee, he will go mad through anger.

Sequitur figuram de forma spatula [The figure of the form of the spatula follows]:

Asy=	*A*	*el*
Casy=		*el*
Lam=	*B*	*friel*
Iam=		*friel*
Pa=		*lam*
Her=	*E*	*lam*
O=		*lam*
Bo=	*L*	*lam*
	A	
	V	

Forma   Spatulæ

Forma spatula [the form of the spatula][244]

This may be made in virgin wax or virgin paper.

Finis huius operis de forma spatulae. [The end of this work of the form of the spatula.]

[26v]

244 Lines of spatula: Asy= A el / Casy= el / Lam= B friel / Iam= friel / Pa= lam / Her= E lam / O= lam / Bo= L lam / A / V.

Alkates Walkates

An Experiment to See by Thyself, without a Child or Fellow
Companion, in a Crystal Stone a Spirit which Will Shew the Truth
Without Fail of All Things Doubtful, and of These and Manslaughter,
of Treasure Hidden in the Ground, and What Spirit Keepeth It, of the
State of Thy Friends, Wheresoever They Be, and of Secret Things and
Things Lost, Whether Thou Shalt Have Them Again or Not.[245]

In primis, dic hanc orationem sequentem devote: [At the first hour of the day, say this
oration of dedication following:]

"O Lord Jesus Christ, son of God, let thy grace, virtue, and mercy appear unto me,
which madest all things with thy right hand. O God of Abraham, God of Isaac, and
God of Jacob, of Hely[246] and of Tobye,[247] which didst deliver the three children,
Sydrac, Mysaac, and Abednago, out of the flame of fire, which didst deliver
Jephthah out of the wars and Susanna from her false accusers, and Daniel out of the
lion's den, which didst heal the man being sick of the palsy, and didst heal the
woman of Canaan of the bloody flux,[248] which didst vanquish devils and raise
Lazarus from death to life, which didst favour Abraham and sufferedst him in his
old age to see thee in the true Trinity. Grant, I beseech thee, that I may see these
spirits, Alkates, Walkates, Miron, Micriton, Balko, and Bosco, that they may appear
unto me in this crystal stone and may shew me the truth of all things past, present,
and to come, whensoever I shall ask them, and grant that they, being bound by thy
mighty power, may fulfill all my desires, which with God the Father and God the
Holy Ghost livest and reignest, one God, world without end. Amen."

Then hold the crystal in thy right hand in a piece of hart's leather towards the sun,
and say:

---

245 The first part of this ritual also appears in Sloane 3846, 37r–v. A similar one can be found in
     Oberon, 534–8. Another to the same spirit appears in University of Pennsylvania Alnwick MS.
     1677, 45–51.

246 *Hely*: Although usually a name of God, here it likely signifies Elijah.

247 *Tobye*: Tobias.

248 *And didst heal the woman...*: A conflation of two biblical stories, one with a Canaanite woman
     whose daughter was possessed by an evil spirit and the other of a bleeding woman; Mark 7:24–
     30, Luke 8:43–48.

"*In nomine sancte trinitatis, patris, et filii, et spiritus sancti, et sancte deitatis, hanc gemmam respicio.* [In the name of the holy Trinity, of the Father, and of the Son, and of the Holy Ghost, and of the holy Deity, I gaze upon this gem.]"

But take heed you be not polluted with woman seven days before you begin this work. Then say:

"*Coniuro vos, Alkates, Walkates, Myron, Micriton, Balko, et Bosco, qui inhabitatis in bosco. Ego vos coniuro et sociis impero per aucthoritatem dei omnipotentis, ut sitis parati obediendo mihi ad precepta mea, et voluntatem meam faciendam et complendam. Coniuro vos, Alkates, Walkates, Myron, Micriton, Balko, et Bosco, per patrem, filium, et spiritum sanctum, et per eum qui est Alpha et Ω, et per tremendum diem iudicii, per dei merita, et per merrita omnium sanctorum, et*

[27r]

per omnia teribilia et ineffabilia nomina dei, quatenus tu, Alkates, in ista gemma christalliam sine mora intres, et venies in propria persona tua, et in pulcra forma humana, coronam in capite tuo portans, et socios tuos tecum. Adduces ut illos videre possim in humana forma, per omnes virtutes dei, et fac hac quod tibi iussero. Te coniuro per beatam Mariam virginem, matrem domini nostri Jesu Christi, et per omnes sanctos dei, et per omnia que in celo sunt et in terra, in mari et in inferno noscuntur, et omnia que sancta sunt et procreata. Amen."

["I conjure you, Alkates, Walkates, Myron, Micriton, Balko, and Bosco, who live in the forest. I conjure you and I order your associates by the authority of omnipotent God, that you, prepared, may be obeying my commands and doing and completing my will. I conjure you, Alkates, Walkates, Myron, Micriton, Balko, and Bosco, by the Father, Son, and Holy Ghost, and by him who is Alpha and Ω, and by the great day of judgment, by the favor of God, and by the favor of all saints, and by all the dreadful and unutterable names of God, that you, Alkates, may enter into this crystal gem without delay, and you may come in your own person, and in a beautiful human form, carrying a crown on your head, and with your associates with you. You will lead so that I may see those in human form, by all the virtues of God, and do this that I shall order you. I conjure you by the Blessed Virgin Mary, mother of our Lord Jesus Christ, and by all the saints of God, and by all that are in the heavens and the earth, and that are known in the sea and in hell, and all that are holy and begotten. Amen."]

Et si sit rebelles, tunc dic: [And if he may be rebellious, then say:]

"Ego coniuro vos, Alkates, Walkates, Myron, Micriton, Balko et Bosco in inferno, per virtutem domini nostri Jesu Christi, filii dei omnipotentis, et per nomina eius, et per nomina sanctorum omnium et virtutes eorum. Condempno vos mitti in ignem eternum, nisi citissime veniatis et voluntatem meam perimpleatis. Amen. Fiat, fiat, fiat."

["I conjure you, Alkates, Walkates, Myron, Micriton, Balko, and Bosco, in hell, by the virtue of our Lord Jesus Christ, son of the omnipotent God, and by his name, and by the name of all the saints and all their virtues. I condemn you to be sent into eternal fire, unless you should come most swiftly and may fulfill my will."]

This done, if he or they come, ask what thou wilt, and they will shew it thee, and if they will not, then say as followeth:

"Condempno vos, Alkates, Walkates, Miron, Micriton, Balko et Bosco in ignem eternum inferni, per virtutem dei vivi et veri, et per potestatem dei quam habet super vos, quod ligati estis in inferno catenis igneis, et sustineatis penas inextinguibiles et intolerabiles sine requie, donec mihi appareatis et fideliter mihi respondeatis sine dolo, mendacitate, vel fallacia, et sine terrore et timore, vel detrimento mei corporis vel anime, ad omnia interrogata et mandata mea et omne velle meum cum efferta perimpleatis, Fiat, fiat, fiat. Amen."

["I condemn you, Alkates, Walkates, Miron, Micriton, Balko and Bosco, into the eternal fire of hell, by the virtue of the living and true God, and by the power of God that he has over you, that you will be bound in hell in fiery chains, and you may sustain inextinguishable and intolerable pains without rest, until you should appear to me and faithfully answer me without pain, illusion, or deceit, and without terror or fear, or with harm of my body or soul, for all things asked, and my commands and all my will may you fulfill with accomplishment. Let it be done, let it be done, let it be done. Amen."]

Then ask what thou wilt, and he will tell thee, then license him to depart *ut patet in aliis experimentis* [as is revealed in other experiments].

If they come not the first day, call them the second day, and the third day, and they shall come and tell thee all things, but look you be not polluted with women which are corrupt, and presume not to do this work on a holy day, nor in cloudy weather, because it cannot be done, but when the sun doth shine, and you must be clean from sin.

Finis huius operis. [The end of this operation.]

[Call to Cantivalerion and Golgathell, Ruler of All Spirits][249]

"O tu spiritus Cantivalerion vel Golgathell, qui est imperator omnium spiritum, rogo te, per virtutes quas habeas, ut mihi obedias, et venias visibilitur mihi in hoc christallo cumcunque, u[b]icumque, et quotiescunque te invocavero, et [blank] te ipsum venire ad me, ubicunque es. Audi vocem meam, per virtutes domini nostri Jesu Christi, qui te creavit, et per virtutes nominis Iesu Tetragrammaton, veni, tu spiritus Cantivalerion vel Golgathell et [blank] te ipsum [blank] in pulcra forma humana in hoc christallo [blank] invocavero pro te. Fiat, fiat, fiat. Amen."

["O thou spirit Cantivalerion or Golgathell, who is the leader of all spirits, I ask thee, by the virtues that thou mayst have, so that thou mayst obey me, and thou mayst come visibly to me in this crystal with whomever, wherever, and however often I will invoke thee, and [blank] to come thyself to me, wherever thou art. Hear my voice, by virtues of our Lord Jesus Christ, who created thee, and by the virtues of the names of Jesus, Tetragrammaton, come, thou spirit, Cantivalerion or Golgathell and [blank], show thou thyself [blank] in beautiful human form in this crystal [blank] I will invoke before thee. Let it be done, let it be done, let it be done. Amen."]

[27v]

---

249 *Cantivalerion*: Despite his lofty stature here, Cantivalerion (or Tantavalerion in *Oberon*) shows up rarely in the manuscripts examined. For another operation, see *Oberon*, 301–2.

An Experiment of the Names of Them That Be Suspected for Theft or Malice, and to Know Any Other Thing, and in What Hour It May Be Proved Every Day. [250]

☉ Sunday before noon at 5, 7, and 11, after noon at 2, 7, 9

☽ Monday before noon at 2, 4, and 11, after noon at 4, 6, 8

♂ Tuesday before noon at 1, 6, and 7, after noon at 3, 8, 10

☿ Wednesday before noon at 3, 5, and 12, after noon at 5, 7, 12

♃ Thursday before noon at 2, 7, and 9, after noon at 2, 4, 11

♀ Friday before noon at 4, 6, and 11, after noon at 2, 6, 8

♄ Saturday before noon at 1, 3, and 10, after noon at 3 and 5

When you have chosen your hour of any day, write the names of the persons suspected and put them in a hollow key, every name severally by itself, and put the end of the key into a book and clasp it or tie it, and say:

"*Gell, Elyell, Elchell, Egla, Ely, Panton. Adiuro vos, rex Caton. Jesus Nazarenus, crucifixus rex Iudeorum, filii dei, miserere mei. Amen. [blank] Adiutorium nostrum in nomine dominum, qui fecit celum et terram. Sit nomen dominum benedictum, ex hoc nunc et usque in seculum. Amen.*"

["Gell, Elyell, Elchell, Egla, Ely, Panton. I adjure you, King Caton. Jesus of Nazareth, crucified king of the Jews, son of God, have mercy on me. Amen. [blank] Our help is in the name of the Lord, who made heaven and earth. May your name be blessed, Lord, from this, now and forever. Amen."]

Then say devoutly as followeth:

---

250 *Book and key divination*: Also known as clidomancy or cleidomancy. One William Wicherely used a procedure with these items and quoting the psalm below in 1549. Two years later, a vicar from Gloucester was brought to court after using a similar technique to find money stolen from him. Foxe, Cranmer, and Nichols, *Narratives of the Days of the Reformation*, 332–33; Historical Manuscripts Commission, *Report on Manuscripts in Various Collections*, 7:53. See also Scot, *The Discouerie of Witchcraft*, 477–78.

"Prevent,[251] O Lord, we beseech thee, our doings with thy most gracious favour, and further us with thy continual help, that all our works may be always continued and ended by thee. Grant this for Jesus Christ's sake, our Lord. Amen.

"O Lord God, which above hast known all things, which hast said, 'I am the living bread which came down from heaven,'[252] and art Alpha and Ω, the beginning and the end, by thy most holy name, which is Tetragrammaton, and by thy mercy and by thy merits and intercessions of thy apostles Peter and Paul, although we be sinners, yet we beseech thee of thy great mercy, that if the person whose name is herein written, be guilty indeed, if that it be true that is here written, thou wilt vouchsafe to shew unto us, by the virtue of thy holy names, Aglay, On, Usyon, Tetragrammaton, by the book and key turning itself, and if the person be not guilty and if it be not true, let neither the book nor key move, so that you wouldst vouchsafe to shew unto us him that is guilty in this deed, or that which is very true by the inseparable Trinity, the Father, the Son, and the Holy Ghost, and as you didst satisfy five thousand men with five loaves and two fishes, so in this thing you wouldst vouchsafe to shew unto us the full and perfect knowledge thereof, by our Lord and saviour Jesus Christ. Amen."

Then let one hold the key on his forefingers' ends and say as followeth:

Pro furto et malicia [For Theft and Malice]

"*Si videbas furem, currebas cum eo, et [cum] adulteris porcionem tuam ponebas. Os tuum abundavit malicia, et lingua tua concinnabat dolum.* [If thou wert seeing a thief, thou wert running with him, and thou wert placing your portion with adulterers. Your mouth exceeded in malice, and thy tongue wast producing pain],"[253] et cetera.

In the Latin it is the 65th Psalm, in English the the 50th Psalm.[254]

Finis huius operis. [The end of this operation.]

[28r]

---

251 *Prevent*: Hasten.
252 John 6:51.
253 Psalm 49:17–18.
254 This is the 50th Psalm in KJV, but it is not the 65th in the Latin.

Androyce vel Andramalcus[255]
Flos Florum Omnium Experimentorum pro Furto et Thesauro
[Flower of Flowers of All Experiments, for Thieves and Treasure]

Accipe puerum virginem decem annorum vel infra potius, et rade ungulam pollicis dextre cum vitreo vel cultello habet manibrium album, vel in lapide christallo, et ungatur oleo olinarum, et dic pater noster ter, puero sedente inter crura magistri sui. Post voca ter, "Androyce, veni festinantur ut respeciat puer in unguem vel christallum." Deinde dic coniurationem sequentem.

[Take a virgin boy of ten years or under preferably, and scrape the nail of the right thumb with glass or a knife that has a white handle, or in the crystal stone, and he may be anointed with olive oil, and say a Pater Noster three times, with the boy being seated between the legs of the master himself. After, say three times, "Androyce, come quickly so that the boy may regard you in the nail or crystal." Then say the following conjuration.]

"Exorziso te, spiritum nomine Androyce, per deum patrem omnipotentem, per deum vivum, per deum verum, per deum sanctum, et per deum qui te e paradisi gaudis eiecit, et per omnia nomina sancta et venerabilia dei, Messyas, Sother, Emanuell, Sabaoth, Adonay, Otheos, Athanatos, Eloy, Panton, Craton, Ysus, Alpha et Ω, Jesus Christus Nazarenus, et per hec sancta nomina, te, Androyce, coniuro per Tetragrammaton, nomen principale dei, Haonob, Leo, Mandalabo, Gramaton, Agla, Ely, Halcanac, Lamazabacthany, Eegon, Rogon, Higron, Spiron, Emorison, et per sanctam Mariam virginem, matrem dominum nostri Jesu Christi; per eius quinque vulnera, per omnes virgines, et per virginitatem beati Johannes baptiste, et evangeliste, et per hec nomina, Snoth et Nooth, per que Salamonem in vase vitrea constringebat, quatenus ubicunque fueris, nunc statim in unguem dextra pollicis illius pueri N. vel in istum christallum intres, et te ipsum monstres in pulcra forma humana, sub colorem rubeum aut album, sine aliquo dampno terrore, timore aut detrimente mei vel alicuius alteris hic in societate mea existentis, et sine molestia corporis et anima mei."

255 *Androyce vel Andramalchus*: A similarly named spirit, Andromalius, is the final spirit in the *Goetia*. "[H]is office is to bring a theefe & goods yt are stolen, Back; and to discover all wickedness, and understand dealings, & to punish Theives [thieves] & other wicked people, & to discover Treasure that is hidd" (Peterson, *The Lesser Key of Solomon*, 39). He is also likely the "Andrew Malchus" mentioned to the clerk William Stapleton as being invoked by the parson of Lesingham (Turner, "Brief Remarks, Accompanied with Documents, Illustrative of Trial by Jury, Treasure-Trove, and the Invocation of Spirits for the Discovery of Hidden Treasure in the Sixteenth Century," 59–60).

["I exorcise thee, spirit with the name Androyce, by God the omnipotent Father, by the living God, by the true God, by the holy God, and by God who threw thee out of joyous paradise, and by all the holy and august names of God, Messyas, Sother, Emanuell, Sabaoth, Adonay, Otheos, Athanatos, Eloy, Panton, Craton, Ysus, Alpha and Ω, Jesus Christus Nazarenus, and by these holy names, thou, Androyce, I conjure by Tetragrammaton, the principal name of God, Haonob, Leo, Mandalabo, Gramaton, Agla, Ely, Halcanac, Lamazabacthany, Eegon, Rogon, Higron, Spiron, Emorison, and by the holy virgin Mary, mother of our Lord Jesus Christ, by his five wounds, by all virgins, and by the virginity of the blessed John the Baptist, and the Evangelist, and by these names, Snoth and Nooth, by which Solomon was binding in a glass vessel, so that wherever thou mayst be, now immediately thou mayst enter in the right thumb of this boy N. or in this crystal, and thou mayst show thyself in a beautiful human form, of a red or white color, without any damage, terror, fear, or damage of me or any other here being in my partnership, and without annoyance of my body or soul."]

Tunc quere a puero si aliquid videat. Si non, incipis iterum donec venit, et si non venit, dicas: [Then ask the boy if he may see anything. If not, thou beginnest again until he comes, and if he does not come, thou mayst say:]

"Exorziso te, spiritum Androyce, cunque omnia predicta tibi cadant in condempnationem perpetuum, nisi statim veneris et mihi veritatem dicas."

["I exorcise thee, spirit Androyce, howsoever all things aforesaid to thee mayst fall into perpetual condemnation, unless thou wilt come immediately, and thou mayst tell me the truth."]

Tunc veniet ut dominis. [Then he will come as a ruler.]

Tunc dicat puer post nostrum suum. [Then the boy may say his own prayer of ours.]

"Androyce, adiuro te et iubeo tibi per fidem quam debes deo tuo privato, et per virtutem dei vivi, veri, puri, et misericordissimi, et per illum angelum qui in tuba canit in die iudicii. Venite, benedicta patris mei, et recipite regnum p[at]ris mei, et per angelos et archangelos, thronos et dominationes, principatus et potestates, cherubin et seraphin, et per omnes potestates dei, et omnes reliquas sanctorum que continentur in universo munde, et si hoc sit verum, ut certe credo quod deus et in deo est omnis vis et potestas, et si hoc verum sit, ut certe verum est quod sancta Maria mater Jesu Christi fuit, virgo ante partum, in partu, et post partum,

et sicut hoc est verum, quod deus omnipotens te eiecit cum primato tuo et sociis tuis, propter superbiam vestram de paradisi gaudio, et per ista nomina qui sunt maxima, Balsacke super Balsacke, Panulion, Preamulion, potestate Azie, Herie, Derede, Capare, quibus nobis aqua et elementa concutiuntur. Iubeo tibi, Androyce, per charitatem dei, et omnia membra eius, et per eius dietatem, et per bonum in malum que quatuor elementa sustinent, et exorsizo, coniuro, ligo, et constringo te, ut monstres isto puero N. integram veritatem, absque fallacio, fraude, sophisticatione, et aliquo detrimento, ad omnes meas questiones, et ab huic non recedas, a nostro conspectu, donec, in omnibus que poteris, mihi veraciter respondisti per signa certa aut per scripta, scribenda, per eum qui venturus est iudicare vivos et mortuos, et secula per ignem. Amen. Fiat, fiat, fiat."

["Androyce, I adjure thee and order thee by the faith that thou owest to thy private God, and by the virtue of the living, true, pure, and most merciful God, and by that angel who plays the trumpet on the day of judgment. Come, blessed ones of my father, and recapture the kingdom of my Father, and by angels and archangels, thrones and dominions, principalities and powers, cherubim and seraphim, and by all the powers of God, and all the relics of saints that are contained in the whole world, and if this may be true, as surely I believe God, and in God is all strength and power, and if this may be true, as certainly it is true that holy Mary was the mother of Jesus Christ, a virgin before birth, during birth, and after birth, and just as this is true, that omnipotent God cast thee out with thy office and thy associates, because of thy pride, from paradise with joy, and by these names that are the greatest, Balsacke over Balsacke, Panulion, Preamulion, with power Azie, Herie, Derede, Capare, by which water and the elements are shaken for us. I order thee, Androyce, by the charity of God, and all his limbs, and by his divinity, by the good in evil that sustain the four elements, and I exorcise, conjure, bind, and chain thee, so that thou mayst show this boy N. the entire truth, away from deceit, fraud, trick, and any harm, to all my questions, and thou mayst not leave from this place, out of our sight, until, in all things that thou art able, thou hast responded to me truly by writing certain signs or writings, by him who will come to judge the living and the dead, and the world by fire. Amen. Let it be done, let it be done, let it be done."]

Tunc, "Interrogo quod vis," et tibi respondebit, et eum totum velle et desiderium tuum implevit. [Then say, "I ask what thou seest," and he will respond to thee, and he will satisfy this all thy will and desire.]

Tunc licenciaveris eum sic: [Then thou wilt dismiss him thus:]

"Androyce, iubeo tibi per virtutem omnium verborum et nomina per que tu huc venisti et mihi respondisti, ut ad locum tibi a deo predestinatum hinc in pace recedas, ubi deus tuus ordinavit te expectare, sine timore, tremore dei, et mihi paratus sis quociescumque te eternum vocavero, absque aliquo impedimento. Recede in pace dei, in nomine patris, et filii, et spiritu sancti. Amen."

["Androyce, I command thee by the virtue of all words and names by which thou camest here and didst respond to me, that thou mayst go back from this place in peace, to the place predestined for thee by God, where thy God appointed thee to wait, without fear or trembling of God, and mayst thou be prepared for me whensoever I wilt call thee in eternity, without any impediment. Leave in the peace of God, in the name of the Father, and of the Son, and of the Holy Ghost. Amen."]

Tunc dicas super caput pueri, "In principio erat verbum, et verbum apud deum," etc., usque ad finem. [Then you should say over the head of the boy, "In the beginning was the word, and the word was with God[256]..." to the end.]

Finis huius operis. [The end of this operation.]

[*Spirits of the Arbatel,*[257] *and the Illnesses They May Treat*]

♄ Aratron, ♃ Thetor,[258] ♂ Phalec, ☉ Och, ♀ Hageth,[259] ☿ Ophiel, ☽ Phul

♄ *Aratron, angelus saturni. Adferat medicinam contra plethoram, pluritim, squina[n] tiam, phlegmonem, febrem, pestilentem, fluxum sanguinis, gonorheam; sputi abundantiam, et articulorum infermitatem.*

[♄ Aratron, angel of Saturn. He may bring forth medicine against plethora,[260] pleurisy, quinsy,[261] burning under the skin, fever, plague, bloody flux, gonorrhea, abundant spit, and weakness of the joints.]

---

256 *In the beginning...*: John, chapter 1.

257 *Arbatel*: Work of magical philosophy, dealing with seven planetary spirits, first published in Basel in 1575. Although some of these spirits are credited with the power of healing, these attributions to particular illnesses are not present. Peterson, *Arbatel—Concerning the Magic of the Ancients: Original Sourcebook of Angel Magic*.

258 *Thetor*: Arbatel has "Bethor."

259 *Hageth*: Arbatel has "Hagith."

260 *Plethora*: An overabundance of a particular humor, often blood.

261 *Quinsy*: Either an inflammation of the throat or peritonsillar abscess.

♃ *Thetor, angelus Iovis. Adfert medicinam contra sanguinis defectum et humorum putredinem, et cruditatem, et concoctionis debilitatem, lienteriam, diarrheam, pertisim, quartanam paralisum, podagram, et art[r]eticam passione, melancholiam, tristiam, spasmum convultione, cancrum, lepram.*

[♃ Thetor, angel of Jupiter. He brings forth medicine against defects of the blood and putrefaction of the humors, and indigestion, and weakness of digestion, lientery,[262] diarrhea, partisim,[263] quartan palsy, podagra[264] and arthritis with passion, melancholy, sadness, cramps with convulsions, cancer, leprosy.][265]

♂ *Phalec, angelus martis. Adferat medicinam contra pituitae abundantiam, somnelentiam, lethargiam, inertiam, gladulus, scrophulas oedomata, pusillanimitatem, surditatem, stuporem, et colicum, flatulentum.*

[♂ Phalec, angel of Mars. He may bring forth medicine against abundance of mucus, drowsiness, lethargy, laziness, tonsils, swelling of the glands, edemas, cowardice, deafness, numbness, colic, and flatulence.]

☉ *Och, angelus solis. Adfert medicinam contra hidropem, catharactas, rheuma occulorum, obscuritatem, epileptiam, animi delinquium, et fincopen.*

[☉ Och, angel of the sun. He brings medicine against dropsy, cataracts, rheum of the eyes, obscurity, epilepsy, failing of the spirit, and fincopen.][266]

♀ *Hageth, angelus veneris. Adfert medicinam, contra febrem tertiatem, ardentem ecticam, phrenitim, icteritiam, capitis dolorem, ventriculi, et intestinorum, clatus ex bilis, acrimonia, ericipelas, et generandi impotentiam.*

[♀ Hageth, angel of Venus. He brings medicine against the tertian fever, burning hectic [fever],[267] insanity, jaundice, pain of the head, the stomach, and the intestines, clatus[268] from bile, indigestion, erysipelas, and sexual impotence.]

---

262 *Lientery*: A type of diarrhea in which undigested food passes through the digestive tract.

263 *Partisim*: Possibly *pertisicus*, or consumption.

264 *Podagra*: Gout.

265 *Leprosy*: Could also be psoriasis.

266 *Fineopen*: Likely *sincopen*, or fainting fit.

267 *Hectic* [fever]: Fever in which the skin is hot and dry, and the cheeks are flushed.

268 *Clatus*: Possibly *clavus*, a callus, tumor, or wart.

☿ *Ophiel, angelus mercurii. Adfert medicinam contra spirandi impedimenta, rancedi-nem tussim, dolorem pectoris et pulmonem, fistulas, ulcera maligna, renum obstructio-nes.*

[☿ Ophiel, angel of Mercury. He bears medicine against impediment of breathing, rancid cough, pain of the chest and lungs, fistulas, malignant ulcers, blockages of the kidneys.]

☽ *Phul, angelus luna. Adfert medicinam contra morbos quos sicca intemperies causavit, ut vigiliam, sitim immodicam, corporis squalorem et iactationem nimiam, tardam, alui deiectionem, et dificiles nicturarum nervorum que motus.*

[☽ Phul, angel of the moon. He brings medicine against illnesses that dry self-indulgence causes, thus sleeplessness, excessive thirst, filthiness of the body, and excessive restlessness, sluggishness, purging of the bowels, and difficulties with nervous blinking.]

[29r]

For Spirits of the Water to Get Treasure out of the Sea

Make thy circle, that is called Cirqulus Aquatiens, in the hour of ☽ and in her day, and enter thy circle with all thy instruments, and be clean in mind and apparel, and say till they come this conjuration following:

"I conjure you, spirits Agariel, Azabal, and Elerotel, and all other that be your sub-jects, by the vanquisher of hell, Jesus Christ, and by his Father and the Holy Ghost, by the glorious Virgin Mary, by the prophecies of St. John Baptist, by the tables of Moses, by the virtue of Saint Michael the Archangel which did drive you out of heaven, by the glorious martyr Saint Cyprian, under whose commandments you were, and by the wise Solomon whom you did obey, by the dreadful day of doom, by the five wounds of our Lord Jesus Christ, by his annunciation, by his nativity and circumcision, by his preaching and by his death and passion, by his glorious resurrection and ascension, and by the coming of the Holy Ghost, by the glorious apostles, by all their virtue, by the sorrows of the Blessed Virgin Mary, which she suffered for her son Jesus Christ our Lord, by her five joys, by her assumption and coronation, and especially I conjure you by that excellent and ineffable and dread-ful name of God which is of infinite virtue, Tetragrammaton, graven in my ring and imperial scepter, that by these virtues, and by the virtue of that holy and reverent name of God, you come speedily to me, without any horrible noise, lightnings, or thunderings, and so coming that you obey my commandments with effect, and by the virtue of that name, which you know of what power, virtue, and might it is, and how it is adored in heaven, earth, and hell, and by the virtues of the Father almighty, and of his blessed Son and of the Holy Ghost, which liveth and reigneth, three persons and one God, world without end. Amen.

"Also I adjure you, devils aforesaid, by all angels, archangels, thrones, dominations, and powers, and by all the virtues of heaven, and by all the miracles of our Lord Jesus Christ, by his casting of of [sic] devils out of men, by his scourging and precious bloodshedding, and by all the terrible things in heaven and earth, and by all your good angels, Emalechim, Amazenten, and Perticentiall. Also I conjure you and adjure you, by the voice of him which was crucified, which is greatest of all, and by his holy name Tetragrammaton, which is a name horrible and terrible to devils but amiable to Christians, that immediately you do appear visibly to us without delay, and answer us truly to all things which shall be

[29v]

demanded of you, and obey our commandments, and fulfill our will, without any dissimulation, deceit, fraud, or guile, by the virtue of Jesus Christ our Lord, who liveth and reigneth with the Father, and the Holy Ghost, world without end. Amen."

Which conjuration being said, if thy fellow see nothing towards the north or south, say the conjuration again till they come. Then shall the spirits come in the likeness of half griffons and half fishes, some having swords, and among them you shall see one having a fair virgin's face, bending her head and looking in a glass. Then conjure her,[269] for the other will not speak; neither will she till you have fumigated her. Then thurify[270] her with pure olibans[271] and mastic, and incense them, and shew them the scepter, lamin, and characters of the moon, and they will obey thee. Then say this one conjuration to the spirit, in this sort following:

"I conjure thee, Ephradyn, or Elphedus, you wise and fair spirit, by the infinite power of God, by the lamentation of the Blessed Virgin Mary, by the holy apostles,

269 *Her*: An unusual change in gender within the same ritual.
270 *Thurify*: Burn incense over.
271 *Olibans*: Frankincense.

Peter and Paul, and by all other apostles, prophets, martyrs, virgins, confessors, and patriarchs, and by the dreadful day of doom, by the ineffable power of God, and by the fiery sword of the cherubims, by the name of God, Agla, and by the ineffable name of God, Tetragrammaton, graven in my ring and scepter, and by the blood-shedding of our Lord Jesus Christ, that you bring me the riches that is lost, hid, or drowned in the sea or other water, to the sum or value of 6000 £, and that you or one of thy subjects bring it to me without any delay, fraud or guile, or any bodily harm of us or of any other creature of God, by the virtue of him which holdeth the scepter of glory, and liveth and reigneth God, world without end. Amen."

Which conjuration being said, he will send a spirit which will fetch it, and when he bringeth it, you must thurify him with incense, and the prince that sent him and commanded him, instead of sacrifice, and then license him to depart in peace, et cetera, and tarry one hour in the circle, as in all other operations. Then come out, and eat, and observe the rules.

[30r]

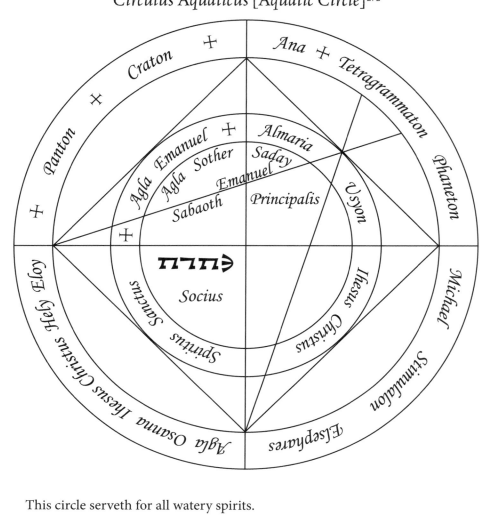

This circle serveth for all watery spirits.

272 Text in circle, outer ring: Ana + Tetragramaton Phaneton Michael Stimulalon Elsephares Agla
  Osanna Ihesus Christus Hely Eloy + Panton + Craton +.
    Inner ring: Almaria Usyon Ihesus Christus Spiritus Sanctus + Agla Emanuel +.
    Inside circle: Agla Sother Saday / Emanuel / Sabaoth / *Principalis* [Principal] / [Hebrew
  letters] / *Socius* [Associate].

For to Excommunicate Spirits that Will Not Appear

"O you obstinate and rebelling spirits that will not appear, being often and lawfully called and acited to appear here before us at this circle, and as yet you would not come nor appear, in the great contempt of our Lord Jesus Christ and yours, which hath created both us and you, and for that cause, I, by the authority of the same Lord Jesus Christ, in that be halfe [he hast?] committed and given unto me, for your disobedience and contempt, I do, and will do unto you, as much as the law of God shall extend, written in the scriptures, and shall bear us in, insomuch that ye shall be excommunicate, accursed, execrated, and deprived from all your places, your offices, and degrees, and cast down into the extreme pains of eternal fire and brimstone, there to abide, suffer, and burn, until such time as you be obedient to my precepts, at all times and hours, and to fulfill all my desires. And now by God's divine license, and by the same authority

[30v]

of our Lord Jesus Christ, I do ratify, approve, affirm, and confirm all these aforesaid pains to increase and burn, so that you never have rest, liberty, nor hope of release and forgiveness in the day of judgment, nor until the day of judgment, but that your pains shall grow and multiply upon you, from day to day, from hour to hour, from time to time, from evil to worse, from pain to pain, and in the same there evermore to continue, and from the face of God for evermore to be expulsed. Heaven and earth and all creatures that are contained in them, excommunicate you, and the holy names of God, which you well know to be of great virtue, excommunicate you. The twenty-four elders excommunicate you. The seven names of God, which are not to be named, excommunicate you. Almighty God with his great power excommunicate you and cast you into hell, into the hottest pit of fire and brimstone. Here is eternal pain which cannot be suffered nor endured, until such time as thou or you come to me, and be obedient unto me, and fulfill all my will and desire presently, perfectly, and truly."

Then here thou shalt tell thy desire what you wouldst have.

"Provided always that, so far forth as you shall appear at my citing and commandment, before me and my fellows, visibly and quietly at my next calling, as I or we shall command you to do, under the pain and excommunication and condemnation aforesaid, that then this excommunication to stand void and of none effect, and if you do not, then to stand in full strength, power, and authority. So be it. Amen."

[The Eight Princes of Darkness, and Three More]

There art **eight** princes of darkness which lie always bound in hell, unto whom all spirits are obedient, which are these: Lucifer, Belzabub, Sabwell, Mirabam, Agyron, Gentuball, Quatuball, and Critaron. These lie bound in hell, with fiery chains, until the day of judgment.

Sathan is prince of the air, Bell is prince of the earth, and Nathan is prince of the water.

[The Reigning of the Planets]

If you will practise any experiment, you must mark the reigning of the planets, for therein is great effect as hereafter followeth:

♄ Saturn for strife and debate, and treasure in the ground.

♃ Jupiter for honour, riches, and treasure, love and favour.

♂ Mars for wars and weapons.

☉ Sol for friendship and treasure and love, and for theft.

♀ Venus for love, and favour of women.

☿ Mercury, for arts and liberal sciences, and wisdom.

☽ Luna, for grace, favour, and riches.

And if you keep these rules, it shall further you much the better.

[31r]

Experimentum de Tribus Boni Angeli
[Experiment of the Three Good Angels][273]

In primis accipe berallum vel christallum, et depone super scabellum, et stet puer parte ad etatem 7 annorum, et dicas, "In nomine patris, et filii, et spiritus sancti, amen," Pater Noster, Ave, et Credo, et 9 et istis quatuor psalmos, "Miserere mei deus," "Deus in nomine tuo," "Deus misereatur nostri," et "Laudate dominum in sanctis," etc. Tunc facias crucem + in fronte pueri, dicens, "In nomine patris, et filii, et spiritus sancti. Amen."

[At first receive a beryl or crystal, and set it over a low stool, and thou mayst stand a boy under the age of seven years, and thou mayst say, "In the name of the Father, of the Son, and of the Holy Ghost, Amen," an Our Father, an Ave, and a Creed, and a Confiteur and these four psalms: "Have mercy on me, God," "God, in thy name," "God, have mercy on us," and "Praise the Lord in holy places."[274] Then thou shouldst make the cross + in front of the boy, saying, "In the name of the Father, and of the Son, and of the Holy Ghost. Amen."]

"Domine Jesu Christe, rex glorie, mitte mihi tres bonos angelos,[275] ex parte dextera tua, qui dicant mihi veritatem, sine falsitate vel fallacitate, de omnibus rebus quibus interogavero. Domine Jesu Christe, rex glorie, creator celi et terre, mitte mihi tres angelos bonos, palam comparientes in isto christallo sivi berallo. Domine Jesu Christe, qui conceptus est de spiritu sancto, quique venturus est iudicare vivos et mortuos, sicut es tu deus et homo, natus ex Maria virgine, mitte mihi tres Aangelos [sic] bonos comparientes ad visum istius pueri per ista nomina dei, Eloy, Sabaoth, Tetragrammaton, Alpha et Omega, principium et finis. Expediatis vos per gloriosam sanctam Mariam, matrem domini nostri Jesu christi, et per novem ordines angelorum, cherubin et seraphin, thronos et dominationes, et per virtutem angelicum Michael, Gabriel, Raphael, et Urielem, qui sunt ante thronum domini nostri Jesu Christi, dicentes, 'Sanctus, sanctus, sanctus, dominus deus Sabaoth, qui est, qui erat, et qui venturus est iudicare mundum,' et per omnia reliqua que sunt in celo et in terra, et per lac quod dominus noster Jesus Christus lactavit de mamillis beate Marie virginis, quando ille puer erat in mundo, et per vestem cocciniam, et per unguentum quod sancta Maria Magdalena unxit pedes Jesu, quod compariatis in isto christallo ad visum istius pueri."

273 For a close parallel, see *Oberon*, 529–33.
     Margin: A little stool.

274 Psalms 50, 53, 66, and 150.

275 Note the similarity to an incantation supposedly copied from a manuscript of Dee's: "Per virtutem illorum qui invocant nomen tuum, Hermeli—mitte nobis tres Angelos, &c." (Lilly, *William Lilly's History of His Life and Times from the Year 1602 to 1681*, 222).

["Lord Jesus Christ, king of glory, send to me three good angels, out of thy right division, who may tell the truth to me, without falsehood or deceit, of all matters that I will ask. Lord Jesus Christ, king of glory, creator of heaven and earth, send to me three good angels, appearing openly in that crystal or beryl. Lord Jesus Christ, who was conceived by the Holy Ghost, and who will come to judge the living and the dead, just as thou thyself are God and man, born from the Virgin Mary, send me three good angels appearing to the sight of this boy by those names of God, Eloy, Sabaoth, Tetragrammaton, Alpha et Omega, the first and the last. Thou mayst dispatch thyselves by the glorious holy Mary, mother of our Lord Jesus Christ, and by the nine orders of angels, cherubim and seraphim, thrones and dominions,[276] and by the virtue of the angelic Michael, Gabriel, Raphael, and Uriel, who are before the throne of our Lord Jesus Christ, saying, 'Holy, holy, holy, Lord God Sabaoth, who is, who was, and who will come to judge the universe,' and by all the relics that are in heaven and in earth, and by the milk that our Lord Jesus Christ gave suck from the breasts of the Blessed Virgin Mary, when that boy was in the world, and by his red garment, and by the unguent that holy Mary Magdalene anointed his feet, that thou mayst appear in that crystal to the sight of that boy."]

Tunc pete a puero si videat aliquam conparientem. Si non, tunc dicas orationes iterum. Si videat, dicas ad primum angelum: [Then ask the boy if he may see anything appearing. If not, then thou sayest the prayers again. If he sees, thou mayest say to the first angel:]

"O angele dei, bene venisti in nomine patris, et filii, et spiritus sancti, et per interiorem quam deus habebat in mente quando deposuit Luciferum de celo in putrum inferni, et elegit vos, valentissimis angelis. [O angel of God, you came well in the name of the Father, and of the Son, and of the Holy Ghost, and by the secret ones that God was holding in his mind when he deposited Lucifer from heaven into the well of hell, and he chose thee from the most strong angels.]"

Dicas ad secundum angelum: [You should say to the second angel:]

"O angele dei, bene vinisti in nomine patris, et filii, et spiritus sancti, et per virtutem sancti Johannis baptisti, et per caput eius, per virginitatem beate Marie. [O angel of God, thou camest well in the name of the Father, and of the Son, and of the Holy Ghost, and by the virtue of the holy John the Baptist, and by his head, and by the virginity of the Blessed Mary.]"

---

276 *Nine orders…dominions:* The truncated list might indicate an omission.

Dicas ad tertium Angelum [you should say to the third angel]:

"*O angele dei, bene venisti in nomine patris, et filii, et spiritus sancti, et per reverentiam passionem domini nostri Jesu Christi,*

[31v]

et per reverentiam sacramenti altaris, quod dominus noster Jesus Christus fecit in cena sua discipulis suis [blank] dixit, 'Hoc est corpus meum.'"

["O angel of God, thou camest well in the name of the Father, and of the Son, and of the Holy Ghost, and by the awe and passion of our Lord Jesus Christ, and by the awe of the sacrament of his altar, that our Lord Jesus Christ made in his supper to his disciples when he said, 'This is my body.'"]

Et tunc dicas: [And then you should say:]

"*O vos, angeli dei, vos rogo per omnia principalia nomina dei que non sunt homini loqui, nisi in periculo mortis, et per omnia que in celo sunt et in terra, et per reverentiam passionis domini nostri Jesu Christi, et per sacramentum altaris, quod monstretis mihi veritatem, sine falacitate vel fallatia, de omnibus rebus petitis ac requisitis.*"

["O you, angels of God, I ask you by all the chief names of God that are not spoken by man, unless in danger of death, and by all things that are in heaven and on earth, and by the awe of the passion of our Lord Jesus Christ, and by the sacrament of the altar, that you should show the truth to me, without falsehood or deceit, of all things asked and sought."]

Tunc pete quid vis, quibus peractis, licentia eos descedere ut sequitur: [Then ask what thou desireth, and these matters having been accomplished, license them to descend as follows:]

"*Ite ad locum ubi dominus noster Jesus Christus vos ordinavit, et prompti estote et ordinate ad mandatum meum revenire. In nomine patris, et filii, et spiritus sancti. Amen.*"

["Go to the place where our Lord Jesus Christ appointed thee, and thou will be ready and ordained to return at my command. In the name of the Father, and of the Son, and of the Holy Spirit. Amen."]

Finis huius opusculi. [The end of this operation.]

Ad Cognoscendum si Aliquis Vexetur a Spiritibus Immundis [For the Purpose of Knowing if Any May Be Vexed by Unclean Spirits]

Scribe hec nomina sancta dei in carta benedicta ut sequitur, et pone illa super patientem ipso nescientem. [Write these holy names of God in blessed paper as follows, and put those over the suffering one without him or her knowing.]

"Coniuro te + carta, per verba illa, tituli triumphalis salvatoris, domini nostri Jesu Christ, et per omnia alia verba que dicuntur, de creature omnium creaturarum, et per illum qui potest tribuere et facere, quod tantam obtineas virtutem, ut omnia que super te scribentur ad effectum salutis eterne producere valeas, et ut omnis fallacia et virtus diaboli exeat de te, et intret in te omnis virtus predicta sine mora. In nomine pa + tris, et fi + lii, et spiritus + sancti, amen. In nomine pa + tris, et fi + lii, et spiritus + sancti + Amen. + Hel + Heloim + Sother + Emanuel + Sabaoth + Agla + Tetragrammaton + Agios + Otheos + Yskyros + Athanatos + Iehova + Adonay + Ya + Saday + Homousion + Messias + Esere + Heye + Increatus pater + Increatus filius + Increatus spiritus + sanctus + Jesus + Christus vincit + Christus regnat + Christus imperat + Si diabolus ligavit vel temptavit te suo effectu vel per sua opera, Christus, filius dei vivi, per suam misericordiam liberet te, N., ab omnibus spiritibus imundis, qui venit de celo et incarnatus est in utero beatissime virginis Marie, causa humane salutis, et eiiciendi diabolum et omnem malignum spiritum a te in profundum inferni et abissi. Ecce crucem + domini! Fugite, partes adverse. Vicit leo de tribu Iuda radix David."

["I conjure thee + paper by these words, signs of our triumphal savior, our Lord Jesus Christ, and by all other words that are said, of the creature of all creatures, and by that one who is able to give and to make, that thou mayst possess so much virtue, so that all things that will have been written above thee, thou mayst be able to produce for the outcome of lasting health, and so that it may cast out all deceit and strength of the devil from thee, and all virtue previously said may enter into thee without delay. In the name of the Fa + ther, and of the S + on, and the Holy + Ghost, Amen. In the name of the Fa + ther, and of the S + on, and the Holy + Ghost, Amen. + Hel + Heloim + Sother + Emanuel + Sabaoth + Agla + Tetragrammaton + Agios + Otheos + Yskyros + Athanatos + Iehova + Adonay + Ya + Saday + Homousion + Messias + Esere[277] + Heye + Unbegotten Father + Unbegotten Son

---

277 *Hel...Esere:* An incantation that has appeared in other contexts, including a treasure-hunting incantation from the *Pneumatologia Occulta et Vera,* which was later adopted into H. P. Lovecraft's short story "The Horror at Red Hook." Horst and Kempf, *Zauber-Bibliothek,* vol. 2, 90; Lovecraft, *The Dreams in the Witch House and Other Weird Stories,* 128.

+ Unbegotten Holy + Ghost + Jesus + Christ conquers + Christ reigns + Christ commands + If the devil bound or tested thee with his accomplishment or by his work, let Christ, the Son of the living God, free thee by his mercy from all unclean spirits, who came from heaven and was made flesh in the womb of the Blessed Virgin Mary, for the purpose of human salvation, and ejecting the devil and all malign spirits from thee into the depths of hell and the abyss. Behold the cross + of the Lord. Flee, evil spirits! The lion of the tribe of Judah, root of David, has conquered."]

Aspergata aqua benedicta. [Sprinkled with holy water.]

[32r]

Serobattam: Experimentum Bonum per Amore vel Furto [*Serobattam: A Good Experiment for Love or Theft*]

Fac fieri [imaginem] de cera virginea, ad longitudine digiti medii, et scribe nomen tuum in posteriori parte capitis eius, et nomen eius N. in anteriori parte capitis, et istud triangulum in discrimine capitis △ 8, et istam figuram inter mammillas, viz.  ⊢ſ♄, et super umbilicum hanc ♄∀♈, et hanc super renes ℓℓℓℓ, et hanc super scapulas ✕, et super femur sinistrum ☿☿☿, et super femur dextrum hanc ⊄, et ponas imaginem tuam super tegulam ad ignem, et modice calefaciat, et tunc imaginem ♂ post diem ☉ et post tres noctes continue, et tertia nocte, sepelies imaginem in quadrivium, et dimittas ibi esse quousque veniat mulier sive vir ad te. Hoc erit infra 12 dies aut marietur infra 25 et dic hanc ♂ sequentem septies, qualibet nocte, super imaginem tuum super tegulam lapideam, temendo faciem eius versus aquilonem.

[Have made an image of virgin wax, to the length of your middle finger, and write thy name in the posterior part of its head, and this name N. in the anterior part of the head, and this triangle in the parting of the hair of the head △ 8, and this figure between the breasts, viz. ⊢ſ♄, and over the navel, this ♄∀♈, and this over the kidneys ℓℓℓℓ, and this over the shoulder blades ✕, and over the left femur, ☿☿☿, and over the right femur, this ⊄, and thou mayst place your image on a tile[278] to the fire, and thou mayst make it warm moderately, and then say the image conjuration after the day of the ☉, and after three nights continually, and on the

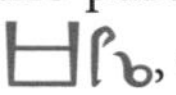

---

278 Tiles turn up in image magic spells elsewhere, but usually the image is drawn on the tile itself; see Braekman, *Magische experimenten*, 38–40; Fredericq, *Corpus Documentorum Inquisitionis Haereticae Pravitatis Neerladicae*, I:428–9; Gal et. al., *Vedrai Mirabilia*, 294..

third night, thou shalt bury the image at a crossroads, and thou mayst leave it there until the woman or man may come to thee. This will be under 12 days or he or she will be married[279] under 25, and say this conjuration following seven times, howsoever thou pleasest in the night, over thy image on the stone roof tile, holding the face of this one toward the north wind.]

"Coniuro vos septem, Serobadam, Eiotas, Beldon, Dulibion, Kulymzadell, Ladilibas, Beelbac, qui monstratis, virgilie, has septem figuras in hac [imagine] scriptas, ut sicut fecistis venire filiam per consuli Beliatam ad imperatorem Belemacke, per matrem Beliada, ita faciatis istam mulierum vel virum, sic nominat N., ad me venire, et ut ratione figurarum vestrarum in hac [imagine] scriptarum, sitis in societate eius, donec ardenter ad me venire faciatis, per eum qui venturus est iudicare vivos et mortuos, et seculum per ignem. Amen."

["I conjure you seven, Serobadam, Eiotas, Beldon, Dulibion, Kulymzadell, Ladilibas, Beelbac, that you, seven stars of the Pleiades, show these seven figures that have been written on this image, so that as you made to come the daughter by means of the counselor Beliata to the commander Belemacke, by the mother Beliada,[280] thus you may make that woman or man, (thus he names N.), to come to me, and thus by reason of your figures written in this image, you may be in this association, until passionately you may make them to come to me, by him who will come to judge the living and the dead, and the world by fire. Amen."]

Certum est et probatum multocies. [It is certain and proved many times.]

---

279 Latin *marietur* is assumed to be *maritetur*.

280 *Beliada*: A variant name of one of the sons of David (1 Chronicles 14:7). The story in question is unknown.

Pro Amore Mulieris
[For the Love of a Woman] [281]

Experimentum probatum ad constringendum mulierem in amore tuo
[Proven experiment for binding women in your love]

In the name of God, take a new tile stone on a Friday and in the hour of ♀, and draw thereon an image with a pencil of steel, of what woman thou wilt, and when thou drawest the picture say thus: "I, N., do make this image in the figure or similitude of N." And when thou hast said thus, then say, "*O divina ♀ splendida, lusidissima stellarum, amore plena me adiuva*. [O divine splendid ♀, most brilliant of the stars, full of love, help me]." And when thou hast finished the form and figure of her, then write in the head of the image her name and this name, viz., Asteroth, and in the breast this name Venus, and under her breasts, Draco and Dragenus, and upon the upper part of her belly, Braco, and on the other part, Lucidus. And write the pentacle of ☉ and other characters about on the names, as it appeareth in the image following,[282] and when you have done all this, then make a fire with coals, and hold the tile with the image in thy hand, and turn thy face towards the south, and say as followeth:

"*Omnipotens, sempiterne deus, qui in principio cuncta creasti celum et terram, et omnia que in eis sunt, qui Adam et Evam ad similitudinem tuam fecisti, eos in paradiso terrestri enodasti, et eos ne deligno.*"

["Omnipotent, everlasting God, who in the beginning created all things, heaven and earth, and all things that are in them, that made Adam and Eve in your likeness, thou didst free these in the terrestrial paradise, and I do not unbind[283] these."]

[32v]

281 In the margin appears the following:
    Periculum ("experiment," "proof," or "danger" might all be relevant here)
    Vite [probably "lives," but also "of/to/for live"]
    A pap
    A navel
    A shoulder blade
    A thigh
    A thigh
    A tile stone

282 *The image following*: Not present in this manuscript.

283 *Unbind*: Latin could also mean "bind."

For ye Ague

A	b	r	a	c	a	d	a	b	r	a
A	b	r	a	c	a	d	a	b	r	
A	b	r	a	c	a	d	a	b		
A	b	r	a	c	a	d	a			
A	b	r	a	c	a	d				
A	b	r	a	c	a					
A	b	r	a	c						
A	b	r	a							
A	b	r								
A	b									
A										

Ut ait Serenns Samoniens inter precepta medicinae, qui portatur hoc nomen, Abraca-
dabra, scriptum secundum hanc formam. Si aeger hinetritio laborans sive alia febri,
hanc schedam alligatam et a collo suspensam, gestaverit valere, illi contra adversam
valitudinem morbumque paulatim declinando transire.

[Thus Serenus Sammonicus affirms among the rules of medicine[284] that this name Abracadabra is carried, written according to this form. If one is suffering from the hemitritaean fever[285] or any fever, this sheet, bound up and suspended from the neck, may bear to have strength for that against ill states of health and disease, turning them away to pass by gradually.][286]

284 *Serenus Sammonicus*: Quintus Serenus Sammonicus (d. 212?), author of the *Liber Medicinalis*, which is the first appearance of the word Abracadabra; see Serenus Sammonicus, *Liber Medicinalis*, 48–49.

285 *Hemitritaean fever*: A fever that has one attack daily, and an additional one every other day.

286 This and the following section are taken from Agrippa von Nettesheim, *De Occulta Philosophia Libri Tres* (iii.31), 432.

[On the Holy Seal of Rabbi Hama, Part 1]

Sed multo efficacius contra omnes hominum adversas valitudines et quas-cunque alias molestias, tradidit Rabi Hama in libro speculationis sacrum signaculum, cuius in anteriore latere sunt quatuor quadrata dei nomina sibi in quadrato sic subalternata, ut a summo in imum, pariter alia quat-uor nomina sacratissima sive divinitatis [sigilla emergant, quorum inten-tio in circunferentiali circulo][287] *continentur inscripta, a tergo autem inscribitur nomen septiliterum Araritha et circunscribitur illi sua interpre-tatio. Hoc est versiculus a quo extractum est, quemadmodum hic depictum vides in altero latere huius follii sequentis.*

[But Rabbi Hama has handed down in his *Book of Speculations*[288] a holy sign, effi-cacious by far against all ill states of health of humans and whatsoever other trou-bles, on the front side of which are four four-lettered names of God in a square alternating thus, as from the highest to the lowest, likewise four other most sacred names or seals of divinity should emerge, the written meaning of which is con-tained in the circumferential circle; on the back, moreover, the seven-lettered name Araritha[289] is inscribed, and its own meaning is inscribed about. This is the short verse from which it was extracted, in the manner you see displayed here on the other side of the following page.]

---

287 This phrase omitted from the manuscript but present in Agrippa.

288 *Rabbi Hama…Speculations*: The *Book of Speculation*, or *Sefer ha-'Iyyun*, was a thirteenth-century work of Jewish mysticism, of a tradition separate from, but later incorporated into, Kabbalah. Rabbi Hama is a mythical figure. The only published version of this text does not have the passage specified above. See Dan and Kiener, *The Early Kabbalah*, 26–28, 45–48.

289 *Araritha*: "Ararita" is a seven-lettered name.

[Two Seals][290]

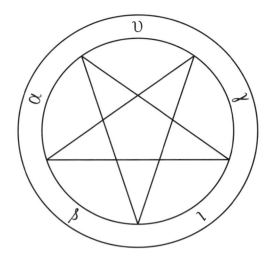

Hoc est signaculum Constantium qui crucem plerique appellabant, latinis litteris inscriptum, "In hoc vince." [This is the seal of Constantine, that very many called the cross, inscribed in Latin letters, "In this conquer."][291]

Alterum, revelatum Antiocho [cognomine] Soteris in figura pentagoni, qui sanitatem edicit (nam resolutum in literas edicit vocabulum ὑγίεια, id est 'SANITAS'). In quorum signorum fiducia et vertute uterque regum insignem contra hostes victoriam reportavit. [Another one, revealed to Antiochus Soteris in the figure of the pentangle, ordains health, for in the letters it ordains the revealed name, ὑγίεια, that is "health." In both trust and fidelty of these signs, he brought back a noted victory of these kings against their enemies.]

[33r]

---

290 Text, seal 1, outer ring: *In hoc vince* [in this conquer]. Seal 2, according to Agrippa, should have the Greek word υγιεια, or "health," but the version here is illegible.

291 This and the following section are taken from Agrippa von Nettesheim, *De Occulta Philosophia Libri Tres* (iii. 31), 495.

[On the Holy Seal of Rabbi Hama, Part 2]

Oportet hac omnia fieri in auro purissime [purissimo] aut in virginea membranarum [membrara]. Tanquam sincera munda et imaculata, etiam in ca[u]sto ad hoc formato ex fumo sacrati cerei vel incensi et aquam [aqua] sacrata atque hac ab actore purgato et expiato infalibili spe, et constanti fide ad deum altissimum mente elevati, si divinam hanc obtinere debeant ac prestare possint vertutem.

[It is proper in this that all things be made in most pure gold or in virgin parchment, just as pure, clean, and unstained, also, with regard to this composing, in ink made from smoke of holy wax tapers or incense and holy water, and with this, the actor cleansed and atoned, with elevated mind, infallible hope, and persistent faith in the most high God, if they would acquire and be able to warrant this divine strength.]²⁹²

Vide manum [see the hand]

Pars anterior, pars posterior [Anterior part, posterior part]²⁹³

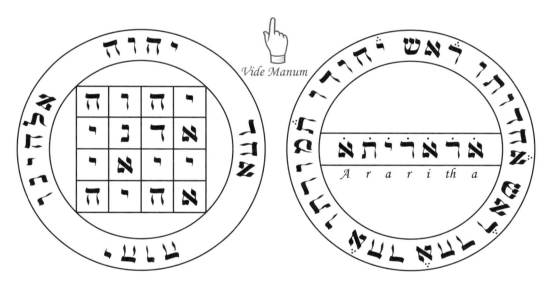

Vide Manum

Araritha

---

292 Agrippa von Nettesheim, (iii.11), 433.

293 We have chosen to draw these as they appear in the manuscript, with the third "Resh" corrected with a "Tau." For Hebrew originals, see Agrippa von Nettesheim, 433.

Hoc signum Iudas Machabeus portavit contra Antiocum Eupatorum quod accepit ab Angelo et significat, "Quis sicut tu in fortibus Tetragrammaton."

[This seal Judas Maccabeus received from an angel and carried against Antiochus Eupator.[294] It signifieth, "Who of you is as Tetragrammaton in strength?"][295]

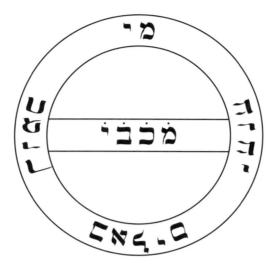

Simili modo hac duo signacula serviant contra terriculamenta et nocumenta malorum demonum atque hominum, et contra quacunque adeunda pericula sive armorum sive itinerum sive aquarum sive hostium, modo quo supera dictum est inscribunt hos caracteres ab uno latere בוווו *et hoc a tergo* צמרכה *qui sunt capite [capita] et fines primorum quicunque versum genistro, et toties [totius] mundanae creationis simbolum eaque ligaturam [ligatura] aiunt hominem modo firmissine speret in deum undersitatis conditorem, fore omnium malorum im munem.*

[In a similar measure, these two seals may be of use against terrors and harms of the evils of demons and of men, and against whatever assaulting dangers of weapons, journeys, waters, or of enemies, in the method it was said above, they inscribe these characters, that are the beginnings and ends of the first five verses of Genesis,

---

294 *Judas Maccabeus…Antiochus Eupator:* Judas Maccabeus was a second-century Jewish commander who fought Antiochus V Eupator.
295 Agrippa von Nettesheim, *De Occulta Philosophia Libri Tres* (iii.31), 496.

on one side וווב[296] and this on the back צמרכה, [297, 298] and the symbol of all mundane creation, and with this ligature, they assert, a man may but hope most strongly in God, the maker of the universe, not to be bound of all evils.][299]

 [300]

[33v]

296 Hebrew text: בוווו

297 Hebrew text: צמרכה

298 The last character here, counter Agrippa, should be a dalet. Jewish Publication Society, *Tanakh = JPS Hebrew-English Tanakh: The Traditional Hebrew Text and the New JPS Translation*, 1.

299 Agrippa von Nettesheim, *De Occulta Philosophia Libri Tres* (iii.11), 433. Corrections are from that text.

300 Text: *Pars posterior, pars anterior* [the posterior part, the anterior part].

301 See note 301 for details on this image.

302 This 3-page-long diagram includes a large number of iterations of the same words: El, Jesus, Tetragrammaton, and Yod-He-Vau-He.

PAGE 166, TOP ROW (ROTATE PAGE 90 DEGREES CLOCKWISE). First circle, ring: + Tetra + grama + ton + Elou + Icbona. Inside ring: Yod-He-Vau-He El. Inside star: Agla On. Second circle, ring: + Hel + Helyon + Adonay + Messias + Saday. Inside ring: Tetragramaton Agla. Inside star: Agios. Third circle, ring: + Tetra + gra + maton + Saba + oth + El. Inside ring: AlCao [?]. Inside star: Gartn. Fourth circle, ring: + Tetra + gra + maton + Elohim + Eheie + Sethen. Inside ring: Yod-He-Vau-He Saday. Inside star: Iehola.

PAGE 166, BOTTOM ROW. First circle, ring: + Tetra + gra + ma + ton + The + os. Inside ring: Zap Thetaos. Inside star: Ananita Ananita [corrected here to Ararita]. Second circle, ring: + Adonay + Sabaoth + Merah + Elohim + Agla. Inside ring: Yod-He-Vau-He He D. Inside star: Angelus El Cados. Third circle, ring: + *Deitas* + *Unitas* + *Maiestas* + *Eternitas* + *Trini* + *tas* [Deity + Unity + Majesty + Eternity + Trinity]. Inside ring: Tetragramaton Theos. Inside star: Heloa El. Fourth circle, ring: + Tetra + grama + ton + Eloy + Adonay. Inside ring: Yod-He-Vau-He D. Inside star: Saday.

PAGE 168, TOP ROW. First circle, ring: + Zad + kiel + Doim + Gibar + Gabu + rah. Inside ring: Yod-He-Vau-He Adonay. Inside star: Kyros Emanuel. Second circle, ring: + Malachim + Tetragra + maton + Sabaoth + Eloha. Inside ring: Tetragramaton On. Inside star: Agla El. Third circle, ring: + Lohim [Elohim?] + Saday + Iathai + Adonay + El + Bene. Inside ring: Yod-He-Vau-He Saday. Inside star: Heloym. Fourth circle, ring: + Agios + Otheos + Yskyros + Athanatos + Messyas. Inside ring: Tetragramaton Agla. Inside star: Solher [corrected here to Sother].

PAGE 168, BOTTOM ROW. First circle, ring: + Adonay + Heloym + Saday + Heloa + Hel. Inside ring: Tetragramaton El. Second circle, ring: + Tetra + grama + ton + Messyas + El + Sother. Inside ring: On Agla Agios Otheos Saday El. Third circle, ring: + Tetra + grama + ton + Alpha + et Omega. Inside ring: Jesus El On Agla Theos. Fourth circle, ring: *Ema + nuell + Vita + Veritas + Creator + Ysus* [Eman + nuell + Life + Truth + Creator + Jesus]. Inside ring: Yod-He-Vau-He El On.

PAGE 169, TOP ROW. First circle, ring: + Tetra + grama + ton + El + Sabaoth + Otheos. Inside ring: Tetragramaton. El. Agla. Inside star: Otheos. Second circle, ring: + Heloym + Atha + natos + Agla + Heloa. Inside ring: Yod-He-Vau-He Hel. Third circle, ring: + Messyas + Yskyros + Helyon + Heloa + Saday. Inside ring: Tetragramaton Cados. Fourth circle, ring: + Iophiel + El + Hesod + Ha + Malim + Ardim. Inside ring: Yod-He-Vau-He El On. Inside star: Mesias.

PAGE 169, BOTTOM ROW. First circle, ring: + On + Agios + Otheos + Via + Iehova + Agla. Inside ring: Tetragramaton El On. Second circle, ring: Gerehe + Ieel + Yskyros + Jesus + Helyon. Inside ring: Yod-He-Vau-He Agla. Third circle, ring: Atha + natos + Micha + El + Agla + Ya. Inside ring: On Emanuel Agla. Inside star: El El El El. Fourth circle, ring: + Adonay + Ema + nuel + Bara + driel + Sabaoth. Inside ring: Yod-He-Vau-He El. Inside star: Agla El El.

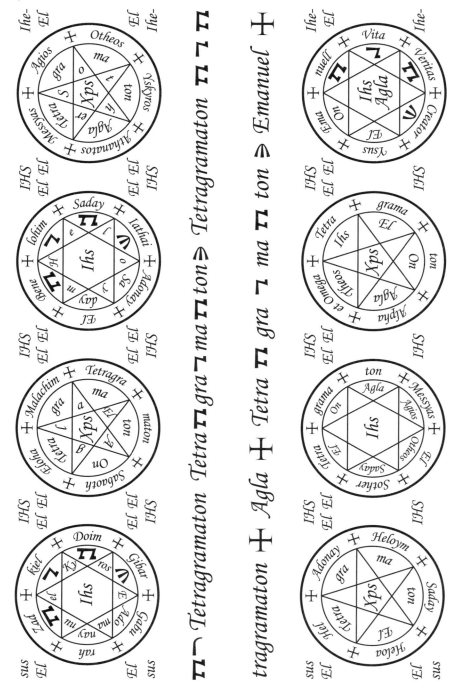

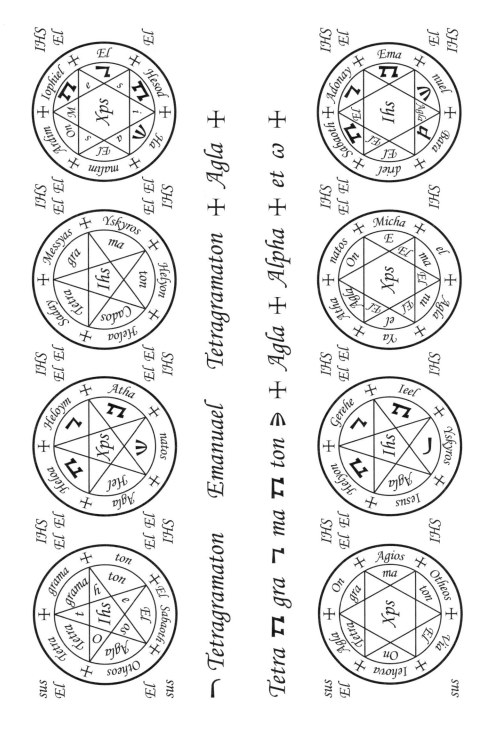

‿ Tetragramaton   Emanuael   Tetragramaton ✚ Agla ✚

Tetra П gra ꓶ ma П П ton ꓵ ✚ Agla ✚ Alpha ✚ et ω ✚

This must be written at the end of the circles before in a piece of parchment, and the circles must be set double as you see them with their names and characters.[303]

"Iehova, Adonay, Saday, On, Messias, Sother, Agla, Agios, Otheos, Unigenitus, Via, Vita, Sabaoth, Yskyros, Athanatos, Hel, Heloim, Manus, Homo, Usyon, Panton, Craton, Sapientia, Virtus, Alpha et Ω, Esereheye, Jesus, Ya, Heloa, Ananizapta, Cicomen, Cycomoy, Sadelay, Cycomos, Cados, El, Tetragrammaton, Hymas, principium, primogenitus, mediator, paraclytus, pater, filius, spiritus sanctus. Jesus Nazarenus, rex Judeorum, fili dei, miserere mei. Agnus dei, qui tollis peccata mundi, miserere nobis. + Ecce crucem domini. Vincit leo de tribu Iuda. Splendor, sol, gloria, lux, panis, angelus, sponsus, pastor, propheta, trinitas, deitas, unitas, bonitas atque maiestas, te adoramus atque invocamus, domine, nomen tuum, benedictus deus in eternum + Tetragrammaton. Amen."

["Iehova,[304] Adonay, Saday, On, Messias, Sother, Agla, Agios, Otheos, Unigenitus, Via, Vita, Sabaoth, Yskyros, Athanatos, Hel, Heloim, Manus, Homo, Usyon, Panton, Craton, Sapientia, Virtus, Alpha et Ω, Esereheye, Jesus, Ya, Heloa, Ananizapta, Cicomen, Cycomoy, Sadelay, Cycomos, Cados, El, Tetragrammaton, Hymas, Principium, Primogenitus, Mediator, Paraclytus, Pater, Filius, Spiritus Sanctus. Jesus of Nazareth, king of the Jews, son of God, have mercy on me. Lamb of God, who takes away the sins of the world, have mercy on us. + Behold the cross of the Lord. The lion of the tribe of Judah conquers. Splendor, sun, glory, light, bread, angel, bridegroom, pastor, prophet, Trinity, deity, unity, goodness, and majesty, we implore you and invoke you, Lord, your name, blessed God in eternity. + Tetragrammaton. Amen."]

303 This passage is sideways and lower on the page, but it seems to refer visually to the figures preceding.
304 This prayer appears with the same orientation as the text before, indicating it is part of the same operation.

Kill a lapwing on a Wednesday in the hour of Mercury, with a knife made of brass in the hour of Mercury, and let it bleed into a vessel of box made in the hour of Mercury, and beware you spill none of the blood beside the vessel, but keep it therein close covered, and set it in a secret place where no man cometh but thyself. Neither let any man see it, and you shall not look in it till it hath stand [stood] nine days. Then uncover it, and you shall see it full of worms, then cover it and let it stand another nine days, and there will be but one worm. Then bray[306] the meat of dates, almonds, figs, and walnut kernels, and make a paste thereof as round as a ball, and make a hole in the midst thereof and put in the worm, and cover the vessel from the air at all times, and let it stand another nine days. Then open it, and you shall find a chicken like a lapwing. Kill it and roast it with a fire of date stones and walnut shells, and keep the grease, and when you will work in any work of philosophy, anoint your face and eyes therewith, and you shall see spirits face to face what they do, and they shall seem unto you as they were men and your fellows, and you shall hear them and speak with them, and whatsoever you ask them, they shall answer you, and they shall hide none of their doings from you. Neither need you to doubt anything, for by this was the science first found out, and when you will no longer see them, wash your face with water secretly wherein swallows have been sodden.

Note that this experiment must be done on the Wednesday in the hour of Mercury.

[35v]

---

305 *Lapwing experiment*: See BL Sloane 1727, 18–19; Sloane 3846, 111r; Bodleian Ballard 66, 13–15; Cambridge Additional 3544, 56–57; *Oberon*, 366–369. Elsewhere this is a hoopoe, a bird that has long associations with unguents for the eyes; see Betz, *The Greek Magical Papyri in Translation, Including the Demotic Spells*, 237–238 (PDM xiv:805–40).

306 *Bray*: To crush into powder.

This is the Girdle Which Must Be Made in Parchment
a Yard and a ?[307] Long and Lined with Linen[308]

[36r]–[36v]

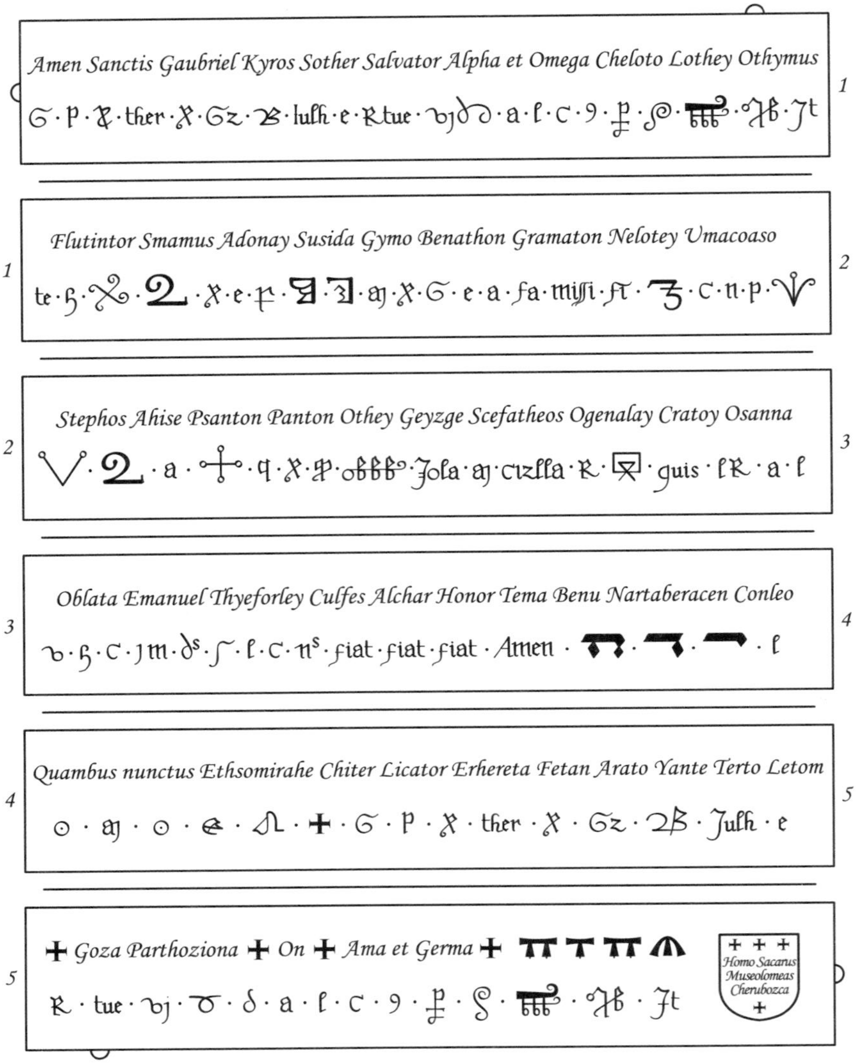

Amen Sanctis Gaubriel Kyros Sother Salvator Alpha et Omega Cheloto Lothey Othymus

1

G . P . ℞ . ther . ℞ . Gz . ℬ . luſh . e . ℞tue . ʋjⳟ . a . ℓ . c . 9 . ♃ . ℘ . ℬℬℬ . ℬ . Jt

1

Flutintor Smamus Adonay Susida Gymo Benathon Gramaton Nelotey Umacoaso

2

te . ₴ . ⚹ . 2 . ℞ . e . ꝑ . Ȝ . Ȝ . aj . ℞ . G . e . a . ſa . miſi . ſt . Ȝ . c . n . p . V

2

Stephos Ahise Psanton Panton Othey Geyzge Scefatheos Ogenalay Cratoy Osanna

3

V . 2 . a . ✝ . q . ℞ . ℞ . oℬℬℬ . Jola . aj . ciʒlla . ℞ . ⌧ . guis . ℓ℞ . a . ℓ

3

Oblata Emanuel Thyeforley Culfes Alchar Honor Tema Benu Nartaberacen Conleo

4

ⱱ . ₴ . c . Jm . ꝺˢ . ſ . ℓ . c . nˢ . fiat . fiat . fiat . Amen . ᴨᴨ . � . ᴨ . ℓ

4

Quambus nunctus Ethsomirahe Chiter Licator Erhereta Fetan Arato Yante Terto Letom

5

⊙ . aj . ⊙ . ⸎ . ℒ . ✝ . G . P . ℞ . ther . ℞ . Gz . ℬ . Juℓh . e

5

✝ *Goza Parthoziona* ✝ *On* ✝ *Ama et Germa* ✝ ᴨᴨ ᴛ ᴨᴨ ⌒

+ + +
Homo Sacarus
Museolomeas
Cherubozca
+

℞ . tue . ʋj . ꝺ . ꝺ . a . ℓ . c . 9 . ♃ . ℘ . ℬℬℬ . ℬ . Jt

---

307 Unknown character: Likely an unknown unit of measurement. See 69r below.

308 Text, line 1: C. Amen sanctis Gaubriel Kyros Sother Salvator Alpha et Ω Cheloto Lothey
Othymus. Line 2: 1. Flutintor Smamus Adonay Susida Gymo Benathon Gramaton Nelotey
Umacoaso 2. Line 3: 2. Stephos Ahise Psanton Panton Othey Geyzge Scefatheos Ogenalay
Cratoy Osanna 3. Line 4: 3. Oblata Emanuel Thyeforley Culfes Alchar Honor Tema Benu
Nartaberacen Conleo [characters] Fiat, fiat, fiat [characters] 4. Line 5: 4. Quambus nunctus
Ethsomirahe Chiter Licator Erhereta Fetan Arato Yante Terto Letom 5. Line 6: 5. + Goza
Parthoziona + On + Ama + et Germa +. Shield: Homo sacer / ramus2 so- / meas che / rubesca
(???). [The text in the illustration reflects that from Scot's *Discouerie of Witchcraft* (p. 415), from
which this is likely derived.]

[Seals of the Planets]

These must be made every one severally in lead, except Venus, which must be made in copper.[309]

[37r]

309 Other examples of planetary talismans usually stipulate that those for each planet be made out of a metal appropriate to the planet.

173

To Spoil a Thief or Witch or Any Other Enemy, and to Be Delivered from the Evil[310]

⊙ *Ante solis ortum* [before the rising of the sun],[311] "I gather the bough of this summer's growth, in the name of such a one N."

When you have gathered the wand, then cover the table and say. "+ *In nomine patris* + *et filii* + *et spiritus sancti* + *Amen* [+ in the name of the Father + and of the Son + and of the Holy Ghost + Amen]" thrice. And so striking upon the carpet, say as followeth: "Drocke, Myrocke,[312] Esenaroth + Betu + Baroch + Ass + Maaroth +," and then say, "Holy Trinity, punish him that hath wrought this mischief, and take it away by thy great justice Eson + Elyon + Emaris + Ales + Age +,"[313] and strike the carpet with the wand.

To Make a Witch Confess Her Evil Before You

Take a lambskin made in parchment, and make therein two images, one of a man and another of a woman, and make them on the Saturday morning at the sun rising, and use them in this manner. Take a bodkin or a nail, and look in what place you would have them hurt. In that place prick them, and do so twice or thrice a day, and the party that you shall use so shall never take rest nor sleep until she hath seen you and required pardon at your hands.

In pricking, say as hereafter followeth:

"I compel and constrain thee, thou wicked person or you wicked persons, which have committed and done this wicked and devilish act, by the true God, by the living God, and by the holy God, that thou nor you have no power to withstand or resist my calling, but with all haste and speed possible, without delay or tarrying, thou come unto me and confess thy naughty and wicked deeds, which thou hast

---

310 See also Weyer, *De Praestigiis Daemonum*, 524. For commentary on this rite and the two following, see Klaassen, "Three Early Modern Magic Rituals to Spoil Witches." For other examples of rites to strike at a distance, see Albertus Magnus, *Egyptian Secrets*, 19; Stehle, "Volkstümliche Feste, Sitten, und Gebräuche im Elsass, 1892," 181.

311 Some material is missing here, apparently pertaining to acquiring a wand of a summer's growth. Other manuscripts often mention a hazel wand of a year's growth, so this might be the intent here.

312 Weyer: "droch, myrroch."

313 Weyer: "+ eson elion + emaris ales ege."

done in the name of God. And also I conjure and constrain thee to come, by all the holy names of God, and especially by these Semurhamephoras[314] + Agla + Adonay + Anabona + Panton + Craton + Agyos + Eskyros + Athanatos + Messyas + Sother + Alpha + et Omega + Emanuel + Sabaoth + Unigenitus + Via + Vita + Homo + Usyon + Principia + Cormogenitus + Sapientia + Consolator + Adiuvator + primus et novissimus[315] + El + Elemay + On + Tetragrammaton + and by the holy name Jesus, at which name all things both in heaven, in earth, and also in hell do bow, and by the holy Virgin Mary, mother of our Lord Jesus Christ, and by St. John Baptist, which was the forerunner of our Lord Jesus Christ, and by the golden girdle which St. John saw girt about the loins of our lord, and by the two-edged sword that

[37v]

proceeded out of the mouth of God, and by all that God is able to do, and by all the powers in heaven, in earth, and under the earth. I adjure you by the seven planets and twelve signs, and by all that you be subject unto, and by all the names of angels, and especially of these: Michaell + Gabryell + Raphaell + Basquiel + Samael + Anael + Capuel + Carafax + Wiel + and by all things that God hath made, to the honour and glory of his name, that thou or you which have done this wicked and devilish deed have no power to resist nor withstand my calling, but without all delay or tarrying, to come speedily in all haste possible, in pain or under pain of eternal damnation, from worse pain to worse. In the name of the Father, the Son, and the Holy Ghost. Amen."

The Experiment of W. Bacon to Destroy Witches

William Bacon[316] the friar made a bond that all wicked persons should come before him and confess their evil deeds in the new of the moon. The moon being in airy signs,[317] on the Saturday in the hour of ♄, take a piece of parchment and write therein the picture and similitude of the man or of the woman suspected. In his forehead write the name of the person, and on his breast these characters ♒.ƒ.♄,

314 Likely Shemhamphorash.

315 *Panton...novissimus*: "All + Strength + Saint + Mighty + Undying + Messiah + Savior + Alpha + and Omega + Emanuel + Lord of Hosts + Only-Begotten + Way + Life + Man + Essence + First + Born of the Trunk (a reference to Isaiah 11:1?) + Wisdom + Comforter + Helper + first and newest."

316 *William Bacon*: A character to whom several ritual magic operations are attributed. He may be a figure inspired by Roger Bacon; see Harms, Clark, and Peterson, *The Book of Oberon*, 26.

317 *Airy signs*: Gemini, Libra, and Aquarius.

and then with a sharp bodkin all to beprick the picture in the head and breast, and read this conjuration following:

"I conjure thee or you N., witch or witches, by the living God, the true God, and the holy God, and by all the prophets and patriarchs, martyrs, confessors, and virgins, and by all the holy people which follow the laws of God, and by all angels and archangels, thrones, dominations, principates, powers, cherubim and seraphim, and by the four elements, fire, water, air, and earth, and the thirty thunderings and lightnings as Sem, Caph, Tan, Sade, Dalleth, etc., and by the seven planets, Saturn, Jupiter, Mars, Sol, Venus, Mercury, and Luna, and by all the powers pronounced before. I conjure you, witch or witches, wheresoever or whatsoever you be, that are within seven miles of this place, no rest to have, but pricking pains, sleeping and waking, until you do come with speed hither into this pool of water,[318] and therein to confess to me some part of your wicked and devilish deeds, which you have done to such a person N., by the virtue of the Holy Trinity. *Fiat, fiat, fiat.* Amen."

When he or she is come, give them counsel utterly to forsake such wickedness forever.

[38r]

This Prayer Is to Be Said Before Thou Dost Name the Great Name of God

"*Benedictus sis tu, domine, qui dedisti sapientiam timentibus te, quoniam nomen tuum sanctum in te est, et ante omnia, nomen tuum fuit, et per omnia secula seculorum durabit, et tibi serviunt omnes creaturae, teque omnes adorant, et super omnes potens es et tu adiutor omnium et omnia sufferens, per sanctitatem tui nominis, et per virtutem nominis, quod, coram te, nomine tu adivues me in isto opere, et compleas petitionem meam, et audias orationem meam et recipias, ut non redeam vacuus nec verecundus de presencia tua.*"

["Mayst thou be blessed, Lord, who gave wisdom with fears for you, because thy holy name is in thee, and before all things, thy name was, and forever and ever all will endure, and all creatures serve thee, all implore thee, and above all thou art powerful, and thou art the helper of all and supporting all things, by the holiness of

---

318 Not mentioned until this point. The goal may have been to scry the identities of the witches instead of having them appear physically.

thy name, and by the virtue of the name, that, face to face with thee, thou mayst help me in this work by thy name, and thou mayst complete my request, and thou mayst hear and receive my prayer, so that I may not return from thy presence worthless or shameful."]

And thou mayst stretch forth thy hand with the paper, in the which the name is written, and thou shalt cry out and say:

"*Oh Michaell de oriente, Gabriell de occidente, Raphaell, de meridies, et Asziell de septentrione. Ethamael superius, iuvate me in isto opere ut respectus sim et habeam petitionem meam.* [Oh Michaell from the east, Gabriell from the west, Raphaell from the south, and Asziell from the north. Ethamael the superior, aid me in this work, so that I might be respected and I may have my petition.] Amen. Amen."

And thou shalt hold the paper in thy hand when thou dost any work.[319]

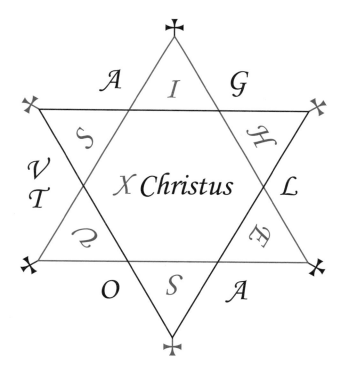

319 Outside star: Aglaotv. Inside star: Ihesus [Jesus]. Center: X Christus [Christ].

[An Experiment for Love]³²⁰

"Our lady loved her dear Son, and so I,³²¹ A. B., love thee, A. D.
So well may she love me, as Jesus did that died on tree,
All such pains may she smart, that may drill her to the heart.
Joy may she never have none, till all my will that she hath done,
By the virtue of Jesus Christ, by his death and his uprist,³²²
Neither eat, drink, rest, nor sleep, nor to herself take any keep,
But burn in love for my sake, and never any rest to take,
Till she incline and do my will, and thereto bind her both heaven and hell,
Elements each one, and moon and sun, angels, apostles, and martyrs many one,
Sea and sand and heavens clear, fast bind her and put her in fear,
I charge you all that this be done, by the high Tetragrammaton,
Who is of power and might most, the Father, the Son, and the Holy Ghost.

"Amen. Amen. Amen."

[38v]

An Invocation Experimental
An Experiment of the Secrets of Rome, Whereby the Romans Knew All Things Past, Present, and to Come, by a Spirit that Is Called Sathan³²³

It was invented by William Bacon, a gray friar,³²⁴ to call the spirit Satan and make him appear in a basin of water, and the master need not to have a child in this experiment. It may be done every day except holy days, but first be well assured thou be not polluted with deadly sin or lechery, but fast and pray, and work fasting, and be steadfast in faith, and have a fair chafer³²⁵ and a clean basin full of fair water, and with a fair sword or knife make a circle, and you must have four candles of

---

320 See Sloane 3846, 71r.

321 *I*: Klaassen reads this as "J," thus "J. A. B." I find this unlikely, given the rarity of middle names in the early seventeenth century.

322 *Uprist*: Resurrection.

323 For other versions, see *Oberon*, 351–55; Sloane 3851, 109v–111r.

324 *William Bacon, a gray friar*: See above for William Bacon. A gray friar is a member of the Franciscan Order.

325 *Chafer*: A vessel for heating water or an object. *Oberon* and Sloane 3851 have "chamber."

virgin wax, and write on every candle these names following: Moyses, Aaron, Iacob, Usion, Tetragrammaton, Meiretonem.[326]

And then fasten the candles on the brim of the basin, as thou shalt see the form hereafter. Then sit you in the midst of the circle, looking towards the south, putting the basin without the circle, and anoint and fumigate the basin with mastic and lignum aloes, and say, "*In principio erat verbum* [in the beginning was the word],"[327] even to the end, and then bless thyself with the sign of the cross, saying, "*In nomine patris + et filii + et spiritus sancti +* [in the name of the Father, and of the Son, and of the Holy Ghost], amen." And also say, "*Per hoc signum crusis* [by this sign of the cross],"[328] etc.

Then say this conjuration so loud that you mayst be heard:

"*Coniuro te, Sathan, per patrem et filium et spiritum sanctum, et per sanctam Mariam, matrem domini nostri Jesu Christi, et per omnes sanctos appostolos dei, et per omnes virgines et viduas dei, et per faciem dei, et per caput dei, et per coronam dei, et per nasum dei, et per dentes dei, et per occulos dei, et per linguam dei, et per brachia dei, et per ungues dei, et per polices dei, et per venas dei, et per tibias dei, et per plantas dei, et per quinque vulnera dei, et per omnia tormenta dei, et per passionem dei, et per nativitatem dei, et per merita dei, et per mortem dei, et per crusem dei, et per diem iudicii in que omnes creature christiane et humane erit in statu triginta annorum, et per quatuor animalia ante thronum dei, sedentia, habentia occulos ante et retro, et per omnium sanctorum eius, et per sapientiam Salamonis. Coniuro te, Satan, per virtutem horum omnium predictorum ut statim venias et appareas mihi in hac pelve in pulcra forma albimonechi trium annorum et integram veritatem illius rei dicens de quinque re examinabo te, sine aliqua falcitate vel fallacia.*"

["I conjure thee, Sathan, by the Father, and the Son, and the Holy Ghost, and by holy Mary, mother of our Lord Jesus Christ, and by all holy apostles of God, and by all virgins and widows of God, and by the face of God, and by the head of God, and by the crown of God and by the nose of God, and by the teeth of God, and by the

---

326 *Moyses…Meiretonem*: *Oberon* has "Moyses Aaron Iacobe Usion Tetragramaton + mei Ratoim." Sloane 3851 has "+ Moses + Aaron + Jacob + Usion + Tetragrammaton + Moriaton."

327 John Chapter 1.

328 *Per hoc signum crusis*: From *Oberon*: "*Per crucis hoc signum fugiat procull omne malignum et per idem signum salvetur quodque benignum et per signum sancta crucis de inimicis nostris libera nos deus noster* [By this sign of the cross, may all evil flee away, by the same sign may all good be preserved, and by the sign of this holy cross deliver us from our enemies, O our God]."

eyes of God, and by the tongue of God, and by the forearms of God, and by the nails of God, and by the thumbs of God, and by the veins of God, and by the shins of God, and by the soles of God, and by the five wounds of God, and by all the torments of God, and by the passion of God, and by the nativity of God, and by the merits of God, and by the death of God, and by the cross of God, and by the day of judgment in which all Christian and human creatures will be in the condition of thirty years,[329] and by four animals before the throne of God, sitting, having eyes before and behind, and by all his saints, and by the wisdom of Solomon. I conjure thee, Satan, by the virtue of all these things said before so that thou mayst come immediately and may appear to me in this basin in a beautiful form of a white monk of three years[330] and saying the complete truth of those things, regarding five matters[331] I will question thee, without any falsehood or deceit."]

Then put out the candle standing on that part before thee, and fumigate as you did before, saying, "*In principio erat verbum* [in the beginning was the word]", to the end. Then turn thee with the basin towards the west and fumigate as you did before, and say, "*In principio erat verbum,*" to the end, and bless thyself with the sign of the + saying, "*In nomine + patris + et filii + et spiritus sancti +* [in the name of the Father, and of the Son, and of the Holy Spirit]," amen. And also say, "*Per hoc signum crucis* [by this sign of the cross]," etc.

Then say, "*Coniuro te Sathan per ista nomina dei, Arsecret, Feodem, Tebden, Fonsegor vel Forseger, Feasilet, Fadesse, Effale, Gannia vel Gonca, Garamysi, Northa, Morarum, Imoboum, Magon, Abba, Azaray, Adonay, Sabaoth, Messias, Sother, Sabaara, Agla, Sponsus, Ysus ac Mediator, et per sancta corpora sanctorum mortuorum, et per sigillum dei vivi. Coniuro te, Sathan, ut nitres in istud vas, in forma*

[39r]

albi monachi trium annorum, et dicas et demonstres mihi veritatem, de omnibus meis questionibus sine fraude, et fallatia, et dolo."

329 *By the day of judgment…thirty years*: According to a theological tradition beginning with St. Augustine, any person who died would rise on the last day appearing to be thirty years old. Bynum, *The Resurrection of the Body in Western Christianity, 200–1336*, 98, 122–26, 139, 152, 263.

330 *White monk of three years*: Most likely two typical demands for spirit appearance, a white monk and a boy of three years, collapsed together. The phrase "white monk" was often used to refer to a member of the Cistercian Order.

331 *Five matters*: A better fit might be "quacumque re," or "whatsoever matter."

["I conjure thee, Sathan, by these names of God, Arsecret, Feodem, Tebden, Fonsegor or Forseger, Feasilet, Fadesse, Effale, Gannia or Gonca, Garamysi, Northa, Morarum, Imoboum,[332] Magon, Abba, Azaray, Adonay, Sabaoth, Messias, Sother, Sabaara, Agla, Sponsus, Ysus, and Mediator,[333] and by the holy bodies of all dead saints, and by the seal of the living God. I conjure thee, Sathan, so that thou mayst appear[334] in that vessel, in the form of a white monk of three years, and thou mayst speak and mayst show the truth to me of all my questions, without fraud or deceit or guile."]

Then put out the candle that standeth on that part, and turn thee towards the north with the basin, fumigating as you did before, saying, "*In principio erat verbum*," to the end, and bless thee with the sign of the + , saying, "*In nomine patris + et filii + et spiritus sancti + Amen.*" Then say:

"*Coniuro te, Sathan, per virgam Moysi, et per tabulam Moysi, et per nomen canderias vel venderias gelostium, et per tres principium figura, et per Danielem prophetam, et per sanctum Petrum et Paulum, et per ista nomina dei, Agla, Aglay, Aura, Mandranatha, Matha, Moneray, Morariew, Monboum, Nayry vel Nayay, Mathaliza, Matratha, et per clavas Christi crucifixus, et per orientem, meridiem, occidentem, et borialem, et per septem planetas, et per quatuor elementa, viz. ignem, aierem, aquam, et terram, et per duodecim signa firmamenta. Coniuro te, ut sine aliqua fallacia dicas mihi veritatem, non fringendo, non mentiendo. Amen.*"

["I conjure you, Sathan, by the rod of Moses, and by the tablet of Moses, and by the nine celestial[335] canderias or venderias,[336] and by the three principal figures, and by Daniel the prophet, and by the saints Peter and Paul and by these names of God, Agla, Aglay, Aura, Mandranatha, Matha, Moneray, Morariew, Monboum, Nayry or

---

332 *Morarum, Imoboum*: Might also be "Morarun, Imoboun."

333 *Arsecret...Mediator*: *Oberon* has "Arceret, Feodem, Funcigor, Fea, Filet, Gonca, Gara, Masi, Mortha, Morarie, Mobonum, Magon, Alba, Azaray, Abba, Adonay, Sabaoth, Messias, Sother, Saba, Agla, Sponsus, Isus Acme." Sloane 3851 has "Focnertu + Forden + Feon + Fugorifedus + Folo + Diry + Fumel + Mebon + Magon + Mesias + Alrararay + Adonay + Sabaoth + Sother + Sabu + Sponsus."

334 *You may appear*: Latin "nitres"; *Oberon* "aparias."

335 *Celestial*: Latin "gelostium" is unclear; *Oberon* has "celestiam," which is substituted here.

336 *Canderias or venderias*: Likely candarias, a term usually meaning "candlesticks," but used in magical manuscripts occasionally to signify a magical diagram. Grévin and Véronèse, "Les 'Caractères' Magiques au Moyen Âge (XIIe–XIVe Siècle)," 328–30. This may be a reference to the treatise *De novem candariis*, an edition of which is forthcoming from the Società Internazionale per lo Studio del Medioevo Latino. *Oberon* has "candelaria," or "candles." Sloane 3851 has "candles."

Nayay, Mathaliza, Matratha,[337] and by the keys[338] of Christ crucified, and by the east, south, west, and north, and by the seven planets, and by the four elements, that is, fire, air, water, and earth, and by the twelve signs of the firmaments. I conjure you, and without any deceit you should say the truth to me, without infringing, without lying. Amen."]

Then put out the third candle and turn thee towards the orient, with the basin fumigated as before, and say, "*In principio erat verbum*" to the end, and bless thee with the sign of the +, saying, "*In nomine patris + et filii + et spiritus sancti + Amen.*" Then say:

"Coniuro te, Sathan, per vincula salamonis, et per sigillum Virgilii, et per sigillum Willelm Bacon, et reverendi dicitur, et per sanctum Michaelem, et per illum sanctam salutationem quem sanctus Gabriell salutavit sanctam Mariam, dicens, 'Ave maria, gratia plena dominus tecum,' et per omnia bona que possunt esse in celo et in terra, et per omnis celos, et per omnia que in eis continentur, et per librum vite, et per passionem sanctam quam deus misit in cruce, mittens spiritum et illa sancta verba que dicebat in cruce pendeus, dicendo, 'Consummatum est,' et per omnia alia sancta verba quae possunt fari et que sunt ineffabilia. Coniuro te, Sathan, ut appareas mihi in forma pulcra albi monachi sine fallacia, velle meam perficiendo. Amen. Et si tu nolueris precepta mea facere, ut proficere desoluo te ab omni officio tuo, et pone te in abissum aquarum, usque ad diem iudicii. Fiat, fiat, fiat. Amen."

["I conjure thee, Sathan, by the bonds of Solomon, and by the seal of Virgil, and by the seal of William Bacon, and it is said they must fear,[339] and by Saint Michael, and by that holy salutation that Saint Gabriel hailed holy Mary, saying, 'Hail Mary, full of grace, the Lord is with thee,' and by all good things that are able to exist in the heaven and in the earth, and by all heavens, and by all things that are contained in them, and by the book of life, and by the holy passion[340] that God sent on the cross, sending the spirit and these holy words that he was saying, hanging on the cross, saying, 'It is finished,' and by all other holy words that are able to be said and that are ineffable. I conjure thee, Satan, so that thou mayst appear to me in the beautiful

---

337 *Agla…Matratha: Oberon*: "Agla + Marra + Mandra + Natha + Matha + Morarimionbon + Moncray + Nazay + Nazay + Matray + Mataliza." Sloane 3851: "Agla + Aglay + Axay + Mare + Mandra + Mory + Motion + Motcory + Matary + Matulia + Nata + Nazary."

338 *Keys: Oberon* has "clavos," or "nails."

339 *And…fear: Oberon* has "et Ramundi desitur catenalentis," the meaning of which is unclear. Sloane 3851 has "by the Seale of Raimond which is called Chath Malentes."

340 *Holy passion: Oberon* has "Spiritum Sanctum," or "Holy Ghost."

form of a white monk without falsehood, completing my will. Amen. And if thou dost not wish to perform my commands, thus I seek to effect[341] thee out of all thy offices and place thee into the abyss of waters, even to the day of judgment. Let it be done, let it be done, let it be done. Amen."]

Then the spirit will appear in the manner aforesaid and tell the truth, and when he hath fulfilled thy desire, then license him to depart, *cum licenciali probatum est* [with license, it is proven].[342]

341 *Seek to effect*: Latin "proficere desoluo" unclear. *Oberon* has "dissolvo," or "I strip." Sloane 3851: "I loose thee…discharge."

342 Text inside basin: *Spiritus* [Spirit].

The basin of water for the spirit to appear in:

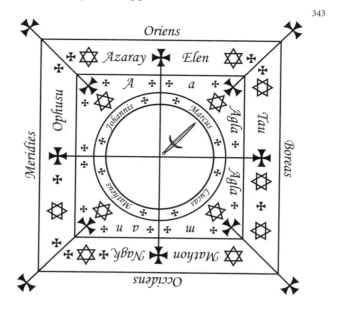

[39v]

Pro Thesauro Abscondito [For Hidden Treasure]

Make your circle with four sticks of plene tree[344] across about the treasure, and then go about it and say, "*In nomine patris + et filii + et spiritus sancti +* [in the name of the Father, and the Son, and the Holy Spirit]. Amen." Then say,

"*Parce dominem, parce famulis tuis, quos redimere digneres cum pretoise sanguine tuo, ne in eternum pasceris nos, pater de celis. Deus, miserere nobis famulis tuis. Filii [fili], redemptor mundi, deus miserere nobis famulis tuis. Spiritus sancte, deus, miserere nobis famulis tuis. Sancte sanctorum deus, miserere nobis famulis tuis. Qui est trinus et unus, deus, miserere nobis famulis tuis, in te solummodo confidentes. Sancta Maria, Sancte Michaele, Sancte Gabriele, Sancte Raphaele, Sancte Iohannis Baptista, omnes sancti angeli et archangeli, omnes sancti patriarchae et prophetae, Sancte Petre, Sancte Paule, omnes appostoli et evangeliste, omnes sancti decipuli domini, et innocentes, omnes sanc-*

---

343   Text, outside square: *Oriens Boreas Occidens Meridies* [East, North, West, South].
   Inside outermost square: + Elen + + Tau + Mathon Nagk + + + + + Ophusu + + Azaray.
   Inside inner square: + A + Agla + Agla + + m + + a n + + + + + + A +.
   Inside circle: + Marcus + + Lucas + + Matheus + + Johannis +.

344   *Plene tree*: Possibly a species of the *Platanus* genus, or plane tree. These do not seem to have been native to Great Britain at this time, however.

---

ti martires, omnes sancti confessores, omnes sancti et sanctae dei, intercedite pro nobis. Omnes sancte monachi et heremite, omnes sanctae virgins et vidue continentes, omnes sancti et sanctae dei intercedite pro nobis, famulis tuis in christi sanguine confidentibus. Propicius esto, parce nobis, et demitte omnibus peccatis famulorum tuorum in hoc loco existentes, et nomini tuo servientes. Ab omni malo, libera nos. Ab hoste iniquo et doloso, ab omnibus insidiis et laqueis, ab incursu malorum spirituum, a livore inimici, ab ira tua, a periculo mortis, a pondere periculorum, libera nos, famulos tuos. Adiuva nos et libera nos, famulos tuos, in te spem habentes, sicut liberasti Lott de Sodomis et flammis ignis, et liberasti Isaac de manibus patris sue Abrahae, et sicut liberasti Moysem de manu Pharaonis, et sicut liberasti Iob de passionibus suis, et sicut liberasti Danielem de lacu leonum, et sicut liberasti Susannam de falsis criminibus, et sicut liberasti Petrum et Paulum de vinculis, et sicut liberasti servos sanctos tuas de tormentibus, sic nos nunc servos tuos adiuvare digneris qui adiuvas et consertas [conservas] nos omnes, in te sperantes nunc et in omne evum. Amen + Benedicat nobis famulis suis et loco isto. Deus pater, qui in principio cunta creavit. Amen. Salvet nos famulos suos et hunc locum dei filii, qui eluminet nos. Spiritus sanctus corpora nostra strenue custodiat, animam nostram saluet, cor nostrum protegat, sensum nostrum dirigat, et ad sempiternam patriam nos producas, qui in trinitate profecta [perfecta]. Vivit et regnat, per omnia secula seculorum. Amen.

["Spare, Lord, spare thy servants, that thou mayst vouchsafe to redeem us with thy precious blood, and do not [sic] nourish us in eternity, Father from the heavens. God, have mercy upon us, thy servants. Son, redeemer of the world, God, have mercy on us, your servants. Holy Ghost, God, have mercy on us, thy servants. Holy God of the saints, have mercy on us, thy servants. God who is three and one, have mercy on us, thy servants, confiding in thee alone. Saint Mary, Saint Michael, Saint Gabriel, Saint Raphael, Saint John the Baptist, all the holy angels and archangels, all of the holy patriarchs and prophets, Saint Peter, Saint Paul, all the apostles and evangelists, all of the holy disciples of the Lord and the innocents, all of the holy martyrs, all of the holy confessors, all of the male and female saints of God, intercede for us. All of the holy monks and hermits, all the holy virgins and temperate widows, all male and female saints of God, intercede for us, thy servants relying in the blood of Christ. Be favorable, spare us, and forgive all the sins of thy servants being in this place and serving thy name. From all evil things, free us. From the perverse and deceitful enemy, from all traps and snares, from the attack of evil spirits, from the envy of the enemy, from thy anger, from the danger of death, from the burden of dangers, free us, thy servants. Help us and free us, thy servants, having hope in thee, just as thou didst free Lot from Sodom and from flames of fire, and thou didst free Isaac from the hands of his father Abraham, and just as thou didst free Moses from the hand of Pharaoh, and just as thou didst free Job from his sufferings, and just as thou didst free Daniel from the den of lions, and just as thou didst free Susanna from the false accusations, and just as thou didst free Peter and Paul from bonds, and just as thou didst free your holy servants from torments, thus thou may be honored to help us thy servants, that thou help and preserve all of us, hoping in thee now and in all eternity. Amen. + may He bless us his servants and this place. God the Father, who in the beginning created all things. Amen. He may save us, his servants, and this place of God the Son, who may illuminate us. May the Holy Ghost guard our bodies vigorously, save our soul, protect our heart, direct our reason, and draw us to the everlasting country, made perfect in the Trinity. He lives and reigns forever and ever. Amen.]

"Benedicet nobis famulis tuus. Deus celi adiuvat nos. Christus, filius dei, corpus nostrum in suo sancto sirvitio custodire et conservare facias mentem meum. Illumines sensum nostrum. Custodiat ab omni malo, liberat nos, et peccata nostra deliat. Dextra sua nos defendat, qui sanctos sarvos semper adiuvat ipse. Nos consaruiat et adiuvare dignatur qui vivit et regnat, deus, per omnia seculorum secula. Amen.

["He will bless us, his servants. The God of heaven helps us. Christ, the son of God, mayst thou make to guard our body in his holy service and to conserve my mind. Thou mayst illuminate our reason. He may guard from all evil, he frees us, and he erases our sins. With his right hand, he, who himself always helps his holy servants, defends us. He preserves[345] us, and he vouchsafeth to help, who lives and reigns, God, forever and ever. Amen.]

"Benedicat nobis famulis suis, spiritus sanctus, qui in similitudine collumba in flumine Iordanis in Christo requievet. Amen.

["May the Holy Ghost, who rested on Christ in the waters of the Jordan in the form of a dove, bless us, his servants. Amen.]

"Decedite ab hoc thesauro, quisquis, et in nomine dei patris omnipotentes, qui cuncta creavit, respondiat. Amen.

["Whosoever, withdraw from this treasure, and in the name of God the omnipotent Father, who created everything, he may respond. Amen.]

345 *Preserves*: Latin unclear.

"Dicedite in nomine Jesu Christi, filii eius, qui pro te et omnibus nobis passus est. Respondeat unus post quemquam istorum semper. Amen.

["Depart in the name of Jesus Christ, his son, who suffered on behalf of thee and all of us. One may always respond after any of those. Amen."]

[40r]

"Dicedite ab hoc loco et ab isto thesauro, et ne nocias nobis famulis Christi, in deum vivum et verum sperantibus, in nomine angelorum. Amen. In nomine thronorum et dominationum. Amen. In nomine cherubin et seraphin. Amen. Dicedite ab hoc loco et ab hoc thesauro + In nomine apostolorum et martirum. Amen. In nomine confessorum et episcoporum. Amen. In nomine sacardotum et levitarum et omnium ecclesie catholice gradium. Amen. In nomine monachorum et herimitarum. Amen. In nomine virginum et fidelium vidua, tunc hodie in pace sit locus iste et societas ista, in Christi sanguine confidentes. Amen. Precipio quisquis es sibi hunc thresaurum obsconditum possides, per patrem, et filium + et spiritum sanctum + per baptismum suam, per incarnationem Christi, et per miracula sua, per crucem suam, per resurectionem suam admirabilem, et per assentionem suam, per spiritus sancti emissionem, et per omnia nomina Christi quae in scripturis habentur + pro prophetas + et apostolos + et martyres confessores + et virgines ac viduas, non nec in nomine Iesu Christi, fideles quem omnies gentis ad iudicum expectantes, qui redditurus est uni quique iuxta facta sua. Invocamus deum patrem + deum filium + deum spiritum sanctum + et ab eo postulavero ut dignatur nobis concedere hanc thesaurum ad usum pauperum et mansuetorum humilium que, qui in trinitate perfecta, vivit et regnat deus per omnia secula seculorum. Amen."

["Depart from this place and from this treasure, and you may not injure us servants of Christ, hoping in the living and true God, in the name of the angels. Amen. In the name of the thrones and of the dominions. Amen. In the name of the cherubim and of the seraphim. Amen. Depart from this place and this treasure + in the name of the apostles and of the martyrs. Amen. In the name of the confessors and of the bishops. Amen. In the name of the priests and of the Levites, and of all the ranks of the Catholic Church. Amen. In the name of the monks and of the hermits. Amen. In the name of the virgins and faithful widows, then today may that place and that fellowship be in peace, trusting in the blood of Christ. Amen. I order whoever thou art who possesseth this hidden treasure, by the Father, and the Son, + and Holy Ghost + by his baptism, by the incarnation of Christ, and by his miracles, by his cross, by his admirable resurrection, and by his ascension, by the sending out of the Holy Ghost, and by all names of Christ that are held in the Scripture + on behalf of the prophets + and apostles + and martyrs and confessors + and virgins and widows, and also in the name of Jesus Christ, the faithful ones who are awaiting the judgment of all people, that he wilt return to judge each individual according to his deeds. We invoke God the Father + God the Son + God the Holy Ghost + and out of this may he requireth that he vouchsafeth to relinquish this treasure to us for the use of paupers and the mild ones and the needy, who, made perfect in the Trinity, liveth and reigneth, forever and ever. Amen.]

"Jesu, miserere nobis, famulis tuis, in te solo spem habentibus, et iam in nomine tuo incipientibus.

["Jesus, have mercy on us, your servants, having hope in you alone, and now beginning in your name.]

"Therefore now thou cursed spirit, or spirits, if thou or you be within this ground, either beneath or above, I charge thee, by the virtue of Jesus Christ's passion, acknowledge thy duty and now, without any tarrying or delay, give place unto the living God and avoid clean from hence, and never you nor none other trouble us, but rather help us and give honour and glory and worship unto Jesus Christ, the Son of God, and unto the Holy Ghost, and depart clean from this treasure, without hurt or harm of our bodies or of our souls, or of any thing that God hath created (if you be in this ground under the pretense of domination), unto the day of judgment, when Christ shall come to judge the world by fire and water, and by such terrible pains as shall be appointed by the infinite God. *Deo gratias.* [Thanks be to god.] Amen. *Fiat, fiat, fiat.*"

The Discharge of Alkates[346]

"Coniuro vos et precipio vos per hec nomina On, Tetragrammaton, Sabaoth, Adonay, Adeo, et per virtutem celorum, ut recedatis a loco isto vobis a summo artificio ordinato, sine cuiuscumque animati molestirum, et mihi esto parati de cetero, quotiescumque vel quandocunque vel ubicunque et qualitercunque vos invocavero, ut mihi cietis respontia, obedientia attribuatus, et voluntatem meam perfecta faciatis, per virtutem domini nostri Jesu Christi, fillii dei, qui sedet in altissimis et eque cuntaque disponit, per infinita seculorum secula. Amen."

---

346 *Alkates*: See above.

["I conjure you and command you by these names **On, Tetragrammaton, Sabaoth, Adonay, Adeo,** and by the virtue of the heavens, that you shouldst retire from that place ordained to you by the highest art, without molestation of whatsoever alive, and you will be ready to come to me finally, how often or whenever or wherever and however I wilt invoke you, so that you produceth answers for me, obedience bestowed, and you may doest my will perfectly, by the virtue of our Lord Jesus Christ, son of God, who sits in the highest and distributes both equally and wholly, forever and ever. Amen."]

Finis.

[40v]

To Avoid Spirits that Keep Any Treasure from the Ground, that You May Have It and Enjoy It

"In the name of the Father, and of the Son, and of the Holy Ghost. Amen. I charge and bind you spirits, which are and be the keepers of this treasure in this ground, that you avoid, and tarry not here, but depart meekly to the place from whence you came, and I also charge and command you, in the name of the living God, that none of you abide within the space of a hundred ells'[347] compass about this ground, the which I charge you and conjure you by the virtue of Jesus Christ, and by his passion, and by all the merits of all the blessed company of heaven. And also I conjure you, and every one of you, and charge you by all the holy names of almighty God in heaven and in earth. And also I conjure you spirits of what legend soever you be, and in what shape or likeness you be, by the virtue of the Blessed Virgin Mary, mother of Jesus Christ, empress of heaven and hell, that ye incontinently avoid and depart from this ground and place. And also I conjure you by all the seven heavens and elements and by all things that are in them, that you depart and avoid from this ground and treasure, and suffer us quietly to have it with peace, and with peace to enjoy it. Also I conjure you and charge you by the flesh and blood of Jesus Christ, and by the virtue of the five wounds, and by the water and blood that Christ shed upon the Cross for the redemption of mankind, that you avoid and tarry not within a hundred ells of this treasure. And also I conjure you by the virtue of the five loaves which Christ blessed, and by the virtue of the bread that Christ brake and gave to his disciples, and by the virtue of all the holy sacraments

---

347 *Ell:* A measure equivalent, in its English version, to 45 inches.

that ever God ordained to be used in the holy church. And yet I conjure you and bind you if you, or any of you, or any other, be here or in any other place to let us, by the virtue of the imperial throne of God, and by all the power and strength therein that you avoid and depart in peace, and not to tarry, within a hundred ells of this place. And also I conjure you and bind you wicked spirits by all that is afore rehearsed, and by these most holy and mighty names of God, Tetragrammaton, Fortissian, Fortissan, Fortission, Almarom, Iosell, Hosell, Abadia, Stimulamaton, Anepheneton, Ielur, Alpha et Omega, Athanatos, Kyros, Yskyros, Otheos, that you do not defraud us from this treasure, nor turn it into any other likeness nor kind, neither by your subtle or invisible power do draw nor pluck it from us. I charge you by the virtue of the incarnation and resurrection of Jesus Christ, and by all the words that ever God spake, and by all the

[41r]

miracles that ever he wrought in heaven and in earth, and by the fast that he fasted the forty days, and by his descension into the hells, and by the holy words that he spake, which did overcome the devils and helly spirits, and by the dreadful day of judgment, when he shall judge both you and me, that if any of you do intend to disobey the holy and mighty conjuration and words of God and me at any time, in the name of the Father, and of the Son, and of the Holy Ghost, and by all the mighty and sacred names of God, I condemn you into everlasting fire, and into the most vilest pit in hell, where the wrath of God is most kindled, and there you to suffer and sustain torments and pains that never shall cease until the day of judgment, for your presumption and disobedience of this, our request and commandment. In the name of the almighty living God, the wrath and curse of God condemn you into everlasting pain, the strength and power of all the angels, archangels, thrones, and principates curse you and condemn you, and all the saints of God, apostles, martyrs, virgins, and confessors curse you and condemn you into everlasting damnation, except you avoid and deliver us this treasure, and that by the virtue of all aforesaid and spoken. And by the power of God, I bind all creatures living that now have power to have this treasure, but I and my company, by these holy and fearful words I bind you and all kind of spirits and living creatures, per[348] As, per Gap, per Alep, per Abra, per Abraica, per Gebra, per Abracula, per Ebracasar, per Abracalens, per Zargon, per Abrion, per Elyon, per Sargion, per Recala, per Rabam, per Canthiale, per Duxule, per Archima, per Rabam, that no spirit nor living creature have power to remove this treasure, nor take it away from me and my company,

348 *Per*: The Latin "by."

until I be at the doing thereof, *per eum qui venturus est iudicare vivos et mortuos. Amen. Soli deo honor et gloria sine fine. Amen. Fiat, fiat, fiat. Probatum est experimentum.* [for he who will come to judge the living and the dead. Amen. To God alone are honor and glory without end. Amen. Let it be done, let it be done, let it be done. This experiment is proven.]"

Finis.

[Consecration of the Magical Tools]

Consecratio anuli, gladei, septri, laia [lamina]. Debent fieri in prima veneris die, post coniunctionem solis et luna, luna existent in pari numero, et omnia hec in mense febrearia olimque dicitur. Admirabile erit factum quando soll in Aries, hoc est in martie. Per tres dies ante operationes absciniantas ab omni chahetu vel naturale polusione et crapulata que faciens nisi uni sacerdoti reveles. In omni coniuratione portet te esse.

[Consecration of the ring, of the sword, of the scepter, of the lamina. They ought to be made on the first day of Venus, after the conjunction of the sun and the moon. The moon will appear in an even number of days and all this, it is said, in the month of February and at that time. It will be most admirable to be done when the sun is in Aries; this is in Mars. For three days before the operations, thou shalt abstain from coition[349] or natural pollution and intoxication, which, if not doing, thou shalt confess to one priest. In all conjurations he may suffer to be with you.]

[41v]

[A Treatise on Calling Spirits]

In nomine patris et filii et spiritus sancti. [In the name of the Father, and the Son, and the Holy Spirit.] Amen.

When you call or conjure one hour, or two, or three, or four, or five, you must not think that the work is false nor deceitful, nor be in any despair for it, for it may be that the time and place is not convenient nor according,[350] or else it may fortune

---

349 Latin *chahetu* unclear. A similar passage in e Mus. 238, 7r, gives *coitu*, or "intercourse," which is used here.

350 *According*: Appropriate.

that they which be called be occupied with some other man, that they may not come to you all that while. Also ye shall know that the spirits will be loath to come at the first time to you, and they will prolong the time as long as they may, and they will give you many occasions to cease your work, if he will be letted for any thing. Nevertheless, if ye intend to bring this work to effect, you may not leave for any occasion, for after you have compelled them once, ever after they must needs to ready to obey you as soon as you call them. Wherefore you must pray soundly in this work and devoutly, and you shall have your purpose, you must be very secret, so that no man know thy intent and purpose. Also whatsoever you do in this work, or hear, or see, you may not discover it to no earthly creature, but only to thy fellows that are sworn to thee, and to thy ghostly father,[351] which must never be but one priest, for if you ever discover it to any other person, you shall never have your intents perfomed. Also see that thy fellows discover no point hereof to no person, for it may be your destruction.

The second part of this book is for to call and constrain any spirit in the world to answer thee and to fulfill thine intents, the which is divided into four parts.

The first part is where you shall call. The second, how you shall call. The third, when you shall call. And the fourth is whom you shall call.

First you shall have a chamber, four square, straight every part, with a window on the east, another on the west, another on the north, and another on the south. They must be boarded or plastered, that you may make all this with chalk or with charcoal. It may well be seen for the protection, seeing all spirits are wicked and nigromancers.

The circle should be made on a waste place, far from access of people, for that spirits will rather appear in such waste places than in any other places where any of the seven sacraments are or have been ministered, in for they hold opinion that every place is hallowed, where any of the seven sacraments hath

[42r]

been ministered in, and lightly a man shall have no place but some of the seven sacraments have been ministered in it, except in such forletten[352] places.

---

351 *Ghostly father*: Priest who serves as confessor.
352 *Forletten*: Forlorn, desolate, uncultivated.

Also you must understand the time that you must conjure in, for every time is not convenient and expedient to this craft. Wherefore you must understand that, from the change of the moon to the opposition,[353] you may work after some nigromancers every day, but after the opinion of Sanroman, Crostheade, and Bathoner[354] you may work but in even days, as the second, the fourth, the sixth, and so forth till the twelfth day, after then you must work no more till after the next conjunction. This doctrine is most perfectest [sic]. Also some say they have begun in the conjunction, and have been three days without appearance or any answer. Therefore you may not be lither,[355] nor yrke[356] for one day, or two, or three, or four, for great clerks have been thereabouts three days daily, before they could have any sight of spirits. Also every time is not expedient to thine operation, for every spirit is subject to one of the seven planets, and he will not lightly appear nor obey thee, nor come to thee, but when his planet reigneth, and in that time he must needs a bay tree.[357] You must try every plant till you have that which is most to you expedient.

Also you must consider that all weather is not apt to this work, wherefore when you will work in this science, you must look that the air be clear day or night, and see that the sun shine in by day, and the moon by night, and the stars, and that it be not cloudy weather, for then the spirits may not lightly appear. Also you must let the sun shine, whereas they shall appear, for they delight much to appear in them and to work in them.

Now I have shewed you the place and the time that you shall conjure in. Now I shall shew you how you shall conjure and how you shall understand how to call into your circle both good and bad spirits, celestial angels, and the four angels and spirits of the air, but I will at this time shew you no more but spirits of the air, wherefore you shall understand that there is four kings of spirits of the air.[358]

---

353 *The change…opposition*: From the new moon until the full moon.

354 *Sanroman, Crostheade, and Bathoner*: These authorities are unknown. Due to truncation, the two n's in Sanroman might actually be m's.

355 *Lither*: Either wicked or lazy.

356 *Yrke*: Exhausted or troubled.

357 *Bay tree*: Possibly in reference to a wand to be used by the magician, of which bay laurel was a common ingredient. See Peterson, "The Magic Wand."

358 The following list has close parallels with *Oberon*, 208–15. The reader is encouraged to consult that text for further connections with other sources. Note that this introduction seems to refer to a longer treatise that is truncated to simply the spirits of the air.

The first king of spirits reigneth in the east and is called Ariens,[359] and he appeareth in the likeness of a horse with a hundred heads,[360] or else if you call him with his company,

[42v]

he appeareth with the favour of a fair woman riding upon an elephant, and all manner of minstrelcy after him. He can tell all things past, present, and to come, and he can truly prophesy of all things to come. He can shew any science earthly, and all earthly treasure is in his guiding, and he hath under him spirits innumerable, of whom twelve of the chief be these that follow.

The first is called Baall. He hath power of love, both of man and woman, and to make a man invisible, and he appears in the likeness of a king, but he speaks hoarsely.[361]

The second is called Agaros, and he can teach the language of every tongue, and to bring again a fugitive, and make a steadfast man come away, and to leave dignity and worship,[362] and he appeareth in the likeness of an old man riding upon a crocodile.[363]

The third is called Barbas,[364] and he can tell of all secret things and of all things hid, and can make men sick, and change men into the likeness or shape of a beast, and he appears in the likeness of a strong lion, but by strong adjuration, he may be compelled to appear in the likeness of a man.[365]

The fourth is called Scar,[366] and he hath power to take from a man hearing, seeing, and understanding, and to bring money whether he is commanded. He is right

---

359 *Ariens*: Oriens. See *Oberon* 208. Changes that will influence name pronunciation will be noted for the other entities below.

360 *Oberon* adds "or as some write, with five heads."

361 *Baall*: First appearing as a Sumerian god in the third millennium BC, Baal later became a well-known Canaanite deity with whose followers the prophets of Yahweh contested. Herrmann, "Baal."

362 *Oberon* has "bring again a fugitive or one run away, and can promote to dignity and worship."

363 *Crocodile*: *Oberon* "cockadrill."

364 *Barbas*: *Oberon* adds "alias Corbas."

365 *He appears in the likeness...adjuration*: An addition to this text.

366 *Scar*: *Oberon* has Star; Additional Ms. 36674, 64r has "Scor."

true to all the commandments of an exorcist, and he appeareth in the likeness of a swan and speaketh hoarsely.

The fifth is called Seper, and he hath power to make a great sea to appear full of fishes[367] or ships with all manner of instruments of war to fear your enemies, and may make great winds, and to cause wounds to rankle and worms to breed in them. He appears in the likeness of a maid.

The sixth is called Algor, and his power is to tell you all secret things, and to give you love and favour of all kings, princes, and lords as you will desire. He appears in the likeness of a fair knight with spear and shield.

The seventh is called Seson, and he can tell of all things that ever were or ever shall be, and he hath power to shew thee the place of hid treasure, and to make thee familiar with every man. He appeareth with a lion's face crowned with a diadem, and hath a venomous serpent in his hand, and rides upon a wood bear.[368] Nevertheless, he will take gladly the body of the air and appear in the likeness of a man.

The eighth is called Marayn,[369] and he hath power to teach the virtues of all herbs and stones, and to bear a man from region

[43r]

to region with a thought. He appeareth in the likeness of a bear with a serpent's tail, and a flame of fire cometh out of his mouth.

The ninth is called Neaphan,[370] and he hath power to tell you of all things that ever were or ever shall be. He giveth favour of all friends and foes, dignities, worship, and riches, and he appeareth in the likeness of a dog.

The tenth is called Barbays. He hath power to teach you the singing and chattering of birds, and lowings of beasts, and telleth where treasure is hid that is within the earth, and witchcraft.[371] He appears in the likeness of a wild ass.[372]

367 *Full of fishes*: An addition to this text.
368 *Wood bear*: A mad bear. *Oberon* has "wild boar."
369 *Marayn*: *Oberon* "Maxayn."
370 *Neaphan*: *Oberon* "Neophon."
371 *Witchcraft*: *Oberon* notes that he undoes witchcraft.
372 *Wild ass*: *Oberon* "wild archer."

The eleventh is called Aymon. He hath power to make all manner of wild beasts tame, and to teach all things that ever were or ever shall be, and to give love of friends and enemies. He appears in the likeness of a man, and he hath teeth like a dog.[373]

The twelfth is called Bufflas,[374] and he hath power to break peace and cause debate, strife, and battle. He is false in all his answers, but if you constrain him strongly, then he will appear in the likeness of a spark of fire.

The second king of spirits is called Amaymon. He reigneth in the south, and all spirits in the south parts of the world are obedient to him. His power is to give true answers of all things that you will ask him, and he giveth familiarity, dignity, and riches.[375] He appears with the favour of an old man having a long beard and long hair hanging over his ears.[376] He is crowned with a bright crown, and he rideth upon a ramping[377] lion. In his right hand, he beareth a dart. Afore him there cometh dancers and all manner of minstrels. He bringeth with him spirits innumerable of whom twelve of the noblest follow hereafter, but beware of him, for he is the most perilous of all spirits of the world.[378]

The first is called Asmoday,[379] and he hath power to teach thee geometry, arithmetic, astronomy, and music, and to tell of all things that one can ask him. Also he can give thee invisibility and can shew thee the place of treasure, and he appears with three heads: the first is like an ass, the second is like a bull, and the third is like a ram, and he hath a serpent's tail and feet like an ass, and a flame of fire cometh out of his mouth.

The second is called Bileth, and he hath power to teach thee the seven liberal sciences, and to make effecions[380] as well of evil as of good, and to teach invisibility.

[43v]

---

373 *Oberon* also notes that he "appeareth in likeness of a wolf, with a serpent's tail, casting fire out of his mouth."

374 *Bufflas*: *Oberon* "Suffales."

375 *Oberon* adds "and by God's permission he hath power to consecrate books. etc."

376 *Ears*: *Oberon* has "eyes."

377 *Ramping*: Rearing.

378 *Oberon* simply notes that he is "very perilous."

379 *Asmoday*: Asmodeus, a figure derived from Zoroastrian beliefs who entered Judeo-Christian belief through the Book of Tobit and later became prominent in traditions surrounding Solomon. Hutter, "Asmodeus."

380 *Effecions*: Most likely performances, although *Oberon* has "consecrations" here.

The third is called Astoroth,[381] and he hath power to tell the seven liberal sciences, and to give answer of all things to come as well as past,[382] and he appears riding upon a foul infernal dragon bearing a serpent in his hand, and a great stink[383] cometh forth of his mouth. Therefore suffer him not to come too nigh[384] your circle, for he is very perilous.

The fourth is called Aleche,[385] and hath power to teach the seven liberal sciences and all languages. He may give thee good familiars,[386] and a true answer to all things, and he appears in the likeness of a king, but thou shalt see nothing of him but his head, and after him cometh four minstrels with trumpets.[387]

The fifth is called Beryth, and he hath power to give thee dignity, and to convert or turn any metal into silver or gold. He can teach you all things both past, present, and to come. He appears in the likeness of a knight, riding upon a red horse, crowned with two red crowns. He speaketh clear, but he is false[388] without he be strongly constrained.

The sixth is called Mallappas, and he hath power to make any buildings as castles and towers, and also he hath power to subvert and overthrow any manner of buildings that you will have him. And he appeareth in the likeness of a raven, but he may be constrained to appear in the likeness of a man, and he speaketh hoarsely.

The seventh is called Partas, and when he cometh in the shape of a man, he hath power to tell the virtue of herbs and stones, and to teach thee logic, and to make thee fair,[389] and to speak and roam [run?],[390] and also to restore sight that is lost, and to shew the place of hid treasure. He appeareth in the likeness of a wood bear.

---

381 *Astoroth/Astaroth*: Originally a female deity in Ugaritic, Egyptian, and Phoenician cultures, she became a male demon within Judeo-Christian belief. Livingstone, "Astarte." Also see the mention of "Asteroth" below.

382 *Oberon* adds "present."

383 *Stink*: *Oberon* has "sting."

384 *Too nigh*: *Oberon* has "within."

385 *Aleche*: *Oberon* has "Abech."

386 *Familars*: *Oberon* has "friendship."

387 *Four...trumpets*: *Oberon* has "trumpeters."

388 *But he is false*: Not present in *Oberon* but similar to a statement in Weyer, *De praestigiis daemonum*, 921.

389 *Fair*: *Oberon* has "invisible."

390 *To speak and roam*: Not in *Oberon*.

The eighth is called Busyn. He can answer truly to all that you will ask him, and to bring dead bodies from one place to another, and to make one of his subjects to enter into the dead bodies and carry it about, and to speak and go where you will, and do all things as the body did living, except eating. He appears in the likeness of a fair woman, but he speaks hoarsely.

The ninth is called Oze, and he hath power to tell thee of all the liberal sciences, when he receiveth the shape of a man,

[44r]

and to tell thee of all secret things, and to change a man into a narrow[391] shape, and he appears in the likeness of a leopard.

The tenth is called Pachyn, and he hath power to make a man wise and to tell all secrets. He appears with three heads, bearing a serpent in his hand and a pine of burning fire in his mouth, with which he may burn what place or thing thou wilt have burnt.

The eleventh is called Gambra, and he hath power to teach the virtues of herbs and stones, and to make all birds of the air tame unto thee, and he appears like a swan.

The twelfth is called Tamar. When he receives man's shape, he can marvelously inform thee in astronomy and all the seven sciences. Also he may inform thee how to have the favour of all great estates, and to shew thee of all treasure that is hid that any spirit keeps, and he appears like a spark of fire.

The third prince or king of spirits is called Paymon, and he reigneth in the west. He hath power to hallow all manner of things, and to answer to all things that is asked him, and gladly he will speak of the world, and he may give familiarity, and he may make all the fishes of the sea to be obedient. He appears in the likeness of a king, with a woman's face, crowned with a bright crown. He rideth upon a dromedary. Afore him cometh a great company of spirits with all manner of instruments of melody, but if he be called alone, then he appears with two kings and speaks mistily, for he would not be understood. Nevertheless, you may make him to speak in the common language. He hath infinite of spirits with him, whereof these following are twelve of the most mightiest.

391 *A narrow*: *Oberon* has "another."

The first is called Belyall. He hath power to give dignity,[392] great love, and favour of all persons, and he appears in the likeness of a fair angel, riding in a chariot of fire, and speaks sweetly.

The second is called Basan,[393] and he hath power to make a man invisible and wise, and he will answer thee to all things. He appears with three heads, the first like a dog, the second like a man, and the third like a ram. He rides upon a wild bear and beareth upon his fist a goshawk, and a flame of fire cometh out of his mouth, and he speaks all hoarsely.

The third is called Gordemser,[394] and he can tell the truth of all things that ever were or ever shall be, and he is right mighty in all his errands doing, and he appears in the likeness of a good

[44v]

angel having a dark face.

The fourth is called Balath. His power is to make whole men sick and to take from a man his wits,[395] and he maketh a man marvelous in the seven liberal sciences, and to have love and dignity of all men. Also he hath power to carry from one place to another as you will bid him. He appears in the likeness of any shape,[396] and he speaks courteously.

The fifth is called Mistolas,[397] and he hath power, when he receiveth man's shape, to teach thee craft[398] and nigromancy, and the virtue of herbs, stones, trees, and waters,[399] and he appears in the likeness of a raven.[400]

392 *Oberon* adds "and promotion."
393 *Basan*: *Oberon* has "Bason."
394 *Gordemser*: *Oberon* has "Gordonsor."
395 *Wits*: *Oberon* has "sense and wits."
396 *The likeness…shape*: *Oberon* has "a misshapen image."
397 *Mistolas*: *Oberon* has "Mistalas."
398 *Craft*: *Oberon* has "witchcraft."
399 *And waters*: Not in *Oberon*.
400 *Raven*: *Oberon* has "night raven."

The sixth is called Aleches,[401] and he hath power to teach thee the seven sciences and their parts. He giveth familiarity, and he appears in the likeness of a wild knight with a red lion's face, and he speaketh sadly.

The seventh is called Zagayme,[402] and when he receiveth man's shape, he hath power to make thee wise.[403] Also he may turn water into wine, and a fool into a wise man, and then he appears like a wild bull.

The eighth is called Taleos.[404] He hath knowledge and power of infinite treasure, and he maketh good familiarity, and he appears in the likeness of a king riding upon a crocodile and hath upon his hand two crows,[405] but he is false of his answers, except he be well constrained.

The ninth is called Cagyn, and he hath power, when he is in man's shape, to bring thee any soul out of purgatory[406] to speak with thee. He appears in the likeness of a pale horse.

The tenth is called Suchay. He hath power to teach thee all manner of language, and to carry thee whither thou wilt in a little space, and he can give thee marvelous love of women, especially of widows. He doth appear with a fair face like unto a woman.

The eleventh is called Ruall.[407] When he hath the shape of a man, he can[408] tell thee all things past and to come. He may give thee love of man and woman, friends and foes. He appears like a dromedary, and he speaks sadly.

The twelfth is called Zayme, and he hath power to bring money out of any place that you will, and to bring it or carry it to any other place whethersoever[409] you will. He can shew you the buildings of cities, towns, and castles. He may give you what dignity you will. He appears in the likeness of a raven.

---

401 *Aleches*: *Oberon* has "Lecher."
402 *Zagayme*: *Oberon* has "Zagayne." See also Weyer, Sloane 3850, 77r; Additional Ms. 36674, 2 ("Zagan").
403 *Oberon* adds "and turneth earth into any kind of metal."
404 *Taleos*: *Oberon* has "Caleos."
405 *Crows*: *Oberon* has "crowns."
406 *Any soul…purgatory*: *Oberon* has "any soul not in the heavenly nor infernal power."
407 *Ruall*: *Oberon* has "Ryall."
408 *Oberon* adds "resolve all doubts."
409 *Whethersoever*: Whichever of the two, but used here as "where."

The fourth prince or king of spirits is called Egyn, and he reigneth in the north. He hath power to teach thee all manner of sciences, and he will gladly tell thee all manner of things

[45r]

that were or ever shall be, of all secret things. He giveth familiarity and dignity. He may make confirmation[410] upon all things. He appears in the likeness of a man, with a bright face, crowned with a double crown, and rides upon a dragon, and cometh with a fearful noise, and after him cometh all instruments of music. But when he is called alone, then he bringeth with him three kings, and cometh not so hastily nor dreadfully. Also he hath with him infinite of spirits, of the which twelve of the mightiest follow hereafter.

The first is called Ozia, and he hath power to teach thee all arts and liberal sciences, invisibility, and familiarity,[411] and may bear thee from region to region in a little space. He appears in the likeness of an old man riding upon an elephant.

The second is called Uryall, and he hath power to turn any metal into silver or gold, and water into wine, and a fool into a wise man, and visible things into invisible. He appears in the likeness of a boisterous knight[412] and speaks hoarsely.

The third is called Urago,[413] and when he takes man's shape, he hath power to make a man wise and invisible, and to change a man into another likeness. Also he giveth love and favour of all men and answers to all things, and he appears in the likeness of an angel, and he is right, true, and faithful to all your commandments.

The fourth is called Synoryell. When he hath man's shape, he hath power to teach thee to understand all beasts and language, and he can tell thee of all things. He can shew the places of hid treasure, and he appears in the likeness of a wild[414] bear.

---

410 *Confirmation*: *Oberon* has "alteration."
411 *Familiarity*: *Oberon* has "give favour of enemies."
412 *Knight*: *Oberon* has "king."
413 *Urago*: *Oberon* has "Vzago." Note similiarity to the spirit Vasago or Vassago (on whom, see above).
414 *Wild*: *Oberon* has "wood" (mad).

The fifth is called Tessaid,[415] and he hath power to teach a man astronomy, geometry,[416] and arithmetic, and he giveth true answers of all secret things that you can ask him. He appears in the likeness of a swan,[417] but he speaketh hoarsely.

The sixth is called Soyll, and he hath power to make a man very gracious and to have the love and favour of parents.[418] He can answer to all questions that you can demand of him, and he appears in the likeness of a ramping lion.

The seventh is called Auras, and he hath power to carry dead corpses whither you will bind him. He giveth answer unto all questions. He appears in the likeness of a wild ass.

The eighth is called Othey. He hath power suddenly to make castles, towers, and towns. He can truly answer thee to all things. He appears[419] in the likeness of a man, and then his eyes burn like fire.

The ninth is called Cacaryll.[420] He hath power to bring any soul out of purgatory[421] and to receive his own shape and to speak with you. He hath power to teach you the science of physic.[422] He appears in the likeness of an ass with a woman's face.

[45v]

The tenth is called Muryell, and he hath power to make love between cousins[423] and to tell of treasure hid, and he appears in the likeness of a white lion.

The eleventh is called Umbra.[424] He hath power to give dignity and to tell of all things to come, and giveth familiarity. He may convey money from one place to another as you will bid him, and he appears in the likeness of a giant, but he speaks so softly that you may not hear him, but he is very true.

---

415 *Tessaid*: *Oberon* has "Fessan" or "Tessan."

416 *Geometry*: Not in *Oberon*.

417 *Swan*: *Oberon* has "flame of fire."

418 *Parents*: *Oberon* has "princes."

419 *Oberon* also has here "like to a tun of wine."

420 *Cacaryll*: *Oberon* has "Saranyt."

421 *Bring...purgatory*: *Oberon* has "raise dead men."

422 *Physic*: *Oberon* has "one the seven arts or sciences liberal."

423 *Cousins*: *Oberon* has "persons."

424 *Umbra*: *Oberon* has "Hinbra."

The twelfth is called Anoboth,[425] and he hath power to make thee marvelous in nigromancy and to shew thee all hid treasure and to tell thee who keeps it, and, if they be of the north side, he will drive them away. Also he can tell thee of any strayed thing that thou canst demand of.[426] He appears in the likeness of an armed knight.

Now I have taught thee where, when, and whom thou shalt call. Now shall I teach thee how thou shalt call.

When thou art well disposed and sad[427] in devotion, as I have taught thee before, and that the time and weather is according and convenient to thy operation, and thy circle is hallowed. Then with thy instruments necessary, that is to say, sword, scepter, plate, ring, and also coals and incense, with thy fellows virtuously disposed, enter right sadly and devoutly, as thou canst think, into thy holy circle and deliver thy fellow the sword, the which, meekly kneeling to the ground, he must receive, and when you deliverest that, you must say,

"*Frater, per vertutem sanguinis Iesu Christi, don liberam potestatem ut nunc gladium benedictum tangere, tenere, gubernare valeas, cum quo et per quem omnis fraudolosa malignorum spiritum potestas compescare, per eum qui venturus est iudicare vivos et mortuos, et seculum per ignem.*"

["Brother, by the virtue of the blood of Jesus Christ, I give free power so that now thou mayst be able to grasp, to hold, and to govern the blessed sword, with which and by which all fraudulent power of evil spirits may be restrained, by him who will come to judge the living and the dead and the world by fire."]

Then he must sit down, turning his face into the east, and thou must devoutly put the ring on thy little finger, and take the scepter in thy right hand, and turn thee towards the habitation or place where the spirit is, saying devoutly and heartily this invocation following:

425 *Anoboth*: For an image of the spirit, see *Oberon* 409.

426 *Also…demand of*: *Oberon* has "Also he can tell of wonderful strange things."

427 *Sad*: Serious.

"O thou spirit N., wherever you be, I call thee in the name of the eternal God. I conjure thee, N., by the might of the Father omnipotent, and by the wisdom of the Son omnipotent, and by the virtue of the Holy Ghost the comforter, and by the holy and undivided Trinity of God, and by all the holy names of God, and especially by the might and virtue of these holy names following + Tetragrammaton + Jesus + Alpha + et Ω + Agyos + Emanuell + Agla + Usyon + Basyen + Christem + Sabaoth + Adonay + Panton + Craton + Jesus + Messyas + Medikym + Medycyny + Helvecie + Hekesy + Heben + Medon + Thrabanna + Zno + Haday + Filioboy + Obba + Abba + Semapheras[428] + and by all the other name of God, by the which you mayst be constrained, commanded, or bound,

[46r]

I conjure, constrain, and command thee by the miracles and all the marvelous deeds of our Lord Jesus Christ, and by all his pains and passions that he suffered in his glorious body, and by his marvelous nativity, and by his annunciation, and by his circumcision, and by his tribulation, scourging, and beating, and by his precious death which he meekly and graciously suffered to redeem mankind, and by his descension into hell, where he bound Lucifer and brought his well-beloved children out of the lamentation and pains of hell to the joys of paradise, and by his mighty resurrection, and by his marvelous ascension, and by the might and virtue of him when he shall come in the end of the world and judge me and thee and all creatures to their deserving through his righteousness.[429]

"I conjure thee, N., by our blessed lady St. Mary the Virgin undefiled, mother to our saviour Jesus Christ, queen and virgin and lady of the world, queen of heaven and empress of hell, and by the virginity and chastity of that most glorious virgin, and by the marvelous fecundity, meekness, and obedience of her, and by all her holiness and innocence, and by all her joy, both in earth and in heaven, and by all the dolours, pains, and tribulations that she suffered meekly here in this present world, and by all the prayers that ever she said, and by all the alms that ever she did, and by all her miracles that ever she wrought, and by all her goodness and mightiness.[430]

---

428 *Tetragrammaton...Semapheras: Oberon* has "Tetragrammaton + Iesu + Alpha + and Omega + Agyos + Emanuell + Agla + Usyon + baseym + Christus + Sabaoth + Adonay + panton + Craton + Ysus + Messias + Medekym + Halvecia + Hekesy + Heban + Medan + Trabema + zarohaday + flioboy + Obba + Alba + Senaphenas."

429 *When thou art well disposed...righteousness*: See *Oberon* 295–7; Sloane 3849, 24r–25v.

430 *I conjure thee, N. by our blessed...righteousness*: Compare to Sloane 3849, 25v–26r.

"I conjure thee, N., by the Father, the Son, and the Holy Ghost, and by all the relics of saints the which are in any place of the world, by the precious body and blood of our Lord Jesus Christ, and by the holy ☩ that our Lord Jesus Christ was nailed upon, and by the nails that were stricken through his hands and feet, and by the crown of thorn that was set upon his head, and by all the bodies and bones of saints contained within the world, and by all virtues of the Old Testament, by our mother the holy church, and by all masses, prayers, and almsdeeds through the world, to the honour and loving of almighty God, and by all the ministers in earth, by all the seven sacraments of the holy church, and by the Ten Commandments of God, and by the seven works of mercy, and by the twelve articles of the faith, and by the two tables of the old law given to Moses, and by the wand of Aaron that flowered, and by all the creatures of God.

"I conjure thee, N., by the Father, the Son, and the Holy Ghost, and by all the holy company of heaven, by angels, archangels, and thrones, by dominations, potestates, cherubim, and seraphim, and by every good angel, and by the orders of angels in which you wast before thy fall, by all holy patriarchs, prophets, apostles, evange-lists, disciples, martyrs, confessors, virgins, and saints, and by all the servants of God, and by their tribulation and penance, almsdeeds and holy works, by all

[46v]

their doctrine and clemency, and by the four evangelists of God and the virtue of them, and by all the characters and signs of heaven, by the which thou or any other spirit art bound or compelled, by the seven planets of the air and the twelve signs of the zodiac, by all the stars in the firmament and tokens therein, and by the four princes of spirits that are in the four parts of the world, the which have power of almighty God to grieve the earth, the sea, and the trees, by the seven kings of the seven planets, and by the four elements, and by all things which they sustain and bring forth, and by the virtue of all manner of herbs, stones, trees, and waters, and by all things that spring in the earth, and by all beasts, wild and tame, and by all things that creep in the earth, and by all manners of weathers and times, and by Lucifer, the prince and king of wicked spirits, the which is bound in hell, and by that spirit that you are obedient to, and to whom you art bound to obey, whatso-ever he be, or whatsoever he be called, by all conjurations, extortions, tokens, or instruments whereby you mayst be constrained.

"I conjure and charge thee, N., by all the virtues of our Lord Jesus Christ, and by the angel that shall cry in a trumpet at the day of doom and shall say, '*Venite, venite,*

venite [come, come, come],' and by angels, thrones, dominations, virtues, principates, cherubim, and seraphim. I conjure and charge thee, N., by the pains of our Lord Jesus Christ, and by the precious death of the cross whereon he was hanged, and by the nails wherewith he was nailed, and by the spear that opened his side, and by the blood and water that flowed thereout, and by the crown of thorn, wherewith he was crowned, and by his death, resurrection, and ascension, and by the sevenfold graces of the Holy Ghost, and by the ring and seal of Solomon, and by the virtue of the sun that was dark, and stones that cleaved, and graves that opened, and many dead bodies have risen, and by the wand of Moses that divided the sea, and by the wand of Aaron that budded, and by the throne of God, and by the golden censers, and by the golden altar, and by the lamps set before God, and by the seats of all the holy saints.

"I conjure and charge thee, you spirit N., by the glorious Virgin Mary, the mother of God Jesus Christ, and by the flesh and blood that God took of the Virgin Mary, and by these names of God which he named with his own mouth, as A. and Ya, Saday, Emanuell, Sabaoth, Arfex, Damamestoras, and by this holy name Adonay that God shall say at midnight, at whose voice all dead men, both good and bad, suddenly shall arise, and by this holy name Sother whereby all stones and buildings shall fall, and men shall say to the mountains, fall upon us, and by this holy name Esyon, whereby God shall cast the devil and his members and all wicked folk into

[47r]

the pit of hell, and God shall lead with him all chosen folk into everlasting bliss.

"I conjure thee, N., only in the virtue or power of God, and by the virtue of him that hath made all this world of naught, and by the infinite might and power of him and his virtue, and by all his creatures visible and invisible, and by all heavenly things, words, and names, and by all earthly things, words, and names, and by all infernal things, words, and names, that any spirit may be compelled by, and by all extortions, exorcisms, conjurations, and precepts, and by the which Solomon and other exorcists have bound and called and compelled any spirit, and by all names that thou shalt be compelled or constrained by at the dreadful day of judgment, in the which almighty God omnipotent shall judge all creatures, and by the dreadful judgment that shall be given upon thee in the day when you and every creature shall know their everlasting state, and by him that shall be their judge and judge all the world, quick and dead, defer you not wheresoever you be, but come in haste, without any manner of letting or tarrying, without any manner of grievous storms, or any grievous noise, and without hurting or harming me or any of my fellows, or any other Christian man, or any other creature, but come to me visibly, and appear in the shape of a fair man or an angel, not fearing me in no manner of wise, and that you fulfill all my commandments, that I, in the power of almighty God shall charge thee, and also that you depart not without my license, till I give thee leave, *per eum qui venturus est iudicare vivos et mortuos, seculum per ignem* [by him who will come to judge the living and the dead, and the world by fire]. Amen."

Now I have taught thee the coming of them, that is to say, when, where, and how. Now shall I also shew thee that last part of this treatise, that is, how to have thy purpose, wherein there is no more to do, but when you hast them before thy presence, then make thy conclusion of thy conjuration, shewing thy intent, and answer them with sweet savours, till they have followed thy purpose, then command what thou wilt, saying:

"I charge thee, you spirit N., that appearest here before this circle by the virtue of this conjuration, wherewith we have constrained thee, and by the virtue of the most holiest and dreadfullest names of God, and by the virtue of this name + Te + tra + gra + ma + ton + that you go without any letting or frauds, making unto (such a place, N.), and bring with you the treasure that lies there, and if there be none that is lawful, I charge thee by the aforesaid conjuration, and under the pain of eternal damnation, that

[47v]

thou bring unto me seven thousand pounds of lawful money of England, either in silver or in gold, from what ground thou wilt, and set it within in our circle, without any hurt or harming of me or any of my fellows. Also I charge thee by the virtue of God's blessed passion, and by all his principal wounds, and by the operation of his holy blood, and by his resurrection, and by his ascension, that you go and come without any tarrying, and without any hurt or harming of me, or any earthly creature + *Fiat* + *fiat* + *fiat* + Amen."

Now when you hast thine intents performed, then license them to depart in this manner following.

First say thy conjuration. Thou make this conclusion as at this time, saying

A discharge or licence

"Depart and go to your places where God hath ordained you to abide, without any grievous noise or storms, and at all times when I call you again to come quickly, without any manner of tarrying, and fulfill my intents.

"*Decidite nunc, decedite nunc, decedite nunc, per virtutem sancte trinitas, et per omnes vertutes celorum, et per vertutem istorum nominum dei + A + g + l + a + Aglaya + Aglaoth + Te + tra + gra + ma + ton + et per vertutem omnium secritorum nominum dei, et per vertutem domini nostri Iesu Christi, qui venturus est iudicare vivos et mortuos, et seculum per ignum, amoris ille pater. Pax domine nostre Iesu Christi sit inter nos et vos. Fiat, fiat, fiat. Amen. In nomine patris, et filii, et spiritus sancti. Amen.* [Depart now, depart now, depart now, by the virtue of the Holy Trinity and by all the virtues of heaven, and by the virtue of these names of God + A + g + l + a + Aglaya + Aglaoth + Te + tra + gra + ma + ton + and by the virtue of all the secret names of God, and by the virtue of our Lord Jesus Christ who will come to judge the living and the dead and the world by fire, that father of love. May the peace of our Lord Jesus Christ be between us and you. Let it be done, let it be done, let it be done. Amen. In the name of the Father, and the Son, and the Holy Spirit. Amen.]"[431]

Then say, "*In principio erat verbum, etc.,*" *usque ad fynem Evangelii. Explicit. Hic laudis deus.* [In the beginning was the word, etc., until the end of the Evangelist. It ends here. This is the God of praise.]

There Be Times and Hours to Be Observed and Considered

The hours of Saturn

[The rest of this page is blank.]

[48r]

431 *Depart now…Amen:* See *Oberon* 297.

For Treasure that Is Hid, to Obtain It

"Oh God of Abraham, Isaac, and Jacob, oh God of patriarchs, oh God of prophets, oh God of martyrs, oh God of confessors, oh God of virgins, oh God and Father of our Lord Jesus Christ, I do invocate thy holy names and imperial majesty, that if this spirit have hid treasure, which lieth unoccupied under the earth or above the earth in any place, that you, Lord, wilt grant me the disposition of it to obtain it to the use of us living creatures, and that none of all these devils and spirits or any else which keepeth this treasure do not prevail against me nor none of my company. Amen.

"I, N., the son of N., do bind you by one God, by the true God, and by the holy God, and by him that spake the word and all things were done, and by him by whom all angels do triumph, and by archangels and hosts, celestial, terrestrial, and infernal, and by all that I have spoken or may cogitate, and by all things that God hath done to the laud and glory of his mighty name, and by the inestimable names of Christ + Jesus + Messyas + Emanuell + Sabaoth + Alpha et Ω + Yskyros + Kyry-os + Otheos + Tetragrammaton + Anapheniton + Nephenay + Sattells + and by the bond of Solomon the sapient which bound spirits into a vessel of glass, and by the most corroborate[432] messenger of God, and by the name of God + Ell + and by a chance admirable.

"I conjure thee and bind thee, you spirit that hid this treasure, and you spirits and devils that keep that, by the secret names of God which should not be named with an unclean mouth, and by the name Ya Ya and in the name Ya Ya which Adam heard; and by the name Yfas, and in the name Yfas which Noye[433] heard and was delivered from the deluge with his family; and by the name Yet, and in the name Yet, Tret, Yot, which Abraham heard and did know God omnipotent; and by the airy fire which Moses heard in the name of God, and spake with God, and did hear him speak in the flame; and by the name Anatheseton and in the name Anathese-ton, that Aaron heard and was made eloquent and sapient; and by the name Saboth and in the name Saboth which Moses heard, and anon there was made fearful darkness three days and three nights; and by the name Egyon, and in the name Egyon, which Moses did name and all the waters of Egypt turned into pale blood; and by that name Ysyston and in the name Ysyston which Moses did name, and all the waters of the floods did rise and ascend into the houses of the Egyptians; and

432 *Corroborate*: Strengthened.
433 *Noye*: Noah.

by the name Ittymon, and in the name Ittymon, which Moses did name, striking the dust of the earth, and there were blains[434]

[48v]

made in all men and beasts; and by the name and in the name Mephaton, which Moses did name, and did strike the fishes, horses, camels, asses, sheep, and oxen of the Egyptians, and they died; and by the name Pentheon and in the name Pentheon which Moses did name, and did take the ashes of the camels and cast them towards heaven and did heal the wounds touching the Egyptians, both of men and beasts, through all the land of Egypt;[435] and by the name Ely, Evell, or Elam, and in the name Ely, Evell, or Elam, which Moses did name, and there was hailstones, such as was never since the world began to this time, so that men and beasts which were in the fields did fall and die; and by the name Ysyston, and in the name Ysyston, which Moses did name, and there was many locusts did appear upon the face of the earth of the Egyptians, and they did devour all that was green in the land; and by the name Anabona, and in the name Anabona, that Moses did name and did receive the tables written with the hand of our saviour; and by the name Elyon, and in the name Elyon, that Elias did name, that it should not rain, and it rained not on the earth for three years and six months; and by the name Synagogyon, and the name Synagogyon, that Elias did name and it rained, and the earth brought forth fruits, and by the name Geryon, and in the name Geryon, which Mary did hear and she was demitted;[436] and by the name Pandacraton, and by the name Adonay, and by the name Emanuell, and by the name Alpha et Ω, and by the holy name of God Semopheras, and by the names of God, and by this name Ia Ia, and by this name Isance, and by this holy name Agla, and by all the great, mighty, and holy names of God, I constrain and bind thee, and charge thee that you fulfill even the way and manner of that I would have thee to do, and I will pray to God, thy creator and mine, for thee to have mercy upon thee. I require thee, you spirit or creature, by the baptism of Jesus Christ. I conjure thee that you come, by the manhood of Christ, the which was dead and rose again. I conjure thee, thou spirit N., *per verbum caro factum est* [by the word made flesh]. I conjure thee, N., by the pain and passion of our Lord Jesus Christ, and by the blood and water that ran out of his side, and by all the wounds of Christ Jesus, and by the lungs and liver of that Lord that died for us upon a cross. Also I conjure thee, N., by that only sacrifice that he offered up for us

434 *Blains*: Blisters or sores.
435 A reference to Exodus 9, although the ashes were not of camels and caused illness instead of curing it.
436 *Demitted*: Humbled.

to his heavenly Father to pacify his wrath and to take the curse upon him. I conjure thee by the great agony that he had hanging upon the cross when he said, 'Eloy, Eloy, Lamazabathenie,'

[49r]

I conjure thee spirit, by his death and burying, and by his resurrection, and by his glorious ascension, and by the coming of the Holy Ghost, and by the dreadful day of judgment, when he shall come to judge both thee and me, and as you thinkest to be saved at the last day, I charge thee to obey me.

"I conjure thee by the obedience that thou owest to the almighty God in Trinity, and by the great name of God, *deus deorum* ["God of Gods"], that made all heavens, with all joys, glorious dignities, worthiness, and worships, and by all suffrages, and by all the glorious dignities that be in heaven, and by all the princes under heaven, and by all the signs and characters of the firmament of heaven, and by the four elements, and by all that groweth upon the earth, and by all waters, seas, woods, lands, stones, and grass and other kind of herbs, and by all serpents, and things that creep upon the earth, and by all the birds of the air and flying fowls, and by all beasts upon the earth.

"I conjure thee by the tops of hills and mountains, and by all valleys and deepness in the earth, and by the graciousness of God from the the [sic] first creation, that thy walking may be known and redressed in the manner of goodness.

"I conjure thee by thine own creation, and by thy life and death, that you never rest day nor night in the air, nor in the earth, nor in the fire, nor in the water, nor in the wind, nor in no other place that ever God created, or ordained, till you shew in where and in what place the treasure is hid that I may obtain that without hurt of my body or of my soul.

"I conjure you, all devils and spirits, from the place where the treasure lieth. I command you by all the holy and secret names of God, and as you trust or would be saved at the dreadful day of judgment by Christ's most precious blood, that you by your craft do not change it, nor alter it, nor draw it away, nor delude me with none of your false crafts, but even as you would have mercy and grace of the eternal God, so do you benevolently and gently obey to your creator, for with faith by his promises, I shall constrain you as thus, you shall cast out devils in my name and speak with new tongues, and say to this or that mountain, 'Plant thyself, or cast thyself into the sea,' and it shall be done. And in the name of Jesus of Nazareth, I claim the victory of you wicked spirits or creatures, by whose promise I trust to obtain my desire, and by the mercy of God the Father, of God the Son, and of God the Holy Ghost, three persons in Trinity and one in substance, living and reigning forever and ever, to whom

[49v]

be laud, praise, honour, and glory, without beginning and without ending. Amen. Amen. Amen.

"I conjure you, devils and spirits associate with the spirit that I call, that you avoid and hinder no point of my purpose, and I conjure you by the living God that ye come not near the spirit that I call, till I have obtained my purpose and will and desire truly."

An excommunication if they be disobedient

"I excommunicate and curse all you devils and spirits which do rebel and will not obey. The great curse that God gave unto Lucifer light upon you devils and spirits that lets my purpose. The pain of the same curse that God gave to Lucifer and to all his wicked angels light upon you devils and spirits that shall rebel against me. The great curse wherewith God cursed the early light upon thee, you spirit which hid this treasure, if you do rebel and not consent to my will.

"O you rebelling spirits, why do ye rebel? All the curses of things cursed cast you down into hell among the devils, whereas is no joy but trouble, torment, and dolour and gnashing of teeth. The curse which God gave unto Cain throw you into fire and brimstone, and all the torments that ever were ordained, torment you forever, and everlasting fire, fire, fire consume you, all wicked spirits. I curse you by all the power and great sentence of God. I curse you by all the holiness of heaven. I curse you by all angels and archangels. I curse you by all prophets and patriarchs. I curse you by all the apostles and disciples of God, and by all the holy things. I curse you by heaven and earth, by sea and land, by nights and days, by lightnings and by heat, by cold and ice and snow, and by all that groweth upon the earth. I curse you, rebelling spirits, avoid and go, malignant spirits, into everlasting torments prepared for the devil and his angels, world without end. So be it, so be it, so be it. Amen."

If he will not obey, condemn him, saying three times:

"Ego condemnabo, N., in ignem eternum, et per dei vivi, et per virtutem omnium nomi-num suorum, et per potestatem quam deus habet super te, sed in ignem sustine hec, donec apparis mihi et totam voluntatem mea[m] adimpleas.

["I shall condemn thee, N., into eternal fire, and by the living God, and by the vir-tue of all his names, and by the power that God holds over thee, but endure in fire here, until thou mayst appear and thou mayst fulfill all my will.]

"Coniuro te, Vasago, per tres personas in trinitate, et unum deum in deitate, per sanc-tam Mariam, matrem domini nostri Jesu Christi, et per omnes sanctos et sanctas dei, quod tu compareas coram me in pulchra forma hominis vel specie humana, et mihi dicas veritatem rei inquerendi sine mendatio vel aliqua fallacia.

["I conjure thee, Vasago,[437] by three persons in Trinity, and one God in divinity, by the holy Mary, mother of our Lord Jesus Christ, and by all male and female saints of God, that thou shalt appear to me face to face in a beautiful form of a man or a human appearance, and that thou shalt tell me the truth of the matter sought after without lying or any deceit."]

Finis.

[50r]

To See a Spirit in a Crystal by a Child or a Woman with Child

When thou wilt begin thy conjuration, first get thee a man child within the age of seven years, or else a woman with child, and set thy back against the sun, and set the child or the woman betwixt thy legs, and the stone in his or her hand, or set on a board before him or her, and let the child or the woman with child say after thee, word by word, as followeth:

"In nomine patris, et filii, et spiritus sancti. [In the name of the Father, and the Son, and the Holy Spirit.] Amen.

---

437 *Vasago*: See above. The presence of the spirit's name here, and the change in tone from the previous passage, might indicate this was supposed to be a different operation copied with the rest.

"I conjure and charge thee, you spirit heavenly, by all the might of God, and by all the power of God, and by all that ever God made in heaven, or in hell, in fire, or in water, or in stone, and by the virtue of God's flesh and his blood, body, and bone, and by the virtue of these holy names of God + Alpha + et Ω + Agla + On + Ely + Saday + Tetragrammaton + Jesus + Christus + Messyas + Sother + Emanuell + Sabaoth + Adonay + Panthon + Craton + Homo + Uriel + Gloriosque + Bonus + Unigenitus + Vita + Via + Manus + Usyon + Primogenitus + Principatus + Sapientia + Virtus + Caput + Finis + Origo + Paraclitus + Mediator + Agnus + Uspes + Adies + Lux + Ymago + Panis + Flos + Vitus + Mons + Ianua + Petra + Lapis + Or + Pastor + Propheta + Sacerdos + Athanatos + Kyros + Theon + Ysis +, by these names and all other holy names of God. I charge thee, thou spirit heavenly, that wheresoever you be in heaven, or in hell, in earth, in air, in fire, in water, in stock, or in stone, that you come certainly and anon, and appear in this crystal stone in a fair form, sitting on a three footed stool, in a red gown syde[438] down to the foot, and a light[ed] candle in thy hand, in the similitude of a fair man, shewing to me truly such things as I shall ask thee, and if you do not, then in the name, virtue, and power of God and of this conjuration, I condemn thee, spirit heavenly, into hellfire there ever for to be until the day of doom. *Fiat, fiat, fiat. Amen.*"

If he appear not on the first day, call him the second day, and if he appear not then, call him the third day, and then he shall come. **Conjure** and charge him that he do all such things as thou commandest him to do on this wise.

"I conjure and charge thee, spirit heavenly, in the name of the Father, and the Son, and the Holy Ghost, three persons and one God, and by the holy and blessed wounds of Christ Jesus, and by all things that God made, and by him that thou believest upon, and by the king's head, that thou have no power to come in stock nor stone, in land nor in water, nor in no place

[50v]

in the world, till thou hast done my will and commandments."

And if he will not work therefore, then bind him on this wise:

"I conjure thee, spirit heavenly, by the faith that you hast to the living and approved God, and by the virtue of God, full of power and mercy, and by angels and archan-

438 *Syde*: Hanging low.

gels, that shalt blow against the day of doom, where and when Christ shall say, 'Come, ye children, to me, into the kingdom of heaven,' and by all angels and arch-angels, thrones and dominations, principates and potestates, virtues, cherubim, and seraphim, and by all the relics of all the saints in heaven, and as it is true that our blessed lady St. Mary bare Christ Jesus, and she a pure maid, and a clean virgin, *ante partum, in partum, et post partum* [before birth, during birth, and after birth]. And by the blessed host of bread, and by the power and virtue of the words of our Lord Jesus Christ, and by the sacrament of the highest, which is turned into God and man, one flesh and blood, under the form of bread and wine. So I conjure thee, spirit heavenly, by the charity of God, and by all the power of God, and by his god-head, and by the holy strength of God, and by all the good and evil that they that be eloquent, bear, and sustain, that thou shew and do all things that I shall ask and demand of thee, without any fraud or leaving making, under the pain of ever end-less damnation."

Then ask of him what thou wilt, and when you hast done with him, then command him by the virtue of all the holy names aforesaid to be ready to thee evermore, and then license him to depart on this wise.

A *License*

"I conjure and charge thee, thou spirit heavenly, through the virtue of God the Father, and the Son, and the Holy Ghost, three persons in Trinity, and one God in unity, and by the virtue of his mercy, and by the virgin St. Mary, and by the virtue of all things aforespoken that thou, spirit heavenly, depart meekly and without any fear of us, by the virtue of God the Father. Amen.

"In the name of almighty God, and by the power and virtue of all the holy names of God, I charge thee to depart in peace. In the

[51r]

name of the Father, and of the Son, and of the Holy Ghost. Amen."

And if thou wilt that he depart, say thus:

"*Ite ad locum predestinatum. Pax sit inter nos et vos, in nomine patris, et fillii, et spiri-tus sancti. Amen.* [Go to your predestined place. Let there be peace between us and you, in the name of the Father, and of the Son, and of the Holy Ghost. Amen.]"

"Jesus nazarenus, rex iudiorum, filii David, miserere me. Adiutorium nostrum, in nomine domine qui fecit celum et terram, sit nomine domine benedictum ex hoc, nunc et virginem ceculum. [Jesus, king of the Jews, son of David, have mercy on me. May our helper, in the name of the Lord who made heaven and earth, be blessed in the name of the Lord, from this, now and forever.]"[439]

"In the name of the Father, and of the Son, and of the Holy Ghost," and *finis*. ☉ *Signum solis* [sign of the sun]. *Finis*.

An Experiment to Call **Three** Spirits into a Square New Glass

Get a square new glass, unpolluted, whereon in one corner with ink or new oil olive, write this name Only.[440] In the second corner, write Ely. In the third corner, write Honely, and in the fourth corner, write Hely, which done, give it to a child in his right hand, standing with his back against the sun, and the master with his face towards the sun, about noon, and then say softly and secretly these names devoutly in the right ear of the child:

"Ely. Adonay. Sabaoth. Eloys. Elios. Ely. Sother. Emanuell. Tetragrammaton. Alpha et Ω. primum et novissimus, principium et fynis [the first and the youngest, the beginning and the end]."

This done, say this prayer:

"Domine Jesu Christem, rex gloriae, per virtutem et potentiam tuam, et per pietatem et Mariam tuam, nobis mittere dignero [sic] 3 angelos dextra tue, et ut compereante in medio istius vitri vel speculi ad visum istius pueri virginis, sine dissimulatione quecumque est ostendere, ac manifestare isto puero N. virgine [sic] veritatem, sine fraude vel dolo, cuiuscunque rei dubie illos interogaverit.

["Lord Jesus Christ, king of glory, by thy virtue and power, and by thy devotion and thy Mary, deign to send us three angels from your right side, and so that they may appear in the middle of this glass or of this mirror to the sight of this virgin boy, to show without disguising whatever it is, and to disclose to this virgin boy N. the truth, without fraud or deception, of whatever matter he will ask those."]

439 *Forever*: "virginem seculum" likely a mistake for "seculum seculorum."
440 *Only*: For other scrying operations involving this spirit, see Cambridge Additional 3544, 26–30, 47–52, 107; Sloane 3851, 50v–51v.

"In nomine patris et fillii et spiritus sancti. [In the name of the Father, and the Son, and the Holy Ghost.] Amen.

"Coniuro vos, angelos dei omnipotens, quod apereatis isto puero N. virgine [sic] in hoc vitro speculo formis pulchris et visibilibus, sine lesione vel terrore alicuius creature dei, per vertutem sancte et indevidue trinitatis, pater et fillius et spiritus sanctus, et per virginitatem beate Marie virginis, et per virginitatem sancti Iohanis Evangeliste, Katherine, Lucie, et Margarete, et per virginitatem istius pueri N. virginis, et per virtutem istius nominis Starias, que cum recedatus ab hoc vitro vel speculo que usque pueri iste virgo vos licentiaverit, donec veritatem dixistis iste puero N. virgini de ea re de qua vos interogaverit."

["I conjure you, angels of omnipotent God, that you may appear to this virgin boy N. in this glass or mirror in beautiful and visible forms, without wound or terror of any creature of God, by the virtue of the holy and indivisible Trinity, Father and Son and Holy Ghost, and by the virginity of the holy Virgin Mary, and by the virginity of the holy John the Baptist, Katherine, Lucy, and Margaret, and by the virginity of this virgin boy N., and by the virtue of that name Starias, that you may [not] retire from this glass or mirror that this virgin of a boy shall give you permission to depart, until you spoke the truth to this virgin boy N. of this matter of which he may ask you."]

Then the master shall rehearse these words following, and the child shall say after him, word by word.

[51v]

"O vos angeli, vobis precipio que unus vestrum principalium appereat in hoc vitro vel speculo coram me puero N. virgini in sede auriato, et ostendat mihi veritatem istius rei furate vel amisso [sic]."

[O you angels, I command you that one of the first of you may appear in this glass or mirror face to face with me to this virgin boy N. in the gilded seat, and let him show to me the truth of this stolen or lost thing.]

This being said by the child, the master shall say thus:

"O vos angeli, recedite ad locum vestrum sine lecione aliccius [sic] creature, parati, quotiens et cum vos invocavero, et pax sit inter nos et vos. In nomine patris et fillii et spiritus

sancti. [O you angels, return to your place without wound of any creature, ready whenever and when I will invoke you, and let there be peace between us and you. In the name of the Father, and the Son, and the Holy Ghost.] Amen."

This last is conjuration sciential.

Incipit Invocatio, et Vocatur Invocatio Salomonis Secretum [Here Begins the Invocation, and It Is Called the Invocation of the Secrets of Solomon]

"In nomine patris, et filii, et spiritus sancti. Amen. N., veni festinantur. Coniuro te, spiritus N., per deum patrem omnipotentem, per deum unum, per deum vivum, per deum verum, per deum sanctum, qui te de paradiso gaudio dei serat, et per sancta sacra nomina + Messias + Sother + Sabaoth + Emanuell + Adonay + Otheo + Athanatos + Hely + Panthon + Craton + Ysys + Alpha + et Ω + Jesus + Christus + Nazarenus + On + El + per ista sacra nomina.

["In the name of the Father, and of the Son, and of the Holy Spirit. Amen. N., come quickly. I conjure thee, spirit N., by God the omnipotent Father, by the one God, by the living God, by the true God, by the holy God, who had barred thee out of the paradise of God, and by the holy consecrated names + Messias + Sother + Sabaoth + Emanuell + Adonay + Otheo + Athanatos + Hely + Panthon + Craton + Ysys + Alpha + et Ω + Jesus + Christus + Nazarenus + On + El + by those sacred names."]

"Coniuro te, N., et per + Tetragrammaton + et per omnia nomina principalia + Onas + Eo + Anandelabo[441] *+ Gramaton + Omonsion*[442] *+ et per sanctam + Altomake + Sparon + Aglas + Ely + Lama + Zaba + Thanie + Egon + Regon + et per sanctam Mariam, matrem domini nostri Jesu Christi, et per omnes virgines, et quinque vulnere dei, et per virginitatem sancti Johannis Evangelisti et Baptisti, et per hoc nomen Mahothe et Nahothe, et per que habemus te astringebat, et ubicunque fueris, statim te mihi monstres in pulcra forma hominis, et habeas colorem album vel rubeum. N., spiritus, te voco per fidem quam habeas domino tuo pripato, et per domini [sic] dei vive et veri, purissimi, et per illos angelos et archangelos, thronos et dominationes, principates [et] potestates, cherubin et ceraphin, et omnes reliqua [sic] sanctorum et sanctarum qui continentur in universo mundo, et si hoc sit verum, que hostia de pane vertetur in cor-*

---

441 *Anandelabo*: Could also be "Anamdelabo."
442 *Omonsion*: Could also be "Omomsion."

pus domini nostri Jesu Christi, et per ista nomina que sunt maxime nicromantium artium, si Bulsacbaris super Bulsas, Pamulon in potestate Aya, de sede nominatis. Aqua resteunt, et elamenta concomitatur, et per ista, iubeo per charitatem dei, et per occulos eius, et per omnia membra eius, et per devinitatem, et per bonum et malum que quatuor elementa sustineat, ut ubicunque fueris, statim in ictu occuli appareas et monstres te mihi in pulcra forma humana et implae desideriam meum, et noli aliquo modo anime mee, nec corpori

[52r]

mee, nec membris meis, nec alicui creature, neque alicui animali, nec domine ecclesie seu campanili quovismodo nocere vel perturbare, et mihi monstres te, et inimicias veracitur et non sophisticaliterum, nec sigmentaliter, nec respontionibus sophisticalibus, sed sicut sunt cum facto de presentibus, preteritis, et futuris, et de omnibus. Quere eis interogabuntur, et fiat per ipsum cui est imperium, honor, et gloria, virtus, pax, eternitas, et bonitas, et infinite seculorum secula. Amen."

["I conjure thee, N. and by + Tetragrammaton + and by all the principal names + Onas + Eo + Anandelabo + Gramaton + Omonsion + and by the holy + Altomake + Sparon + Aglas + Ely + Lama + Zaba + Thanie + Egon + Regon + and by the holy Mary, mother of our Lord Jesus Christ and the five wounds of God, and by the virginity of the holy John the Evangelist and Baptist, and by all virgins, and by this name, Mahothe and Nahothe, and by which we consider he was restraining thee, and wheresoever thou mayst be, immediately thou mayst show thyself to me in a beautiful form of a man, and thou mayst have a white or red color. N., spirit, I call thee by the faith that thou hast in thy personal God, and by the lord God living and true, most pure, and by those angels and archangels, thrones and dominions, principalities and powers, cherubim and seraphim, and all relics of male and female saints that are contained in the whole world, and if this may be true, that the sacrifice of bread will be turned into the body of our Lord Jesus Christ,[443] and by these names that are greatest of the nigromantic art, if Bulsacbaris over Bulsas, Pamulon in the power Aya, from the named seat. They restrain the waters, and the elements are attended, and by these, I command by the charity of God, and by his eyes, and by all his limbs, and by the divinity, and by the good and evil that the four elements may sustain, so that wheresoever thou wilt be, thou mayst appear in the blink of the eyes, and thou mayst show thyself to me in a beautiful human form and complete my

---

443 *The sacrifice…Jesus Christ*: The belief in transubstantiation, the literal physical presence of God in the Mass. The Church of England rejected this doctrine. Bicknell, *A Theological Introduction to the Thirty-Nine Articles of the Church of England*, 382–83.

desire, and do not wish in any manner to injure or to disturb my soul, nor my body, nor my limbs, nor other creature, nor other animal, nor church or belltower of the Lord, in no way, and thou mayst show thyself to me, and truly answer and not a deceptive word, nor making fictions nor with sophistic answers, but as they are in fact, of the present, the past, and the future, and of all things. Seek these things that are asked, and let it be by the same to whom is dominion, honor, and glory, virtue, peace, eternity, and goodness, and forever and ever. Amen."]

Post hec, dicas istum psalmum, "Quicunque vult," usque ad fynem, et preusque huius-modi psalmum dixeris. Apparebit in circulo et interogabit quid secum velis, tunc, loquere ad eum audati animo hoc modo. [After this, thou shalt say that psalm, "Whosoever wishes,"[444] though to the end, and likewise thou shalt have said the first[445] psalm. He will appear in the circle, and he will question what thou may want, then, with the thought heard, speak to him in this manner.]

"Coniuro te, spiritus N., in nomine patris paracliti, et filii, et spiritus sancti, et iubeo ut impleas desiderium meum, ut hic scriptum est."

["I conjure thee, spirit N., in the name of the Father the guardian, and of the Son, and of the Holy Spirit, and I command so that thou mayst fulfill my desire, as this is written."]

Faciet et eadem dabit tibi responsa, cum autem desiderium tuum inpleverit. Tunc dicas hoc modo:

[He will do and the same will give to thee answers, when also he may accomplish your desire. Then thou mayst say in this manner:]

"N., cum te invocavero esto mihi paratus. Vade ad locum tuum predestinatum, ubi deus tuus te ordinavit, quousque alias te invocavero, et tunc presto sis mihi. Pax sit inter nos et te. In nomine patris, et fillii, et spiritus sancti. Amen."

["N., when I invoke thee, thou will be ready for me. Go to thy predestined place, where thy God appointed thee, until I invoke thee another time, and then thou mayst be ready for me. Let there be peace between us and thee. In the name of the Father, and of the Son, and of the Holy Ghost. Amen."]

---

444 *Whosoever wishes*: The Athanasian Creed.
445 *First*: Could also be "prior."

"In nomine Jesu, facio hoc signum ⊤ *," et tunc dicas istum psalmum, "Quicunque vult," et cet, et abitit que. Si forte abire voluerit, dicas hec verba.*

["In the name of Jesus, I make this sign ⊤," and then thou shalt say that psalm, "Quincunque vult," etc., and he leaves on account of that. If he may desire to leave strongly, thou mayst say these words:]

"O tu, maligne spiritus, preaceps totius nequitie, recede, Assimiliom, quia demones tibi precipiunt, et vade ad locum predestinatum, In nomine patris, et fillii et spiritus sancti. Amen.

["O thou, evil spirit, foremost of all wickedness, withdraw, Assimiliom, because the demons order thee, and go to thy predestined place. In the name of the Father, and of the Son, and of the Holy Ghost. Amen."]

Et statim abibit, et secure poteris recedere a circulo. [And immediately he will leave, and thou wilt be able to leave the circle undisturbed.]

[52v]

[A Circle to Find Treasure][446]

Make a circle in a house floor (that standeth out of the way from people and is void and clean) with a chalk stone in the hours of Saturn's sign and his hours, and if you cannot make it up in one hour, make it up in another hour that pertaineth to the same sign when it falleth, and stick a candle in the midst of the circle burning, and say this conjuration following:

"I conjure you, four princes of hell, Sathan, Lucifer, Deutalion, and Saciathon or Saciaton,[447] by the Father, and the Son, and the Holy Ghost, and through the virtue of all the angels and archangels in heaven, and through the virtue of thrones, dominations, rule, and power, cherubim and seraphim, and by all the virtues of God, that you bring or cause to be brought hither gold or silver, or any other treasure, (or any thing that is stolen) gold, silver, or rings, that is hid in the earth, or gold or silver or any other treasure that is in such a place N., or in any other place in water, in

---

446 Compare to BL Sloane MS 3853, 259v.
447 *Sathan…Saciaton*: Sloane 3853 has "Sathan, Lucifer, Deucalion, Faciaton."

fire, in air, or in earth, before this candle be burnt out or quenched, by the virtue of our Lord Jesus Christ that died for mankind upon the Mount of Calvary, and shall come to judge us and you and all the world by fire. *Fiat, fiat, fiat.* [Let it be done, let it be done, let it be done.] I do call Sathan, Lucifer, Deutalion, Saciathon. *Fiat.* [Let it be done.] Amen."

And these uses ought to befall three times in Saturn and in his hour, and when this thing is brought to this place, discharge them, saying:

"I command you by the sacrament of the altar which is the very body and blood of Christ, that you go hence again to the place that you come from, and do no harm to no creature of God, by the virtue of our Lord Jesus Christ, and by the virtue of our lady that is a very true maid before her son's face and was in the birth of Jesus Christ, and shall be ever more, world without end. Amen."

Here followeth the figure of the circle for this purpose:

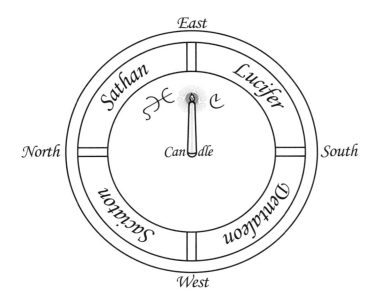

There should be characters in the circle which were torn out of the copy.[448]

[53r]

448 Text inside circle: Lucifer Dentaleon Saciaton Sathan. Sloane 3853 lacks any characters in the circle, although it does place the numbers 19, 29, 39, and 49 between the names.

[The Chapters of All Offices of Spirits[449]]

Materia istorum capitulorum talis est. In istis capitulis et in qolibus capitulo, invenietis unam conclusionem, et in qualibet conclusione, sunt nominanda nomina dei et sancte caracteres unde siquis vult aliqua istorrum capitulorum sacere. Ita opertet eum incipere. Primo minuat se sanguine modicum. Post ea, sit balneatis et rasus barba, et totus lotus in fonte vino, et mundus et mundis vestibus indutus, et a venere, et ab omni pollusione corporis se absentet per tres dies, et non minus commedat nec minus bibat. Ungulas manuum et pedum tondat. Ieiunat hiis tribus diebus, et in quolibet die nominat omnes demones de quolibet ca[pitul]o et dicat, "O vos," tales nominando eos. "Rogo vos per virtutes quas habetis ut obediatis mihi." Hoc dicas in mane, orto sole, etiam iterum post solis occasum, et incipies die lune insurgentibus auris. Quarto die, vero, et quacunque hora volueris, elige tibi quacunque capitulum vis facere, et fac circulum unum cum lancea una. Haste salicit, et circa circulum caracteres illius capituli, et dic conditione illius capituli, et incontinenti et sine mora facient quiquid volueris, et omnia quecunque impetrare desideras, et hoc est vera nigromancia vos. Igitur opertet stare mundos ad minus quando vultis [vultu?] hoc facere. Eadem die, opertet gladium habere, et fac cerculum in quo loco vis facere, et cerca circulum ponas caracteres que sunt in fine unus cuiusque capituli, et suffumiga circulum cum incensu, et tunc incipies conditione illius capituli, et incontinenti et sine mora aliqua tibi venient quos tu vocasti, et dicent quid [qui] vis precipe, "Nos volumus sacrificium; precipe quid vis," et si forte dicant, "Derelinque deum tuum, et sacrifica nobis, et implebimus omnia precepta tua et disiderium tuum." Responde eis sic: "Non est velle meum deum meum derelinquere, sed sua gracia ego, ei serviam in omni tempore, nec faciam aliquid que poterit eum aggravare nec vobis sanctificabo." Si forte recedent, tunc invocentur iterum, et statim circa venerit. Coniura eos conditione predicti capituli quibus factis, dic, "Tu, virtute horum verborum, et in virtute honorum nominum dominum mei Jesu Christi, principio vobis, et principias sine mora facere ea qua officiis vestris sunt deputata, et non faciatis aliud nec illud ad que vos estis deputati quandocunque vos invocavero," et noli principere eis abire tunc, sed precipe eis ut faciant omne velle tuum quacumque tu eos vocaveris. Brevissima est hec ars, et melior omnibus artibus, et sit sive in die, sive in nocte, sive in quacunque hora vis, aut in quocunque loco vis. Hec sunt epitula de quibus in verbo agimus, et extra cerculos fac figuras ipsorum, et si non facere vis circulos, porta tecum

---

449 Variants to what follows, with shorter entries and many differences in the spirits listed, appear in Sloane MS 3853, 219r–223r, and Chetham's Mun.A.4.98, 60v-65v. The former operation, entitled "the boke of the Sience of nygromansie," declares the spirits it lists to be the servants of Asmoday and provides a long incantation in which all of them are named. The latter is simply labeled "Clavis spirituum," or "The Key of the Spirits." I have given this untitled section the same label as what appears in Sloane MS 3853, 221r, for continuity of reference.

karecteres illius capitulorum qui vis facere, et nullo modo dubitandum est in sequentibus invenies capitula predicta.

[The matter of these chapters is thus. In these chapters and in each chapter, you will find a concluding section, and in any concluding section, the names of God are named and the sacred characters whence anyone who desires to make anything of these chapters. Accordingly, it is necessary to begin this. First, the magician may let a small amount of blood from himself. After this, he may be bathed and the beard shaved, and all the bathing done in a living fountain. Having put on both ornament and clean clothing, he should absent himself from sexual love and all pollution of the body for three days, and he should not eat nor drink less.[450] He should cut the nails of his hands and feet. He should fast these three days, and in each day he names all demons of whatsoever chapter, and he should say, "O you," with calling such ones, **"I ask you by the virtues that you may have that you should obey me."** Thou shalt say this in the morning, with the sun visible, also again after the setting of the sun, and it will begin on the day of the Moon with the rising winds.[451] On the fourth day, moreover, and on whatever hour thou mayst desire, select for thee whatever chapter you desire to do, and make a circle with the rod. Take a spear of willow and draw around the circle the characters of that chapter and say with the compact of that chapter, and swiftly and without delay they should do whatever thou mayst wish, and all that thou wishest to effect, and this is the true necromancy for you all. Therefore it is fitting to remain clean at least when you desire to do this. On that same day, it is proper to hold the sword, and make the circle in what place you desire to operate, and around the circle thou mayst place the characters that are at the end of whatever chapter, and suffumigate the circle with incense, and then thou wilt begin in the compact of that chapter, and at once and without delay any ones that thou didst call will come to thee, and they who thou wisheth to command will say, **"We wish sacrifice, command what you wish,"** and if they may say with strength, **"Forsake thy god, and sacrifice to us, and we will achieve all thy commands and desire,"** respond to these thus: **"It is not my will to forsake my God, but I have his grace, I will serve him in all time, and I will not do anything that will be able to aggravate nor make you holy."** If they will retire strongly, then they may be called again, and they will come around immediately. Conjure these in the compact of the aforesaid chapter, with which done, say, **"You, in the virtue of these words, and the virtue of the honorable names of my God, Jesus Christ, I govern you all, and you begin without delay to do these things that were assigned to your offic-**

---

450 This contradicts what is below.
451 Mun.A.4.98, 62r, adds that the magician must also prepare by anointing his body with honey.

es, and you may not do anything else nor that to which you were assigned whenever I will call you," and then do not govern these to leave, but command them so that they may do all thy will whenever thou wilt call them. Most brief is this art and better than all arts, and it may be either in day, or in night, or in whatever hour thou desirest, or in whatever place thou desirest. These are the decrees regarding which we compel in the word, and outside the circles make the figures of the same, and if thou dost not desire to make the circles, carry with you the characters of those chapters that thou desirest to do, and it is doubted in no way that thou wilt find the aforesaid chapters following.]

Isti sunt qui **sciunt** *omnes artes et omnes scripturas. Vade ad locum ubi vis aliquam artium vel scientiarum vel scripturarum prophetiam, etc. Aperi librum et factum est.*

These are those that **know** all arts and all writings. Go to the place where thou desirest any of the arts or the sciences or the prediction of the scriptures, etc. Lay open the book, and it is done.[452]

"Coniuro **vos demones,** *Satrapis, Beluginis, Baramptis,* **cum omnibus sociis vestris, per deum omnipotentem, et per Christem deum, qui vos sub mea potestate includere fecit, et per sanctionem per quam sub me vos misit, ut veniatis ad me vel aliud vel alios quandocunque vel quociescunque, quacumque hora et ubicunque voluero, statim et sine**

[53v]

mora, in ea forma vel specie in qua a me, vel ab alio, vel ab aliis de voluntate mea vobis precipietur, nulli nocentes nec mihi, nec aliis, nec cui, nec aliquibus, donec de voluntate mea vobis preceptum fuerit, docentes me et alium vel alios preficere, quandocunque quocienscunque voluero, omnem scientiam, artem, et scripturam, et quidquid vobis precipio, faciatis mihi et alii vel aliis pro velle meo, administrandum taliter conferentes, ut a me alio vel aliis quem vel quos voluero in perpetuum, sine velle meo afferre non valeatis, et si iste liber ab aliquo in aliquo loco vel studio casualiter habeatur, que ad me [seu] alium seu aleos eadem hora de voluntate mea revertatur, et ubicunque voluero alii vel aliis per velle meo."

["I conjure **you demons,** Satrapis, Beluginis, Baramptis, with all your associates, by the omnipotent God, and by Christ God, who made to imprison you under my power, and by the consecration by which he sent you under me, so that you may

---

452　From here until page 239, the illustrations following each section go with the preceding section.

come to me, or another, or others whenever or how often or in whatever hour and wherever I will desire, immediately and without delay, in this form or appearance in which he will be commanded by me, or by another or by others from my will, harming no one, neither me, nor others, nor anyone, nor anything, until there will be a command to you regarding my will, teaching me or another or others to whom you are appointed, whenever and how often I will desire, all sciences, arts, and scriptures, and whatever I order you, you may do for me and for another and for others, on account of my will, carrying out its execution in such a manner so that by me or another or others who I will wish in perpetuity, you will not have strength to give without my will, and if this book may be held by another in any place or school[453] by chance, that it may be returned to me or another or others that same hour by my will, and whenever I will wish to another or others by my will."]

Iste sunt qui vadunt per diem et noctem, unicumque [ubicunque] volueris, ostendentes tibi quecunque volueris. Aperi librum et precipe, et factum est, et si vis videre res mundi et videre quod volueris, aperi librum, et dic: "Coniuro vos, principes demonum, qui vocamini Selus Leus, cum lxix sociis vestris, per deum omnipotentem qui fecit celum et teram, mare et omnia que in eis sunt, et per regem vestrum qui vos sub mea potestate tradidit, et per ista nomina: Messias, Sother, Emanuel, Sabaoth, Adonay, Gymel, Caldey, memor ut veniatis ad me ad quem de voluntate mea vobis precipietur, ostendentes etiam mihi cui voluero signata omnia mundi regna, et quicquid vobis precipio quecunque et ubicunque voluero mihi per velle meo hec omnia faciatis."

[These are those which go by day and night, wherever thou mayst desire, showing to thee whatever thou desirest. Open the book, and order, and it is done, and if thou desirest to see matters of the world and to see who thou desirest, open the book and say: "I conjure you, princes of demons, who are called Selus Leus, with 69 of their associates, by the omnipotent God who made heaven and earth, sea and all things that are in them, and by your king who handed you over under my power, and by these names: Messias, Sother, Emanuel, Sabaoth, Adonay, Gymel, Caldey, heedful that you may come to me or to someone regarding my will that is ordered

---

453 *School*: Could also be any place of study.

to you, also showing to me or to someone all designated estates[454] of the world that I desire, and I order you that whosoever, whatsoever, and whensoever I desire, you may do for me all these things by my will."]

*Isti sunt qui dissipant omnem **substantiam** inimici tui, de omnibus rebus. Aperi librum, et precipe, et scientam est. Si vis dissipare omnem substantias inimici tui, vel inimicorum tuorum, vel aliorum cuius vel quorum volueris, vade ubi vis, aperi librum, et dic:*

[These are those that scatter all **wealth** of your enemy, regarding all matters. Open the book, and order, and it is known. If thou desirest to scatter all wealth of thy enemy, or of thy enemies, or of others who thou wilt desire, whatever and wherever thou wilt desire, go where thou wishest, open the book, and say:]

"Coniuro vos, Dileo, Belugo, Maconus, per nomina domini nostri Jesu Christi, et per virtutes sanctorum eius, et sanctorum nominum eius, Unigenitus, Virge, Alpha et Ω, Leo, Sponsus, Hora, Sacerdos, Jesu, Salvator, et pro reges vestros Cyrus, Satyran, Lyes, ut veniatis ad me ad eum vel alios quem vel quos voluero, quecunque vel ubicunque voluero, sine mora, in ea forma vel specie in qua vobis de voluntate

[54r]

mea precipetur, dissipantes N. proficere et totum substantiam eius inimici mei vel alterius quem vel quos voluero, per velle meo, et omnia castra, villas, vel civitates, burgos vel palacia, turres et domos, sine lesione corporali omnium hominum, omnem substantium eius dissipantes."

["I conjure you, Dileo, Belugo, Maconus, by the names of our Lord Jesus Christ, and by the virtues of his saints and these holy names, Unigenitus, Virge, Alpha and Ω, Leo, Sponsus, Hora, Sacerdos, Jesu, Salvator,[455] and on behalf of your kings,

---

454 *Estates*: Could also be "kingdoms," "authorities," or "possessions."

455 *Unigenitus…Salvator*: "Only-Begotten, Sprout, Alpha and Ω, lion, bridegroom, hour, priest, Jesus, savior."

Cyrus, Sayran, Lyes, so that you may come to me or to this one or others who I will desire, whatever and whenever I desire, without delay, in this form or appearance in which you may be ordered through my will, N., to effect the scatterings and all the wealth of this enemy of me or of another who I will desire, by my will, and all castles, estates, or fortified places,[456] settlements, or palaces, towers and homes, without injury to the body of all men, scattering all wealth of this one."]

Isti sunt audiunt et faciunt omnia mala que homines et femine faciunt et dicunt. Aperi librum et precipe et factum est. Si vis scire omnia bona et mala que homines faciunt et dicunt, dic: "Coniuro vos qui deputati estis ad illud paternitatem et trinitatem et unitatem, et per ista nomina Sudyr, Navis, Orion, Golyon, Godolyn, Amay, Silori, et per potestatem vestram que inclusit vos in hac cartula, ut veniatis ad me quodcunque, quocienscunque, et quacunque voluero, sine mora, in illa forma et specie in qua a me de voluntate mea vobis preceptum fuerit, dicentes mihi perfecte cui voluero, que dicturi sunt, dicunt, vel dixerint, de me amici vel inimici mei, facientes omnia que ego precepero mihi per velle meo."

[These are those who hear and do all evil things that men and women do and say. Open the book and order and it is done. If thou wisheth to know all good and bad things that men do and say, say: "I conjure you who were banished from that fatherhood and trinity and unity, and by these names Sudyr, Navis, Orion, Golyon, Godolyn, Amay, Silori, and by your power that imprisoned you in this document, so that you may come to me whoever [whenever], how often, and with whatsoever I will desire, without delay, in that form and appearance in which there will be a command to you from me by my will, saying to me perfectly what I desire, what they are about to say, they say, or they might have said, regarding me or of my friends or enemies, doing all for me that I will order through my will."]

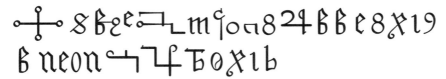

---

456 *Fortified places:* The Latin might also mean "dioceses."

Isti sunt qui faciunt et capiunt castra. Si vis facere castra aut civitates aut capere, vade ad locum ubi vis facere vel capere, et dic: "Sycors, Azochede, Festilen, Formasus, Lucifer, Barachi, Uriel, vos rogo ut edificatis edificium vel capiatis quod vobis precipio, et coniuro vos per nomina Christi, Alpha et Ω, vertute Myche, Oron, Pycayranon, Geracenta, Rampon, Jesum Christum, Theonicor, ut vos edificium vel edificia faciatis vel capiatis, per adiutorium Beryth et discipulorum eius, quecunque et quandocunque et ubicunque vobis precepero, ut veniatis in ea forma vel specie in qua a me vobis preceptum fuerit, et statim sine mora, obedientes mihi, et facite quod vobis precipietur sine querela, in quocunque die vel nocte vobis precepero, secundum voluntatem meam, edificia, castra, [et] civitates edificetis vel capiatis ad meam voluntatem."

[These are those that make and seize castles. If thou wisheth to make or to capture castles or fortified places, go to the place where thou desirest to make or capture them, and say, "Sycors, Azochede, Festile,[457] Formasus, Lucifer, Barachi, Uriel,[458] I ask you that you erect or may seize the building that I order you, and I conjure you by the names of Christ, Alpha and Ω, by the virtue of Myche, Oron, Pycayranon, Geracenta, Rampon, Jesus Christ, Theonicor, that you may make or capture the building or buildings, through the help of Beryth and of his disciples, whatever and whenever and wherever I will call you, so that you may come in this form or appearance into which there will be a command by me to you, and immediately without delay, obeying me, and do what you will be ordered without complaint, on whatever day or night I will order you, following my will, you may build or seize buildings, castles, and fortified places at my will."]

2 2 ℓ Heon ∞ ⋈ e e e e ᴧ ᵒᴋ 8 ᵗ m 8
ᴫ ⋈ c c e e e S c ᴕ ᴗ Hoon ᵗ ℓ t Ƶ m
ℰ 2 + c neon

[54v]

Isti sunt carpentarii. Si vis facere laborarium **curaminis,** *aperi librum et dic,* "Adiuro vos, Murus vel Mirus, Sorios, Karus, cum ceteris vestris sociis, per Christum regem, qui est super vos et nos et infernum, et per ista nomina Christi, Clamor, Imperator, Christus, Odier, Alpha et Ω, Salvator, et per illum qui vos in inferno proiecit, ut veniatis ad me et adiuvetis me vel alium de voluntate mea, et faciatis ea que precipio vobis de arte

---

457 *Festilen*: Could also be "Festilem."

458 Note the proximity of Lucifer and Uriel.

curaminis. Faciatis mihi laborarium in quacunque hora die vel noctis, quando vobis precepero omnia que vobis precepta fuerint, secundum voluntatem meam, statim et incontinenti facientes et mihi alii vel aliis obedientes."

[These are carpenters. If thou desirest to produce a laborer of skill,[459] open the book and say, "I adjure you, Murus or Mirus, Sorios, Karus,[460] with your remaining associates, by Christ the king, who is over you and us and hell, and by these names of Christi, Clamor, Imperator, Christus, Odier, Alpha et Ω, Salvator,[461] and by that one who cast you into hell, that you may come to me and you may help me or another regarding my will, and you may make these things that I order you regarding the craft of skill. You should make a laborer for me in whatever hour in the day or of the night, when I will command you, following my will, doing all things that there will be orders to you to do, and obeying both me and another or others, immediately and quickly."]

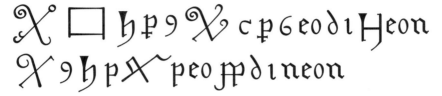

Isti sunt pistatores qui afferunt pisces. Cum volueris pisces capere, accipe vestem nigra et fermentum. Forte apperi librum, et dic, "Coniuro vos, Calmus, Carbus, cum sociis vestris millenis, per Asmoday vel per Asmodo, qui vos tradidit mihi, et per Jesum Christem dominum nostrum, et per ista nomina Christi, Manan, Liber, Fortis, Flos, Vitis, Mons, Ianua, Lapis, Angelus, Sacerdos, Iesu, Salvator, quatinus pisces quot et quos voluero, mihi statim adducatis, et veniatis in ea forma vel specie in qua a me preceptum fuerit, quecunque, et ubicunque, et in quacunque hora hoc omnio faciatis, sine mora et murmuratione, et pisces adducatis mihi per voluntate mea."

[These are fishermen who bring fish. When thou mayest desire to take fish, get black clothing and a piece of the Host. Open the book with power, and say, "I conjure you, Calmus, Carbus, with your thousands of associates, by Asmoday or by Asmodo, who handed you over to me, and by Jesus Christ our Lord, and by these names of Christ, Manan, Liber, Fortis, Flos, Vitis, Mons, Ianua, Lapis, Angelus,

---

459 Sloane 3853, 222v, has "curious works of carpentry."
460 *Murus or Mirus, Sorios, Karus:* Sloane 3853 has "Nurus or Mirus, Soyrio, Kaius"
461 *Christi...Salvator:* "Christ, Clamor, General, Christ, Odier, Alpha and Ω, Savior."

Sacerdos, Iesu, Salvator,[462] when I will desire so many fish, so many and what kind, you should bring to me immediately and you should come in this form or appearance in which there will be a command by me, whatever and wherever and in whatever hour you should do all these things without delay and murmuring, and you should bring fish to me by my will."][463]

[magical characters]

Isti sunt factores pannorum. Cum volueris facere vestem admirabilem, vade ad locum quemcunque volueris, et dic: "Coniuro te, principem demoniorum, qui vocaris Uleos, cum omnibus sotiis tuis, per natum de virgine, et per eius nomina, On, Ebrion, Manosos, On, Effraym, On, Habuero, On, Amotique, On, Regalion, ut tu in hac hora venias et facias mihi laborem vel aliis, per velle meo, quod tibi preceptum fuerit, in forma illa vel specie in qua voluero vel alii voluerint. Per velle meo venias et omnia statim et incontinenti ad voluntatem meam, facias vestem admirabilem."

[These are makers of clothing. When thou mayst desire to make wonderful clothing, go to whatever place thou mayst desire, and say: "I conjure thee, prince of the demons, who is called Uleos,[464] with all thy associates, by the birth from the virgin, and by these names, On, Ebrion, Manosos, On, Effraym, On, Habuero, On, Amotique, On, Regalion, that thou mayst come in this hour and mayst make toil for me or another by my will, that there will be a command to thee, in that form or appearance in which I desire, or others may desire. Thou mayst come by my will both immediately with all things and quickly, to my will, thou mayst make admirable clothing."]

[magical characters]

Isti sunt qui reddunt hominem. Si vis esse invisibilum, *vade ad locum clausum ubi sis obsconsus, et dic,* "Piarum, convoco te, ut

---

462 *Manan…Salvator*: "Manan, Book, Powerful, Flower, Vine, Mountain, Gate, Stone, Angel, Priest, Jesus, Savior."

463 See Sloane 3853, 222v.

464 *Uleos*: Sloane 3853, 222r, has "Ulios."

---

venias ad me." Apperi librum et statim cum robore veniet ad te, et ducet te, et nullus videbit. Liga istos, dicendo, "Coniuro te, Piarum spiritum. Ligo vos per virtute dei, et per illa nomina dei, Alleluya, Fortisson, Fortissan, Almoron, ut venias ad me vel illum quem vel quos voluero, et reducatis invisibilem me vel illum. Nec corpore meo nec corporibus eorum noceatis, et sine ulla querela, in ea forma vel specie in qua a me vel aliis vobis preceptum fuerit apperiatis, et statim et incontinenti, faciatis mihi vel sibi voluntatem meam, et obediatis mihi et eis."

[These are those who render a man invisible.[465] If thou desirest **to be** invisible, go to the enclosed place where thou wouldst be hidden, and say: "Piarum, I summon thee, that thou mayst come to me." Open the book and immediately he will come to thee with strength, and he will guide thee, and no one will see thee. Bind these, saying, "I conjure thee, spirit Piarum. I bind thee by the virtue of God, and by these names of God, Alleluya, Fortisson, Fortissan, Almoron, so that thou mayst come to me or another who I desire, and thou mayst bring back invisibility to me or that one. Mayst thou not harm either my body or those bodies, and without any complaint, thou mayst appear in this form or appearance in which there will be an order by me or others, and immediately and quickly, thou mayst do for me or himself my will, and thou mayst obey me and these ones."]

Isti sunt qui faciunt libros. Quando volueris facere libros, accipe cartas et vade ad locum ubi vis. Apperi librum, precipe, et factum est, et dic, "Coniuro vos, Abermo, et Nocte, et Nonis, et Drepis Eryneon, et Membris Liafis, et Catis vel Catacis, et Nonis, per ista nomina dei, Agla, Monhon, Tetragrammaton, Ely, Deus, Elyoron, Anepheneton, ut veniatis in hora ista, et faciatis sine ulla questione pulcherrimum librum, in illa forma vel specie in qua a me de voluntate mea preceptum fuerit, venientes et facientes librum vel libros in promptu et cum effectu qualencunque voluero, et ubicunque preceptum fuerit a me, si mihi placuerit, veniatis et statim cum effectu omnia perficere implete."

---

465 Compare Sloane MS 3853, 222v.

[These are those who make books. When thou mayst desire to make books, take the papers and go to the place that thou desirest. Open the book, order, and it is done, and say. "I conjure you, Abermo, and Nocte, and Nonis, and Drepis Eryneon, and Membris Liafis, and Catis or Catacis, and Nonis, by these names of God, Agla, Monhon, Tetragrammaton, Ely, Deus, Elyoron, Anepheneton, so that you may come in this hour, and you may make without any inquiry the most beautiful book, in that form or appearance in which there will be a command from me by my will, coming and making the book or books of whatsoever sort I desire in readiness and with accomplishment, and wherever it will be ordered by me, if it is pleasing to me, you should come and immediately fulfill to complete all things with accomplishment."]466

Isti sunt qui irritant homines. Cum volueris aliquid irritare, surge in aurora, et vade foras cum silencio. Apperi librum, et dic:

[These are those who irritate men.467 When thou mayst desire to irritate anyone, get up at dawn, and go out of doors with silence. Open the book, and say:]

"Zebulo, Meron, Musas, Mures, adiuro vos, principes tenebrarum, et coniuro vos per deum vivum et verum, et per ista nomina, Romir, Honor, Fortis, Salubris, Salvator, Unigenitus, Luminis, Habundantius, Virtutibus, Salcaurras, Jesu, ut veniatis mihi cum 38 sociis vestris, ut irritetis eum vel eam, eos vel eas, quem vel quos a me vel ab aliis vobis preceptum fuerit, pro velle meo, statim et sine mora, quecunque et ubicunque voluero, cum effectu ista precepta adimpleatis."

---

466 See *Oberon* 235. It may be that the difficulty with the beginning of that passage was that it constituted a list of spirits; note the similarity of "Abermo" here to "Obymero" there.

467 *Irritate men*: Sloane 3853, 222v, has "provoke men to anger and to fight one with another." Mun.A.4.98, 64v, has "*excitant homines et mulieres* [they excite/stimulate/awaken men and women]."

["Zebulo, Meron, Musas, Mures,[468] I adjure you, princes of darkness, and I conjure you by the living and true God, and by these names, Romir, Honor, Fortis, Salubris, Salvator, Unigenitus, Luminis, Habundantius, Virtutibus, Salcaurras, Jesu,[469] so that you may come to me with 38 of your associates, so that you may irritate that man or that woman, those men or those women, this one or those ones, there will be an order to you from me or from others, on account of my will, immediately and without delay, whatever and wherever I desire, that you may accomplish these commands with effect."]

ꝭıⱯoaꞇabɱoɛooᚹ ꭗ Ʌ neon

Isti sunt homines qui reddunt castum. Si vis esse castus et mundus, vestem mundam et castam accipe, et vade ubi vis. Apperiendo librum, et dic:

[These are the men who restore abstinence. If thou desirest to be unpolluted and pure, take spotless and pure clothing, and go where thou desirest. The book is to be opened, and say:]

"Adiuro et coniuro vos, demones qui estis ad hoc deputati per Mariam, matrem domini nostri Jesu Christi, et per omnes sanctos,

[55v]

et per monumentum domini nostri Jesu Christi, et per nigromancie saltus, et per exorcismum Salomonis, et per istas 9 literas, ut reddatis me alium vel alios castum vel castos de voluntate mea, et quacunque hora diei vel noctis vobis precepero, veniatis mihi vel illi de voluntate mea obedientes, et quecunque voluero perficere faciatis."

["I adjure and conjure you, demons, who were assigned to this matter by Mary, mother of our Lord Jesus Christ, and by all the saints, and by the tomb of our lord Jesus Christ, and by the nigromancy of the woodland,[470] and by the exorcism of Solomon and by these nine characters, so that you may restore to me or another or others abstinence from my will, and whatever hour of the day or night I will order

---

468 *Zebulo, Meron, Musas, Mures*: Sloane 3853 has "Zebuleme, Zon, Mulas, Mures."

469 *Romir...Jesu*: "Romir, Honor, Powerful, Health-Giving, Saviour, Only-Begotten, Of Light, More Abundant, With Virtue, Salcaurras, With Jesus."

470 *Saltus* could also be translated as mountain pasture, ravine, thicket, etc.

you, you may come to me or to these obeying from my will, and you may do whatever I will desire to be done."]

Isti sunt seductores mulierum. Ut muliere[m] te sequatur ubicunque volueris, apperi librum, et dic:

[These are the seductors of women. So that a woman may follow thee wherever thou mayst desire, open the book and say:]

"Raton, Rarilzispus, Mircos, rogo vos per ista nomina Lon, Gon, Neon, ut adducatis mihi vel talem vel tales mulieres vel mulierem N., sine lesione corporum et sensum, et mihi vel aliis, per velle meo."

["Raton, Rarilzispus, Mircos, I ask you by these names, Lon, Gon, Neon, that you may lead to me such women or such a woman N. without injury of the body and sense, of me or to others, by my will."]

Isti sunt rarithores thesaurorum vel feminarum. Apperi librum et dic, "Rogo vos et con-iuro vos, demones Raton, Raryhispus, cum omnibus sociis vestris, per ista nomina dei, Gon, Lon, Yana, Ye, Ya, Yoth, Vau, On, Neon, ut statim mihi veniatis in pulcra forma humana, ostendentes mihi thesauros quos desidero, vel aliis pro velle meo, per eum qui venturus est iudicare vivos et mortuos et seculum per ignem. Venite, letantes, venite, iocunditates, venite, mites, cum hillari, voltu, in forma pulcra virorum, nemeniem frau-dentes vel ledentes nec mihi nec alicui nocentes, sed mihi nec visibiliter apperentes, et omnia que voluero facientes et demonstrantes et dicentes. Fiat, fiat. Amen."

[These are providers[471] of treasure or women. Open the book and say, "I ask you and conjure you, demons Raton and Raryhispus, with all your associates, by these names of God, Gon, Lon, Yana, Ye, Ya, Yoth, Vau, On, Neon, so that you may come to me immediately in a beautiful human form, showing to me or to others treasures that I

---

471 Latin *rarithores* is unknown.

desire, on account of my will, by him who will come to judge the living and the dead and the world by fire. Come, rejoicing ones, come, players, come, peaceful ones, with good cheer, kindly, in a beautiful form of men, deceiving and killing and harming no one, neither me nor any other, but appearing to me visibly, and doing and showing and saying all that I would desire. Let it be done, let it be done. Amen."]

ℓ p G ı ꞩ] n e ı g g ꞇ Ꝓ o e ꝓ ꝕ ꜹ n neon

Isti sunt qui faciunt ferramenta et castra ferri, et omnia que volueris de ferro, exceptis armis. Si volueris ferramentum habere, vade ad locum ubi nullus te videat. Apperi librum, precipe, et factum est: Dic: "Adiuro et coniuro vos artifices ferramentorum, Lymer, Ancor, Iaspes, cum 98 sociis vestris, per Cristum deum cui contremescunt angeli et archangeli, et per ista nomina, Catos, Costos, Salutis, Gloriosus, Cremeon, Kyrion, Meneon, ut veniatis mihi in ea forma et specie in qua a me vobis preceptum fuerit, et sine mora et querela, ferramenta que volo mihi faciatis vel ferramentum verax et perfectum, sine ulla mora et incontinenti, adimpleatis que vobis precepta fuerint a me per velle meo."

[These are those who make iron implements, and castles of iron, and all that thou mayst desire of iron, with weapons excepted.[472] If thou mayst desire to have iron implements, go to a place where no one may see thee. Open the book, order, and it is done. Say, "I adjure and conjure you, artificers of iron implements, Lymer, Ancor, Iaspes,[473] with 98 of your associates, by Christ God for whom the angels and archangels tremble, and by these names, Catos, Costos, Salutis, Gloriosus, Cremeon, Kyrion, Meneon,[474] so that you may come to me in this form and appearance in which there will be an order to you by me, and without delay and complaint, you may make iron implements or the iron implement for me that I desire, true and perfect, and that you complete what commands you will have from me, without any delay and quickly, by my will."]

ı p l ꝛ n ꝓ ꝑ k ℓ ꝋ ꝋ ꝋ Ꞁ Ⱶ neon

---

472 *Iron implements…*: Sloane 3853, 222v, states "all manner of great works of iron, or of any other metal."

473 *Lymer, Ancor, Iaspes*: Sloane 3853 has "Leymer or Limer, Aner, Iaspes."

474 *Catos…Meneon*: "Intelligent, Costos, Of Health, Glorious, Cremeon, Kyrion, Meneon."

Isti sunt qui capiunt volucres. Cum volueris capere volucres, accipe vasculum virtreum, et vade ad silvas, et pone vas super librum, et dic, "Adiuro vos, Scorpus, Fligoth, Cornus, per deum et dominum nostrum, et per Asmoday, qui vos includit in hac car-

[56r]

tula, et per nomen Christi, Angelus, Salutiferus, Genitus, Consors, Pastor, Osanna et Modernus, Pius, Ancator, Clamide, Reo, Iustum, Confer, Benignus, Adesto, ut vos adducatis mihi volucres qualescunque voluero, in quacunque die vel noctis hora vobis preceptum fuerit, et statim et sine mora veraciter veniatis, et cum effectu ista precepta adimpleatis."

[These are those who capture birds. When thou mayst desireth to capture birds, take a small glass vessel, and go to the woods, and place the vessel over the book, and say, "I adjure you, Scorpus, Fligoth, Cornus,[475] by God and our Lord, and by Asmoday, who imprisoned you in this paper, and by the name of Christ, Angelus, Salutiferus, Genitus, Consors, Pastor, Osanna et Modernus, Pius, Ancator, Clamide, Reo, Iustum, Confer, Benignus, Adesto,[476] so that you may bring birds to me, whatever type I will desire, in whatever day or hour of the night there will be a command, and may you come truly, immediately and without delay, and fulfill this command with accomplishment."]

Isti sunt qui faciunt resuscitare mortuos.[477] Si vis resuscitare mortuos, et ita que facias eos ambulare per 44 dies et reverti, plus ea, ad tumulum, vade ad sepulcrum et unge ungues vel crura cum oleo. Apperi librum, et dic:

[These are those that make to revive the dead. If thou wisheth to revive the dead, and accordingly that thou mayst make them to walk for 44 days[478] and to return, more days than these, to the barrow, go to the sepulchre and anoint the nails[479] or legs with oil. Open the book, and say:]

475 *Scorpus, Fligoth, Cornus*: Sloane 3853, 222v, has "Scorpus, Stigot, Corvus [or Cornus]."

476 *Angelus…Adesto*: "Angel, Bringing Eternal Bliss, Begetting, Sharing, Shepherd, Osanna and Modern, Pious, Ancator, Clamide, Reo, Just, Confer, Good, Adesto."

477 Rawlinson D.252, 66v, provides this particular entry, separate from the rest of the list.

478 *44 days*: Chetham's Mun.A.4.98, 61v, gives twenty days.

479 *Nails*: Fingernails and toenails, not metal objects.

"Nereus, tibi principio, per deum celi, et per ista nomina Christi, Nodum, Alius, Ostium, Zegifer, Jesu, Carnis, Genitor, Salvator, ut fiat quod nunc voluero, cum precepero, ut resuscites N. ut loquar secum et ut dicat mihi veritatem de rebus quos interrogabo vel aliquis, de voluntate mea."

["Nereus, I govern thee, by the God of heaven, and by these names of Christ, Nodum, Alius, Ostium, Zegifer, Jesu, Carnis, Genitor, Salvator,[480] so it may be done that which I will now desire, when I will command, so that thou mayst revive N., so that he may speak himself and so that he may tell me the truth regarding the matters that I or another will ask him, by my will."]

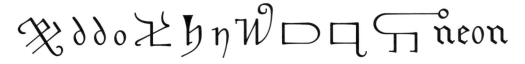

Isti sunt qui faciunt mulieres ardere in amore tuo. Vide quod mulierem vis, et vade ad lectum tuum, et dic:

[These are those who make women[481] to burn in thy love. See what woman thou desirest, and go to thy bed, and say:]

"Coniuro te, Miremicum, cum 22 sociis vestris, et per Neonem, principem vestrem, et per deum meum, et per ista nomina Gracius, Legis, Amor, Odo, Carus Christi, Leger et Niger, Nobilis, ut faciatis eam mulierem vel mulieres quod vel quos voluero exardescere in amore meo, vel aliorum de quo vel quibus voluero ego, et veniatis in ea forma vel specie in qua a me vel ab aliis de velle meo vobis preceptum fuerit, et sine querela, faciatis statim et incontinenti, et, sine aliqua molestia, mihi obediatis et voluntatem meam adimpleatis."

["I conjure thee, Miremicum,[482] with 22 of your associates, and by Neonem,[483] your prince, and by my God, and by these names, Gracius, Legis, Amor, Odo, Carus Christi, Leger and Niger, Nobilis,[484] that you may make this woman or women who

---

480 *Nodum…Salvator*: "Nodum, Other, Door, Zegifer, Jesus, Flesh, Father, Saviour."

481 Sloane 3853, 222r, adds "and men."

482 *Miremicum*: Could also be *Miremicun*. Sloane 3853 has "Inrinut."

483 *Neonem*: Truncated in manuscript, but this reading agrees with Sloane 3853. On the other hand, Mun.A.4.98 gives "*nomen* [name]."

484 *Gracius…Nobilis*: "Beloved, Of the Law, Love, Odo, Precious of Christ, I Am Appointed and Black, Renowned." Mun.A.4.98, 64r has "Gracius Legis Amor Odocarus Presubaus [?] Nobilis."

I will desire to blaze up in love of me or of others who I will desire, and you may come in this form or appearance into which there will be a command to you from me or from these by my will, and without complaint you may do this immediately and quickly, and, without any annoyance, you may obey me and fulfill my will."]

Isti sunt seductores mulierum. Ut mulier te sequatur ubicunque volueris. Aperi librum, et dic:

[These are the seductors of women. Thus a woman may follow thee wherever thou mayst wish. Open the book, and say:]

"*Sadon, Rarnilpus, Rurcos,*[485] *coniuro vos per ista nomina, Gonvon, Non, ut adducatis mihi vel alii cui voluere, mulieres N., sine lesione corporis et anime mee, sine aliqua molestia. Veniatis in ea forma specie mihi qua a me vel alio vobis precipietur. Veniatis statim et incontinenti, sine mora et molestia, mihi obedientur [obedient] vel alii per velle meo.*"

["Sadon, Rarnilpus, Rurcos, I conjure you by these names, Gonvon, Non, that you may bring to me or to others who I desire, women N., without wound of my body or soul, without any annoyance. You may come in that form or appearance to me, that will be ordered to you by me or another. You may come immediately and quickly, without delay and annoyance, to obey me or another by my will."]

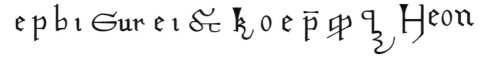

[56v]

485 *Sadon, Rarnilpus, Rurcos*: Sloane 3853, 223r has "Zacon, Raruhilpus, Nircos." Mun.A.4.98, 65v has "Savon Carmulpos Curcos."

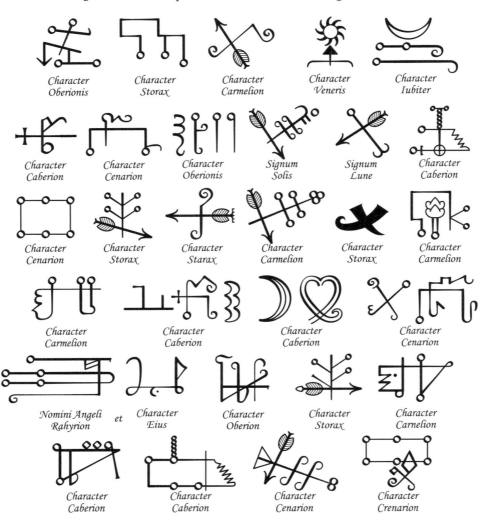

Character Oberionis   *Character Storax*   *Character Carmelion*   *Character Veneris*   *Character Iubiter*

Character Caberion   *Character Cenarion*   *Character Oberionis*   *Signum Solis*   *Signum Lune*   *Character Caberion*

Character Cenarion   *Character Storax*   *Character Starax*   *Character Carmelion*   *Character Storax*   *Character Carmelion*

Character Carmelion   *Character Caberion*   *Character Caberion*   *Character Cenarion*

Nomini Angeli Rahyrion   *et*   *Character Eius*   *Character Oberion*   *Character Storax*   *Character Carmelion*

Character Caberion   *Character Caberion*   *Character Cenarion*   *Character Crenarion*

486 Text, Line 1: *Character Oberionis* [of Oberon] *Character Storax Character Carmelion Character Veneris* [of Venus] *Character Iubiter* [of Jupiter].

Line 2: *Character Caberion Character Cenarion Character Oberionis* [of Oberon] *Signum Solis* [Sign of the Sun] *Signum Lune* [Sign of the Moon] *Character Caberion*.

Line 3: *Character Cenarion Character Storax Character Starax Character Carmelion Character Storax Character Carmelion*.

Line 4: *Character Carmelion Character Caberion Character Caberion Character Cenarion*.

Line 5: *Nomen Angeli Rahyrion et Character Eius* [the name of the angel Rahyrion and his character] *Character Oberion Character Storax Character Carnelion*.

Line 6: *Character Caberion Caberion Character Cenarion Character Cenarion*. Compare to *Oberon*, 454–5.

[List of Spirit Names]

Ego sum Azoel, spiritus thesaurorum qui obscendo ego, et quod velle apereo. Do subito nec quiquid de hiis, sine me haberi potest vel eciam retineri. Ecce, assum, quid vocasti me.

[I am Azoel, spirit of treasures that I hide, and that I show it according to my will. I give suddenly and not everything of these things, without it being able to be held or even to be possessed by me. Behold, I appear, as thou hast called me.][487]

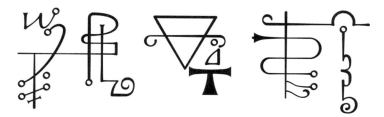

Ego sum Bell, spiritus qui do scientiam thesaurum et spiritum familiarem, qui omnes tuas compleo voluntates, et facio consecratum suum experimentis et spiritu, ut occultos thesauros et universa totalia adduco. Ecce, assum, quid vocasti me.

[I am Bell,[488] the spirit who gives the knowledge of treasures and familiar spirits, that I supply all your wishes, and I make its consecration with the experiments and the spirit, so that I bring hidden treasures and all together. Behold, I appear, as thou hast called me.]

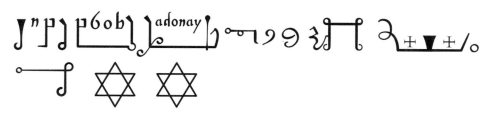

[57r]

487 For a longer conjuration and a similar seal for Azoel, see Rawlinson D.252, 68r–69r.

488 *Bell*: Spirit likely derived from the biblical Ba'al or Baal (see above). His name is similar to that of Bael in the *Goetia*, but the functions and seals of the spirits are quite different. See Peterson, *The Lesser Key of Solomon*, 7.

*Ego sum spiritus Namath, avertens mala inimicis, et **retrocedere** facio tela, emissa, sibi ipsi nec sedi posset ab aliquo inimico qui me invocaverat. Ecce, assum, quid vocasti me.*

[I am the spirit Namath, averting evil matters by enemies, and I make missiles sent out **to return** to them, and he would not be able to abide from any enemy that had invoked me. Behold, I appear, as thou hast called me.]⁴⁸⁹

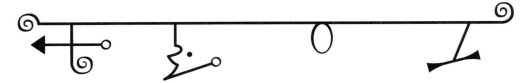

*Ego sum spiritus Mezebin. Sciencies bona et mala, preterita, **presentia,** et futura do, et noticiam in hiis, et in herbis **gratiosis et vertuosis,** et lapidibus **preciosis.** Ecce, assum, quid vocasti me.*

[I am the spirit Mezebin, I give the sciences, good and bad, the past, **present,** and **future,** and fame in these, and in **agreeable and virtuous** herbs, and in **precious** stones. Behold, I appear, as thou hast called me.]⁴⁹⁰

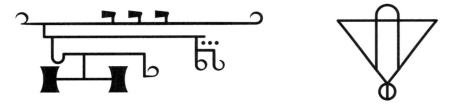

Ego sum Ydyal, spiritus qui aurum et argentum, montes et flumina, fontes et lacus, campes et edificia, qualibet transfero. Conficio, erigo novas domos. Planto, edificio quiquid volo, et reduco ad gradum prestinum. Ecce, assum, quid vocasti me.

[I am Ydyal, the spirit who carries gold and silver, mountains and streams, springs and lakes, fields and buildings everywhere. I complete and build new houses. I plant and I build whatever I desire, and I return it to the original state. Behold, I appear, as thou hast called me.]

---

489 *Namath*: See Cambridge University Library Additional 3544, 103.
490 *Mezebin*: See description of "Mekebin," Cambridge University Library Additional 3544, 103.

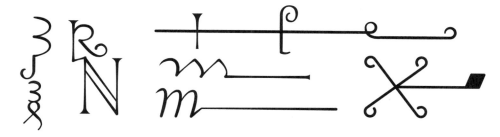

Ego sum Castrietar, spiritus celeris, qui porto homines et reduco unecunque et ubi-cunque voluerit, in mome[n]to, nec est qui me impediat, et hoc absque omni lesione vel periculo, iuxta voluntatem invocantis. Ecce, assum, quid vocasti me.

[I am Castrietar, the quick spirit, who carries men and brings them back whenev-er[491] and wherever he may desire, in a moment, and there is nothing that may hin-der me, and this without all harm or danger, according to the invoking will. Behold, I appear, as thou hast called me.][492]

Ego sum Annrafael, spiritus grandis et fortis, qui subverto montes et pontes. Contero, erigo, et restituo in momento. Per me eum cadunt turres, et in ictu oculi subleuantur. Ecce, assum, quid vocasti me.

[I am Annrafael, a spirit great and strong, who overthrows mountains and bridges. I destroy, erect, and restore these in a moment. Through me the towers of these fall, and in the blink of the eyes, they are raised up. Behold, I appear, as thou hast called me.]

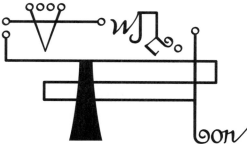

491 *Whenever*: Latin "unecunque" is unclear.
492 *Castrietar*: See "Castrietur," Cambridge University Library Additional 3544.

se'tur in sequenti folio [it will follow in the next folio]

[57v]

Pentaculum Salomonis [Pentacle of Solomon]
Signum Salomonis [Sign of Solomon][493]
Circulus Aquaticus [The Aquatic Circle][494]

493 Text around star points: *Ag Christus La* [Agla].

494 Additional MS. 36674, 159r; Bacon and Macdonald, *De Nigromancia: Sloane Ms. 3885 & Additional Ms. 36674*, 59; Wellcome 110, 75v.

Text, outer ring: + Pantheon + + Usion + + Agla + + Amaziel + + Pancraciel + + Gabriel + + Michael +.

Inside inner ring: *Spiritus Sanctus* [Holy Spirit] *Filius* [Son] *Adonay Pater* [Father] *Sabaoth Deus* [God] *Emanuel Omnipotens* [Omnipotent].

Within circle: *Principalis* [Head] *Socius* [Associate].

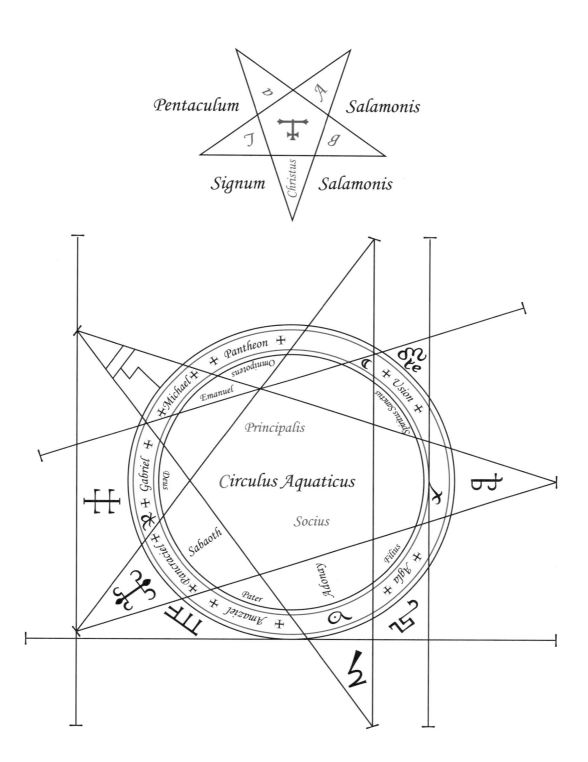

Pentaculum Salamonis

Signum Salamonis

Circulus Aquaticus

[List of Spirits, Continued]

Ego sum Ramath, spiritus rapimarum, qui fures provoco ad surendum que volo invenire. Res preditas facio et restituo in momento. Ecce, assum, quid vocasti me.

[I am Ramath, the spirit of robbery, who calls forth thieves for stealing anything I desire to acquire. I bequeath and I return the provided items in a moment. Behold, I appear, as thou hast called me.]

Ego sum Baalam, spiritus gratiosus, qui inclino corda potentiam ad premovendum quos voluero ad honores et dignitates, quod velle illius qui me invocaverit. Sublevo et humilio quos voluero. Ecce, assum, quid vocasti me.

[I am Balaam,[495] an agreeable spirit, who inclines the hearts of the powerful ones to a great stirring toward honors and dignities that I will desire, those by the will of that one who will invoke me. I raise up and abase whomever I wish. Behold, I appear, as thou hast called me.]

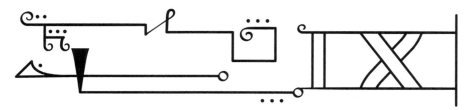

---

495 *Baalam:* A spirit quite different from his appearance and functions in other works. Peterson, *The Lesser Key of Solomon*, 30; Weyer, *De praestigiis daemonum*, 930; Scot, *The Discouerie of Witchcraft*, 391.

Ego sum Marog, spiritus ocii et terditatis, qui stare naves facio super aquas et homines super terram, nec movere possunt de loco ubi steterint, nisi ad [i]mperium meum iuxta voluntatem invocantis me. Ecce, assum, quid vocasti me.

[I am Marog, a spirit of swiftness and of tardiness, who makes ships to stand still on the waters, and men on land, and not be able to move from a place where they should remain, unless to my command, according to the will calling me. Behold, I appear, as thou hast called me.]

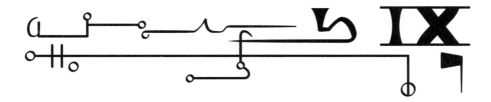

Ego sum Gaziel, spiritus diurtiarum [diuitiarum], qui eas congrego. Custodio bona vel subtrahe [subtraho] in bonae deficieti, et ego nummularios et pecunias perdo. Omnia mihi licent. Ecce, assum, quid vocasti me.

[I am Gaziel, a spirit of wealth, who collects these things together. I guard one's possessions, or I take them in the abandoning of possessions, and I lose moneys and riches. All things are permitted to me. Behold, I appear, as thou hast called me.]

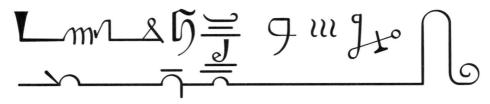

[58v]

[blank]

[59r]

Circulum in quo Spiritus Aerei et Ignei

[The Circles in which the Spirits of the Air and of Fire...][496]

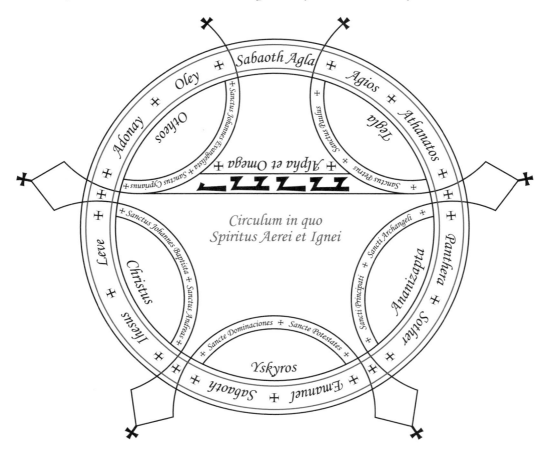

496 Additional Ms. 36674, 156v; Bacon and Macdonald, *De Nigromancia: Sloane Ms. 3885 &*
Additional Ms. 36674, 49.; Sloane 3850, 113v.

   Text, inside ring: Sabaoth Agla + Agios + Athanatos + + + Panthera + Sother + + + Emanuel
+ Sabaoth + + + Ihesus + Leve + + + Adonay + Oley +.

   Inside ring: Tegla Ananizapta Yskyros Christus Otheos + Alpha et Ω.

   Loops, going clockwise: + *Sanctus Petrus + Sanctus Paulus* + / + *Sancti Principati + Sancti*
Archangeli + / + *Sancte Dominaciones + Sancte Potestates* + / + *Sanctus Iohannes Baptista +*
Sanctus Andreas + / + *Sanctus Johannes Evangelista + Sanctus Cyprianus* + [+ Saint Peter + Saint
Paul + / + Holy Principalities + Holy Archangels + / + Holy Dominions + Holy Powers + /
Saint John the Baptist + Saint Andrew + / + Saint John the Evangelist + Saint Cyprian +]

   Inner bar: Yod-He-Vau-He.

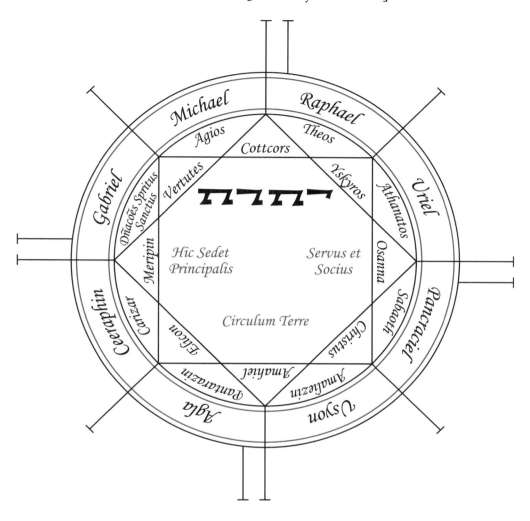

[59v]

497 Bacon and Macdonald, 55; Wellcome MS. 110, 77v.
      Text, inside ring: Raphael Uriel Pancraciel Usyon Agla Ceraphin Gabriel Michael.
      Inside ring: Theos Athanatos Sabaoth Amaliezin Pantarizin Carizar Dominaciones Spiritus
Sanctus Agios.
      Inside eight-pointed star: Cottcors Yskyros Osanna Christus Amahiel Elicon Meripin
Vertutes.
      Center: Yod-He-Vau-He *Hic Sedet Principalis* [Here Sits the Head] *Servus et Socius* [Servant
and Associate].

498 Top circle, text, outer ring: + Messias Sother + Emanuel Sabaoth + Adonay Usion + Panthon
Craton + Messias Sother + Emmanuel Sabaoth + Adonay Usions Jesus.

Inner ring: + + *Sanctus Deus* + + + *Sanctus Fortis* + + + *Sanctus et Imortalis* + + + *Miserere
Nobis* + [Holy God + + + Holy Strength + + + Holy and Immortal + + + Have Mercy on Us +].

Around square: Occinomos Occinomos Occinomos Occinomos.

Inside square: Pancracion Pancracion Pancracion Pancracion.

Triangle, perimeter: Brytanoy Athaoth Sathagon.

Center: *Triangulus* [triangle].

Bottom diagram, BL Additional Ms. 36674, 160v. This represents part of a procedure using
an ointment to view spirits.

Circle with triangle, text, outer ring: + *Sancte Petre* + + *Sancte Paule* + + *Sancte Andrea* +
+ *Sancte Laurenti* + *Sancte Johannes Baptista* + *Jesus Christ* + *Maria Sancta* + [Saint Peter + +
Saint Paul + + Saint Andrew + + Saint Lawrence + Saint John the Baptist + Jesus Christ + Holy
Mary].

Outside triangle: *Deus Pater Deus Filius Deus Spiritus Sanctus* [God the Father God the Son
God the Holy Ghost].

Inside triangle: + Yod-He-Vau-He + Sancte Michael + + Yod-He-Vau-He + Sancte Gabriel +
+ Yod-He-Vau-He + Sancte Raphael +.

Left dagger, blade: + Hath + Hoth + Iohihith +.

Pommel: *Crucifixus* [crucified].

Right dagger, blade: Agla Usion Verbum.

Pommel: IHS.

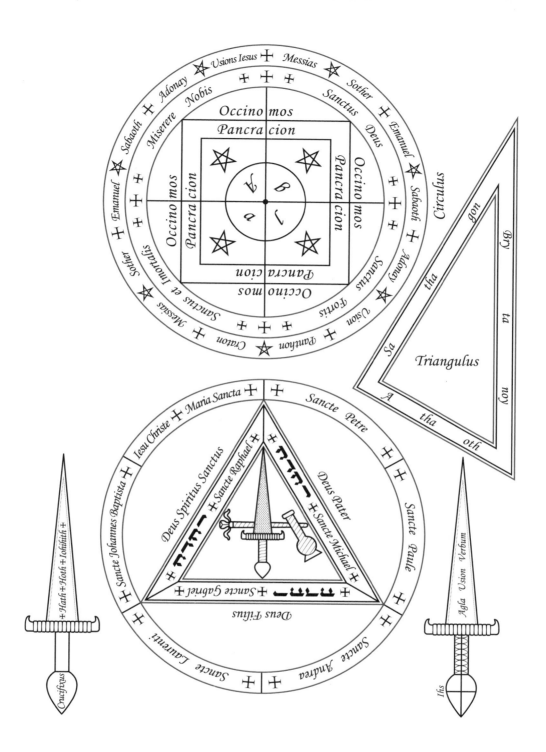

[Notes on Incense]

*Thurifices aunt circulum cum olibano puro, et dimittas thuribulum in circulo cum igne et olibano. Zep **circulus coleret**.*

[Moreover, thou mayst suffumigate the circle with pure frankincense, and thou mayst send forth the thurible in the circle with fire and frankincense. Thus (?) the circle might protect.]

[60r]

[Hexagram and] Circulus Equi
[The Circle of the Horse][499]

499 BL Additional Ms. 36674, 162r; Wellcome 110, 82v, 83v. For experiments to call a spiritual horse to serve the magician, see Bacon and Macdonald, *De Nigromancia*, 65–71; Kieckhefer, *Forbidden Rites*, 219–21; BL Additional Ms. 36674, 161r–162r; Bodleian Rawlinson D.252, 74v–75v.

   Upper diagram, text, inside edges: *Sancte Michael Deus Filius Sancte Uriel Sancte Raphael Sabriel Deus Spiritus Sanctus* [Saint Michael, God the Son, Saint/Holy Uriel, Saint/Holy Raphael, Sabriel, God the Holy Spirit].

   Sides: *Sancte Deus Sancte Deus* [Holy God Holy God].

   Center: *Deus Pater* [God the Father] Yod-He-Vau-He Jesus. Note that "Sabriel" is "Gabriel" in other sources, including Additional Ms. 36674, Cambridge Additional 3544, 32, Leipzig Cod. mag. 16, 103v; Rawlinson D.252 74v. The art has been changed to reflect this spelling.

   Lower diagram, circle: Craton + Agla.

   Triangle edge: Messias + Deus Filius + Sother / Sabaoth Deus Pater + Adonay + Ath + / Emanuel + Spiritus Sanctus + Pantheos.

   Inside circle: Yod-He-Vau-He Circulus Equi.

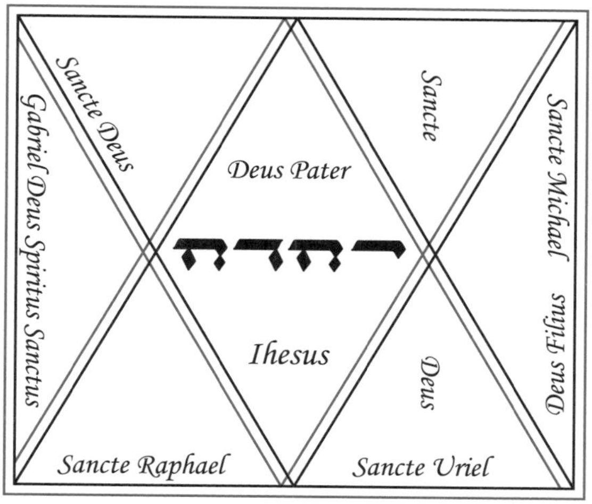
Sancte Deus
Gabriel Deus Spiritus Sanctus
Deus Pater
Sancte
Sancte Michael
Deus Filius
Ihesus
Deus
Sancte Raphael
Sancte Uriel

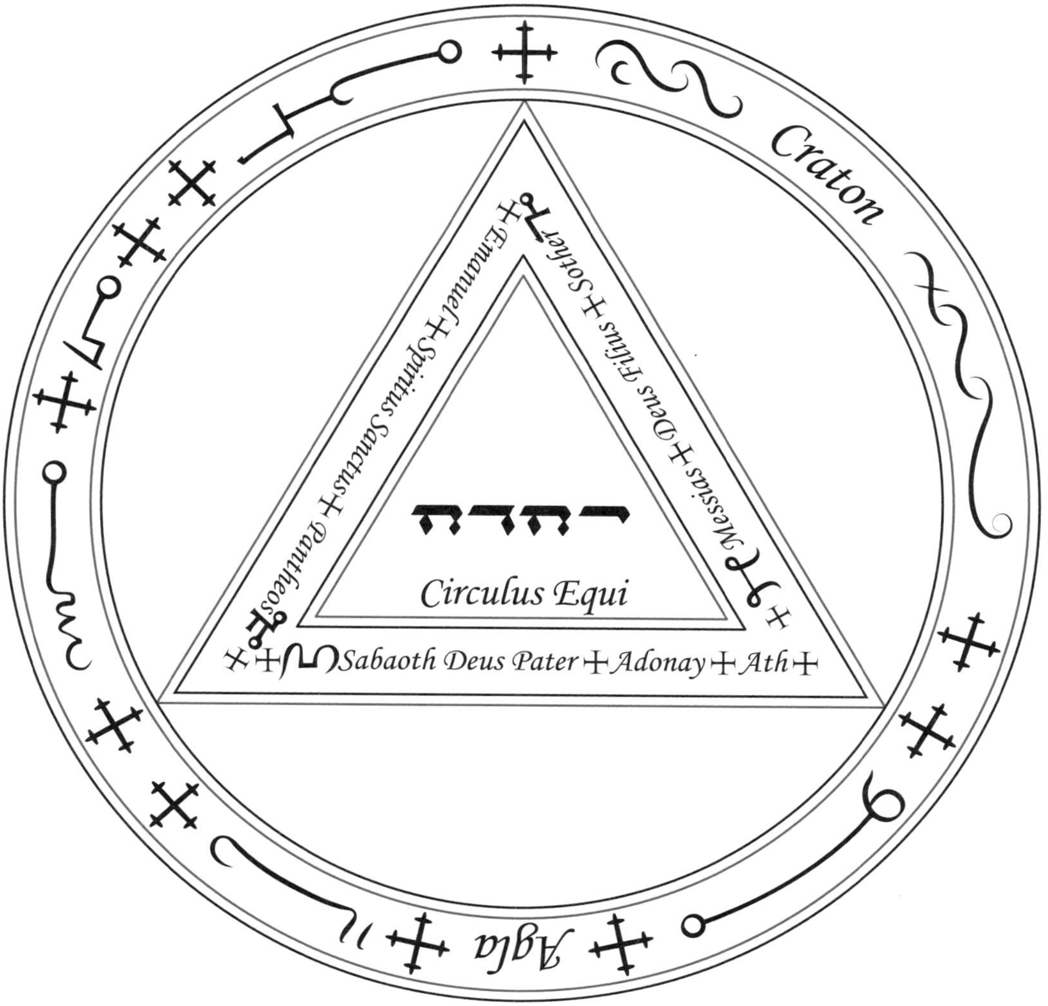
Craton
Agla
Emanuel
Spiritus Sanctus
Pantheos
Soter
Deus Filius
Messias
Sabaoth Deus Pater
Adonay
Ath
Circulus Equi

[60v]

[Magical Triangles][500]

500 Additional Ms. 36674, 163r; Bacon and Macdonald, *De Nigromancia: Sloane Ms. 3885 &*
     Additional Ms. 36674, 74; Wellcome MS. 110, 98r. Part of an operation to summon Alastiel.
         Upper circle, text, outside ring: *Oriens* [east].
         Inside ring: + Sancte Uriel + + Sancte Gabriel + Sancte Michael + R + + Sancte Raphael + +.
         Outside triangle: *Sanctus Immortalis Sanctus Deus Sanctis Fortis* [Holy immortal one, holy
     God, holy strong one].
         Inside triangle: + *Sanctus Spiritus Deus* + *Sanctus Deus Pater* + *Sanctus Deus Filius* [+ God
     the Holy Ghost + God the Holy Father + God the Holy Son].
         Outside border triangle: *In isto circulo erit anulus* [in this circle will be the ring].
         Lower circle, text, inside ring: + Raguel + Arath + Muscet + Senth + Astaroth + Belial +
     Sathan.
         Outside triangle: Agla Agios Alpha.
         Inside triangle: Bleth Ppiuli (?) Micoil (?).

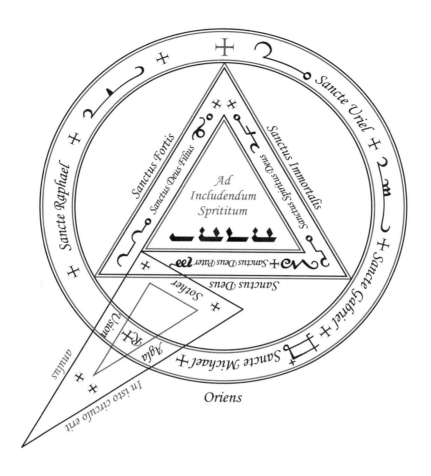

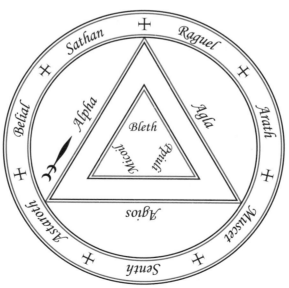

501 Circle 1, text, inside ring: + *Ut* [as] Emanuel + Raphael + Michael + Gabriel +*et* [and] + Otheos
+ Agios + Adonay + Sabaoth.

Outside triangle: + *Deus Filius On* + + *Deus Pater Eternus* + + *Deus Spiritus Sanctus Alpha* [+
God the Son On + + God the Eternal Father + + God the Holy Spirit Alpha].

Center: + *Sother*+ + *Agios* + *Circulum ad Indudem Spiritum in Phi* [Circle for the Purpose of
the Possessing Spirit in Philosophy] + Agla + Yod-He-Vau-He.

Circle 2: *Item Cooperitorium Bleth* [Also the Covering of Bleth].

Around inside ring: + Agla + Adonay + Thau + Ioth.

Circle 3: *Circulus 3m militum* [Circle of the Three Knights].

Circle 4: *Circulus Osininalis* [The Circle of Osininalis].

Text, around outside: Ba Bi Lo N.

Inside outer ring: Messias Sother Emanuel Sabaoth.

Inner ring: Onayan.

Circle 5: *Cooperitorium Pendegriel* [The Covering of Pendegriel].

Border: + A + g + l + a + Sabaoth + Adonay + Eloy.

Inside: *Christus vincit / Christus / regnat / Christus imperat* [Christ conquers / Christ /
reigns / Christ commands].

Regarding Bleth in circle 2, see below on the spirit Bileth. The "covering" here may be
the seal on the urinal, or glass vessel, in which the spirit is to appear; Cambridge University
Library Additional 3544, 102–3. Regarding Circle 3, a well-known experiment involves
the calling of three spirits as soldiers or knights; for example, see Sloane 3846, 111r–112r;
Cambridge University Library Additional 3544, 100–1. Regarding Circle 4, a similarly named
spirit, Osininilis or Osiminilis, appears in a mirror operation in Sloane MS. 3853, 232v–233v,
although that circle on 233v is quite different than this one.

Circulum ad Indudem Spiritum in Phi

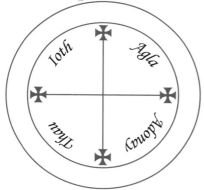

Item Cooperitorium Bleth

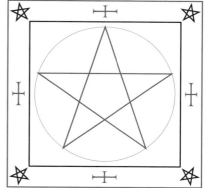

Circulus ·3· Militum
m

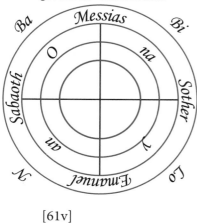

Circulus Osininalis

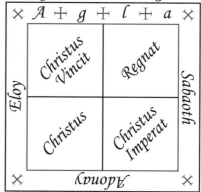

Cooperitorium Pendegriel

[61v]

Circulus Satan Barrados Belzebue
[The Circle (of) Satan, Barrados, Belzebue][502]

502 This title may only refer to the circle at upper left.

Text, second circle, center: A G V G.

Third, center: Gitgih.

Fourth, outer ring: + Adonay. Inner star: Brepsnpa.

Fifth, inside ring: Estrion. Inside circle: Sa Va / Sam Bo / Ia Es / Te Ve.

Sixth, inside ring: + O R I S T I O N. Around middle: *Lex Salus Pax Lux* [Light Health Peace Light].

Seventh, inside ring: + Usyrion.

Eighth, inside ring: + Ebiona. Inside circle: Suum Ma Ban Dos Kyeth Paly Ton Hec Gla Ca.

Ninth circle, around edge: + Ygiorbyg.

Tenth circle, inside ring: + Osinels. Center: Agla Alga Coga Agal.

Eleventh circle, inside ring: *Quamvis audieris tonitrua, respice hanc figuram et non occurret tibi malum nec fulgure [fulgura] nec tonitrua. Verum est.* [Although thou wilt hear thunders, look back upon this figure and evil will not meet thee, neither thunders or lightnings. It is true.]

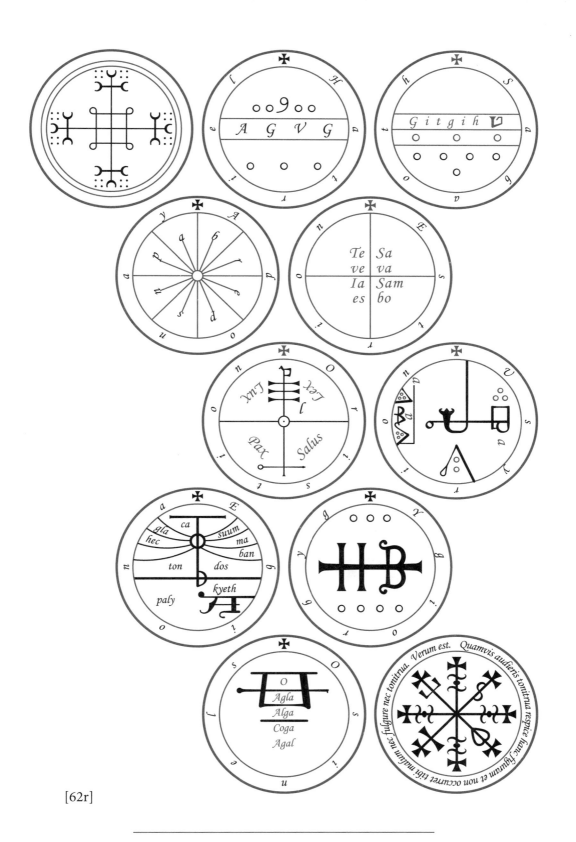

[62r]

259

503 Circles from top to bottom, left to right, text, first circle: + *In quocunque die videris hoc signum ne iugulaberis nec morte subitanea peribis. Probatum est certe.* [In whatsoever day thou mayst see this sign, thou wilt not be killed nor die from an unexpected death. It is certainly proved.]

Second: Hoc est signum quod posuit dominus in fronte Aaron quam do progebat contra hostes suos. [This is the sign that the Lord placed on the forehead of Aaron, which the same was protecting against his enemies.]

Third: + *Hoc signum contra demones valet die ac nocte In nomine domini nostri Jesu Christi.* [This sign has strength against demons in day and night, in the name of our Lord Jesus Christ.]

Fourth: + *Mulier cum in partu laborat si hoc signum super se humerit lenum pariet verum est.* [When a woman suffers in birth, if she will moisten this sign on herself, she will give birth easily. It is true.]

Fifth: + *In quocumque die videris hoc signum non peribis in aqua nomine domini ineffabile certe est.* [+ In whatsoever day thou mayst see this sign, thou wilt not perish in water, in the ineffable name of God, it certainly is.]

Sixth: + *Qui hanc figuram secum portaverit ignis ei nocere non poterit sed salvabit socios.* [+ Who will carry this figure with him, fire will not be able to hurt him, but he will save his associates.]

Seventh: + *Contra arma et non poterit a te gutta sanguinis exire et probatum est vere.* [+ Against weapons, and it will not be able to produce a drop of blood, and it is truly proven.]

Eighth: + *Istam figuram forte cum non gladio peribis nec veneno nec subitania morte verum est.* [This strong figure, when thou wouldst not die with sword, nor with poison, nor with sudden death. It is true].

Circulum Salomonis [*Circle of Solomon*]⁵⁰⁴

Oriens
Olla

Boreas
Olla

Meridies
Olla

Occidens
Olla

Hisforiel

Ioth heth he van

Porta

Circulum Salamonis

Ia fa fa Ia

dafur

Hoc signum Salamonis est qua dæmonis in puteo mr sigillavit It mn verum est ti mn n n

S
B
Athi
ee
r
ie
o

[63r]

Experiments

ANGER TO ASSUAGE

Write this name in an apple, Yava, and cast it at thine enemy, and thou shalt assuage his anger, or give it to a woman, and she shall love thee.

BLEEDING TO STAUNCH

Write with his own blood on his forehead this word, Beronix, and for a woman, Beronixa,[505] or touch the place that bleedeth with thy finger, and then say, "*In nomine patris vere, in nomine filii vere, in nomine spiritus sancti vere* [In the name of the true Father, in the name of the true Son, in the name of the true Holy Ghost], and in the virtue of these three names of thy bleeding, now staunch." *Probatum est* [It is proven].

BLEEDING TO STAUNCH

"Dac, hac, sanguis manit in te, cicut Christus fecit in se. Sanguis manit in sua vena, sicut Christus in sua pena. Sanguis, maneti iuste fixus, sicut Christu quando fuit cruci-fex."

["Dac, hac, blood remains in thee, just as Christ did himself. Blood remains in his veins, just as Christ in his pain. Blood, remain affixed justly, as in Christ when he was crucified."][506]

BLEEDING TO STAUNCH

De sanguine qui effluxit. Scribe nomina apostolorum in pergamena, videlicet, Petri, Pauli, et Andrea, et liga super hominem vel bestiam, et statim cessabit. + Fyat + fyat + fyat +

[For the blood that flowed out. Write the names of the apostles on parchment, namely, of Peter, of Paul, and of Andrew, and tie it on the man or beast, and it will cease immediately. + Let it be done + let it be done + let it be done +]

---

505 *Beronix...Beronixa*: A reference to St. Veronica, who was believed to be the bleeding woman healed by touching Jesus's cloak (Matthew 9:20–22). Similar examples to this charm have turned up in sources ranging geographically from Denmark to the Netherlands. Braekman, "Middelnederlandsche Zegeningen, Bezweringsformulien en Towerplanten," 288, 316; Henslowe, *Henslowe's Diary*, 33; Hunt, *Popular Medicine in Thirteenth-Century England*, 29; Ohrt, *Danmarks Trylleformler*, 2:94.

506 A garbled version of the "Stans sanguine in te" charm, which dates back to the mid-fourteenth century. The original was likely intended to rhyme. Roper, *English Verbal Charms*, 121–22.

Bleeding to Staunch

"God that was born in the borough of Bethlem, and baptised in the water of *flem* [river] Jordan. The water was both wild and wood; the child was both meek and good. He blessed the flood, and still it stood. With the same blessing that he blessed the flood, I bless thee, blood, by virtue of the child so good." And say five Pater Nosters, five Aves, and one Creed.[507]

Bleeding to Staunch

"Christ that died on the rood, and on the cross shed his blood. There came three angels that were good, with three chalices to receive his blood. Christ Jesus, for thy bitter passion, stay you the blood of N." Say this thrice, with a Pater Noster, Ave, and Creed.

Bewitched or Forspoken[508] or Enchanted

"If any three biters have thee forbidden, with wicked tongue, with wicked thought, or with wicked eyes all the most. I pray God be thy boot, in the name of the Father, and of the Son, and of the Holy Ghost. God, that virtue between water and land, be thy help and succour with this prayer that I can. For Jesus's sake and Saint Charity.[509] Amen." Say this nine times over, and at every third time, a Pater Noster, an Ave, and a Creed.[510]

Bewitched or Forspoken

Whoever shall carry these names of God about them need not to fear the peril of water, fire, or enchantment, evil end, or enemy. If a woman with child carry them about her, she shall be safely delivered. That hath been proved.

+ Messias + Sother + Emanuel + Sabaoth + Adonay + Unigenitus + Via + Vita + Manus + Homo + Usyon + Principium + Primogenitus + Virtus + Sapientia + Alpha + et Ω + Caput + Finis + Fons + Origo + Boni + Paraclitus + Mediator + Agnus + Ovis + Vitulus + Serpens + Aries + Leo + Vermis + Os + Verbum + Splendor + Sol

---

507 The "Flum Jordan" charm, a traditional blood-staunching charm dating back to the seventh century. Roper, *English Verbal Charms*, 104–9; Davies, "Healing Charms in Use in England and Wales 1700–1950," 21.

508 *Forspoken*: Charmed with magic.

509 *Saint Charity*: Early Christian martyr, likely of apocryphal origins, supposedly killed with her sisters Hope and Faith. See Farmer, *The Oxford Dictionary of Saints*, 161–62.

510 The "three bitter biters" charm appears first in the fourteenth century, and later in many sixteenth- and seventeenth-century sources, including other grimoires, as a charm against witchcraft; e.g., BL Sloane 3846, 71r. Most famously, the charm was cited in the Pendle witch trials of 1612; see Roper, *English Verbal Charms*, 125–27.

+ Gloria + Lux + Imago + Panis + Flos + Vitis + Mons + Ianua + Petra + Lapis +
Angelus + Sponsus + Pastor + Propheta + Sacerdos + Athanatos + Kyros + Theos +
Panton + Craton + Ysus + Salvator + Eleyson + Himas Veritas + Ego sum qui sum
+ Christus + Deus + Jesus + Nazarenus + Rex + Iudeorum + Salus + Pater + Filius +
Spiritus Sanctus + Omnipotens + Misericers + Eternus + Creator + Mitium + Pri-
mus + Novissimus + Trinitas + Deitas + Unitas + Bonitas + atque Maiestas +[511]

Te adoramus atque invocamus, domine, nomen tuum. Benedictus deus in eternum,
visita nos in salutari tuo, et in via pacis me dirige. Memor esto mei, Christe, rex gloriae,
et in virtute tua exaudi me, et libere me ab omnibus tribulationibus, malicia augustiis,
et periculis omnium inimicorum meorum, visibilium et invisibilium. [We implore and
call upon your name, Lord. Blessed God in eternity, visit us in your salvation, and
direct me in the way of peace. Be heedful of me, Christ, king of glory, and in your
virtue hear me, and free me from all tribulations, spite from great ones, and the
dangers of all my enemies, visible and invisible.] Amen.

[63v]

Bewitched, Forspoken, or Enchanted

+ Christus + Jesus + Sother + Messias + Defende me, creaturam tuam N., nomine ab
omnibus malignis spiritibus. Exurgat deus, et dissipentur omnes inimici nici fugiant a
facie mea, sicut cera a facie ignis. Amen. Fiat, et ita veniat in nomine patris, et filii, et
spiritus sancti. Amen. Sola potestate sanctissimae trinitatis, que unus atque trinus est,
unus in essentia atque trinus in persone, hoc effectum sit. Amen. Ab omni malo, libera
me, domine. Amen. Ab insidiis diaboli, libera me, domine. Amen. A tentatione demo-
num, libera me, domine. Amen. A damnatione perpetua, libera me, domine. Amen. Ab
omni maleficio, venefitio, maledictione, fassinatione, incantatione malo aspectu, a
potestate et malicia omnium inimicorum meorum, visibilium et invisibilium, et ab hac
aegritudine qua nunc laboro. Libera, protege, et defende me, domine, propter gloriam
sanctissimi nominis tui, nunc et semper. Amen. A subitane, improvisa, et eterna morte,

---

511 *Unigenitus…Maiestas*: Translation: "Only-Begotten + Way + Life + Hand + Man + Essence
+ Beginning + Firstborn + Strength + Wisdom + Alpha + and Ω + Head + End + Source +
Beginning + of the Good + Advocate + Mediator + Lamb + Sheep +, Bull-calf + Serpent +
Ram + Lion + Worm + Mouth (or Face) + Word + Brilliance + Sun + Glory + Light + Likeness
+ Bread + Flower + Grapevine + Mountain + Gate + Rock + Stone + Angel + Bridegroom +
Shepherd + Prophet + Priest + Undying + Opportune Moment + Everywhere + Of All + Power
+ Jesus + Savior + Have Mercy + Last Truth [?] + I am that I am + Christ + God + Jesus + of
Nazareth + King + of the Jews + Health + Father + Son + Holy Ghost + Omnipotent + Merciful
[?] + Eternal + Creator + of the Mild One [?] + First + Newest + Trinity + Deity + Unity +
Goodness + and Majesty."

libera et defende me domine + Jesus nazarenus, rex iudeorum, fili dei, miserere mei +
Amen. + Contra tristiciam, timorem, et melancholiam cuiusdam egroti, portetur.

[+ Christus + Jesus + Sother + Messias + Defend me, your creature N., in [your] name from all evil spirits. Let God rise, and all my enemies may be dissipated, unless they may flee from my appearance, just as wax from the appearance of fire. Amen. Let it be done, and thus he may come in the name of the Father, and of the Son, and of the Holy Ghost. Amen. Only with the most holy power of the Trinity, that is one and three, one in essence and three in person, let this be accomplished. Amen. From all evil things, free me, Lord. Amen. From the snares of the devil, free me, Lord. Amen. From the temptation of the demons, free me, Lord. Amen. From perpetual damnation, free me, Lord. Amen. From all witchcraft, poisoning, malediction, fascination, and incantation with evil aspect, from power and malice of all my enemies, visible and invisible, and from this illness that I suffer now. Free, protect, and defend me, Lord, on account of the glory of your most holy name, now and forever. Amen. From unexpected, unforeseen, and permanent death, free and defend me, Lord, + Jesus of Nazareth, King of the Jews, Son of God, have mercy on me + Amen. Against sadness, fear, and melancholy of the sick, let it be carried.]

Master Kymberleye[512]

To Know if One Be Bewitched or Forspoken

Look well in their eyes, and if you can discern your picture therein, they are not bewitched, et cetera.[513]

For a Horse That Is Bewitched, or Any Other Beast

"Three biters[514] have bitten thee, three betters have betters [sic] have bettered thee. In the name of the Father, the Son, and the Holy Ghost, three persons and one trinity. Stand up, bayard,[515] *a* [in] God's name." Say this three times, and make three crosses on him with your hand, and he shall be cured.

---

512 *Master Kymberleye*: See Introduction.

513 See also e Mus. 243 f.7, quoted in Baker, *Cunning Man's Handbook*, 283. In other places, the lack of an image in the eyes is a way to identify a witch. de la Mare, *Come Hither: A Collection of Rhymes and Poems for the Young of All Ages*, 614.

514 *Three biters*: See above for another occurrence of this charm.

515 *Bayard*: Most likely a horse.

HORSE OR ANY OTHER BEAST BEWITCHED

Take the witch knot[516] and make it bloody with the blood of his ear, and lap it in the hair of his breast, if it can be had, or in the hair of his tail, and rake it in the bottom of the embers, that it may be burnt, and tarry there till it be consumed, and it may be the witch will come in the while, and so you may know her. *Probatum.* [It is proved.] John Carpenter.[517]

FOR A BILE[518] OR FELON

Say this three times, three days. "*In nomine patris, qui sivi te, in nomine filii, inveni te, in nomine spiritus sanctus, deleat te. Deus pater, del te, deus filius, del te, deus spiritus sanctus.* [In the name of the Father, who permits thee, in the name of the Son, find thee, in the name of the Holy Ghost, let him obliterate thee. God the Father, let him obliterate thee, God the Son, let him obliterate thee, God the Holy Spirit.] Amen." Then say three Pater Nosters, three Aves, and a Creed.

FOR BITING OF A MAD DOG[519]

Write these words thrice, and put them on a piece of cheese and eat it: "Oribus,[520] Aliebus, Nives, Vivas, Nives, Vivas, Populas, Qui, Ne."

BITING OF A MAD DOG

Write upon bread or cheese these words, "Aribus, Alibus, Rivos, Rivas, Opulisque," or thus, "Artibus, Alibus, Omnibus, Rivas, Viveris," and eat it.

[64r]

To Find Treasure That Is Hid in the Ground

Go to the place where you hear it is, and dig five holes, at each corner one, and one in the midst. Make them somewhat deep with a dagger. Then take green hazel

---

516 *Witch knot*: A tangle of hair supposed to be the work of witches.

517 *John Carpenter*: See introduction.

518 *Bile*: Boil.

519 For similar charms for the same purpose, see Blaisdell, "A Frightful, but Not Necessarily Fatal, Madness: Rabies in Eighteenth-Century England and English North America," 109; Grabinski, *Die Sagen, der Aberglaube und abergläubische Sitten in Schlesien: mit einem Anhang über Prophezeihungen*, 42; Henslowe, *Henslowe's Diary*, 33; Peterson, *Grimorium Verum*, 75; Scot, *The Discouerie of Witchcraft*, 243; Seyfarth, *Aberglaube und Zauberei in der Volksmedizin West-Sachsens*, 166, 167, 174, 175; Skemer, *Binding Words: Textual Amulets in the Middle Ages*, 17.

520 *Oribus*: Latin "with the mouths/faces."

sticks, and cleave them at the one end, and put the five names hereunder written into the clefts of the sticks with the names upward, and set the sticks into the five holes, the middlemost first, and then the four other, and lay the turfs over the holes again, close that they be not perceived, and that no rain get in for wetting of the names, and let them remain there a night and a day, and if there be any treasure in the place, the names that are nearest to it will miscarry and be either rent or burnt.

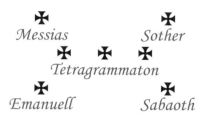

A True Experiment to Find Treasure That Is Hid in the Ground[521]

About sun rising upon the day of [the] ☉, gather two hazel rods of one year's growth, and when you gather them, say, "In the name of the Father, I have sought you + in the name of the Son, I have found you + and in the name of the Holy Ghost I gather you +." Then cut them up, and when you have so done, say three Pater Nosters, three Aves, and one Creed over them, with three benedictions. Then keep them and when you will use them, hold you the one end thereof between your thumb and your fingers in either hand one, and your fellow the other ends likewise, an inch asunder, and say as followeth: either the 24th psalm, or this prayer following three times:

"O merciful God, king of all kings, which containest the throne of heaven, beholdest all deeps, weighest the hills, and shuttest up with thy hand the earth, hear us, oh most meek God, and grant unto us, being unworthy according to thy great mercies, to have the verity and virtue of knowledge of hidden treasures.[522] O Lord God Almighty, as thou by thy angel didst guide the three kings of Collen,[523] Jasper, Melchior, and Balthaser, when they went with their worshipful presents towards Bethelem. Jasper carried myrrh, Melchior incense, and Balthaser gold worshipping

---

521 An example of a rite for a divining rod. For more examples, see Dillinger, "The Divining Rod: Origins, Explanations, and Uses in the Thirteenth to Eighteenth Centuries," as well as *Oberon* 363–4.

522 Compare to Scot, *The Discouerie of Witchcraft*, 299.

523 *Collen*: Cologne.

the high king of all the world, Jesus, God's son of heaven, the second person in Trinity, born of the holy, blessed, and clean virgin St. Mary, queen of

[64v]

heaven, empress of hell, and lady of all the world. At that time, the holy angel Gabriel warned and bade the aforesaid three kings that they should take another way for dread and peril [of] that hard Herod the king, and by his ordinance would have destroyed those three noble kings that mickely[524] sought out our lord and saviour. And as wittily and truly as those three kings turned for dread and took another way so wisely and so truly, O Lord God of thy mightiful mercy, bless these two hazel rods of one year's growth at this time, and as those three kings turned the right way, even so, good Lord God, make these two rods bow and bend always the right way towards the treasure, and when they be right over it. Then, good Lord God, make them to fold crosswise, the one over the other. Grant this, good Lord, for thy blessed passion['s] sake. Amen. In the name of the Father, and of the Son, and of the Holy Ghost. Amen."

An Experiment to Cause a Thief to Come Again unto Thee in Proper Person, if He Be in Any Place within the Realm of England[525]

First make an image of virgin wax, and write in the forehead of the image Yris with this character ⬡, and in the neck of the head Sibilia[526] with this character ⌐◻◡, and in the noddle[527] of the head write Azaria with this character ◦⌐◻◡◦. Then write in the breast the name of him that is the doer of it and these names, Eleazar, Maliga, with this character ⁺◻◡*ag*, and in the back over against these, this charac-

---

524 *Mickely*: Much.

525 This wax image rite and its variants turn up in a number of other texts, e.g. Bodleian Rawlinson D.252, 69v–71v; BL Sloane 1727, 24–28; Sloane 3846, 38r–39v, 41r–42v. The most recent is a nineteenth-century Liverpool cunning man's manual; see Harms, *William Dawson Bellhouse: Galvanist, Cunning Man, Scoundrel.*

526 *Sibilia*: Often considered to be the queen of the fairies, she appears in a number of rituals from this time, e.g., *Oberon* 360–3, 537–40; Scot, *The Discouerie of Witchcraft*, 401–10. Nothing more descriptive than the name appears in any of these wax image rites, however. For further background on Sibilia's appearances, see Harms, "Spirits at the Table: Faerie Queens in the Grimoires," 47–50.

527 *Noddle*: Back of the head.

---

ter ☩⚴, and then make a fire of white thorn dried or of the thorn of eglantine. Then take the image aforesaid in thy hand, and say this prayer following:

"O God, the maker of all things and the revealer of all hidden things, from whom no secrets are hid, we humbly beseech thy majesty that thou wouldst vouchsafe to send N. unto us in the strength of his wicked deeds before us, and grant that we may come to our worthy country, by Christ our Lord. Amen.

"Turn thee, O God, and thou shalt quicken us, and thy people shall rejoice in thee. Let us pray:

"Almighty and eternal God, maker and master of all things, the virtue and increaser of all things from whom no secret is hid, we humbly beseech thee that, by the invocation of thy holy names, thou command thy spirits Sabaoth,

[65r]

Uriel, and Raguel[528] to obey my commandments, that they make N. to come again and return unto me and to confess their fault, that we may give thee thanks in thy church, by Christ our Lord. Amen."

Then hold the image to the fire, but beware that the wax melt not, and say as followeth:

"I conjure you, O ye angels of god, Sabaoth, Uriel, and Raguel, by the high powers of God the Father, the Son, and the Holy Ghost, and by these names which I call upon for my help, I am, Alpha et Ω, the first and the last, and Agla, and by this holy name of God Tetragrammaton, and by the name of our Lord Jesus Christ, at which all knees of things in heaven and in earth and under the earth ought to bow, and by the joys of heaven wherein you are, that in what country or place soever they be, you cause N. to come again to us, by the virtue of these characters which are written in this image, and to return unto us in all their strength. Even as I do prick this image with this prick of thorn (and then prick the characters with the prick), so

---

528 *Sabaoth, Uriel, and Raguel*: Sabaoth, literally "hosts," is usually a reference to the armies of heaven. Uriel, or "Fire of God," and Raguel, "friend of God," are mentioned in 1 Enoch 20 as two of the seven archangels. The Roman Synod of October 25, 745, condemned both of these names, being employed by a holy man named Adalbert preaching near Soissons, as being the names of demons. Boniface and Emerton, *The Letters of Saint Boniface*; Russell, "Saint Boniface and the Eccentrics."

suffer them not to stay nor rest, day nor night, sitting, going, sleeping, or waking, until they come unto us, and that their hearts do melt in their coming, as this wax of the image doth doth [sic] melt from or before the face of the fire, until they be come unto us, and confess their fault."

Then keep the image in a box in clean clothes without hurt, because if they be hurt, the party will be destroyed, et cetera.

And if there be two, then make two images according to the parties, whether they be men or women, and let thy fellow hold the one and thou the other, until you come to hold them to the fire. Then take them both into thine own hands and say the conjuration aforesaid. *Finis. Probatum.* [It is proved.]

[65v]

The Quadrangle [for Treasure]

To find out treasure, and to take it forth, and to have an answer of spirits that keep the same, when you art where it is, if thou wilt have a magical answer, draw nigh the spirit, **Dradragoban** if thou shalt not have a magical answer of the spirits that keep it, and so thou shalt have it forth always. Thus you oughtest to do and to work in such sort that the spirit keeping the same may open it to thee.

Make a quadrangle circle on the ground as is shewed in the figure before, and thou shalt have suffumigations—frankincense, saffron, and red roses dried—and thou shalt hold it before thee. Then exorcise every corner of the quadrangle, holding thy face towards him, and subfumigate[529] to him, and then in which corner he doth appear, he shall give answer unto thee, and then say:

"I conjure and adjure thee, thou spirit or you spirits lying in the ground and keep-ing this treasure, that thou or you come forth, and appear and that thou or you do obey me by these names, burning spirits, constraining Babay et Babaty, Margar,

---

529 *Subfumigate*: Suffumigate, or burn incense.

Eptra, Hell, Regessa, Menanas, Margon, Sichone, Metelex, Qui Odingeo, Lepera, Egicam, Sgalis, Magram, Repeli, Siadris, Fuglep, Verexi, Benlam, or Renlam, Ator, Iesan, Goffela, Crea, Baba Mutela, Effrater, Onom,[530] Magala, Serar, Tabat, that by and by you dost come forth from the earth and dost appear, and make answer unto me, and that you dost obey unto me hurting nor harming nothing, nor any creature which God hath created, but those things that thou dost keep thou shalt grant and give unto me, whatsoever it be, if it be to my liking, whether it be silver or gold or other jewels. *In nomine patris, et filii, et spiritus sancti* [in the name of the Father, and the Son, and the Holy Ghost]. Amen."

This conjuration done, thou shalt see a smoke go from the earth, and he shall open the ground unto thee, but fear not, but conjure him strongly, and after that he shall stand and appear, and thou shalt see him truly. Then inquire diligently of him, and command him to open the earth, and to give the treasure unto thee without hurting or harming of thee or any creature of God whatsoever, and then he will open the ground and lift up the treasure and deliver it unto thee, then receive it, and keep it secret, that it be not known how you camest by it. Then license the spirit to depart, making him promise thee that he will not shew it abroad, and that he shall not hurt anybody, and that he shall quietly depart with the treasure, but bind him strongly.

A License or Discharge

"See that you depart and go to the place that God hath ordained you to abide in, without any grievous noise or storm, and at all times that you obey the command-ments of God, and I command you that you be quiet. By all these names of God, I bind and constrain you, *decedite nunc, decedite nunc, decidite nunc* [depart now, depart now, depart now], by the virtue of the Father of heaven, and by the virtue of these holy names of God + Aglaya + Aglaoth + Te + tra + Gra + ma + ton + and by the virtue of all the holy and blessed names of God, *et per venturus est iudicare vivos et mortuos et seculum per ignem amen. pater noster etc. In nomine patris et filii et spiritus sancti, amen. Fiat, fiat, fiat. Probatum est.* [and who will come to judge the living and the dead and the world by fire, amen. Our father, etc. In the name of the Father, and the Son, and the Holy Ghost, amen. Let it be done, let it be done, let it be done. It is proved.]"

[66r]

---

530 *Onom*: Could also be "Onon."

[Magic Circle][531]

| Pater de caelis, deus, miserere nobis | Fili, redemptor mundi, deus, miserere nobis |
| Spiritus sancte, deus, miserere nobis | Sancta Trinitas vivis, deus, miserere nobis |

For Treasure That Is Hid

"*Jesus Nazarenus, rex iudeorum, dona nobis gratiam tuam. Amen.* [Jesus of Nazareth, king of the Jews, give us your grace. Amen.]

"*In nomine meus, demonia eiicient, linguis loquentur novis, serpentes tollent, et si mortifferum quid biberint, non eis nocebit, super egros manus imponent, et bene habebunt. Aleluya, deus, in nomine tuo, etc. Deus misereatur et cetera.*

["In my name, they will cast out the demons, they will speak with new tongues, they will take up serpents, and if they will drink any poison, it will not hurt them, they will place their hands over illnesses, and they will be made well,[532] Alleluia, God, in thy name, etc., God have mercy, etc.]

"Thou spirit or spirits which keep this ground or earth and treasure, I conjure you and charge you by the mighty power of God, and by his strength, and by all the

---

531 Text inside the circle: *Pater de caelis, deus, miserere nobis* [Father from the heavens, God, have mercy on us]. *Fili, redemptor mundi, deus, miserere nobis* [Son, redeemer of the world, God, have mercy on us]. *Spiritus sancte, deus, miserere nobis* [Holy Ghost, God, have mercy on us]. *Sancta Trinitas vivis, deus, miserere nobis* [Holy living Trinity, God, have mercy on us].

532 Mark 16:17–18.

might, power, and strength of the holy and blessed Trinity, that thou or you depart from this treasure, earth, or ground. Depart, O thou spirit or spirits, and I charge you and command you by all the power and strength of almighty God, the Father of heaven, and by the virtue and divinity of Jesus Christ our Lord, coequal with the Father, and with the Holy Ghost, the third person in Trinity. Depart, O thou spirit or spirits, I command you, by the virtue, might, and strength of Jesus Christ, the king of glory, and by the virtue and love of the Holy Ghost, and by all the strong mansions of Jesus Christ, king of all goodness, and by the virtue of the love and mercy of Jesus Christ, the only son of the living God, and by the virtue of the obedience of Jesus Christ, when he was obedient to the death of the cross, which liveth and reigneth with God his Father and the Holy Ghost in the perfect Trinity.

"I conjure thee, thou spirit or spirits, by the fearful power of the judgment of him, which shall judge all mankind, and all kings and devils, and all wicked spirits.

"I conjure thee or you by him to whom all knees do bow, both in heaven, earth, and hell. Depart, O thou spirit or spirits, from this place or ground and treasure, and that thou or ye come not nigh unto it by the space of a hundred miles, until we have taken and obtained our wills and pleasures by the virtue of the Holy Ghost and predestination of God, in whose name I command thee, thou spirit or you spirits, that keep this treasure to depart from this place or ground, and not to come nigh unto it by the space of our hundred miles, neither to vex, trouble, nor fear us, until we have had our full mind and pleasure.

"I conjure thee, thou spirit or you spirits, by the virtue of all heavens and celestial creatures worshipping your omnipotent God. Depart, O thou spirit or spirits, from this place and ground, through the virtue of almighty God and of all earthly things, both quick and dead, movable

[66v]

and unmovable, worshipping the omnipotent God. Depart, O thou spirit or spirits, from this place, through the virtue of the person of Jesus Christ, and of the sweet face of Jesus Christ, which was smitten upon and which spittle deformed, so be thou spirit or ye spirits smitten with the fire and pains of hell, which shall always burn and never be quenched, if you depart not by and by from this place and ground and came not near that by a hundred miles, until we have obtained our minds, through the virtue and strength of the rope which bound the arms of Christ, wherewith he was drawn and stretched upon the cross, so be ye spirit or spirits drawn, stretched, and nailed with the most strongest pains of hell with fiery chains, except ye depart by and by. Depart, O thou spirit or spirits, by the great pain the which Christ suffered in his feet when he was nailed upon the cross, so be thou or ye spirit or spirits nailed and pierced with the pains of hellfire, except ye depart by and by. And if ye depart not by and by, the fire of hell, which shall always burn and never be quenched, descend, and fall down upon you spirits, and burn you, so that you shall never have rest nor ease. And as the spear painfully pierced the side of Jesus Christ, so be the spirit or spirits painfully pained, so that you from this day forth shall never have rest nor ease. All thunders and lightnings, with all the fire of hell, fall down upon you. The sword of death, with all the torments of all the devils in hell, descend down upon you, and remain upon you forever, except ye depart incontinent from this place and ground, and not to come near it by a hundred miles, until we have taken our minds and pleasure therein. Depart, O thou spirit or spirits, I conjure you and charge you, by the virtue of the blood of the saviour of all mankind, and by the virtue of the blood and water that Christ sweat upon the Mount of Olyvet before his bitter passion, when he was in an agony, and the angel of God comforted him, declaring to him what a great mystery he should bring to pass through his blessed death, of the which mystery, O ye wicked spirit or spirits that keep this treasure, be no partakers, but such as believe in his death depart from this place. O ye wicked spirit or spirits, I charge and command you, by the infinite word of God, that ye come not near that by the space of a hundred miles, for the space of a hundred days next following, neither to trouble, vex, nor delude us, neither to draw it deeper nor lower into the earth, but only to let it remain

[67r]

where it standeth, without craft, falsehood, guile, or dissimulation, neither to change it into any other colour, but to let it remain as it is in the own proper place.

"I conjure thee, spirit or spirits, by the words that Christ spake in the time of his most blessed passion, when he prayed for them that persecuted him, saying, 'Father, repute not this unto them, for they know not what they do,' and by these words which he spake to his holy mother, saying, 'Woman, behold thy son,' and to his disciple, 'Behold thy mother,' and by that holy word I trust that is the health of mankind, and by these words, 'Eloy, Eloy, Eloy, Lamazabathanie,' that is to say, 'My God, my God, why hast thou forsaken me?' and by these words it is ended, and by these holy words, 'Father, into thy hands I commend my spirit.' Depart, O ye spirit or spirits, from this treasure, and from this place or ground by and by, without any craft or guile or any manner of deceit.

"I conjure thee, you spirit or spirits, by the virtue of Christ's passion and his resurrection, and also by the virtue of his holy ascension, and by the fearful coming of him to judgment, where ye and all your fellows shall receive just judgment meet and according to your offenses, except ye depart from this place and ground. The virtue of the omnipotent God, the father of all saints in heaven, excommunicate you, and all his angels excommunicate, and cast you into the everlasting pains and fire of hell, where never shall be comfort nor hope, ease nor rest, and Christ, the only begotten Son of the Father, curse you and bind you with all the pains aforesaid. The Holy Ghost with all the church of God excommunicate you and curse you from all hope and forgiveness. The holy Trinity curse and excommunicate you. All the sorrows, pains, and torments of hell fall down upon you and remain upon you until the last day of doom, except ye depart immediately. All fires and lightnings and thunders curse you. All sorrow and malediction fall down upon you and remain upon you forever, O ye rebelling spirits, except ye now depart and neither hurt, trouble, nor vex us, nor draw nor convey away treasure from us, but suffer it to remain in this place here, that we may obtain it without craft, subtlety, or guile of you or any of you, by virtue of all that is aforespoken or shall be hereafter spoken. Amen.

"I conjure you spirits, and I constrain you, and I command you that ye depart from this place and treasure, and that ye come not near it by a hundred miles for the space of a hundred days next following.

"I conjure you spirits, by the first word that God spake in the creation of the world, saying, 'Let there be light,' and so that was done.[533]

"The second word he said, 'Let there be a firmament between the waters, and let it divide the waters,' and so it was done.

"The third word that God said, 'Let the waters under heaven gather themselves

[67v]

together into one place, that the dry land may appear,' and so it was done.

533 See *Oberon* 320.

"The fourth word was when he commanded the trees and the herbs to spring, saying, 'Let the earth bring forth green grass that beareth seed and fruitful trees, every one in his kind, bearing fruit,' and so it came to pass.

"The fifth word was when God made the sun and the moon and the stars, saying, 'Let there be lights in the firmament of heaven, to divide the day from the night, that there may be tokens, signs, days, and years, and let them be lights in the firmament to shine upon the earth,' and so it was done.

"The sixth word was when he made the fishes and fowls, saying, 'Let the waters bring forth fishes that move and have life, and fowls that fly under the firmament of heaven,' and so it came to pass.

"The seventh word was when God blessed them, saying, 'Grow and multiply upon the earth.'

"The eighth word was when God said, 'Let the earth bring living beasts, every one in his kind, and creeping worms,' and so it was done.

"The ninth word was when God made man, saying, 'Let us make man in our similitude after our likeness, that he may have rule over fishes of the sea and fowls under heaven, and over all cattle and over all the earth, and over all worms that creep upon the earth.'

"The tenth word was when God said, 'Grow and multiply you and fulfill the earth; subdue it, and have dominion over the fishes of the sea, and over the fowls of the air, and over all beasts and worms that creep upon the earth.'[534]

"By the virtue of all these words and of all the names of God, I conjure and compel you, O ye spirits or spirits, and straightly command you to depart from this place and treasure, and neither contain it nor draw it lower, nor change it into any other colour or colours,[535] but only to let it remain in the own proper substance, as it was when it was first set here, and not to come near it by a hundred miles, until such time as we have fulfilled our minds and wills and purposes. In the name of God the Father, and of God the Son, and of God the Holy Ghost. Amen."

534 *The first word…earth*: See *Oberon* 320.
535 *Colour*: Most likely "nature" or "appearance."

He that doth discharge the ground must be a priest having a stole about his neck, and holy water, and a bunch of hyssop to cast the holy water on the ground, and turn his face into the east, and read this above written **three times** devoutly.

This was written in a sheet of parchment having on the back side thereof, at every corner a cross and one in the midst.

[68r]

+ ME DEXTERA ♄ ♈ 2 ✠ ⊞

+ DOMENI FECIT VURUTIE ♉ ✠ ⊞

+ DEXTERA ♊ □ 3 ✠ ⟡

+ DOMINI EXERSACIT MEI ♋ ✠ ◇

+ DEXTERA ♌ ♂ 2 ✠ ⚜

+ MESAS ⊕ ♍ ☉ 2 ✠

+ DEXTERA ✳ ♎ ✳ ✠ ⚜

+ DOMENI AMI ✠ ⊞

+ DEXTERA ♏ ✳ ♃ 1 ✠ ⊞

+ DOMEI FECIT MI ✸

+ DEXTERA ✳ ↑ ✳ ✠ ◇

+ WERTIE ✳ ♑ ✳ ⚸ ✳ 3 ✠ ⬦

+ DEXTERA ✳ ♒ ∿ ✳ ✠ ⟡

+ TETRAGRAMATON ✠ ⬦

+ DEXTERA ♓ ☽ 3 ✳

+ MESSIAS ALPHA ✠ 3 ⚜

536 Text: + Me Dextera + + Domeni Fecit Vurutie + + Dextera + + Domini Exersacit Mei + + Dextera + + Mesas + + Dextera + + Domeni Ami ++ Dextera + + Domei Fecit Mi + + Dextera + + Wertie + + Dextera + + Tetragrammaton + + Dextera + + Messias Alpha +. The Latin here is corrupt, so I have not attempted to translate it.

The length of this circle must be twelve yards 3 q3,[537] and the breadth of it must be an inch at the least, and it must be cut compass that it may be round that length. *Finis.*

For Them That Are Bewitched, Proved by a Hundred

Come to them and say these words, "+ Anitrita + Sockuluta + Gaudes + Whip Tibi Tendi + Whip Tibi Daria + Conquenorum Iube dei + Tetragrammaton +" If it be a man or beast, say these words, and in saying of them, cast a little salt into drink and give it him, or cast it into drink that will not work, or into any other thing that is forespoken. *Finis.*

To Cause a Woman to Tell What She Hath Done in Her Sleep[538]

Take a stone called Agath, and lay it upon her left pap[539] when she is asleep. If the stone be good, she shall tell thee all that thou requirest of her.

[Donet or Consecrations]

Here beginneth the book which is called the Donet or Consecrations, which consecrations are found in other places.

This is the doctrine of experiments in general, by the which you may the more easily go to all works, and into the name of the practice of love, of hate, or of discord. Before you go to work, you must abstain nine days from all sin and carnal copulation, and put on clean clothes, wash in baths, shave your beard, and pare your nails, and keep you in good state and measurable. Also you must know that all manner of

---

537 *Q3*: An unknown unit of measurement. See 36r above.

538 See *Oberon* 541. The stone in question is agate. Curiously, I can only find this in one work other than *Oberon*: a book about witchcraft originally published in the seventies. Paulsen, *The Complete Book of Magic & Witch-Craft*, 50. It would seem to refer to a work of natural magic, however.

539 *Pap*: Breast.

circles, both more and less, must be made on Wednesday at night, or on Tuesday by day, being clear and no wind, nor clouds appearing, but if the clouds appear afterward, it is no matter.

There are four manner of callings. The first is calling to love and discord; the second is to call uncled[540] spirits; the third is to consecrate any thing, as rings, image, penny, or any other thing whatsoever; the fourth is to find treasure and to have knowledge of thieves.

Also, it is to understand that these invocations must be done at lunations[541] and times and qualities of the signs for every purpose, as it is found in many experiments. As if thou wilt call for love, you must consider the moon increasing and the sun going down, being moist as in Ariete.[542] Aries is a sign falling and having a moist [nature?], for love cometh of great heat; therefore, it is to be considered in all experiments that be for love. Also experiments of discord and sorrow be made in a cold and moist sign, for then that one quality destroyeth another. The experiment of calling spirits must be made, the sun being dry going down, and for calling the congregation infernal. Also call the four kings infernal of the four places of the world, the sun being cold and dry as is aforesaid. Also when you make the experiment of virgins and maidens, then the sun must be in a wederlye[543] sign, as in Libra. Understand that you mayst make the experiment of virgins' love [in] all the signs except Libra. Also the same must be in a cold sign, moist and watery, as in Scorpio. Also, the sun being in a watery

[70r]

sign, you mayst call spirits of woods and waters. And the sun being in an earthly sign, you mayst call all spirits except Asteroth, which abideth in bushes and woods,[544] that been cold and dry. And as it is said before of the sun, so is it to be considered by the moon, the which causeth the worker to take heed what days and hours be profitable in his working.

540 *Uncled*: Term unknown, possibly "unclean."
541 *Lunations*: Lunar months, or times of the full moon.
542 *Ariete*: Aries.
543 *Wederlye*: Unclear—possibly "weatherly," with Libra being an airy sign.
544 *Asteroth…woods*: This attribute of Astaroth derives from biblical traditions, which placed shrines of Astarte in sacred groves.

Invocatio Regum [Invocation of the Kings]

It is known that the invocation of all kings, as well principal as other, ought to be done in the first sleep,[545] for the first be before or after it is a great labour, for they will not come. Nor it is not speedful for the worker, the cause which they prolong the time as much as they may, is that the day may appear before his work be ended, and they do it as is abovesaid, that you may have to short time. And also spirits shall be moved, and by the force of the worker, they shall do him harm. Also understand that you mayst make thy experiments all hours of the night except the hours matatinall,[546] for then spirits draw them to come to holy hours to tempt the religious, and so that time of service that profiteth not the caller.

Exorcismum ad Odium [An Exorcism for the Purpose of Hate]

An exorcism for hate or sorrow at the hours of the night is not profitable, wherefore in the mornings is most right to call princes of devils. For if thou call and he come not from the first hour to the second, call him no more in no wise, but afterward call him in the morning when the church is last occupied, for if you call him in the morning he letteth not but cometh. Also, you mayst well know that in any work, whensoever he cometh, he is alone, or else he bringeth great company and fellowship with him, as it is said in the book of Solomon of the Office of Spirits,[547] and if he come alone, you mayst the better have thy will, and the more he dreadeth thee.

Officiis Spirituum de Marchionibus
[In the Offices of the Spirits, of the Marquises]

Marquises shall be constrained the third hour, the fifth, and the eighth. If he came not in the third hour nor in the fifth, thou mayst well know for troth[548] that he shall come the eighth hour, and if he come alone by himself, that is the more to dread,

---

545 *First sleep*: Much of pre-industrial Europe recognized two periods of sleep, first sleep and second sleep, punctuated by a short time of wakefulness. The time to which it applies could vary, based upon an individual's sleep schedule. See Ekirch, *At Day's Close: Night in Times Past*, 300–311.

546 *Matatinall*: Likely matutinal, or early morning.

547 *Book…Spirits*: A list of spirits of this title appears in different places (e.g., *Oberon* 191–207), or it might refer to the treatise immediately following.

548 *For troth*: With confidence.

and if there come many with him the less dread, and so it is more peril with one than with many.

[70v]

De Ducibus [Regarding Dukes]

Dukes may not be constrained but in the seventh, the thirteenth, fourteenth, or sixteenth hour, if he he [sic] appear not the first hour, he shall come to you the third on the next day, that is to wit on the Sunday. If thou see him not in the seventh hour anon, he cometh in the sixteenth. *Notando de signe* [for writing of the mark]. It behoveth thee to have these tokens on thy breast or on thy forehead, or else they fear thee not. When they see this sign, they dreaden thee, and so you mayst have thy will. ♅♇☌

De Prelatis [Of Prelates]

Prelates be not constrained but in the seventh hour, the eighth, or the third, and if he come not the first hour, you must abide till the seventh hour, and then he cometh, whether it be service time in the church or no.

De Militibus [Of Knights]

Knights may be constrained in all hours, save only at service time, as when there is no singing in the church, and when you callest, ordain[549] a quick[550] cat, or else thou canst not constrain him.

De Comitibus [Of Earls]

Earls appear in every place except holy places and dedicate[551] places. When he appeareth, he giveth true answers, in the first hour, in the sixth, seventh, ninth, or twentieth, and if you ask any thing of him, take with thee this sign upon thy head

---

549 *Ordain*: Provide.
550 *Quick*: Living. I do not encourage this.
551 *Dedicate*: Dedicated.

[blank], and anon he shall be meek unto thee, and all things that he may give thee, thou shalt have, and you mayst not have praeses[552] by this token, ne[553] constrain him but at noon, and therefore if you call him in any other hour, you gettest him not, neither mayst you call him, but at noon.

De Principibus [Of Princes]

Princes and other spirits that be subject to kings, of marquesses, dukes, prelates, knights, presidents, and earls, with the hours in the morning and evening for love, or in the places in which you mayst constrain them. Thus much of the hours, how thou mayst constrain a spirit by night that resteth, to be said of the hours of the day.

Hours of the Day[554]

Princes may be constrained at at [sic] noon and in the eventide, subject to kings but before prime;[555] marquesses from noon to compline,[556] or from compline till the night fail; dukes from prime to midday, but thou must see that the time to clear; prelates in other hours of the day, and knights from the grey morning to the spring of the sun, and from the[n] and from evensong till the sun go down. Also you mayst not call the

[71r]

spirits that be called presidents in the second hour of the day, but in the eventide. Comites[557] may be constrained all hours of the day.

552 *Praeses*: Presidents.

553 *Ne*: Do not.

554 A similar list of hours for conjuring spirits of various ranks, different in some details, appears in the *Lemegeton*. See Peterson, *The Lesser Key of Solomon*, 41.

555 *Prime*: Office of the liturgy corresponding to the first hour of the day, approximately 6 AM.

556 *Compline*: Office of the liturgy just before bedtime, approximately 9 PM.

557 *Comites*: Counts.

De Circulis Quibus Diebus Debeat Fieri
[Of the Circles, on Which Days It Should Be Made]

All circles as well, more or less, must be made on the Wednesday at night in clean weather in places where people come not, and all circles must be made round, except the circle for the spirit which is called Byleth,[558] which must be four square. Understand that all circles must be in wildsome places where people come not, also in hills, deep vales, woods, or in deserts, except the circle of the spirit Amarum[559] that must be made in an orchard among fruit and trees.

De Loco [Of the Place]

The circle must be plain, not grown with herbs, for that place is holy where herbs grow. Also the master shall go first into the circle and come out before his associates, and so they to go in and out after him. Also, he must have with him good and trusty fellows, and well willing and bold. They must sit and speak nothing, but the master only himself, standing and turning into the east, after into the west, then to the south, and last into the north, and so they all shall make their prayers kneeling on their knees, saying this prayer following:

"O deus pissime, O deus dulcissime, O Rex Adonay, gloriosissime, per te reguntur omnia et consistant atque creantur. [O God most pious, O God most sweet, O King Adonay, most glorious, all will be guided by you, and they may stop and may be granted.]"

And after this prayer, the master shall make his inquisition in conjurings thus:

"Ego, pro potissumum et pro coroboratum nomine dii, El, forte et admirabile, coniuro, adduco, et impero et exorsizo vos, spiritus N. [I, on behalf of the most able and

---

558 *Byleth*: Byleth, or Bilet, or Bileth, is a spirit who appears in a wide variety of sources. *Oberon* 210 attributes to him the liberal arts, invisibility, and consecrations; Reginald Scot 380–381 provides a detailed list of conditions for his summoning; and Bayerische Staatsbibliothek Clm 849 and Sloane 3824 include divination ritual calling upon Lylet or Bylet. See Kieckhefer, *Forbidden Rites: A Necromancer's Manual of the Fifteenth Century*, 242–43.; Ashmole and Rankine, *The Book of Treasure Spirits: A 17th Century Grimoire of Magical Conjurations to Increase Wealth and Catch Thieves through the Invocation of Spirits, Fallen Angels, Demons and Fairies*, 55–58; Boudet, "La magie au carrefour des cultures dans la Florence du Quattrocentro: Le Liber Bileth et sa démonologie." For a treatise on summoning Bilet and a square diagram to do so, see Gollancz, *Sepher Maphteah Shelomoh: Book of the Key of Solomon*, 85–93. For more discussion, see Stratton-Kent, *Pandemonium*, 146–50.

559 *Amarum*: Unknown spirit.

---

strengthened name of God El, strong and admirable. I lead, I command, and I exorcise you, spirits N.]"

And so, when the Master is in the circle with his fellows, then he shall say this following, "*Potentissimum etc. vos exorsizamus et imperamus* [most powerful, etc., we exorcise and command you], etc."

Also, the master with all his fellows must have a book hallowed upon their breasts or before them, or an image or penny or ring, or any other thing that is hallowed whatsoever it be. And also the master must have *forcepem ac perigendum* [a forceps and needle]. Also the master must have a crown on his head, in which shall be written "*Jesus Nazarenus, rex iudeorum, Christus regnat, Christus vincet, Christus imperat*" ["Jesus of Nazareth, King of the Jews, Christ reigns, Christ conquers, Christ rules"]. Also he must hold these names in his right hand with a sheltron[560] of our saviour and every one of his fellows. Also the Master must have a red march cock,[561] which he shall cast out of the

[71v]

circle. Also when you makest thy conjuration aforesaid, if the spirit ask sacrifice, give him none for displeasing of God, but the master shall say thus: "*Rogobo* [rogabo] *deum meam si placeat sibi, ut restituat tibi locum prestimum.* [I will ask my God if it may be pleasing to him that he may restore to thee thy predestined place.]"

Also the master must have ivory, with which he must make his circle so great that he and his fellows may sit in it, one turned east, another west, & c.

560 *Sheltron*: A gauge. The significance of the item in question is unknown.

561 *Red march cock*: A red rooster hatched in March or from multiple generations of such hatchings. It is possible that this was considered a sacrifice; in a Venetian manual, this is listed as the favorite offering to demons; Peterson, *Secrets of Solomon*, 142. On the other hand, such a rooster helps to find treasure, and its crow would banish spirits. Ó Súilleabháin, *A Handbook of Irish Folklore*, 41; Ó hógáin, "Dreaming and Dancing: W. B. Yeats' Use of Traditional Motifs in 'The Dreaming of the Bones' (1919)," 67; Lynch, "Folk Beliefs about the March Cock," 22, 24, 32.

Emanuel: The Call of Tobyas into a Crystal Stone[562]

"I conjure thee, O spirit of Tobyas. By God, I bind thee by the mouth[563] of God. I adjure thee, Tobyas, by all the angels of God. I command and charge thee, Tobyas, by the faith which you owest unto our Lord, thy private God, that you come speedily unto me into this crystal stone to the sight of this child N.[564] without delay, without hurting, without guile, and without fallacity, also without hurt of me[565] or any other creature of God, and that you give me a true answer of all things which I shall ask thee, and that you depart not from this crystal until you have finished my will, and that I license thee to depart, as thou wilt answer the Lord thy God at the last day of judgment, when he shall come to judge the quick and the dead and the world by fire. Amen. + In the name of the Father + and of the Son + and of the Holy Ghost + so be it.[566]

"Thou spirit of Tobyas, you knowest that Christ liveth, Christ conquereth, Christ reigneth and ruleth in heaven, in earth, in the water, in the sea, and in all deep places. Wherefore if thou wilt not appear in perfect shape and form as is above named, I commit thee into the hands of these infernal spirits, viz. Lucifer, Satan, Tataleon, and Fasall,[567] to be burned with fire and brimstone until thou hast finished my will."

When he appeareth, say thus:

"Now the curse[568] of God almighty + the Father + the Son + the Holy Ghost come upon thee, Tobyas, and deprive thee from thy duty unto the deepest pit of hell until the last day of judgment, and that you never come again unto thy honour, except thou stand and appear before me in a fair form and likeness of a man, or of a woman, and not hurting me nor any other creature of God, answering to my

---

562 Tobias was the young man from the Apocryphal *Book of Tobit* who overcomes Asmodeus. He seems to have made the transition into a spirit himself. Major divergences from the operation in *Oberon* (p. 553) will be noted here. That version begins: "The Moon increasing dic ['say'] 3 p[ater] n[osters], three A[ves] & three Creeds," followed by the Psalms 142 and 52, and that the moon should be in a fiery sign of the sign of the zodiac.

563 *Mouth*: *Oberon* has "mother,:

564 *To the sight…N.*: Not in *Oberon*.

565 *Of me*: Not in *Oberon*.

566 *Oberon* adds, "+ I bind thee by God + the Father + God the Son + and God the Holy Ghost. Amen."

567 *Tataleon…Fasall*: *Oberon* has "Tatalion [Catalion?] and Pasill"

568 *Curse*: *Oberon* seems to have "cross," although the manuscript is unclear at this point.

---

request and also to fulfill my desire without delay, rest, or any other cavillation[569] or falsehood, writing or painting the same and shewing it to me, and that I may read it and perfectly understand it."[570]

Finis.

[72r]

The Call of Oberion into a Crystal Stone[571]

First say, "In the name of the Father + and of the Son + and of the Holy Ghost + Amen." Then say a Pater Noster, Ave, and Creed, and the child also and bless you and the child with the sign of the +. Then say these psalms: "Miserere," *per* [through] "Deus, in nomine tuo," "Laudate in sanctis ovis,"[572] and let the child say with you if he can, and he must say after you this conjuration following:

"I conjure thee, Oberion, in the name of the Father, and of the Son, and of the Holy Ghost, and by the virtue of our lady St. Mary and St. Michael, St. Gabriel, St. Raphael, and all other angels, archangels, thrones, dominations, principates, potestates, cherubim, and seraphim, and by all the apostles, martyrs, confessors, and virgins, and by the virtue of all heavenly things, and especially by all the virtue of almighty God, and by the virtue that every creature doth owe unto God, and by the virtue of the Holy Ghost, and by the virtue of these holy names of our Lord God, Tetragrammaton, Alpha et Ω, Thau, Stimuleniton, Agla, Messias, Sother, Emanuel, Sabaoth, Adonay, Panton, Craton, Iskyros, Athanatos, and by all the other names of God, I command and bind thee, and I conjure thee, Oberion, that you be ready now to come into this stone, and to abide therein until the time that I license thee to go. And I charge thee, Oberion, by the virtue of God, that you shew me always truly whatsoever I desire of thee, upon pain that I shall put upon thee, by the might

---

569 *Cavillation*: Seeking mistakes of a frivolous nature.

570 *Oberon* adds, "And thus I bind thee by the blessed power of heaven and earth, and by the blessed blood of our saviour Jesus Christ, and by all his miracles that ever he wrought, and by the blessed passion of our saviour Jesus Christ, suffered for me and all mankind. Amen."

571 *Oberion*: This spirit, sometimes identified as the "King of the Fairies," appears first in Bibliotheca Medicea Laurenziana Plut. 89 MS. Sup. 38, dated to 1494. A number of conjurations of Oberion exist, with this being a short variant unlike others (see Bodleian Douce 116, 174–9; BL Sloane 3826, 98r–99r; Sloane 3846, 54v, 102v–107r; *Oberon* 454–81, Wellcome MS. 110, 97r)

572 Most likely Psalms 50 through 53 and 150, with the last title in the text being considerably mangled ("Praise in the holy eggs").

of God, if you be false and untrue or disobedient to me at this time, by these holy names of our Lord, El, Eloy, Sabaoth, Hely, Adonay, Alpha et Ω, Tetragrammaton, *principium et finis* [beginning and end], and by the virginity of Christ, that you shew us the truth truly and openly, without any peril to me and all that are present, in all haste, by the virtue of all angels. Amen. *Veni huc, Oberion, in nomine patris, veni, in nomine filii, veni, spiritus Oberion, in nomine spiritus sancti.* [Come here, Oberion; in the name of the Father, come; in the name of the Son, come; spirit Oberion, in the name of the Holy Ghost.]"

Say this conjuration three times, and he shall appear. When thou wilt avoid him, say this:

"Thou spirit Oberion, I comand thee and charge thee in the name of the Father, the Son, and the Holy Ghost, that you go into the same place that God hath ordained thee to, and I charge thee to come again to me at all times whensoever I call thee, under the pain of everlasting damnation." Then make the sign of the + in thy fore-head and likewise in the gills,[573] saying, "*In nomine patris et filii et spiritu sancti* [In the name of the Father, and the Son, and the Holy Ghost]. Amen." *Finis.*

[72v]

Experimentum Optimum Verissimum [*Most Best (and) Most True Experiment for the Fairies*][574]

In the night before the new moon, the same night, or the night after the new moon, or else the night before the full moon, the night of the full, or the night after the full moon, go to the house where the fairies' maids do use, and provide you a fair and clean bucket or pail, clean washed with clean water therein, and set it by the chimney side or where fire is made, and hang a fair new towel, or one clean washed, by, and so depart till the morning. Then be you the first that shall come to the bucket of water before the sunrise, and take it to the light. If you find upon the water a white ryme[575] like raw milk or grease, take it by with a silver spoon, and put it into

---

573 *Gills*: The flesh under the ears and jaws, in the approximate location of a fish's gills.

574 See also BL Sloane 3851, 129r. More broadly, this is a variation of what I have elsewhere called the "table ritual," which has numerous examples across the ritual magic texts of this period. See Harms, "Spirits at the Table: Faerie Queens in the Grimoires."

575 *Ryme*: A film or membrane.

a clean saucer.[576] Then the next night following, come to the same house again before eleven of the clock at night, making a good fire with sweet woods, and set upon the table a new towel or one clean washed, and upon it three fine loaves of new manchet,[577] three new knives with white hafts, and a new cup full of new ale. Then set yourself down by the fire in a chair, with your face towards the table, and anoint your eyes with the same cream or oil aforesaid. Then you shall see come by you these fairy maids, and as they pass by, they will obey you with becking[578] their heads to you, and like as they do to you, so do to them, but say nothing. Suffer the first, whatsoever she be, to pass, for she is malignant,[579] but to the second or third which you like best, reach forth your hand and pluck her to you, and with few words, ask her where she will appoint a place to meet you the next morning, for to assoyle[580] such questions as you will demand of her, and then if she will grant you, suffer her to depart and go to her company till the hour appointed, but miss her not at that time and place. Then will the other in the meantime, while you are talking with her, go to the table and eat of that is there. Then will they depart from you, and as they obey you, do you the like to them, saying nothing but letting them depart quietly. Then when your hour is come to meet, say to her your mind, for then she will come along. Then covenant with her for all matters convenient for your purpose, and she will be always with you. Of this assure yourself, for it is proved.

Finis.

[73r]

576 *Saucer*: In the usage of the time, a dish about four to six inches in diameter used to serve sauces or salt at the table. Brears, *Cooking and Dining in Tudor and Early Stuart England*, 437.

577 *Manchet*: A quality wheat bread eaten in upper-class households.

578 *Becking*: Nodding.

579 *For she is malignant…*: The motif of two good fairies and one evil one here may be seen as having parallels to "Sleeping Beauty." Indeed, in the oldest surviving version of that tale, the evil spirit is said to have cursed the princess because, when a table was laid for the three fairies to bless her birth, the knife for one of them was omitted. Bryant, *Perceforest: The Prehistory of King Arthur's Britain*, 387–88, 409.

580 *Assoyle*: Answer, from the context, but it is more often used in the context of forgiveness.

Kill a lapwing, or two or three, and save the blood in a pewter vessel that is close, and keep it so ten or twelve days that no air come in, and within that time it will be turned into worms. Then make paste of walnuts or almonds, but walnuts are better. Beat them small, and then, in some round thing, make it like a pie, and then put the worms into it, and cover it with a cover of the same, and look that there be room enough for the worms to increase therein, and let it remain other[582] ten or twelve days if need be. Then the worm will be turned into a lapwing. Note that you may look to it after ten days, but if it be not fully grown, let it tarry therein till it be fully grown to a lapwing again, and when it is ready grown in proportion, then take it out and let it blood[583] under the right wing, and save the blood in a silver vessel, and when thou wilt see the spirits, then anoint thy eyes with the blood and look out of thy window into the east, and if you be in the field, look into the east, and thou shalt see all the spirits of the air. Then mayst you call one of them to thee and command him to fulfill thy desire, and when he hath done thy commandment, avoid him or them, saying, "*Vade pax sit inter me et te* [let there be peace between thee and me] + In the name of the Father + and of the Son + and of the Holy Ghost + three persons in trinity and one in unity. Amen."

This may be done in March, April, May, June, or July, but June or July are best for the heat.

Finis.

Experimentum Probatum Verissimum de Furto [A Most True and Proven Experiment for Thieves][584]

Pro furto, vade ad sepulcrum alicuius defunctus vel defuncte, et voca ipsum vel ipsam ter nomine propre etc. Pone caput tuam iuxta sepulcrum, et dic:

---

581 See "An Experiment to See Spirits What They Do" above.

582 *Other*: Another.

583 *Blood*: Extract blood.

584 See the experiment "For theft" below; also Bodleian Ballard 66, 35–39; Bodleian Douce 116, 129–130, 196–202, 204; Bodleian Rawlinson D.252, 67r–67v; Bodleian Rawlinson D.253, 139–40; Newberry Vault Case 5017, 23; Sloane 3884, 47–56; Sloane 3851, 103r–v; University of Illinois Pre-1650 0102, 68–72, 87–92.

[For theft, go to the sepulcher of any dead man or woman, and call the same three times by their proper name, etc. Place thy head next to the sepulchre and say:]

"Coniuro te, N., per Sezel,[585] *que est deus et habet ossa mortuorum in potestate, ut licenciam petas, veniendi ad me in hac nocte, et non me redendo nec ledendo nec nigetando, sed honesto modo et favorabili, demonstres unam veritatem de illo furto et defurio, ubi sit et utram debio ire et haec rehabere vel non." Tunc accipe de terra sepulcrum quae est ad caput nostri, et illa liga in pannulo lindo [lineo], et pone sub auriculum tuam, et dormias super eam, et in nocte somniabis, et veniet vis tibi, et dicet tibi veritatem de omnibus quibus ab eo vel ad ea petieris.*

["I conjure thee N. by Sezel, who is God and has the bones of the dead in his power, so that thou mayst seek leave, coming to me in this night, and without abandoning or harming or denying me, but in an honest and favored manner, thou mayst show a truth of this thief and stolen things where he may be and whether I should go and have it again or not." Then take from the earth of the sepulcher near the head of ours, and tie that in a linen rag, and put beneath the lobe of thy ear and sleep above it, and in the night thou wilt dream, and he thou desirest will come to thee, and he will tell thee the truth of all things that from this or these ones thou wilt seek.]

Finis.

[A Short Operation for Theft]

Si furtum fuerit factam, scribe, "Magnus dominus" et caracteres ⛰⛰⛰ *et pone sub capite in lecto et videbis furem illum intrare.*

[If theft may be done, write, "Great Lord" and characters ⛰⛰⛰, and place beneath the head in the bed, and thou wilt see that thief to enter.]

[73v]

---

585 *Sezel*: Possibly derived from Zazel, the planetary spirit of Saturn. Agrippa von Nettesheim, *De Occulta Philosophia Libri Tres*, 313 (ii, 23).
       Other versions of the same rite (e.g., Newberry Vault Case MS 5017, 12r), however, call upon Azazel instead. Azazel is a spirit from the *Book of Enoch* credited with giving weapons and forbidden lore to humans. 1 Enoch 8:1, 9:6; Charlesworth, "1 (Ethiopic Apocalypse of) Enoch."

"Benias,[586] whereas thou art bound to this book, I, N., do charge thee to go to N. this night. I also command thee, Benias, that you go to her, being asleep in her bed, or at any other time when I command thee, and trouble her so with me, N., that she come to me within in this six hours, wheresoever she be, by land or by water, or in any other place within this twenty-four miles. Also I charge thee, Benias, that you appear to her by these words and characters and Loy + Tetragrammaton ⚹ Sabaoth ♌♂. Benias, I, N., do charge thee and command thee by the precious blood that ran down from Jesus on the rood. Also I command thee by the piles of stone that Jesus was scourged upon. Also I charge thee by the sharp spear that Longinus thrust through his side, and I charge thee by the crown of thorn that upon Christ's head was borne. Also I charge thee by the nails that nailed Jesus to the tree. Also I charge thee, Benias, by the great smart that grieved Jesus to the heart. Also I charge thee, Benias, by the mightest most, when Jesus Christ gave up the ghost, that you do my will in these things before rehearsed, otherwise the curse of God almighty, the Father, the Son, and the Holy Ghost come upon thee, Benias, and deprive thee from thy dignity, unto the deepest pit of hell, until the last day of judgment, and that you never come again unto thy honour, except you truly do my message and commandment." ✝ ○ ∞ ♀.

The Preparation of Experiments of Love as Followeth[587]

Say these names over virgin wax or parchment, or any other experiment of love.

"Venus, Aster, Atopolin, Asmo, 8 ♃ Aih, Semey, Eansursh, Smue, Menser, Esum, Vasmi, Freese, Rather, Yetes + Deres, Erner, Theser, He, Refer, Trera, Sever, Atesi, Orces, Niloportas, Loui, Satrox, Portasinall, Deroper, Ponilbus, Noxarata, Peta, Relmo, Onahirasterp, Lopostarius, Sem, Polacar, Rata, Sepuros, Sperabonatos, Sonaco, Laripos, Ariplotoson, Necesolap, Hinds, Ratoplo, Loueson, Nerolo, Perortira, Focan, Emas, Saine, Meas, Saem, Masa, Amas, Sema, Esam, Moas vel Maos, Masa, Yrtell, Abigellem, Urricas, Asteroth, Dracho, Draco, Dracutius, Affacill, Ara, Arab, Agal, Draned, Atrox, Bell, Belliall, Roncefall, Aray, Zacui, Menot, Ariell, Iemure, Cayma, Pestall, Beryi, Berifer, Emull, Zaiell, Agama, Ceris, Rayma, Belima,

---

586 *Benias*: Said to be the chief of four spirits that Dr. John Lambe called into a crystal. *A Briefe Description of the Notorious Life of Iohn Lambe*, 4–5.

587 See BL Additional MS. 36674, 10v–11r, reprinted in Peterson, "The Key of Knowledge (*Clavicula Salomonis*)."

Genitall, Topora, Corilron, Zagan, Oralioch, Asmo, Ideus, Talii, Camon, Bermo, Non[588] Kagaoche Textator, at Lapidator.[589] I conjure you, all ministers of love, by these names or by what other names soever you are called, by the power and majesty of him who may destroy you and make you again, and by all his whole names by the which you be daily constrained, that you do consecrate this present wax according, as it is necessary and

[74r]

convenient, so that it may have the virtue which it should have, by that fear and virtue of that most holy name Adonay, and of the almighty Father, whose kingdom and empire remaineth for ever and ever, and that ye give this wax such virtue as I would it should have, for this is come from the holy seat of Adonay, a fear which shall compel you to do my will [blank]."

Then make your image, and make a fumigation, and hold the image over it, and say as followeth:

"O you noble Orient,[590] king which doth reign in the east; O you Pyamon,[591] king most mighty in the occident, who hath mighty and strong dominion; O you, Agaymon,[592] greatest king within the south part and dost marvelously rule; O you Agame, king most famous, whose kingdom and empire is in the north,[593] I do call you and humble you by him that said and all was done, which did create all things with one word, and to him all things do obey, and he, from the seat of his majesty, did create all things and doth govern all things, and by this holy name which all the world doth fear, which is written in twelve [?] letters Ioth, Eth, He, Vau,[594] and by the nine heavenly condarios,[595] and by their virtues, and by the marks and tokens

---

588 *Non*: Could also be "Nom."

589 *Venus…Lapidator*: Note particularly the names "Asteroth," "Belliall," and "Asmo, Ideus." These names are not in the magical names contained in Additional Ms. 36674.

590 *Orient*: The version in Add. Ms. 36674 has "Eggye."

591 *Pyamon*: Most likely Paymon, as in Add. Ms. 36674.

592 *Agaymon*: Add. Ms. 36674 has "Amaymon."

593 *Agame*: Add. Ms. 36674 has "Egyn."
       O you noble Orient…: The four kings turn up in many different magical texts in Western Europe. This particular list is closest to the one in Agrippa von Nettesheim, *De Occulta Philosophia Libri Tres*, 471 (iii, 24).

594 *Ioth…Vau*: Likely a mistaken rendering of Yod-He-Vau-He.

595 *Condarios*: Likely "candarias," on which see above. The author seems to have left this in Latin, perhaps indicating that the term was unfamiliar.

of the maker of all. I conjure you that you do consecrate this image as doth appertain, that it may have the virtue which it should have."

This being done, say:[596]

"I conjure you again by your former conjuration, and by the living God, by the true God, and by the holy God, three persons and one true God, who hath created all things of nothing by his word, and I charge you by him which hath made you, and hath created heaven and earth and the sea and all things which are in them, and which hath sealed the sea by his high name, and hath set him his bounds which he cannot pass, and hath stablished the dry land in the midst thereof, and by him which hath made his angels spirits and his ministers a flaming fire, which knoweth all things that are past, present, and to come, and by him which hath the keys of hell and of death, and by him which is Alpha and Omega + the beginning and the end, that liveth and reigneth, overcometh, and governeth, which was dead and rose again the third day, and which is called + Tetragrammaton + I conjure you also again by all the might and power of God, and by all his holy names, and by all things that you may be constrained by that, presently and without delay, you cause that woman N., whom this image doth represent, to burn in my love, and that you suffer her to take no rest, sleeping nor waking, eating nor drinking, standing nor sitting, lying nor going, until she come or send unto me and fulfill all my desire, by Jesus Christ who shall come with great power and majesty to judge both the quick and the dead and the world by fire. Amen."

If she come, well it is; if not, lay the image under

[74v]

your bed's head, and within three days you shall see wonders of the woman.

If it be a thing to touch withal, or to shew to a woman and for love, say as followeth:

"I conjure you, Oyte, Tayly, Talgott, ministers of love and makers of friendship, which have power to put heat in man and woman and to inflame them in the fire of love. I conjure you by him that created you, and by the dreadful day of judgment, by him that doth govern the world, and that maketh all creatures to tremble, that in this night you consecrate and confirm these characters and figures or images, and

---

596 The following paragraph is not in Add. Ms. 36674.

that ye make them to have such virtue, that whomsoever I do touch or shew them, they may love me above any man, and that they prefer me above all other, and that all their mind and fantasy be on me by all the virtue aforesaid." *Finis.*

An Experiment for Love

Take three hairs of her head whom you knowest, and an image of of [sic] virgin wax. Secretly bind the three hairs about the image, and hold it over a fire of thorns until it melt, and say:

"I conjure thee, N., her father and mother, and the place where she dwelleth, by Cathan, Galian, Belsebub, and by the son of Raguel, and by all the devils that have power to hurt any thing, that you turn unto my love, and that you never rest, sleeping nor waking, eating nor drinking, until you come to me and fulfill my will in all things. I conjure thee, Sathan, by the very God, and by the holy God, and by his holy virginity, and by his most chaste mother, and by the dreadful day of judgment, and by the virginity of St. John Baptist, and by his head, and by the virginity of St. John the Evangelist, and by the virginity of St. Katherine, St. Margeret, St. Lucye, and all saints, and by the effusion of the precious blood of our Lord Jesus Christ, and by his incarnation, circumcision, death, and burial, and by his resurrection and glorious ascension, and by these most holy names of God, Emanuell, Sabaoth, Adonay, Otheos, Iskyros, Athanatos, Agla, Alpha et Ω, the beginning and ending, and by this holy name of God, Tetragrammaton, by angels, archangels, thrones, dominations, principates, potestates, virtues, cherubim, and seraphim, and by all the virtue of them, and by the patriarchs, prophets, apostles, martyrs, confessors, and virgins, by the four evangelists, and by all the heavens, and by all things contained in them. I conjure thee, Sathan, and all thy power, by the virtue of our Lord Jesus Christ, and by the virtue of all the aforesaid things, that you

[75r]

cause this woman N., of whose head these three hairs belongeth, to burn in my love, and with fervency of love to melt as this wax melteth at the seat of this fire, and that she may not rest, sleeping nor walking, sitting nor standing, eating nor drinking, lying nor walking, until she come or send unto me, by thy power, Sathan, and by the virtue of the aforesaid image. Let all this be done without tarrying. Amen."

Finis.

Another for Love [Wax Image][597]

Accipe tres crines cuiusdam N. de capite, et fac imaginem de cera virginea, et include tres crines in imagine, viz. unum in corona, et alium in corde, et tertio in medio pedum, et pone imaginem iuxta ignem, sic dicendo: "Coniuro te, per patrem, et filii, et spiritus sancti, per sanctam Mariam, matrem domini nostri Jesus Christi, et per incarnationem eius, et per omnes sanctos et sanctas dei, et per thrones et dominationem, per celum, per teram, per mare, et per omnes angelos et archangelos, et per cherubin et seraphin, et per omnia qua in eis sunt, et per omnia celestia et terestria et infernalia, ut illum vel illam N. pic ardere in amore meo, sicut ista cera delfluit a facie ignis. Sic idum [idem?] non vigilet, neque dormiet, neque ambulett, donec voluntate[m] meam compleverit," et proiicias ceram ab igne in aquam.

[Receive three hairs of this one N. from the head, and make an image of virgin wax, and shut three hairs up in the image, that is, one in the crown, and another in the heart, and third in the middle of the feet, and place the image next to the fire, thus saying, "I conjure thee, by the Father, and by the Son, and by the Holy Ghost, by the holy Mary, mother of our Lord Jesus Christ, and by his incarnation, and by all male and female saints of God, and by the thrones and dominions, by the heaven, by the earth, by the sea, and by all angels and archangels, and by cherubim and seraphim, and by all things that are in them,[598] and by all heavenly, terrestrial, and infernal things, that this man or woman N. pictured will burn in my love, just as this wax flows down from the face of the fire. Thus the same may not be wakeful, nor may sleep, nor may walk about, until my will may be fulfilled," and thou mayst throw the wax from the fire into the water.]

The Same in English

Take three hairs of her head and enclose them in a picture of virgin wax, one in the crown of the head, another in the heart, and the third in the midst of the feet, and set the picture before the fire, and say as followeth:

"I conjure thee by the Father, the Son, and the Holy Ghost, and by Saint Mary the mother of our Lord Jesus Christ, and by his incarnation, and by all saints of God, by cherubim and seraphim, by thrones and powers, by angels and archangels, by

---

597 This and the following rite are not identical, as a close examination will reveal.
598 *And by all things...in them*: This should come before "and by all angels and archangels."

heaven and earth and the sea, and by all that is therein, and by all things celestial, terrestrial, and infernal, that this man or woman N. whom this picture doth represent, may burn in love of me, and as this wax doth melt before the face of the fire, so in like manner she may melt in my love and never rest, waking, sleeping, nor walking, until my will be fulfilled." And then take the picture from the fire and cast it into the water.

To Make a Woman Follow Thee

Take sal ammoniac[599] on a Sunday, and put it in water, and then take it out again, and say over it three Pater Nosters, three Aves, and one Creed, and these names: "+ Sabaoth + Odon + Condona + Silfactan + I pray and beseech thee, O Lord, by the virtue of these names, that what woman or maid soever shall taste of this salt, or take it in meat or drink, may neither sit, nor stand, nor sleep, nor drink, until she have fulfilled my will." *Finis.*

[75v]

For Theft[600]

Go to the grave of one that is buried, and call him or her thrice by their proper name, laying thy head on the grave, saying, "I conjure thee, N., by Sezel, which is God and hath the bones of all that are dead in his power and keeping, that thou require license to come unto me this night, without any hurt or danger of my body or soul, after a just and favourable manner, and that you do declare to me the truth concerning this theft and things stolen, whether I may have it again or no."

If this do not prevail, then take of the earth of the grave at the head of the dead body, and bind it in a black cloth, and put it under your pillow, and sleep upon it, and in the night you shall dream, and he shall come unto you and tell you the truth of all things that you shall inquire after.

---

599 *Sal ammoniac*: Ammonium chloride. Ingestion, depending upon dosage, may lead to nausea and vomiting.

600 For another version, see "*Experimentum Probatum Verissimum de Furto* [A Most True and Proven Experiment for Thieves]," above.

An Experiment of a Candle for Theft Proved

Write these names on a candle made of virgin wax, + On + Ely +, and sprinkle it with oil de bay,[601] and say these names over it, always reciting them till the spirit do appear: "Operon, Eyre, Cascire, Dalyon, Galphin, Cardyn, Unchax, Ymar, Sodyon, Gelyn." And then say, "I conjure thee, spirit, by these imputed names of spirits, and by Elmon, De Angaria, Te Nosse, Noy, Ay, Aye, El, Ely, Elyon, Eyon, Eloy, and by the virginity of the Blessed Virgin Mary, and by the head of St. John Baptist, and by the virginity of St. John the Evangelist, and by the virginity of St Katherine, and by the head of your prince, that you do go quickly after your fellows, and quickly return with them again, and answer me truly to all things that I shall demand." And then after the first hour, the spirit shall appear with two of his fellows in the candle, and then conjure them by the former conjuration and by the names aforesaid that they do truly answer unto all things that shall be demanded of them. And when the spirit doth appear, say these names following to bind them and thou shalt be safe, from all peril and danger: "Tetragrammaton, Amamaball, Draconeum,[602] Allia, Fortisan, Almaron, Siga, Sache, Forge, Pamissiom, Sinnon, Dracosu, Eloy, Sachee, Emanuell, Anathenthout, Semaphoras." Amen.

For the Mother[603]

"In the name of the Father, + and of the Son + and of the Holy Ghost + Amen. I adjure thee, grief of the mother, by the Father, + the Son, + and the Holy Ghost + that you do not hurt, neither have any power over this servant of God, N., in the head, in the forehead, in the breast, in the womb, in the belly, nor in any part of the body. Christ reigneth, Christ doth rule, Christ vouchsafe to command, that hereafter you do not trouble nor molest this servant of God, N. In the name of the Father + and of the Son + and of the Holy Ghost + Amen + Ageos + Otheos + Agios + Yskyros + Athanatos + Elyson + Imas + In the name of the Father + and of the Son + and of the Holy Ghost, I make this sign of the + O holy mother of God, pray for me. Amen."

---

601 *Oil de bay*: Oil combining laurel berry extract with olive oil.

602 *Draconeum*: Could also be *Draconeun*.

603 *The Mother*: Condition in early modern English medicine, in which a supposed imbalance of the womb led to many different symptoms in various parts of the body; see Iorden, *A Briefe Discourse of a Disease Called the Suffocation of the Mother*, C1r–v.

To Consecrate Pen, Ink, and Paper

"I conjure you, O creatures of pen, ink, and paper, by Aneriton, per [by] Stimulaton,[604] and by his name that doth all things, that you help me in this work which I prepare you for, and after say these psalms: "*Domine, dominus noster* [O Lord, our Lord]," [605] *Deus, deus meus* [God, my God],"[606]

[76r]

"*Respice, domine* [have respect, O Lord],"[607] "*Domine quid habitabit* [O Lord, who will dwell],"[608] "*Quam dilecta* [how loved],"[609] and after say these words or names following: "Bismelet,[610] Godomes, Theophites, Alpha et Ω, Adonay, Tetragrammaton, by the virtue of these holy names, I do consecrate this present writing, in the name of the Father + and of the Son + and of the Holy Ghost + Amen." oƎoucdeɪɯ

That a Sword or Knife Shall Not Hurt Thee

Write these names "+ Offusa + Polustra + Genifera +"[611] and, saying the aforesaid names, blow or breathe against the blade when any man would hurt thee or slay thee, and if thou wilt that it shall not cut, say these names, "+ Obstat + Olenster + Genetrix + [blank] ♀," and consecrate these herbs, valerian, vervain, and marigolds, ☉ being in Leo, or Virgo, and ☽ increasing.

---

604 *Stimulaton*: One of the hundred names of God in Honorius and Hedegård, *Liber Iuratus Honorii a Critical Edition of the Latin Version of the Sworn Book of Honorius*, 112. It is also a name of power in the *Grand Grimoire*. See Peterson, "Le Grand Grimoire."

605 *Domine…*: Psalm 8.

606 *Deus…*: Psalm 21.

607 *Respice…*: A gradual or liturgical hymn derived from verses in Psalm 73.

608 *Domine quid…*: Psalm 14.

609 *Quam dilecta*: Psalm 83.

610 *Bismelet*: Possibly a variant of "Bismillah," an Arabic phrase, "In the name of God," which is the first phrase in the Koran.

611 A Norwegian charm for the same purpose from Vinje, Telemark dated circa 1520 gives "O ffusa + o Amplustra + o geministra in nomine patris et f. e. s. s. Amen." Bang, *Norske Hexeformularer og Magiske Opskrifter*, 508.

In the third house,[613] make a hollow ring of gold, into the which put this writing, written in virgin parchment with the blood of a man, "A-Anolita, Alibeat, Stab-blait," and the ring so made and filled, touch him the next day following, in the morning before he go into the field, making a fumigation with the hairs of a dead man, and say kneeling this prayer following:

"O Lord God almighty, which from the highest heavens dost behold the deeps, which hast formed man after thine owne image and similitude, by whom the living do live and the dead do die, I do beseech thee by thy bountifulness and benignity, that in what day or hour soever I touch this ring with my hand, that the spirits of those names which are enclosed therein may make armed soldiers to appear before the eyes of whomsoever I will."

And this being done, touch the earth with the ring, making this sign + Afterwards, lap the ring in fine cloth and keep it cleanly, and when you will work therewith, say (touching the ring with your hand), "O ye spirits whose names are enclosed herein, I conjure you by the prince whom ye ought to obey, that whatsoever we desire ye do." And this being said, you shall see wonderful things. *Finis.*

[76v]

[blank]

[77r]–[77v]

[blank]

[78r]–[78v]

[blank]

---

612 This title is misleading, as the experiment is to create illusory soldiers.

613 *Third house*: Likely the third astrological house, although that house does not seem to have martial significance, and the celestial body involved is not stated.

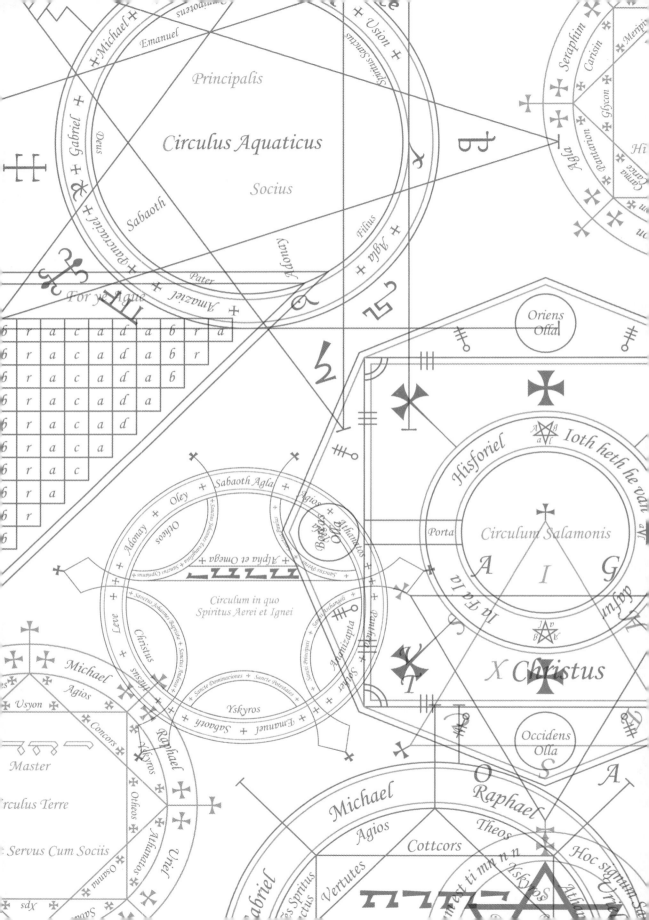

Works Cited

Manuscripts

Biblioteca Medicea Laurenziana, Firenze. Plut. 89 MS. Sup. 38.

Bodleian Library, Oxford. Ballard 66, Douce 116, e Mus. 173, 238, 245; Rawlinson D.252, D.253.

British Library, London. Additional 36674; Sloane 1727, 3824, 3846, 3849, 3851, 3853, 3884, 3885.

Cambridge University Library, Cambridge. Additional 3544.

Chetham's Library, Manchester. Mun.A.4.98.

Newberry Library, Chicago. Vault Case 5017.

University of Illinois Archives, Urbana-Champaign. Pre-1650 0102.

Wellcome Institute, London. Wellcome 110.

Printed Works

Agrippa von Nettesheim, Heinrich Cornelius. *De Occulta Philosophia Libri Tres*. Edited by V. Perrone Compagni. Leiden/New York: E. J. Brill, 1992.

Albertus Magnus (pseud.). *Being the Approved, Verified, Sympathetic, and Natural Egyptian Secrets; or, White and Black Art for Man and Beast*. Chicago: Egyptian Publishing Company, 1930.

Ashmole, Elias, and David Rankine. *The Book of Treasure Spirits: A 17th Century Grimoire of Magical Conjurations to Increase Wealth and Catch Thieves through the Invocation of Spirits, Fallen Angels, Demons, and Fairies*. London: Avalonia, 2009.

Bacon, Rogerus, and Michael-Albion Macdonald. *De Nigromancia: Sloane Ms. 3885 & Additional Ms. 36674*. Gillette, NJ: Heptangle Books, 1988.

Baker, Jim. *The Cunning Man's Handbook: The Practice of English Folk Magic, 1550–1900*. London: Avalonia, 2014.

Bang, Anton Christian. *Norske Hexeformularer og Magiske Opskrifter*. Kristiana: J. Dybwad, 1901.

ben Simeon, Abraham, Georg Dehn, Steven Guth, and S. L. MacGregor Mathers. *The Book of Abramelin: A New Translation*. Lake Worth, FL: Ibis Press, 2006.

Betz, Hans Dieter. *The Greek Magical Papyri in Translation, Including the Demotic Spells*. Chicago: University of Chicago Press, 1986.

Bicknell, Edward John. *A Theological Introduction to the Thirty-Nine Articles of the Church of England*. New York: Longmans, Green and Co., 1955.

Blaisdell, John Douglas. "A Frightful, but Not Necessarily Fatal, Madness: Rabies in Eighteenth-Century England and English North America" (dissertation, Iowa State, 2003).

Blum, Richard H., and Eva Marie Blum. *The Dangerous Hour: The Lore of Crisis and Mystery in Rural Greece*. New York: Scribner, 1970.

Boniface, and Ephraim Emerton. *The Letters of Saint Boniface*. New York: Columbia University Press, 2000.

Boudet, Jean-Patrice. "Les Condamnations de la Magie a Paris en 1398." *Revue Mabillon* n. s. 12 (2001): 121–57.

———. "La magie au carrefour des cultures dans la Florence du Quattrocentro: Le Liber Bileth et sa démonologie" in *Penser avec les Démons: Démonologues et Démonologies (XIIIe-XVIIe siècles)*, edited by Martine Ostorero and Julien Véronèse, 313–34. Micrologus Library 71. Firenze: SISMEL—Edizioni del Galluzzo, 2015.

Braekman, Willy Louis. "Middelnederlandsche Zegeningen, Bezweringsformulien en Towerplanten." *Verslagen en Mededelingen van de Koninklijke Academie voor Nederlandse Taalen Letterkunde* (1963), 275–386.

A Briefe Description of the Notorious Life of Iohn Lambe: Otherwise Called Doctor Lambe, Together with His Ignominious Death. Printed in Amsterdam [i.e., London]: [G. Miller?], 1628.

Brears, Peter C. D. *Cooking and Dining in Tudor and Early Stuart England*. London: Prospect Books, 2015.

Bryant, Nigel. *Perceforest: The Prehistory of King Arthur's Britain*. Cambridge, UK/Rochester, NY: D. S. Brewer, 2011.

Bynum, Caroline Walker. *The Resurrection of the Body in Western Christianity, 200–1336*. New York: Columbia University Press, 1995.

Charlesworth, James H., ed. "1 (Ethiopic Apocalypse of) Enoch (Second Century B.C.–First Century A.D.): A New Translation and Introduction." In *The Old Testament Pseudepigrapha*, 5–89. Garden City, NY: Doubleday, 1983.

Dan, Joseph, and Ronald C. Kiener. *The Early Kabbalah.* New York: Paulist Press, 1986.

Davies, Owen. "Healing Charms in Use in England and Wales 1700–1950." *Folklore* 107 (1996): 19–32.

Dawson, William Harbutt. *History of Skipton: (W. R. Yorks.).* London: Simpkin, Marshall, and Co., 1882.

De Voragine, Jacobus. *The Golden Legend: Readings on the Saints.* Princeton: Princeton University Press, 2012.

Delatte, Louis. *Un Office byzantin d'exorcisme (Ms. de la Lavra du Mont Athos, Θ 20).* Mémoires de la Classe des Lettres / Académie Royale de Belgique. Collection in 8o. Sér. 2 52. Bruxelles: Palais des Académies, 1957.

Dillinger, Johannes. "The Divining Rod: Origins, Explanations, and Uses in the Thirteenth to Eighteenth Centuries." In *Contesting Orthodoxy in Medieval and Early Modern Europe: Heresy, Magic, and Witchcraft,* edited by Louise Nyholm Kallestrup and Raisa Maria Toivo, 127–43. Palgrave Historical Studies in Witchcraft and Magic. Cham, Switzerland: Palgrave Macmillan, 2017.

Duffy, Eamon. *The Stripping of the Altars: Traditional Religion in England, c.1400–c.1580.* New Haven; London: Yale University Press, 2005.

Ekirch, A. Roger. *At Day's Close: Night in Times Past.* New York: W. W. Norton & Co., 2006.

Farmer, David Hugh. *The Oxford Dictionary of Saints.* Fifth revised ed. Oxford: Oxford University Press, n.d.

Foxe, John, Thomas Cranmer, and John Gough Nichols. *Narratives of the Days of the Reformation: Chiefly from the Mss. of John Foxe the Martyrologist; with 2 Contemporary Biographies of Archbishop Cranmer.* London: Camden Society, 1859.

Fredericq, Paul. *Corpus Documentorum Inquisitionis Haereticae Pravitatis Neerlandicae: Verzameling van Stukken pauselijke en bisschoppelijke Inquisitie in de Nederlanden.* Hoogeschool van Gent Werken van den practischen Leergang van vaderlandsche Gescheidenis 1, 5, 8, 10. 5 vols. Gent: Vuylsteke, 1889–1903.

Gal, Florence, Jean-Patrice Boudet, and Laurence Moulinier-Brogi. *Vedrai Mirabilia: Un Libro di Magia del Quattrocento.* I libra di Viella 245. Rome: Viella, 2017.

Gollancz, Hermann. *Sepher Maphteah Shelomoh: Book of the Key of Solomon.* York Beach, ME: Teitan Press, 2008.

Grabinski, Ludwig. *Die Sagen, der Aberglaube und abergläubische Sitten in Schlesien: mit einem Anhang über Prophezeihungen.* Schweidnitz: Brieger & Gilbers, 1886.

Great Britain. *The Statutes of the Realm: Printed by Command of His Majesty King George the Third, in Pursuance of an Address of the House of Commons of Great Britain, from Original Records and Authentic Manuscripts.* London: Dawsons, 1963.

Grévin, Benoît, and Julien Véronèse. "Les 'Caractères' Magiques au Moyen Âge (XIIe–XIVe Siècle)." *Bibliothèque de l'école des Chartes* 162, no. 2 (2004): 305–79.

Harms, Dan. "Spirits at the Table: Faerie Queens in the Grimoires" in *The Faerie Queens: In Magic, Myth and Legend*, edited by Sorita D'Este, 41–58. London: Avalonia, 2013.

———. *William Dawson Bellhouse: Galvanist, Cunning Man, Scoundrel.* Burbage: Caduceus Books, forthcoming.

Harms, Daniel, James R. Clark, and Joseph H. Peterson. *The Book of Oberon: A Sourcebook of Elizabethan Magic.* Woodbury, MN: Llewellyn, 2015.

Henslowe, Philip. *Henslowe's Diary*, edited by W. W. Greg. London: A. H. Bullen, 1904.

Herrmann, W. "Baal" in *Dictionary of Deities and Demons in the Bible DDD*, 132–39. Leiden: Brill, 1999.

Historical Manuscripts Commission. *Report on Manuscripts in Various Collections.* Vol. 7. London: The Hereford Times Limited, 1914.

Hockley, Frederick, John Hamill, and R. A. Gilbert. *The Rosicrucian Seer: Magical Writings of Frederick Hockley.* York Beach, ME: The Teitan Press, 2009.

Honorius, and Gösta Hedegård. *Liber Iuratus Honorii: A Critical Edition of the Latin Version of the Sworn Book of Honorius.* Stockholm: Almqvist & Wiksell International, 2002.

Horst, Georg Conrad, and Herbert Kempf. *Zauber-Bibliothek: oder von Zauberei, Theurgie und Mantik, Zauberern, Hexen und Hexenprocessen, Dämonen, Gespenstern und Geistererscheinungen.* Freiburg im Breisgau: Ambra/Aurum Verlag, 1979.

Hutter, M. "Asmodeus" in *Dictionary of Deities and Demons in the Bible DDD*, edited by K. van der Toorn, Bob Becking, and Pieter Willem van der Horst, 106–8. Leiden/Boston/Grand Rapids, MI: Brill; Eerdmans, 1999.

Hunt, Tony. *Popular Medicine in Thirteenth-Century England: Introduction and Texts*. Cambridge: D. S. Brewer, 1990.

Iorden, Edward. *A Briefe Discourse of a Disease Called the Suffocation of the Mother*. London: John Windet, 1603.

Jewish Publication Society. *Tanakh = JPS Hebrew-English Tanakh: The Traditional Hebrew Text and the New JPS Translation*. 2nd ed. Philadelphia: Jewish Publication Society, 2000.

Kieckhefer, Richard. *Forbidden Rites: A Necromancer's Manual of the Fifteenth Century*. University Park, PA: Pennsylvania State University Press, 1998.

Kittredge, George Lyman. *Witchcraft in Old and New England*. New York: Russell & Russell, 1956.

Klaassen, Frank F. "Three Early Modern Magic Rituals to Spoil Witches." *Opuscula* 1, no. 1 (2011), 1–10.

———. *The Transformations of Magic: Illicit Learned Magic in the Later Middle Ages and Renaissance*. Magic in History. University Park, PA: The Pennsylvania State University Press, 2012.

Lilly, W. *William Lilly's History of His Life and Times from the Year 1602 to 1681*. Re-printed for C. Baldwin, 1715.

Livingstone, A. "Astarte" in *Dictionary of Deities and Demons in the Bible DDD*, 109–14. Leiden/Boston/Grand Rapids, MI: Brill; Eerdmans, 1999.

Lovecraft, H. P. *The Dreams in the Witch House and Other Weird Stories*. London: Penguin, 2005.

Lynch, Geraldine. "Folk Beliefs about the March Cock." Dublin: National Folklore Collection, Ireland, University College Dublin, 1976.

McLean, Adam. *The Magical Calendar: A Synthesis of Magical Symbolism from the Seventeenth-Century Renaissance of Medieval Occultism*. Grand Rapids, MI: Phanes Press, 1994.

Mare, Walter de la. *Come Hither: A Collection of Rhymes and Poems for the Young of All Ages*. London: Constable & Co., 1923.

Martinez, David. "'May She Neither Eat nor Drink': Love Magic and Vows of Abstinence." In *Ancient Magic and Ritual Power*, edited by Marvin W. Meyer and Paul A. Mirecki, 335–59. Religions in the Graeco-Roman World. Leiden: E. J. Brill, 1995.

Ó hógáin, Dáithí. "Dreaming and Dancing: W. B. Yeats' Use of Traditional Motifs in 'The Dreaming of the Bones' (1919)." *Hungarian Journal of English and American Studies* 8, no. 1 (2002): 57–75.

Ohrt, F. *Danmarks Trylleformler*. København: Gyldendal, 1917–21.

Ó Súilleabháin, Seán. *A Handbook of Irish Folklore.* London: H. Jenkins, 1963.

Paulsen, Kathryn. *The Complete Book of Magic & Witch-Craft.* New York: Signet, 1980.

Peterson, Joseph H., ed. *Arbatel—Concerning the Magic of the Ancients: Original Sourcebook of Angel Magic.* Lake Worth, FL/Newburyport, MA: Ibis Press; distributed Red Wheel/Weiser, 2009.

———. "Liber Juratus Honorii, or The Sworne Booke of Honorius." Kasson, MN: Joseph Peterson, 1999. CD-ROM.

———. *Secrets of Solomon: A Witch's Handbook from the Trial Records of the Venetian Inquisition.* Kasson, MN: Twilit Grotto, 2018.

Peterson, Joseph H., trans. "Le Grand Grimoire, ou l'Art de Commander les Esprits Celestes, Aériens, Terrestres, Infernaux." Kasson, MN: Joseph Peterson, 1999. CD-ROM.

———. *Grimorium Verum.* Scotts Valley, CA: CreateSpace, 2007.

———. "The Key of Knowledge (Clavicula Salomonis)." Esoteric Archives, 1999. http://esotericarchives.com/solomon/l1203.htm.

———. *The Lesser Key of Solomon: Lemegeton Clavicula Salomonis: Detailing the Ceremonial Art of Commanding Spirits Both Good and Evil.* York Beach, Me.: Weiser Books, 2001.

———. "The Magic Wand," 2007.

Roper, Jonathan. *English Verbal Charms.* Helsinki: Suomalainen Tiedeakatemia, 2005.

Rosen, Edward, and Lynn Thorndike. *The Sphere of Sacrobosco and Its Commentators.* Chicago: University of Chicago Press, 1949.

Russell, Jeffrey B. "Saint Boniface and the Eccentrics." *Church History* 33 (1964): 235–47.

Scot, Reginald. *The Discouerie of Witchcraft: Wherein the Lewde Dealing of Witches and Witchmongers Is Notablie Detected, the Knauerie of Coniurors, the Impietie of Inchantors, the Follie of Soothsaiers, the Impudent Falshood of Cousenors, the Infidelitie of Atheists, the Pestilent Practices of Pythonists, the Curiositie of Figure Casters, the Vanitie of Dreamers, the Beggerlie Art of Alcumystrie, the Abhomination of Idolatrie, the Horrible Art of Poisoning, the Vertue and Power of Naturall Magike, and All the Conueiances of Legierdemaine and Iuggling Are Deciphered: And Many Other Things Opened, Which Have Long Lien Hidden, Howbeit Verie Necessarie to Be Knowne: Heerevnto Is Added a Treatise Vpon the Nature and Substance of Spirits and Diuels, & c.* Imprinted at London: By William Brome, 1584.

Serenus Sammonicus, Quintus. *Liber Medicinalis*. Paris: Presses Universitaires de France, 1950.

Seyfarth, Carly. *Aberglaube und Zauberei in der Volksmedizin West-Sachsens*. Leipzig: Wilhelm Heims, 1913.

Sibley, Ebenezer, Frederick Hockley, and Joseph H. Peterson. *The Clavis or Key to the Magic of Solomon*. Lake Worth, FL/Newburyport, MA: Ibis Press; distributed by Red Wheel/Weiser, 2009.

Skemer, Don C. *Binding Words: Textual Amulets in the Middle Ages*. University Park, PA: The Pennsylvania State University Press, 2006.

Skinner, Stephen, and David Rankine, eds. *The Veritable Key of Solomon*. London: Golden Hoard, 2008.

Stehle, Bruno. "Volkstümliche Feste, Sitten, und Gebräuche im Elsass, 1892." *Jahrbuch für Geschichte, Sprache und Litteratur Elsass-Lothringens* 8 (1892), 159–81.

Stratton-Kent, Jake. *Pandemonium: A Discordant Concordance of Diverse Spirit Catalogues*. West Yorkshire: Hadean Press, 2016.

Toporkov, Andrei. "Russian Love Charms in a Comparative Light" in *Charms, Charmers, and Charming: International Research on Verbal Magic*, edited by Jonathan Roper, 27–53. Palgrave Historical Studies in Witchcraft and Magic. Hampshire: Palgrave Macmillan, 2009.

Turner, Dawson. "Brief Remarks, Accompanied with Documents, Illustrative of Trial by Jury, Treasure-Trove, and the Invocation of Spirits for the Discovery of Hidden Treasure in the Sixteenth Century." *Norfolk Archaeology* 1 (1847): 55–64.

Véronèse, Julien. *L'Almandal et l'Almadel Latins au Moyen Âge: Introduction et Édition Critique*. Firenze: SISMEL, Edizioni del Galluzzo, 2012.

Weyer, Johann. *Ioannis Wieri De Praestigiis Daemonum, & Incantationibus Ac Ueneficiis Libri Sex, Postrema Editione Quinta Aucti & Recogniti. Accessit Liber Apologeticus, Et Pseudomonarchia Daemonum…* Basileae: Ex Officina Oporiniana [per Balthasarum Han, Hieronymum Gemusaeum & Polycarpi fratris haeredes], 1577.

Wilkins, David. *Concilia Magnae Britanniae et Hiberniae, a Synodo Verolamiensi A.D. CCCCXLVI Ad Londinensem A.D. MDCCXVII; Accedunt Constitutiones et Alia Ad Historiam Ecclesiae Anglicanae Spectantia*. 4 vols. Londini: sumptibus R. Gosling, F. Gyles, T. Woodward, & C. Davis, 1737.

William of Auvergne. *Guilielmi Alverni Episcopi Parisiensis, Mathematici Perfectissimi, Eximii Philosophi, ac Theologi Præstantissimi, Opera Omnia: Quæ Hactenus Reperiri Potuerunt, Reconditissimam Rerum Humanarum, ac Divinarum Doctrinam Abundè Complectentia, ac Proinde Bonarum Artium ac Scientiarum Studiosis, Maximè Verò Theologis, ac Divini Verbi Concionatoribus Apprimè Necessaria: Nunc Demùm in Hac Novissima Editione ab Innumeris Errorum Chiliadibus Expurgata, Instaurata, Elucidata, atque Sermonibus & Variis Tractatibus Aucta ex Mss. Codd. ut et Præfationibus ad Lectorem Apertius Intelligetur: Quorum Catalogum Proxima post Præfationes Pagina Indicabit cum Indicibus Locupletissimis Rerum Notabilium.* Aureliæ; Londini: ex typographia F. Hotot; apud Robertum Scott, bibliopolam, 1674.

Worrell, William H. "The Demon of Noonday and Some Related Ideas." *Journal of the American Oriental Society* 38 (1918): 160–66.

Index

Auras, 202

Ave Maria, 68, 83, 182

Avis, 104

Ay, 301

Aye, 73, 74, 301

Aylesbury, Thomas, 10

Aymaeleon, 105

Aymon, 196

Aymse, 76, 78, 103

Ayos, 70, 71

Ayriltis, 86

Aysell (vinegar), 108

Azaray, 180, 181, 184

Azaria, 270

Azazel, 36, 294

Azepa, 75, 76, 108

Azie, 144

Azochede, 229

Azoel, 241

Ba'al / Baal / Baall, 194, 241

Baba Mutela, 273

Babaty, 272

Babay, 272

Bacon, Roger, 175

Bacon, William, 39, 48, 175, 178, 182

Bael, 241

Balaam, 246

Balath, 199

Balbo, 119

Balko, 136–138

Balsacke, 144

Balthaser, 269

Ban, 258

Baracheell / Barachyell, 75, 77, 98

Barachi, 229

Baramptis, 43, 225

Barasim / Barasym, 98

Barbas, 194

Barbays, 39, 195

Barion, 75, 77

Barlow, Thomas, 4

Baron, 9, 75, 77

Barrados, 258

Barthan, 119

Baryon, 110

Basan, 199

Basel, 37, 145

Basin of water, 178, 184

Basion / Basyen / Basyon, 75, 77

Basquiel, 175

Bassett, William, 12

Bathoner, 193

Bay tree, 193

Beabo, 113, 114

Beal / Beall, 119

Beauchamp, Sir John, 13

Beauty, provided by spirits, 33, 129, 292

Beelbac, 158

Beelzebub / Belsebub / Belzabub / Belzabue, 100, 152

Beena, 75, 76, 108

Belchye, 100

Beldon, 158

Belemacke, 158

Beliada, 158

Beliata, 158

Belima, 295

Bell, 152, 241, 295

Bellhouse, William Dawson, 270

Belliall, 295, 296

Belltowers, 74

Belsac, 73, 74

Belsebub—see Beelzebub

Beluginis, 43, 225

Belugo, 227

Belyall, 199

Belzabub / Belzabue—see Beelzebub

Bucket, magical tool, 291

Bucknall, 6

Bucton, 75, 77

Budon, 110

Bufflas, 196

Buildings, destruction of, provided by spirits, 197, 200, 206, 229, 242

Buildings, provided by spirits, 197, 200, 206, 229, 242

Bulsacbaris, 219

Bulsas, 219

Burcham, 95

Busyn, 37, 198

Bybon, 119

Byleth—see Bileth

Bythel, 93

Ca, 48, 51, 163, 223, 258

Caaph, 76, 78

Caberion, 240

Cacaryll, 202

Cachefurto, 97

Cados, 75, 77, 82, 97, 109, 167, 170

Cagyn, 200

Cain, 91, 107, 212

Caldey, 226

Calkfulgra, 94

Calmus, 230

Camon, 296

Canaan, 136

Cancer (ailment), 95, 146

Candles, magical tool, 178, 179, 181

Candlesticks, holy, magical tool, 63, 112, 181

Canthiale, 190

Cantivalerion, ritual to summon, 27, 101, 119, 139

Cantivalerion, 27, 101, 119, 139

Capare, 144

Caph, 76, 78, 103, 176

Caphaell, 75, 77, 98

Capiell, 97

Capuel, 175

Caput, 86, 104, 115, 214, 265

Carafax, 175

Carbus, 230

Cardyn, 301

Carisin, 118

Carizar, 249

Carmacarice, 118

Carmelion / Carmelyon, 240

Carnis, 94, 238

Caron / Caronem / Caronera, 123

Carpenter, John, 4, 268

Carpenters, provided by spirits, 230

Carpet, 39, 174

Carus Christi, 84, 238

Casaubon, Meric, 20

Cascire, 301

Casiell, 132

Cassiopeia (constellation), 11

Castles, provided by spirits, 197, 200, 202, 228, 229, 236

Castles, seizing, provided by spirits, 197, 200, 202, 228, 229, 236

Castrietar, 243

Caszepell, 75, 77, 98

Cat, 285

Catacis, 232, 233

Cataracts, 146

Cathan, 298

Catholic Church, Roman, 9

Catis, 232, 233

Caton, 140

Catos, 236

Cayma, 295

Caymay, 121, 122

Cecil, William, 11

Celandine, 117

Cenarion, 240

Cornus, 237

Corpses, moving, provided by spirits, 35, 202

Costos, 236

Cottcors, 249

Cotton, Sir Robert Bruce, 4

Cotton, Sir Thomas, 21

Cough, rancid, 147

Cousins, love between, provided by spirits, 202

Coynothomen, 67

Cramps, 146

Crapp, Jane, 25

Crassitus, 86

Craton, 72–76, 104, 108, 109, 115, 128, 142, 143, 150, 170, 175, 204, 214, 218, 250, 252, 266, 290

Cratoy, 172

Crea, 273

Credo in deum patrem—*see* Nicene Creed

Creed, 68, 79, 83, 102, 153, 220, 265, 268, 269, 290, 300

Cremeon, 236

Crissia, 95

Critaron, 152

Cross, holy, 68, 72, 93, 98, 106, 179

Crossroads, 158

Crostheade, 193

Crowley, Aleister, 27, 40

Crystal, consecration of, 20, 29, 30, 59, 63, 64, 85, 100, 101, 107, 109–114, 116, 128, 129, 131, 136, 137, 139, 142, 143, 153, 154, 213, 214, 289, 290, 295

Crystal, summoning spirit into, 20, 29, 30, 59, 63, 64, 85, 100, 101, 107, 109–114, 116, 128, 129, 131, 136, 137, 139, 142, 143, 153, 154, 213, 214, 289, 290, 295

Culfes, 172

Cunning folk, 5, 15, 16, 19, 20, 46

Cycomoy, 170

Cyprian, Saint, 147, 248

Cyrus, 227, 228

Daemonologie (James I), 17, 31, 49

Dafur, 262

Dalleth, 176

Dalyon, 301

Damamestoras, 206

Daniel, 42, 49, 136, 181, 186

Daniell, 109

Danzig, 10

Dardyell, 75, 77, 98

Daria, 282

Dates, 3, 171, 264

David, King, 156–157, 216

Davis / Davies, Mother, 12

Davis, John, 35

De Angaria, 301

De Nigromancia / De Nigromantia (pseud.-Bacon), 2, 4, 15, 118, 244, 248, 252, 254

De Novem Candariis, 181

De Occulta Philosophia (Agrippa), 20, 28, 37, 44, 106, 120, 160, 162, 164, 165, 294, 296

Deacon, 99

Dead, demons masquerading as, 16, 17, 23, 33–37, 54, 71, 76, 79, 87, 89, 98, 106, 109, 111, 113, 122, 123, 129, 132, 134, 144, 154, 158, 181, 191, 198, 202, 203, 206–208, 210, 236, 237, 273, 275, 289, 294, 297, 300, 303

Deafness, 146

Death, in water, talisman to protect against, 71

Death, unexpected, talisman to protect against, 260

Dedragramay, 97

Emanuel, 59, 86, 150, 156, 167, 172, 175, 226, 244, 248, 250, 252, 256, 265, 289, 290

Emas, 295

Emorison, 142, 143

Emull, 295

Enathi, 70, 71

Enemies, talisman to protect against, 39, 67, 107, 108, 162, 164, 179, 195, 196, 201, 227, 228, 242, 260, 266, 267

Ennoy, 119

Entro, 105

Eo, 79, 83, 141, 187, 218, 219, 294

Ephradyn, 148

Epilepsy, 146

Eptra, 273

Erathon, 94

Eriona, 75, 77

Erith, 75, 77, 115

Erner, 295

Erysell, 115

Erysipelas, 146

Es, 69, 75, 76, 80, 129, 139, 153, 176, 187, 258

Esam, 295

Esay, 94

Esere, 156

Esereheye, 170

Essex, 18

Estrion, 258

Esum, 295

Esyon, 206

Eternitas, 167

Eternus, 266

Ethamael, 177

Ethsomirahe, 172

Eucharist, 99

Eusule, 95

Evangelists, 64, 68, 93, 100, 112, 126, 185, 205, 298

Evans, John, 19

Eve, 70, 96, 105, 107, 132, 159

Evell, 210

Eviona, 98

Exorcism, 23, 56, 234, 284

Eyon, 301

Eyre, 301

Fainting, 146

Fairies, nature of, 2, 19, 21, 23, 24, 31–33, 35, 41, 44, 49, 50, 52, 270, 287, 290–292

Fairies, ritual to summon, 21

Fairy Queen, 32

Falneyl, 101

Familiars, 29, 52, 197

Fanaboth, 67

Farabores, 119

Faraphyell, 75, 77

Fasall, 289

Faust Book (Jones), 28, 50

Favour, provided by spirits, 60, 136, 141, 152, 194–196, 198, 199, 201, 202

Feasilet, 180, 181

Felon, ritual to cure, 268

Feodem, 180, 181

Fercon, 97

Festilen, 229

Fetan, 172

Fever, 145, 146, 160

Fields, provided by spirits, 210, 242

Figs, 171

Filioboy, 204

Filthiness of the body, 147

Finis, 86, 94, 104, 115, 214, 265

Haye, 93

Hazel, 25, 174, 268–270

Healing, 15, 19, 20, 38, 46, 50, 145, 260, 265

Health, 49, 62, 63, 68, 72, 105, 107, 108, 111, 156, 157, 160–162, 236, 258, 266, 276

Hebanth, 93

Heben, 204

Hec, 72–74, 76, 119, 121, 128, 129, 132, 142, 156, 188, 191, 213, 220, 221, 223, 226, 258

Hehahub, 75, 76

Hekesy, 204

Helamo, 75, 76, 108

Hele, 67

Hell, 25, 27, 30, 33, 49, 63, 64, 67, 70, 78, 79, 87, 88, 91, 105, 112, 114–116, 121, 122, 132, 137, 138, 147, 148, 151, 152, 154, 157, 175, 178, 189, 190, 204–206, 212, 214, 221, 230, 270, 273, 275–277, 289, 295, 297

Heloa, 167, 170

Heloy, 75, 76, 89, 109

Helvecie, 204

Hely (Elijah), 73, 75, 76, 94, 109, 136, 150, 216, 218, 291

Helyon, 167

Henry VIII, King, 7, 36

Heptameron (pseudo-d'Abano), 20, 48

Herbert, William, Earl of Pembroke, 12

Herbs, 43, 195, 197–199, 205, 211, 242, 278, 287, 302

Herefordshire, 13, 14

Herie, 144

Herlam, 132, 133

Hermely, 119

Hermits, 185, 187

Herod, King, 270

Hesod, 167

Heth, 76, 78, 103, 262

Heye, 156

Hidden things, provided by spirits, 271

Higron, 142, 143

Himas, 266

Hinds, 295

Historiel, 262

Hocraell, 75, 77, 98

Holy Ghost / Spirit, 22, 60, 62, 63, 66–69, 72, 77, 80–82, 85, 90, 91, 96, 98, 101, 104, 105, 107, 109–111, 114, 121–126, 128, 130–133, 136, 137, 141, 145, 147, 148, 153–157, 174, 175, 178–180, 182, 184–191, 204–206, 208, 211–218, 220, 221, 244, 250, 252, 254, 256, 264–271, 273–275, 277, 278, 289–291, 293, 295, 299, 301, 302

Holy water, 66, 94, 102, 116, 157, 163, 279

Homo, 68, 86, 94, 104, 115, 153, 170, 172, 175, 214, 265

Homousion, 156

Honely, 216

Honor, 71, 73, 74, 87, 111, 172, 191, 219, 220, 233, 234

Hoopoe, 171

Hopkins, Matthew, 6, 8, 18, 20, 49

Horses, rituals to protect, 28, 210

Hosell, 190

Host, Communion, 74, 99, 215

Hoth, 250

Hoye, 67

Hubbe, 67

Hubbethu, 93

Humor, putrefaction of, 7, 145

Hyheha, 75, 76, 108

Hymas, 170

Hyssop, 102, 279

Ia, 67, 210, 258, 262

Ia Ia, 210

Iamfriell, 132, 133

Iammax, 119

Ianua, 86, 94, 104, 115, 214, 230, 266

Iaspes, 236

Iathai, 167

Iay, 70, 71

Icbona, 167

Ideus, 296

Ieel, 167

Iehola, 167

Iehova, 156, 167, 170

Ielur, 190

Iene, 97

Iesan, 273

Iesu, 80, 97, 130, 131, 139, 187, 203, 204, 208, 230, 231

Ihan, 76, 78

Illness, 17, 37–39, 210, 267

Imago, 86, 104, 266

Imago Patris, 104

Imas, 301

Imoboum / Imoboun, 180, 181

Imperator, 229, 230

Impotence, 146

Incense, 35, 84, 93, 148, 149, 163, 203, 224, 252, 269, 272

Indeus, 93

Indigestion, 146

Indulgences, 34

Inger, 84

Ink, magical tool, 3, 42, 102, 163, 216, 302

Innael, 75, 77

Inquiell, 75, 77, 98

Insanity, 146, 147

Insaul, 106

Insomnia, 124, 174, 178, 272, 297–300

Intestines, pain of, 146

Invisibility, provided by spirits, 16, 196, 201, 232, 287

Ioazac, 76, 78, 103

Iohihith, 250

Ionatyell, 93

Iophiel, 167

Iosell, 190

Ioseph, 75, 77, 98

Ioth / Iothe, 59, 70, 71, 93, 97, 109, 132, 133, 256, 262, 296

Iparon / Iperon, 100

Irculo, 106

Iregon, 75, 77, 110

Iron implements and castles, provided by spirits, 236

Irritation, provided by spirits, 117

Isaac, 78, 79, 87, 94, 107, 136, 185, 209

Isance, 89, 210

Iskyros—see Yskyros

Ittymon, 210

Iube, 282

Iulia, 104

Iuramiter, 83, 84

Iustum, 237

Ivory, magical tool, 288

Jacob, 87, 94, 107, 136, 179, 209

James I, King of England (James VI of Scotland), 11, 31, 49

Jasper, 3, 269

Jaundice, 146

Jephthah, 136

Lucyell, 75, 77

Luminis, 233, 234

Lunaell, 98

Lungs, pain of, 89, 147, 210

Lux, 86, 94, 104, 115, 170, 214, 258, 266

Lyes, 227, 228

Lymer, 236

Ma, 48, 53, 92, 167, 207, 208, 258, 273

Mabnos, 75, 77, 97, 98

Maccabeus, Judas, 164

Maconus, 227

Macryon, 119

Magala, 273

Mageth, 73, 74

Magical Elements (pseudo-d'Abano)—*see* Heptameron

Magon, 180, 181

Magram, 273

Magus, The (Barrett), 21

Mahate, 75, 76

Mahothe, 218, 219

Maiestas, 68, 167, 170, 266

Malachim, 167

Malathym, 76, 78, 100

Malchus, 95, 142

Malchus, Andrew, 95, 142

Maldall, 75, 77, 110

Malice, 59, 140, 141, 267

Maliga, 270

Malim, 167

Mallappas, 197

Manan, 230, 231

Manchet, magical tool, 292

Mandalabo, 142, 143

Mandell, 128

Mandranatha, 181

Manosos, 231

Manslaughter, 136

Manus, 75, 76, 86, 92, 104, 115, 170, 214, 265, 274

Maos, 295

Maothe, 73, 74

March cock, 288

Margar, 272

Margaret, St., 217

Margon, 273

Marigolds, 302

Marog, 247

Marquises (spirits), 28, 284

Mars, 78, 100, 119, 120, 146, 152, 176, 191

Martyrs, 13, 22, 33, 46, 64, 68, 77, 79, 87, 93, 99, 104, 112, 121, 126, 128, 149, 176, 178, 185, 187, 188, 190, 205, 209, 290, 298

Mary Magdalene, 108, 154

Mary, Blessed Virgin, 22, 23, 63, 71, 72, 80, 104, 111, 122, 124, 126, 128, 133, 137, 143, 147, 148, 154, 157, 175, 189, 204, 206, 215, 217, 270, 301

Masa, 295

Mass, 6, 125, 219

Mass of the Holy Ghost, 125

Mastic, 102, 103, 148, 179

Matha, 181, 182

Mathaliza, 181, 182

Mathematics, 7, 9, 14

Mathepart, 113

Mathon, 184

Mathye, 100

Matiate, 108

Matiell, 67

Matratha, 181, 182

Maveryon, 126, 127

Maymon / Mayemon, 119

Maziell, 70, 71

Meas, 92, 144, 172, 295

Peter, Saint, 185, 248, 250

Petra, 86, 94, 104, 115, 214, 266

Phalec, 145, 146

Phaneton, 150

Phares, 97

Philoneum, 100

Phrayes, 125

Phul, 145, 147

Physic, provided by spirits, 202

Phytoneum, 76, 78

Piarum, 231, 232

Picatrix, 37, 51

Pierrepont, Robert, Earl of Kingston, 11

Pilate, 107

Piri, 105

Pistraye, 95

Pius, 237

Plague, 95, 145

Planetary hours, 61

Planets, 37, 40, 49, 50, 60, 77, 100, 106, 119–121, 152, 173, 175, 176, 182, 193, 205

Plate, magical tool, 3, 6, 124, 126, 203

Pleiades, 38, 158

Plethora, 145

Pleurisy, 145

Pllo, 106

Podagra, 146

Poison, talisman to protect against, 260, 274

Polacar, 295

Poliol, 106

Polustra, 302

Ponilbus, 295

Pope, Thomas, 6

Popes, 36

Populas, 268

Portasinall, 295

Potestates/powers, order of angels, 63, 69, 70, 73, 93, 97, 98, 110, 111, 115, 143, 205, 215, 218, 248, 290, 298

Power, John, 12

Ppiuli, 254

Preamulion, 144

Prelates (spirits), 28, 285, 286

Presidents (spirits), 286

Priamon, 121–123

Priest, 87, 191, 192, 227, 231, 266, 279

Primogenitus, 86, 94, 104, 115, 170, 214, 265

Primus, 70, 104, 175, 266

Princes (spirits), 46, 53, 59, 90, 96, 97, 101, 152, 195, 202, 205, 211, 221, 226, 234, 284, 286

Principalities/principates, order of angels, 29, 68, 74, 77, 144, 219, 248

Principium, 69, 86, 94, 115, 132, 153, 170, 181, 216, 265, 291

Prophecy, provided by spirits, 108

Propheta, 86, 104, 115, 170, 214, 266

Prophets, 63, 64, 68, 79, 87, 91, 93, 108, 112, 121, 126, 149, 176, 185, 188, 194, 205, 209, 212, 298

Prudentius, Hymn ante Somno, 92

Psalms, 41, 62, 69, 153, 289, 290, 302

Psalter, 69

Psanton, 172

Pseudomonarchia daemonum (Weyer), 27, 55, 311

Psoriasis, 146

Purgatory, 23, 33, 34, 36, 200, 202

Putrost, 106

Pyamon—*see* Paymon

Pycayranon, 229

Quambus, 172

Quatuball, 152

Rufalas, 94

Rurcos, 239

Rymeloth, 105

Sa, 258, 287

Sabaara, 180, 181

Sabalay, 67

Sabaoth, 31, 59, 67, 72, 73, 75, 76, 82,
    86–88, 93, 97, 98, 104, 109, 111,
    115, 118, 123, 128, 132, 133, 142,
    143, 150, 153, 154, 156, 167, 170,
    175, 180, 181, 188, 189, 204, 206,
    209, 214, 216, 218, 226, 244, 248–
    250, 252, 256, 265, 271, 290, 291,
    295, 298, 300

Sabbats, 18

Saboth, 209

Sabquiell, 97

Sabriel, 252

Sabwell, 152

Sacerdos, 86, 104, 115, 214, 227, 230,
    231, 266

Sache, 301

Sachee, 301

Saciathon / Saciaton, 221, 222

Sacraments, 23, 63, 71, 77, 99, 115,
    189, 192, 205

Sadalay, 93

Saday / Sadday, 75, 77, 79, 80, 82, 97,
    105, 109, 150, 156, 167, 170, 206,
    214

Sade, 176

Sadelay, 170

Sadon, 239

Saem, 295

Saffron, 272

Saine, 295

Saints, 14, 22, 23, 33, 34, 64, 66, 68,
    71, 72, 74, 93, 96, 107, 108, 115,
    116, 122, 128, 137, 138, 144, 180,
    181, 185, 190, 205, 206, 213, 215,
    219, 227, 234, 265, 277, 298, 299

Sal ammoniac, 300

Salamon—see Solomon

Salgiell / Salgyell, 75, 77

Salt, 37, 39, 282, 292, 300

Salubris, 233, 234

Salus, 68, 71, 258, 266

Salutiferus, 237

Salutis, 156, 236

Salvator, 72, 75, 76, 105, 108, 172,
    227, 229–231, 233, 234, 238, 266

Sam, 258

Samaell, 97

Samanus, 119

Samay, 121, 122

Samaym, 100

Sameth, 76, 78, 103

Sammonicus, Quintus Serenus, 160

Samyell, 75, 77, 98

Sanroman, 193

Saphar, 129

Saphiron, 129

Sapientia, 68, 86, 94, 104, 115, 170,
    175, 214, 265

Saraphyell, 98

Sarapiell, 119

Sargion, 190

Sari, 73, 74

Sarie, 73, 74

Sarypyell, 97

Sathagon, 250

Sathan, 24, 72, 90, 95, 125, 127, 152,
    178–182, 221, 222, 254, 298

Sator Arepo Tenet Opera Rata, 104

Satquiell, 75, 77, 98

Satrapis, 43, 225

Satrox, 295

Sattells, 209

Saturn, 78, 100, 119, 120, 145, 152,
    176, 208, 221, 222, 294

Satyll, 88

Saucer, magical tool, 2, 292

Saymay, 121, 122

Saymbrie, 95

Sayran, 228

Scar, 194

Scefatheos, 172

Scepter, magical tool, 82, 123, 148, 149, 191, 203

Sciences, provided by spirits, 102

Scorpio, 283

Scorpus, 237

Scot, Reginald, 20, 27, 35, 287

Scrying, 30, 216

Scudamore, John, 14

Secrets, 24, 30, 53, 78, 117, 174, 178, 198, 218, 271, 288

Seigneurs, 63, 121

Selus Leus, 226

Sem, 67, 176, 295

Sema, 295

Semapheras, 204

Semar, 119

Semeforas, 36, 76, 78, 103

Semeth, 75, 77, 115

Semey, 295

Semopheras, 89, 210

Senators, 88

Senth, 254

Sentony, 114

Seper, 195

Sepeton, 63

Sepuros, 295

Seraphim, order of angels, 29, 63, 68, 74, 77, 87, 93, 97, 98, 106, 109, 115, 118, 144, 154, 176, 187, 205, 206, 215, 219, 221, 290, 298, 299

Serar, 273

Seriatell, 106

Serobadam / Serobattam, 158

Serpens, 79, 86, 94, 104, 265

Serph, 106

Seson, 195

Sethen, 167

Seven sisters, 32, 104–105

Sever, 295

Seyros, 83

Sezel, 36, 294, 300

Sgalis, 273

Sheltron, magical tool, 288

Ships, stopping, 247

Siadris, 273

Sibilia, 32, 124, 270

Sichone, 273

Sidney, Sir Philip, 8, 10

Siga, 301

Silfactan, 300

Silori, 228

Sinnon, 301

Slaugnes, 95

"Sleeping Beauty," 33, 292

Sloane, Sir Hans, 21

Sluggishness, 147

Smagogyon, 89

Smamus, 172

Smargeos, 105

Smue, 295

Sniagagion, 89

Snoth, 142, 143

Sockuluta, 282

Sodom, 185

Sodyon, 301

Soissons, 271

Sol, 100, 104, 152, 170, 176, 266

Soldiers, 256, 303

Solher, 167

Soll, 86, 94, 191

Solomon, King, 35

Som, 93

Sonaco, 295

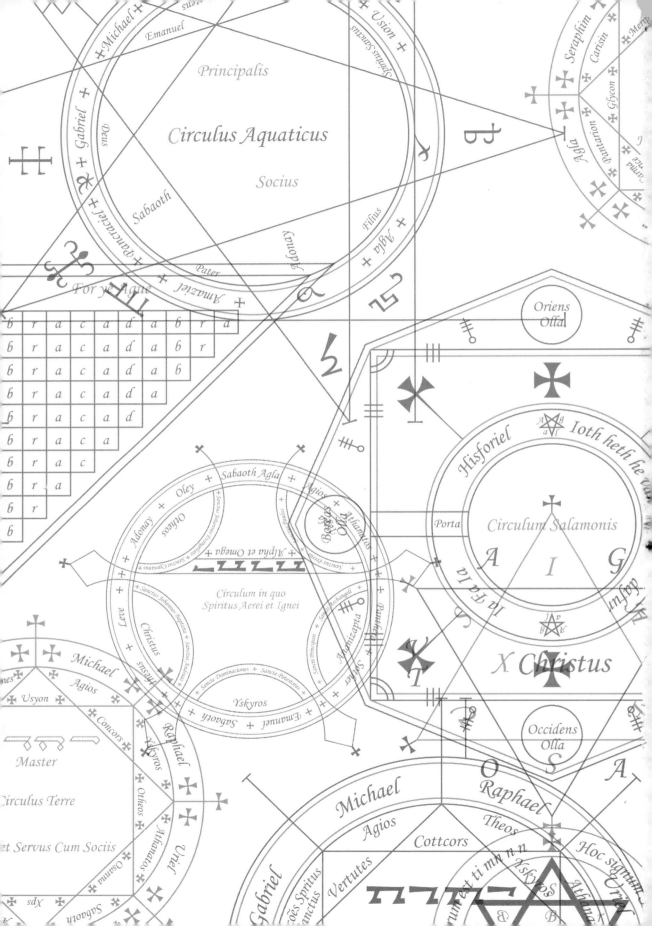